Country
STYLE

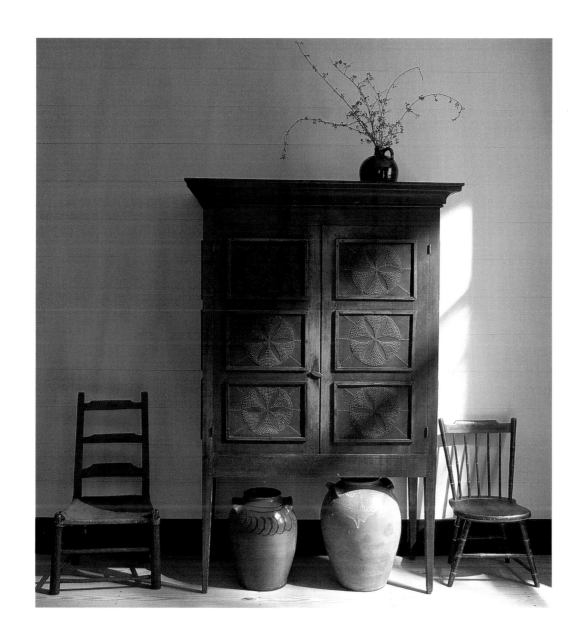

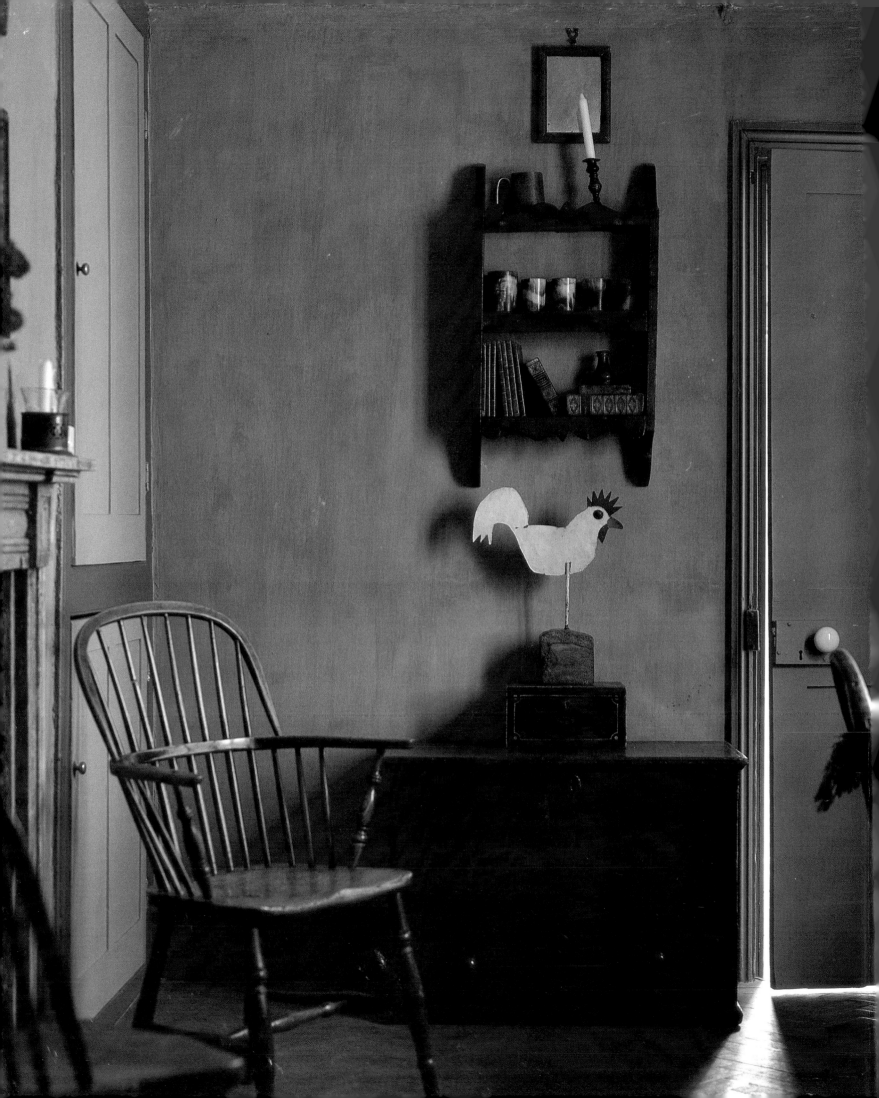

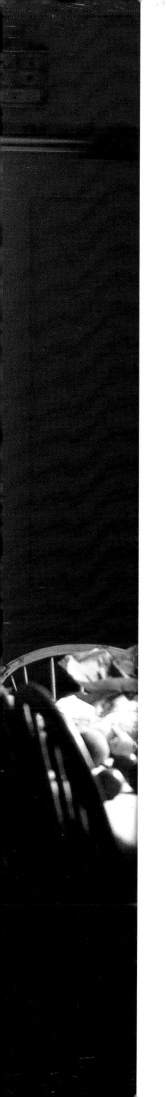

Country
STYLE

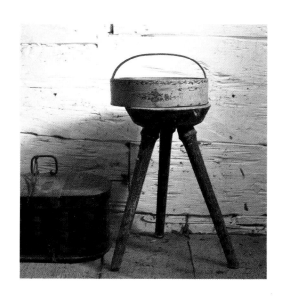

JUDITH AND MARTIN MILLER

Photography by James Merrell

MITCHELL BEAZLEY

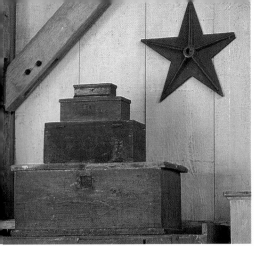
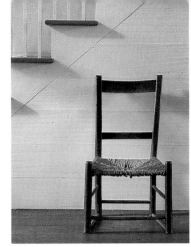
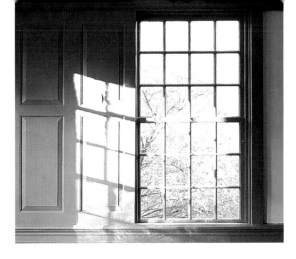
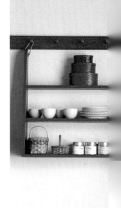

COUNTRY STYLE
Judith and Martin Miller
Photography by James Merrell
Chief Contributor (National Styles): Megan Tresidder

Edited and designed by
Mitchell Beazley International Ltd,
Artists House, 14-15 Manette Street,
London W1V 5LB

Senior Executive Art Editor **Jacqui Small**
Executive Editor **Judith More**
Art Editor **Larraine Lacey**
Editorial Assistant **Kirsty Seymour-Ure**
Production **Ted Timberlake**

A CIP catalogue record for this book is available from the British Library
ISBN 0 85533 7664

The publishers have made every effort to ensure that all instructions
given in this book are accurate and safe, but they cannot accept
liability for any resulting injury, damage or loss to either person or
property whether direct or consequential and howsoever arising.
The authors and publishers will be grateful for any information which
will assist them in keeping future editions up to date.

Typeset in Bodoni Book 12/16 pt Roman and $9\frac{1}{2}/12\frac{1}{2}$ pt Italic by
Servis Filmsetting, Manchester, England
Colour reproduction by Scantrans Pte Ltd, Singapore
Printed in West Germany by Mohndruck, GmbH, Gütersloh.

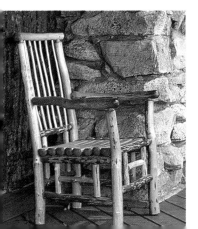
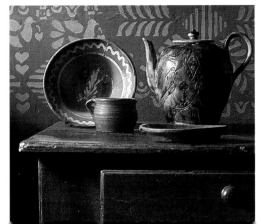
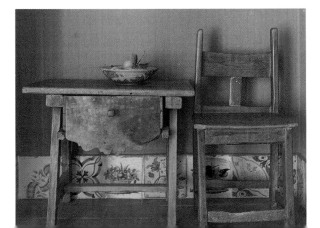
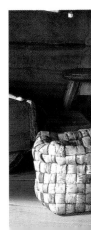

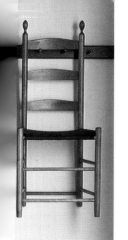
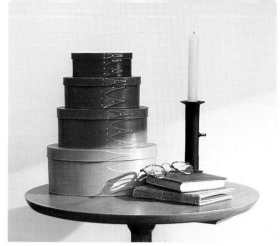
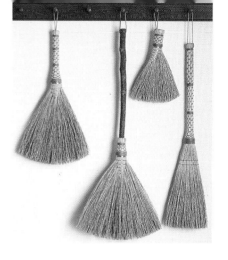
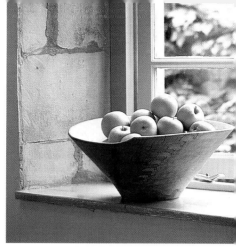

Contents

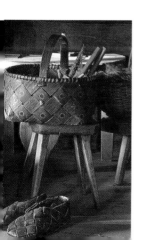
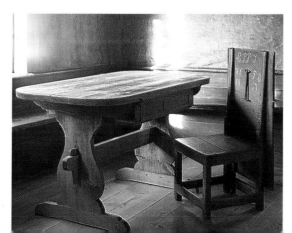
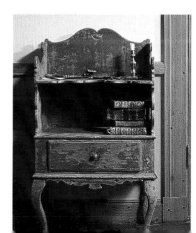
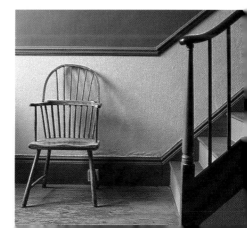

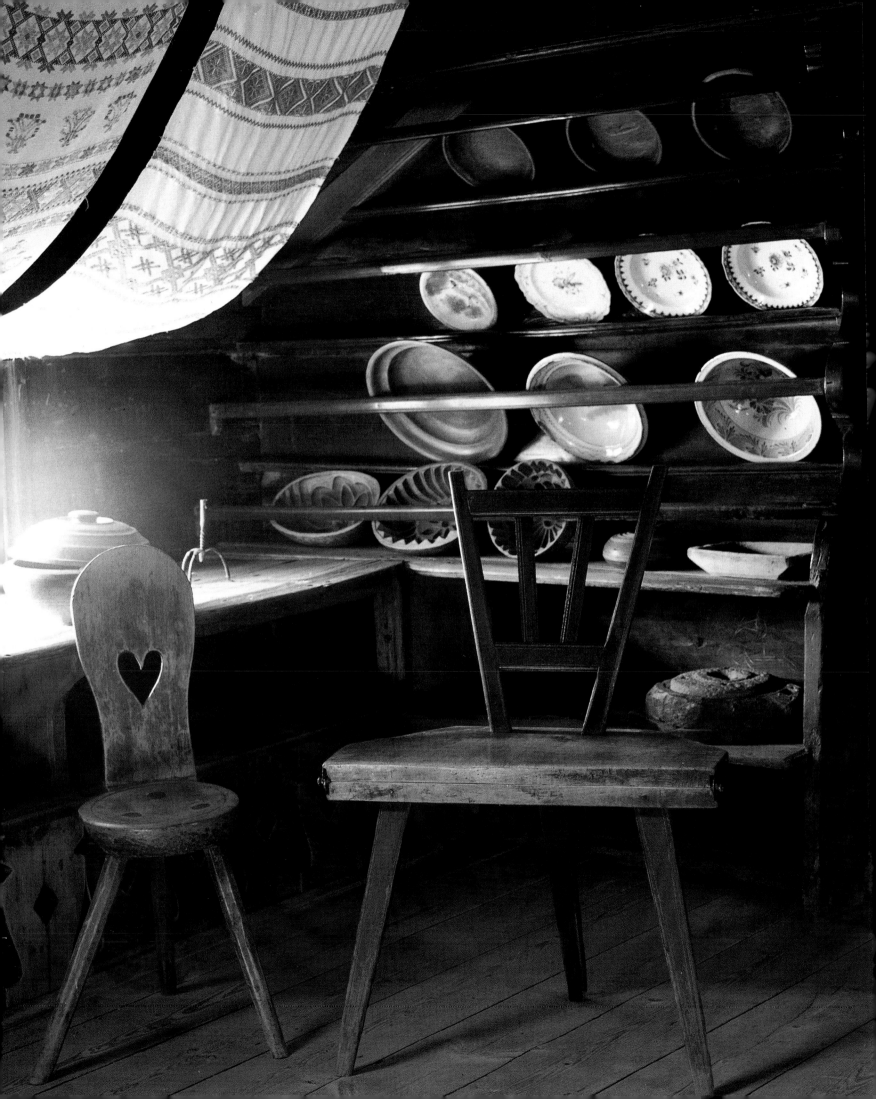

Foreword

No decorating style has been as long-lasting and as universally liked as country. Part of its appeal today lies in the fact that the simplicities of rural life are seen as an effective refuge from urban pressures. Our affection for it may also be a rebellion against those decorating fashions in which elaborate swagging, dragging and draping have held sway. The comfortable, unstructured look of country style seems, by contrast, relaxingly natural.

Although the term style suggests a planned design that is at odds with the basic unselfconsciousness of country homes we have used it here because certain rural traditions have deeply influenced international styles of decorating, and it is these we have featured in this book. For example, to call the Tuscan tradition a style is not to deny its spontaneity but rather to recognize the particular harmonies and contrasts of colour, texture and furnishings that make it so distinctive.

It can be argued that country style can't be transplanted as it relies on the very landscapes and nuances of light from whence it grew. Yet scores of photographs throughout these pages show how successfully elements of these styles have been exported worldwide. The distinctive features of *le style Provençal* – the brilliantly coloured faience, the golden patinated furniture and the richly coloured printed fabrics – can be purchased all over the world. So, too, can Spanish tiles, Swedish painted furniture, American patchwork quilts, English floral wallpapers and chintzes and Italian terracotta pots. With enough research, these elements can be happily adapted to an apartment in New York or London or a country cottage in Devon or Maine.

You don't have to stick to products from one country either; individual elements, all drawn from craft traditions, can blend delightfully, as is evident in Stephen Andrew's rustic *finca* in Spain (see page 105). Country style can be an eclectic magpie. The people who create successful country homes, like the ones shown in this book, don't copy designs, they allow their homes to evolve, within the constraints of modern life, in a natural way. Every home we visited had a comfortable, unselfconscious feeling. Everything belonged, although many of the elements came from different cultures, countries and centuries. Such engaging mixtures characterize American country style in particular, which evolved from a melting pot of immigrant cultures.

To an extent it is still true that country style, which belonged essentially to the poor, can be achieved without a lot of money. It comes from a tradition of simplicity and making do. But while this book celebrates authentic country style it is not a call to martyrdom. In seeking to recreate the feel of an original cottage we don't advocate cooking over an open fire, raising water from a well or eschewing modern bathroom facilities.

Most of us have a picture in our minds of country living. This may be of the stark simplicity of Shaker-influenced rooms or the comfortable clutter of the English cottage; it may even include scents like the smell of woodsmoke from a glowing hearth, or of a kitchen filled with the aroma of drying herbs and baking bread. The magic of country style lies in its naturalness, honesty of design, and directness. In this sense, creating a country style requires the opposite of effort; it succeeds most where it tries least.   JUDITH MILLER. 1990

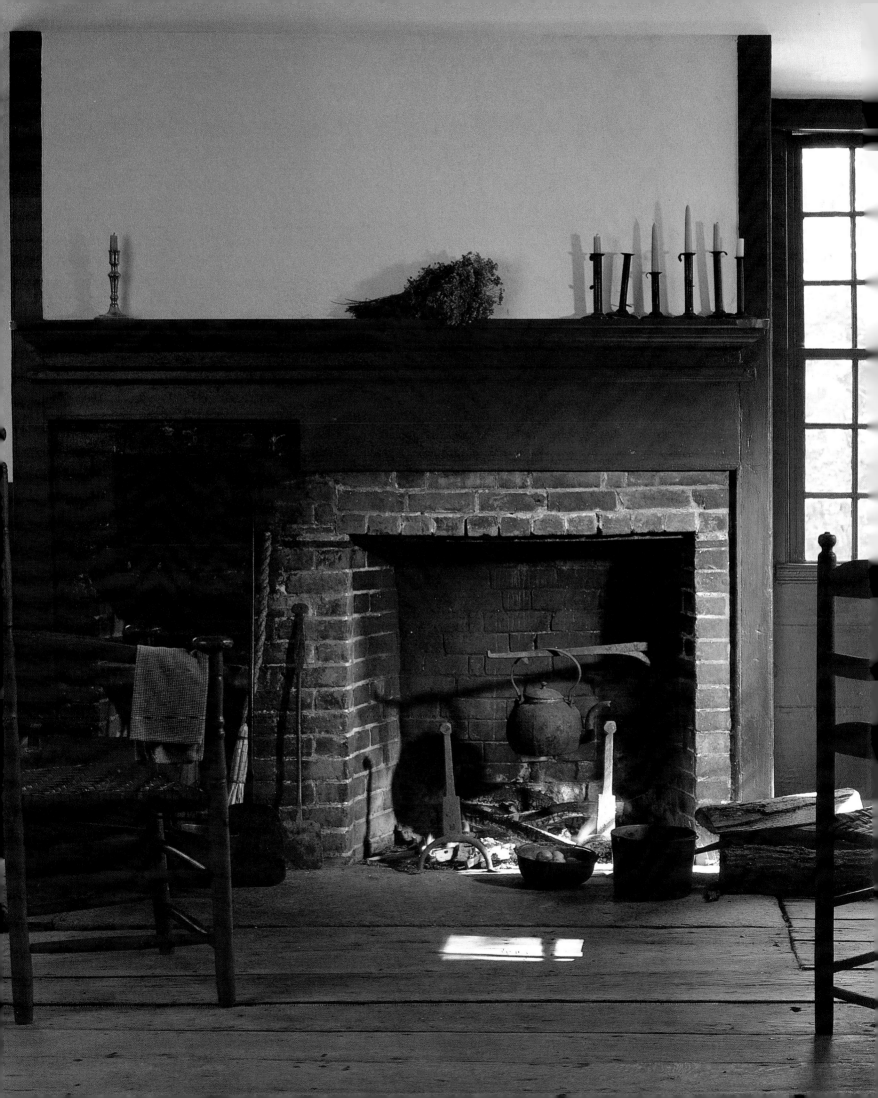

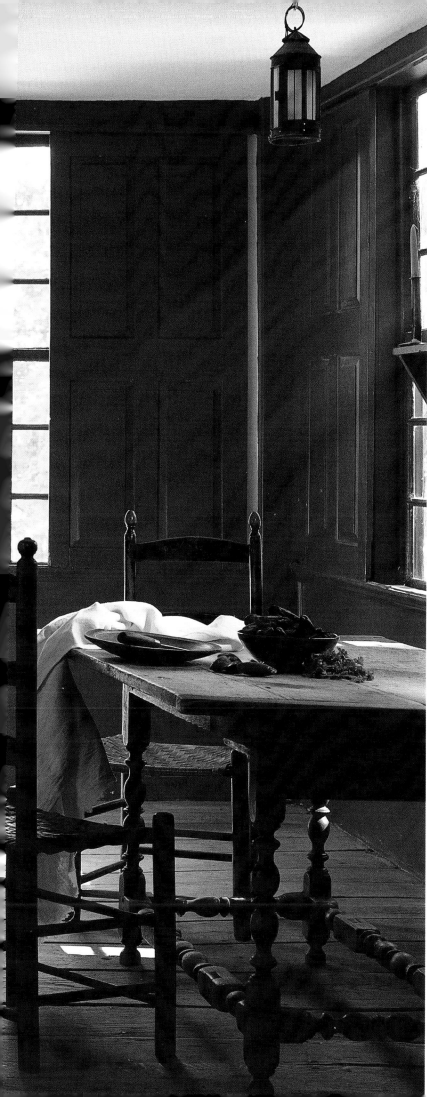

THE ESSENCE
of Country Style

C ountry runs through the history of interior decoration like the rogue thread of a style that is somehow stronger and more durable than the rest. Simple, instinctive and traditional, it has easily outlasted Baroque, Rococo, Empire and the rest of the changeling fashions of the rich. It is not hard to understand why. Because country style was created by those without the money to follow new trends, it has a timelessness to it. By applying the criteria of what was natural, comfortable and would last, the rural poor created their own classics of interior design and furnishing. Two of the most enduring chair designs, for instance – the English Windsor chair and the American rocker – were invented by local craftsmen as simple solutions to the need for comfortable seats.

If there is a current "vogue" for country style, it is not a new one. The simplicity at the heart of the country look answers a very old impulse in those who have money and possessions to experiment with having less. "Country" became established as a deliberately sought-after style in the 19th century, when as a reaction to the bourgeois excesses of the period the rural interior became the symbol not just of an ideal way of life but of a fast-disappearing one. No wonder, then, that country style has on occasion become overworked, especially in the chintz-choked living rooms of so many English houses.

As the homes in this book prove, true country style today remains based on the same fundamentals of ease and simplicity and a love for craftsmanship. Since it belonged to the poor, and was born from the necessity to make-do and mend, the style can be achieved without spending a lot of money, even now. The magic of country style is that it is created from elements which sound almost too wholesome to be appetizing – naturalness, honesty of design, directness, non-exhibitionism yet it has more warmth and broad appeal than any other style.

Left:
The honesty of country style is evident in this American keeping room,
with its brick hearth and bare boards.

Period themes

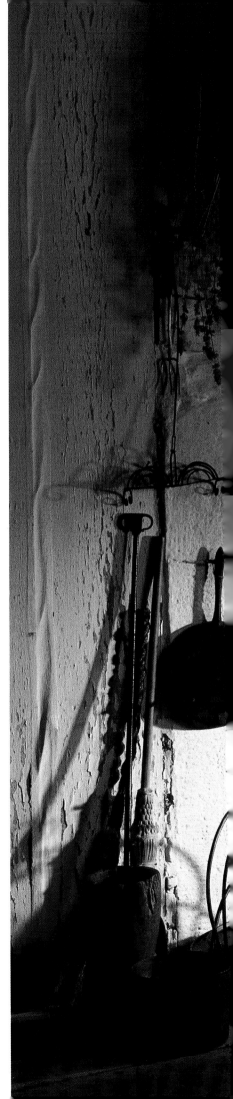

*P*eriod themes are a very strong strand in the fabric of country style. If you own an old building you may want to research and recreate its original look. Bear in mind that this is not always a quick or simple option. For example, Stephen Mack is so painstaking in his reconstruction of 17th and 18th century New England homes that he often cooks in iron cauldrons suspended over open fires in the age-old manner and uses candlelight whenever possible. (But the electricity is there, in carefully concealed conduits, triggered by hand-whittled wooden switches.) For many people, this approach is time-consuming to carry out and can be difficult to live with. These country home owners follow an easier path to a period mood by simply choosing country antiques and then creating a sympathetic background for them.

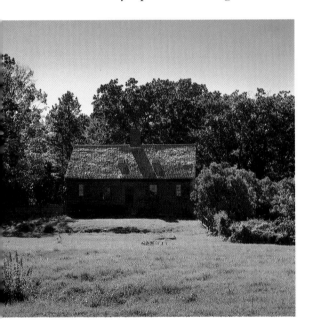 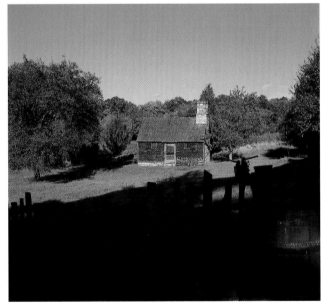

Stephen Mack's two-storey late 18th century timber-framed clapboard home (above left) is in the classic American central chimney design, with two parlours and a keeping room on the ground floor. The house was derelict when Stephen bought it and having restored it completely he now specializes in restoring 18th and early 19th century buildings, like the 18th century Simon Huntingdon Tavern in Connecticut, shown above.

Right:
The keeping room was originally the main – and often the only – room in early American homes. It was used for cooking, sleeping and other household activities. Here, culinary implements cluster either side of a log fire laid on traditional andirons, while herbs dry in bunches suspended from the ceiling beams.

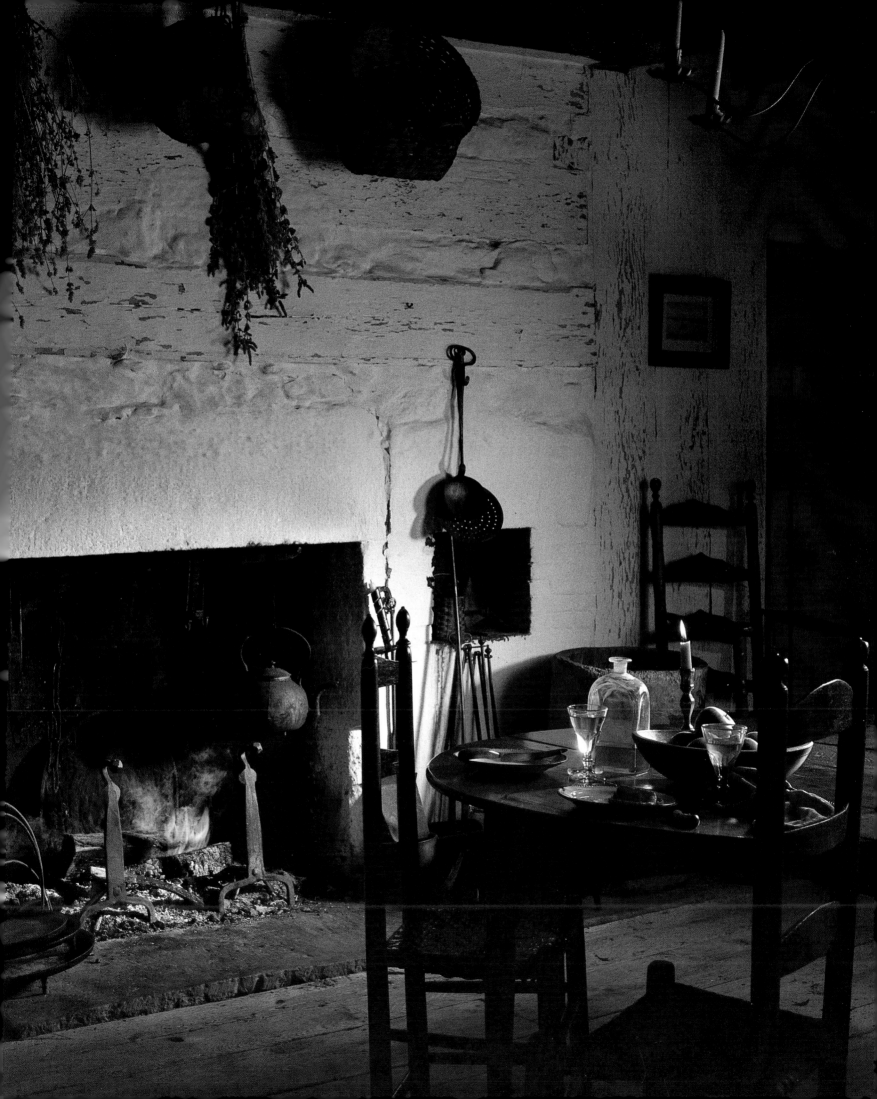

Period themes

Right:
On a mud room door wrought-iron fittings are locked by a wooden wedge. Note the whittled wooden light switch just visible on the right-hand wall; Stephen takes great care that 20th century practicalities such as electricity and plumbing are unobtrusive.

Right:
In the pantry open shelves are lined with period serving dishes, pots and plates made from copper, pewter, earthenware and wood.

Below:
Another view of the keeping room shown on p. 10. The panelling is painted in an authentic colonial red.

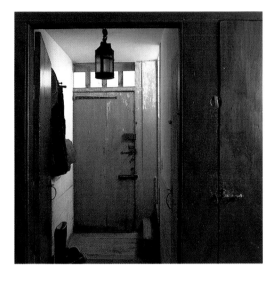

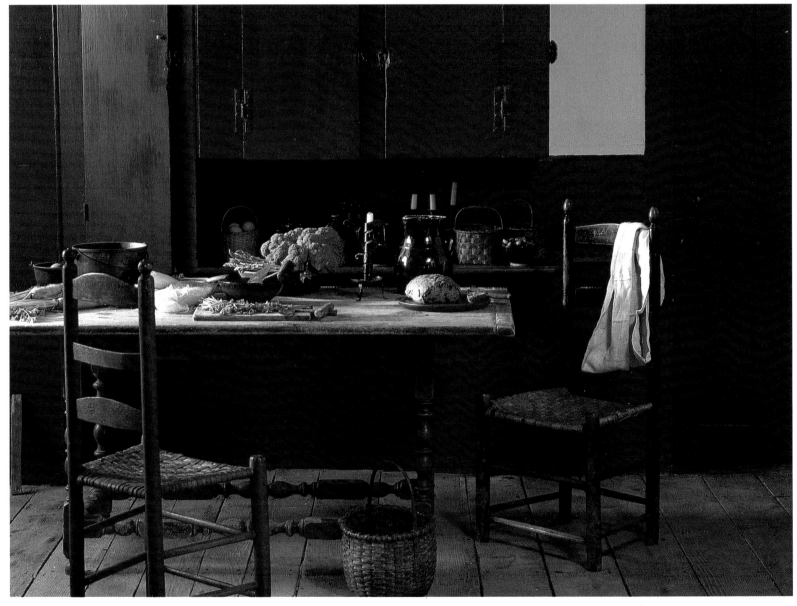

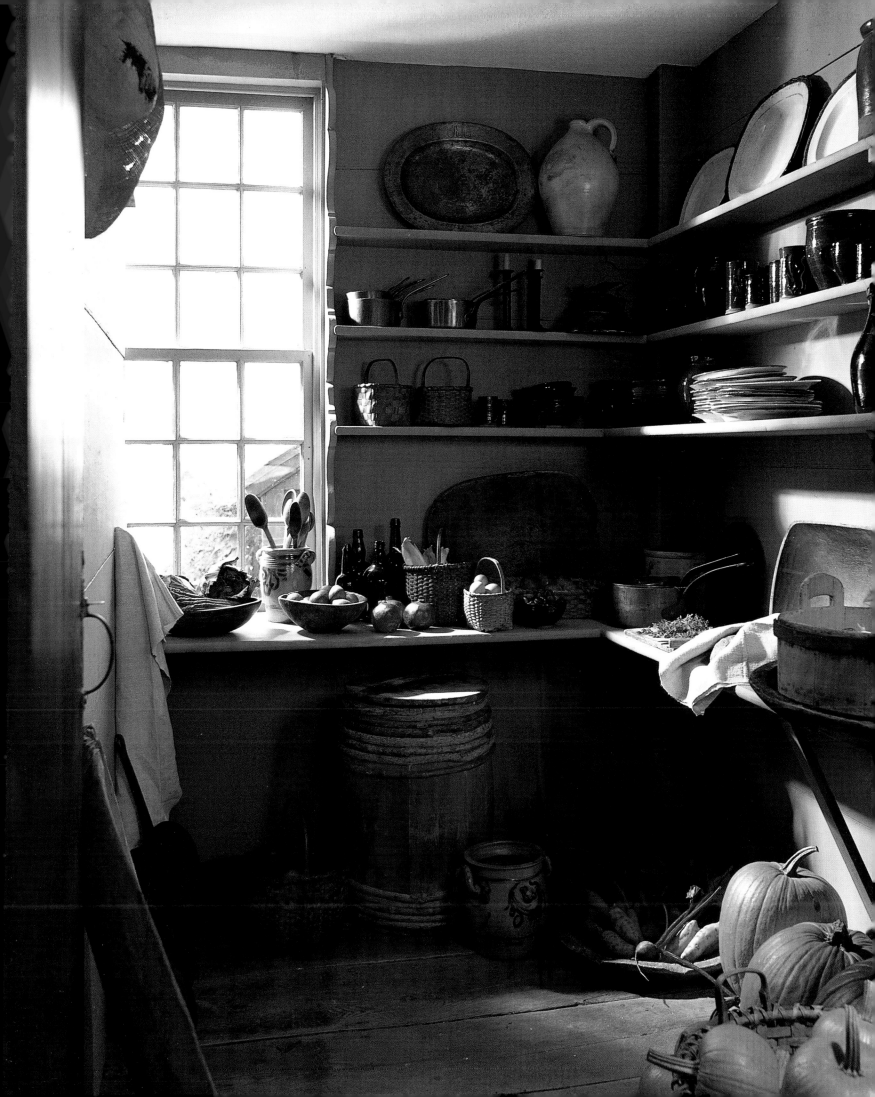

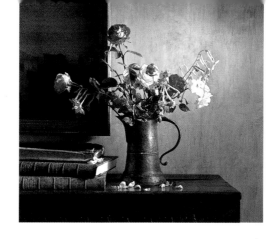

Frog Pool Farm, in Avon, England, a medieval house which dates back to the reign of Edward III, is the home of Trevor Micklem, an antique dealer who specializes in furniture, needlework, metalware and pottery of the 17th and early 18th centuries.

Right:
In the beamed 16th century dining room Cromwellian chairs are arranged around a 17th century oak gateleg table. One wall is dominated by a vast fireplace; the others are washed in ochre and Indian red. The wainscot chair is early 18th century.

Above:
Wild flowers or old-fashioned garden varieties, like these roses informally arranged in a 17th century pewter jug, are preferable to hothouse blooms.

Below left:
A James II walnut chair stands to the left of the door while on the right is a mid-17th century Lancashire chair.

Below right:
This 15th century door was probably the original front entrance, but is now an internal door. Such changes are common in country homes because they grow and evolve over the centuries. Furniture spans the centuries too. The walnut table dates from the 17th century, while the Windsor chair is 18th century.

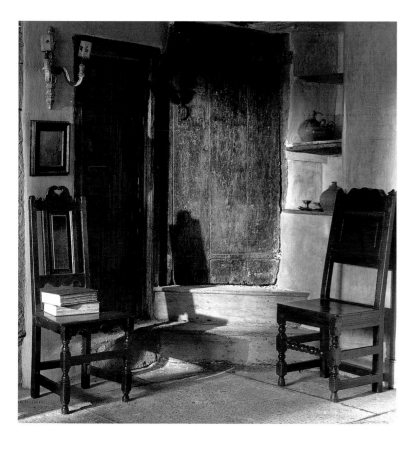

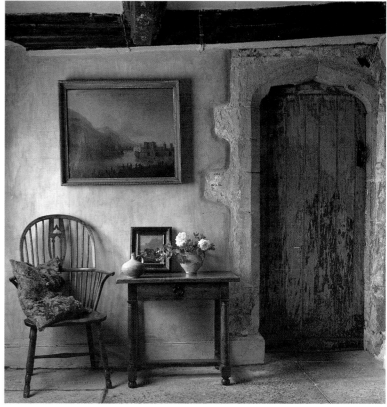

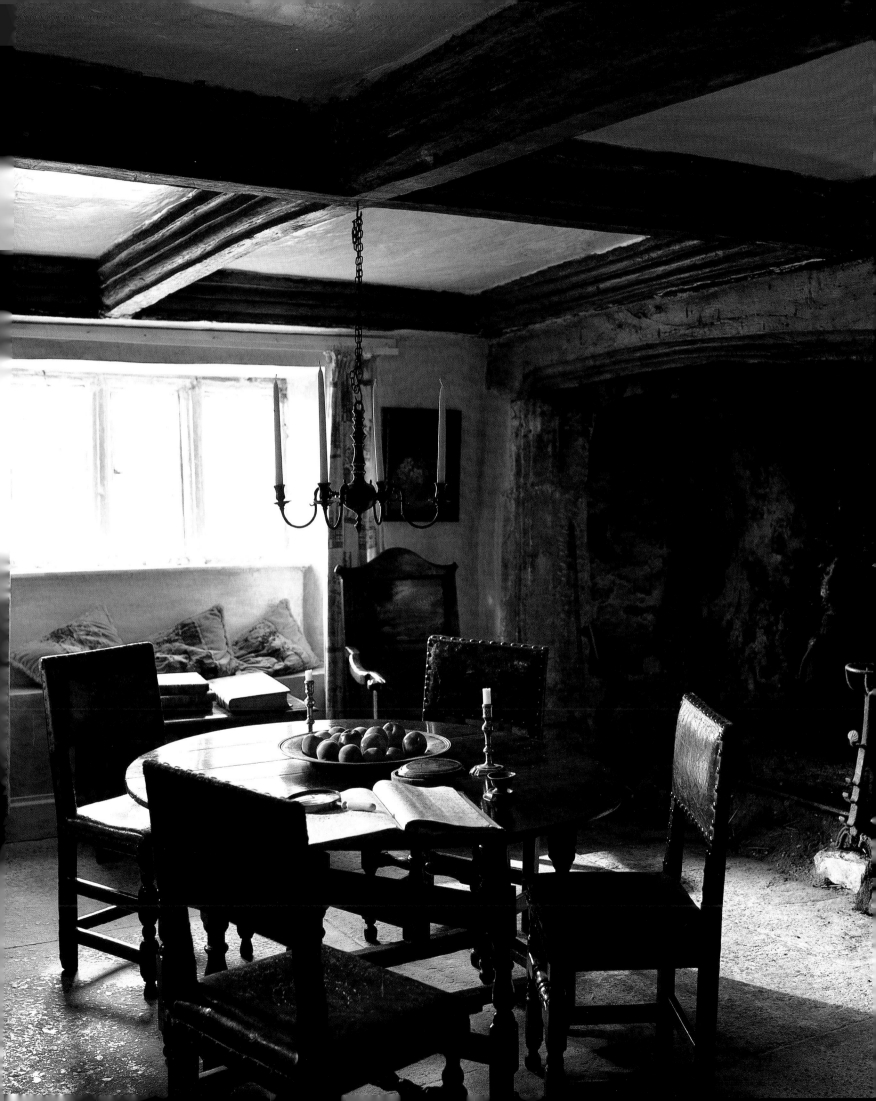

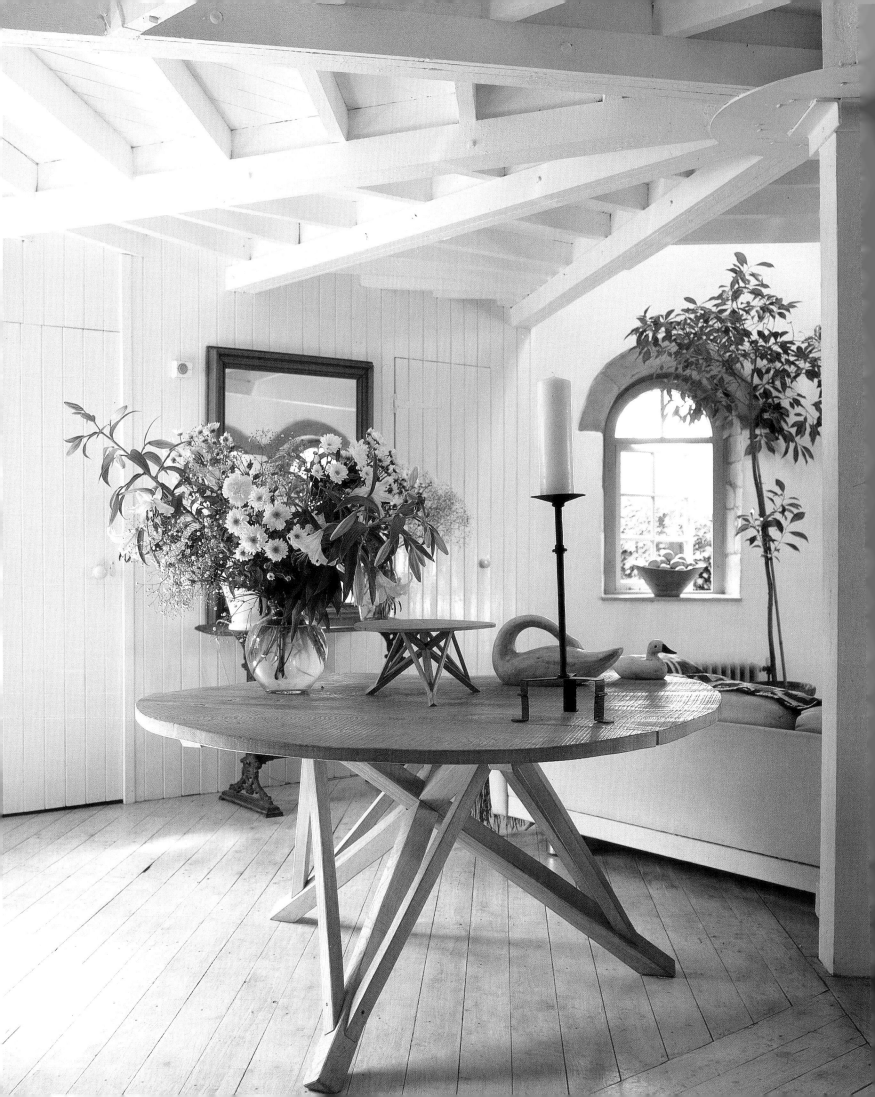

Modern mood

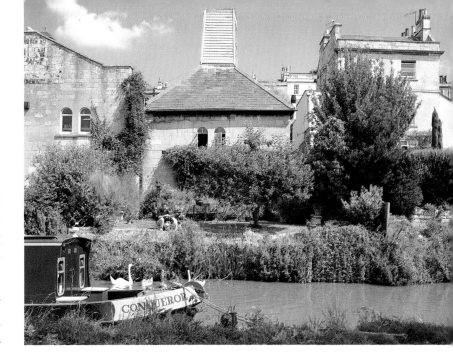

*I*t is becoming increasingly hard to distinguish between country style and sheer nostalgia, where almost anything goes as long as it is old. But the new isn't ruled out, as the home shown here proves. Country style is liberating because, having evolved continuously over the centuries it can't be forced into any one era. Just as the original homes of rural people changed with each generation – the furniture swapped, added to or discarded, the walls repainted – so their modern counterparts can defy period definition. The key to country style, ancient or modern, is a naturalness and honesty of design.

On the outskirts of Bath, Somerset, by the edge of a canal, stands The Malt House. Its site was dictated by its former function since the barley used to be brought by barge for malting. Although this house is in a city, it has true country style and – best of all – country views. Built about 1840 and used commercially until 1956, it was converted into a domestic dwelling in 1974. When the present owner acquired it he gutted the original conversion work to open up and reveal the strong structural contours of the building.

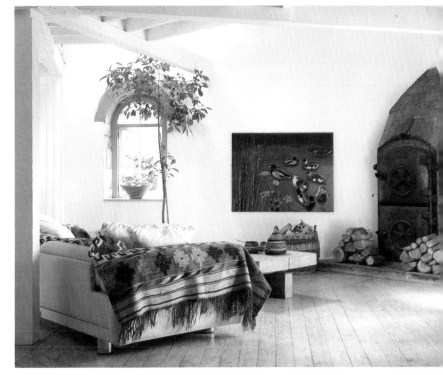

Left:
The principal living area is one
large, open space on the first floor, broken up only by the main
structural support post (to the right of the picture) which goes right
down through the malt house furnace on the ground floor. New white-
stained floorboards have replaced the original tiles, which were covered
with holes to transmit the heat from the furnace through the barley. These
tiles have now been relaid on the ground floor (see page 180). The shape
of the modern table, and its prototype sitting on top of it, designed by
Richard Latrobe Bateman, echoes
the strong lines of the beams.

Middle right:
The door to the furnace makes a stunning piece of industrial sculpture.
The furnace itself is practical as well as decorative. The owner uses it both
as a fire and a slow oven (the top part is ideal for casseroles). The strong,
clean form of the English elm coffee table, a modern piece which was
made by Richard Latrobe Bateman, is a perfect complement to the
architectural quality of the room. Despite its appearance, the kelim over
the sofa is not an antique. Vegetable-dyed ethnic textiles fade
wonderfully quickly, losing their bright, brash newness to become
comfortably mellow.

Below right:
The Malt House no longer produces malt, but it is still a workplace. Many
of today's exponents of country style continue the strong tradition of
combining their home and industry, although drawing boards and
computer workstations are now more common than looms and lathes.

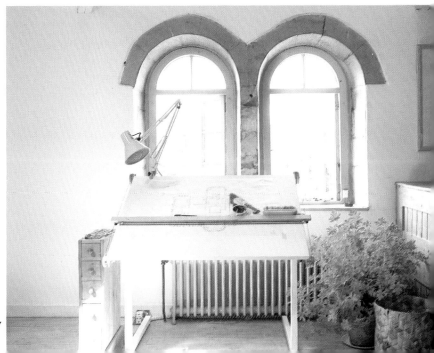

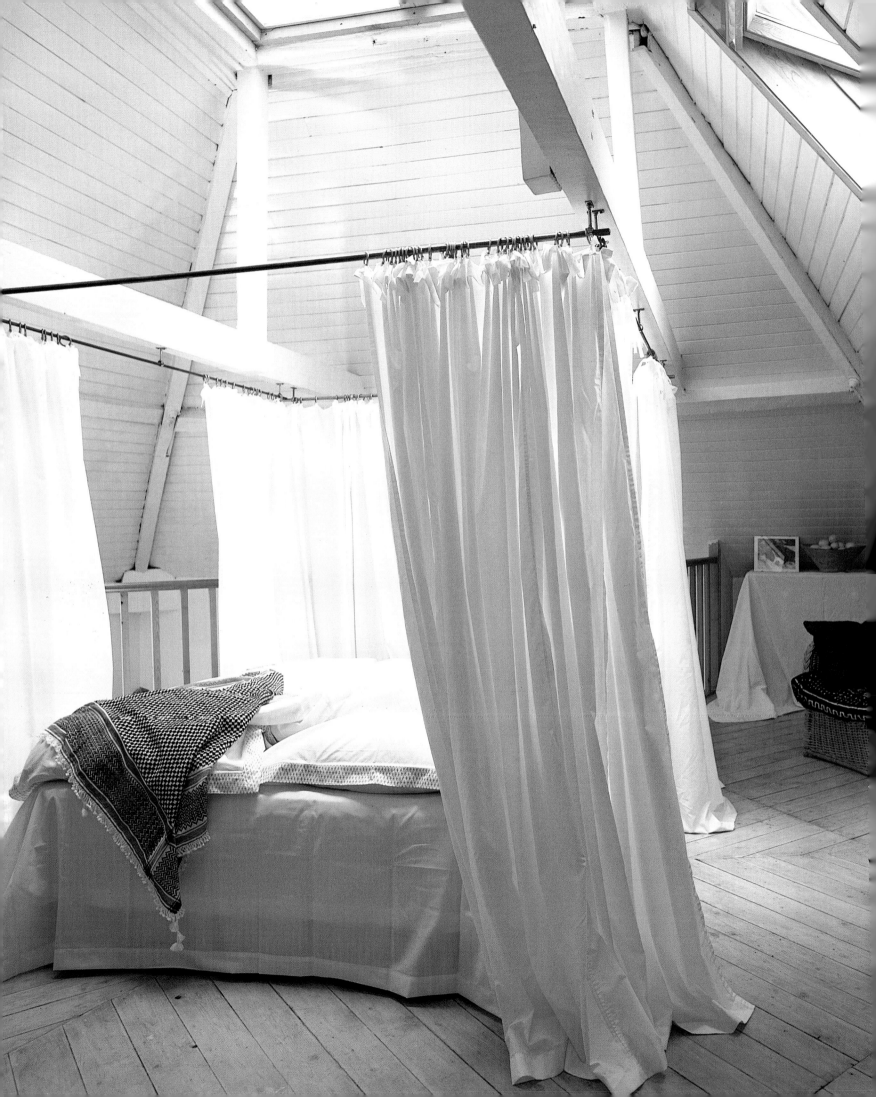

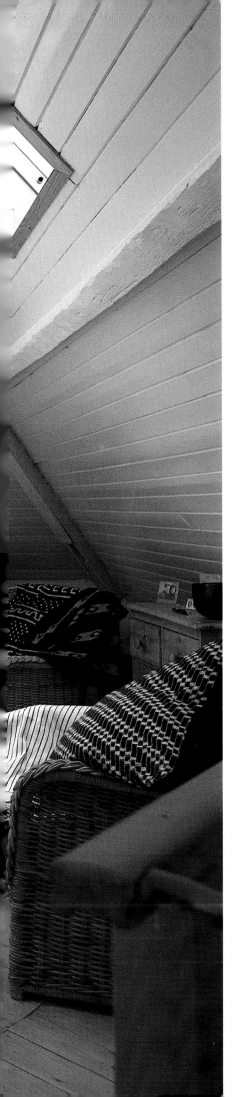

Modern mood

On the top floor, under the sloping malthouse roof, sit a bedroom and bathroom reached by a spiral staircase from the main living area below.

Left:
Supporting beams have been utilized to hold generous white drapes for a four-poster, while the bed itself stands in a pool of light from the rooflights above. The wicker armchairs are cushioned with African mud-painted fabrics.

Below:
The bathroom is furnished with a freestanding rolltop bath, its black exterior painted to match the stained-wood chair by Richard Latrobe Bateman. Unobtrusive recessed lights add to the uncluttered feel.

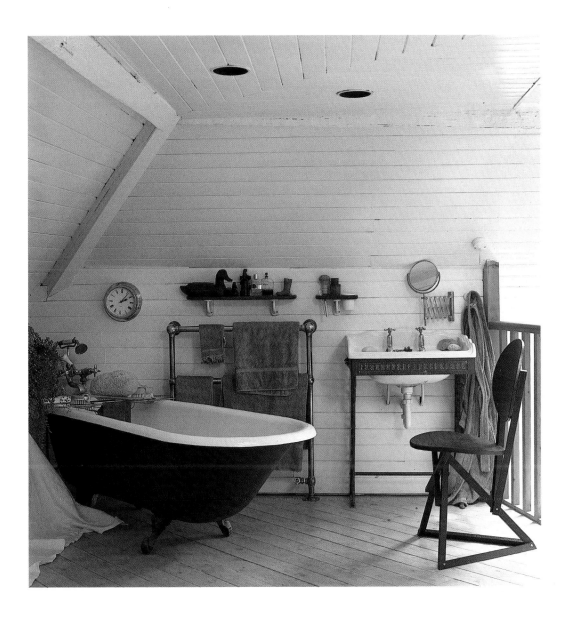

Retro mood

*Y*ou don't need to own a historic country home to indulge in period-style interior decoration. A modern house which has been built with traditional materials and features, or has had them added in a sympathetic manner, can be furnished with antiques to provide the perfect compromise for today.

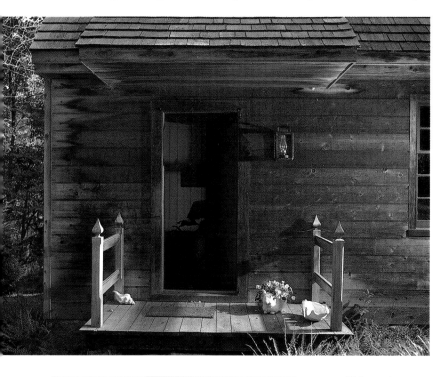

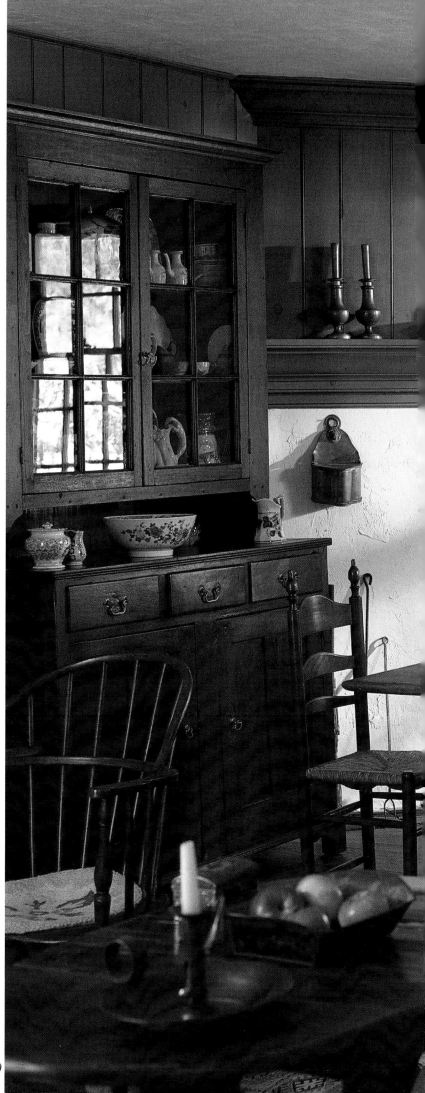

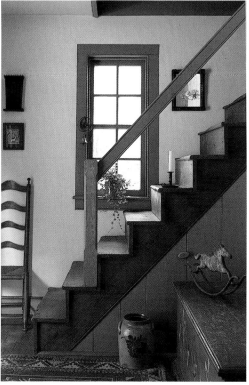

This modern American house is made to look like a Chester County plank house. Authentic paint colours, country furniture and artefacts have transformed a new dwelling into an ageless country home.

Left:
Although the house is new, the stairs were salvaged from a period barn.

Right:
The woodwork is an authentic Williamsburg blue.

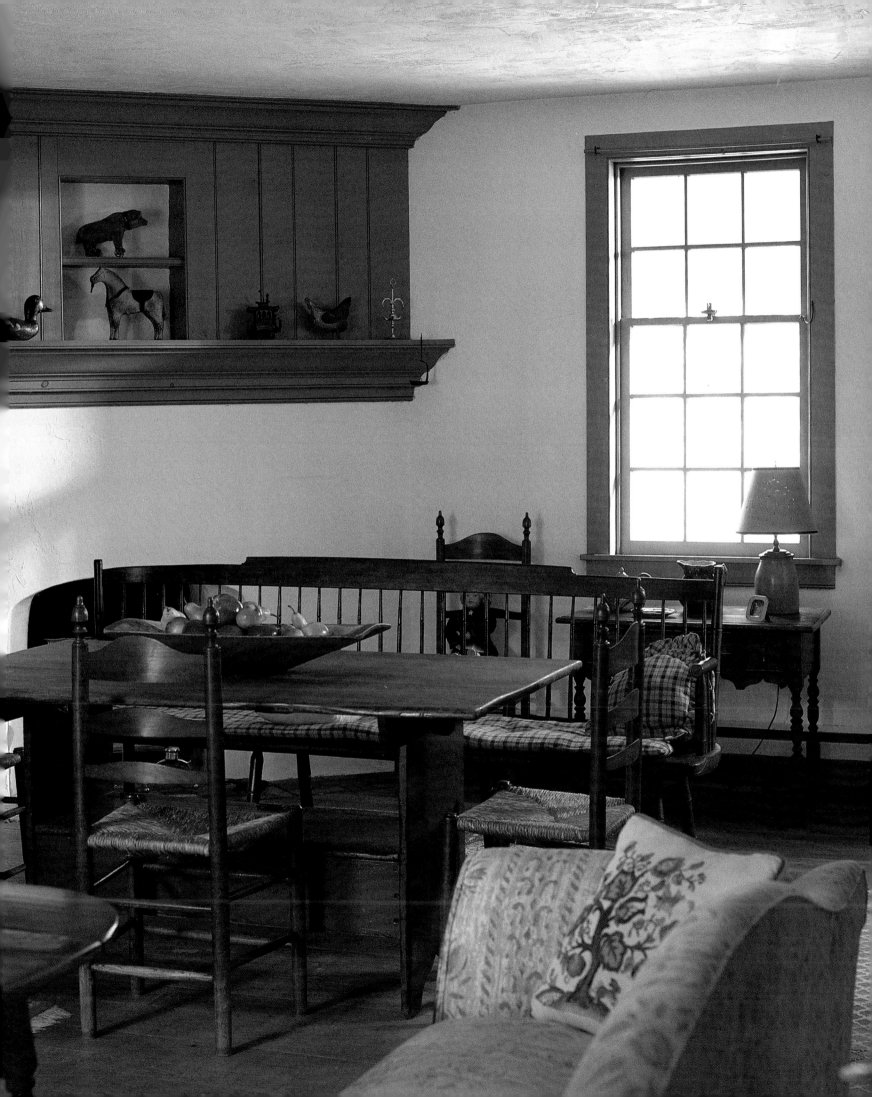

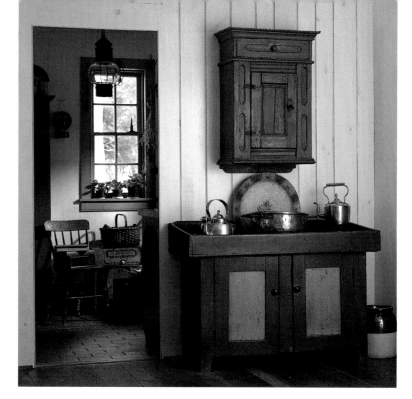

Below:
The triangular window, with a sill that is low and deep enough to be used as a window seat, gives a fine view of the countryside in both directions. The period feel of this room is enhanced by the hickory pine Windsor chair with writing slope, dating from circa 1760-80, and the early New England butterfly table that dates from circa 1700.

Right:
Late 18th century rush-seated fruitwood ladderbacks and an 18th century Windsor settee are grouped around an 18th century settle table.

Left:
Because fine woods were scarce in colonial America, most furniture was made from inferior wood and then painted.

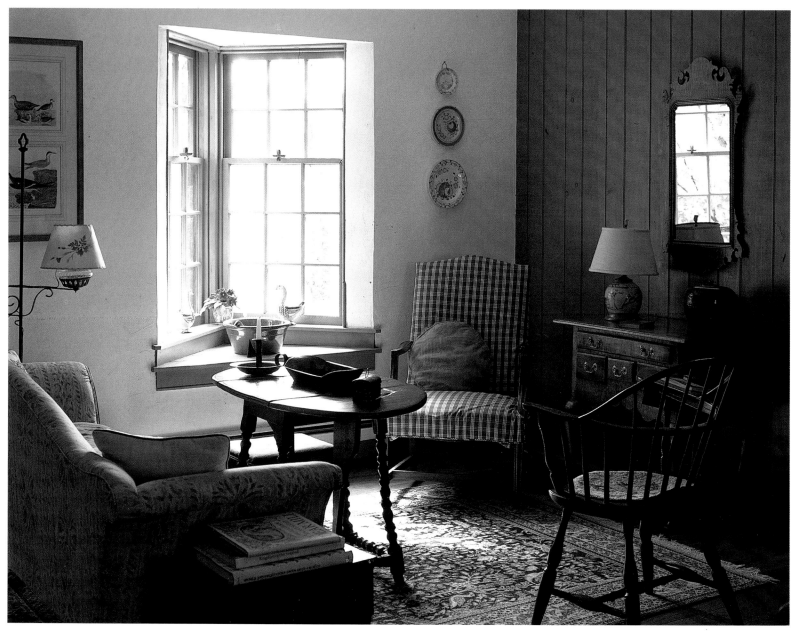

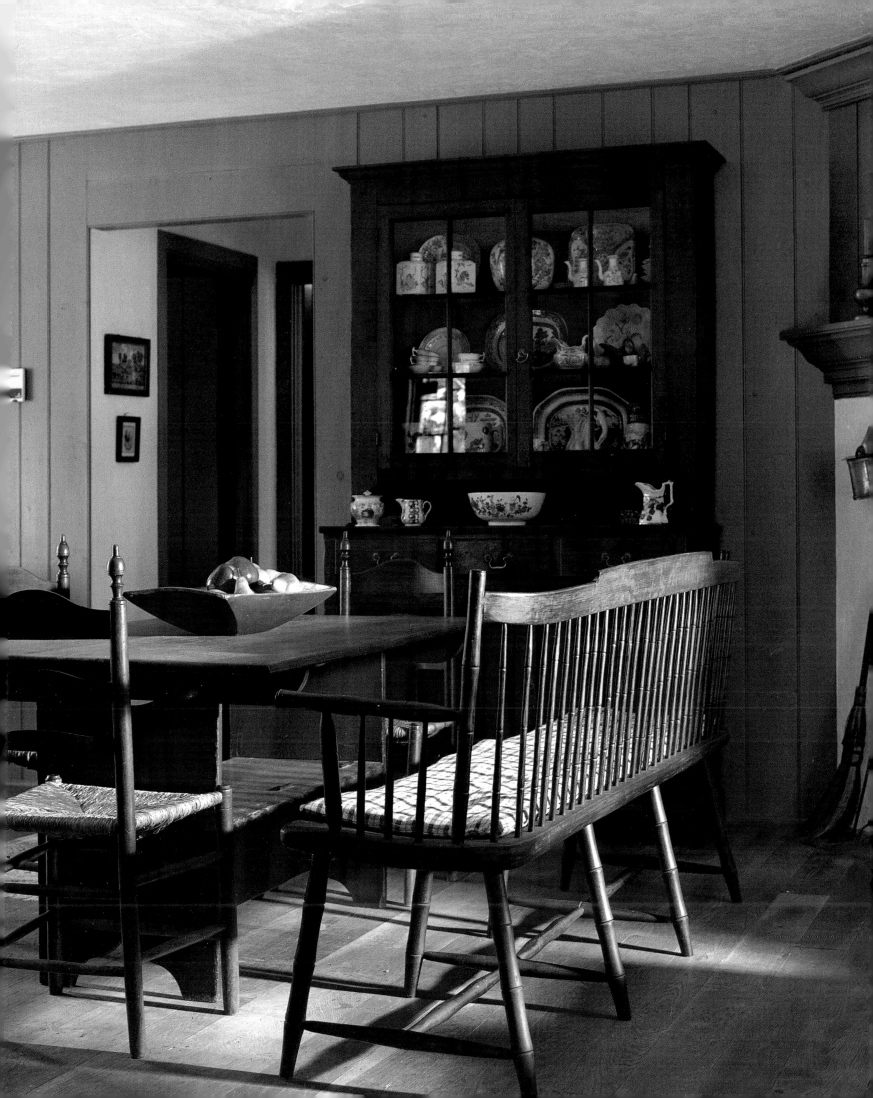

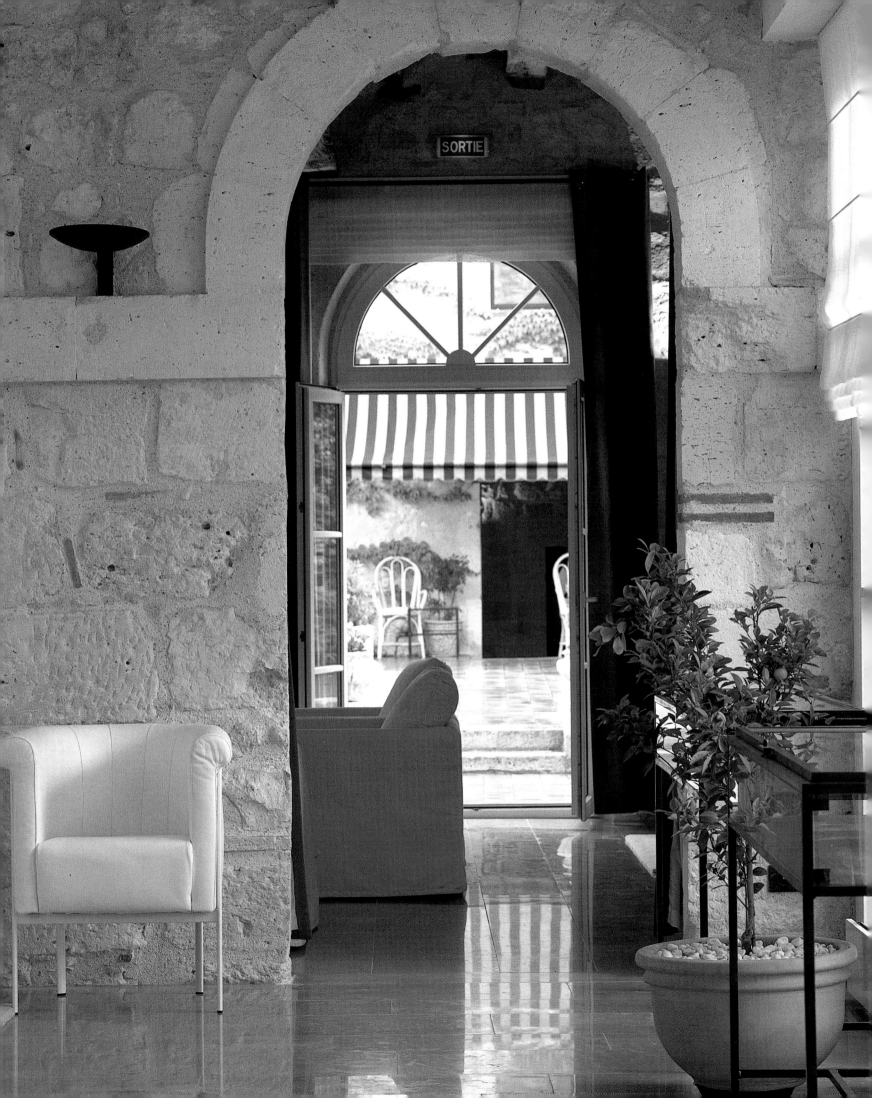

New looks, old setting

*T*he essence of country is its continuing absorption of the world around it; it is a living style. There is no reason why well-made new pieces which have simple lines and are made from natural materials cannot be used to furnish old country barns, farmhouses or cottages.

L'Aubergade, *a 13th century stone country house in the French village of Puymirol, is furnished in a modern adaptation of country style.*

Left and below:
Tall windows reflect light onto the highly polished marble floor of the entrance hall, where stone archways and ancient walls washed in white provide a spacious setting for classic white furnishings. Touches of colour – the blue of the canvas curtains and the orange of the fruits on the tree set in a cream-glazed tub – echo the traditional hues of Provençal prints.

Below right:
Plain blinds diffuse and whiten the brilliant sunlight. The striped canvas curtains are threaded directly onto their pole – a device that is very suitable in a country setting. Rough-hewn beams and a well-worn brick floor make a textural counterpoint to the glossy modern desk and mellow wooden antique chair.

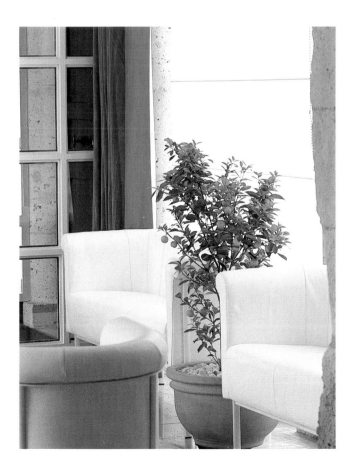
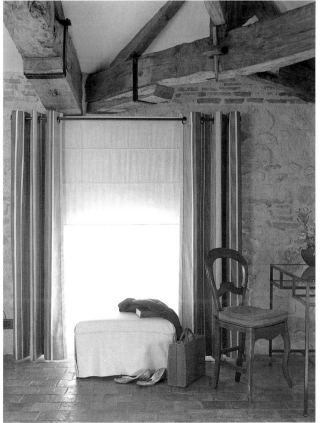

Cottage clutter

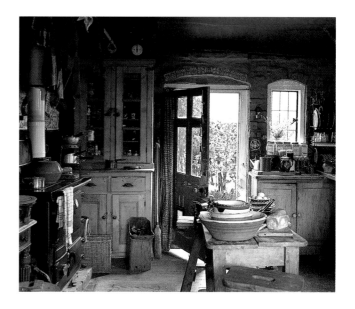

P art of the fascination of country style is that it is a such a
mixture of the real and the idealized. The cluttered
cottage is the prime example. It exists in everyone's mind's eye
as a treasury of English blue-and-white china and spongeware,
the whole delicious muddle enhanced by a riotous profusion of
flowers on the wallpaper behind. In the same mind's eye, a
small Italian hillside villa is an airy space, punctuated here and
there by terracotta urns. The English rural class had no more
possessions than the Italians, but their houses tended to be
smaller so their belongings went further in filling up space.
What was the logical result of the difference in scale between
English and Italian homes eventually became the hallmark of
their respective styles. And this cluttered style is not purely
English, although the English cottage is the epitome of it. In
any country home where space is at a premium, the cluttered
look will prevail.

*Mary Wondrausch, potter and artist, lives and
works in a brick-built Surrey cottage dating
from around 1550. As this English house has
evolved over the centuries, so it has continued
to develop during the 35 years it has been
Mary's home. Mary has added her own craft to
the fabric of the cottage: for example, the wall
tiles above the pine cupboard in the kitchen
were made by Mary herself, as were the ceramic
cupboard handles. Mary's absorption in
international folk art is expressed throughout
the house in her exuberant use of potteries,
textiles and wall finishes.*

*Far right:
Drying herbs hang
from the 16th century
cross beam.*

*Top right:
Log baskets and coal
hods feed the range
which doubles as a
source of heat. As
well as cooking
country food it dries
the linen.*

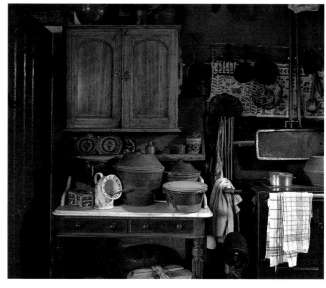

*Middle right:
The total antithesis
of the modern fitted
look, this is a true
country kitchen.*

*Bottom right:
Above a splashback
of hand-potted tiles,
shelves hold egg cups
and jars of herbs.*

*Overleaf:
A profusion of
textiles fill the room
with pattern, texture
and colour.*

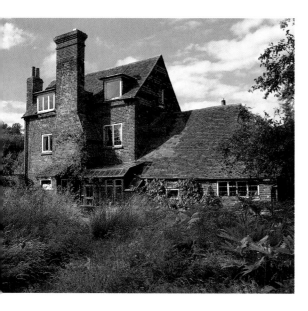

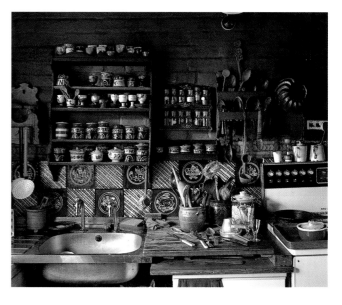

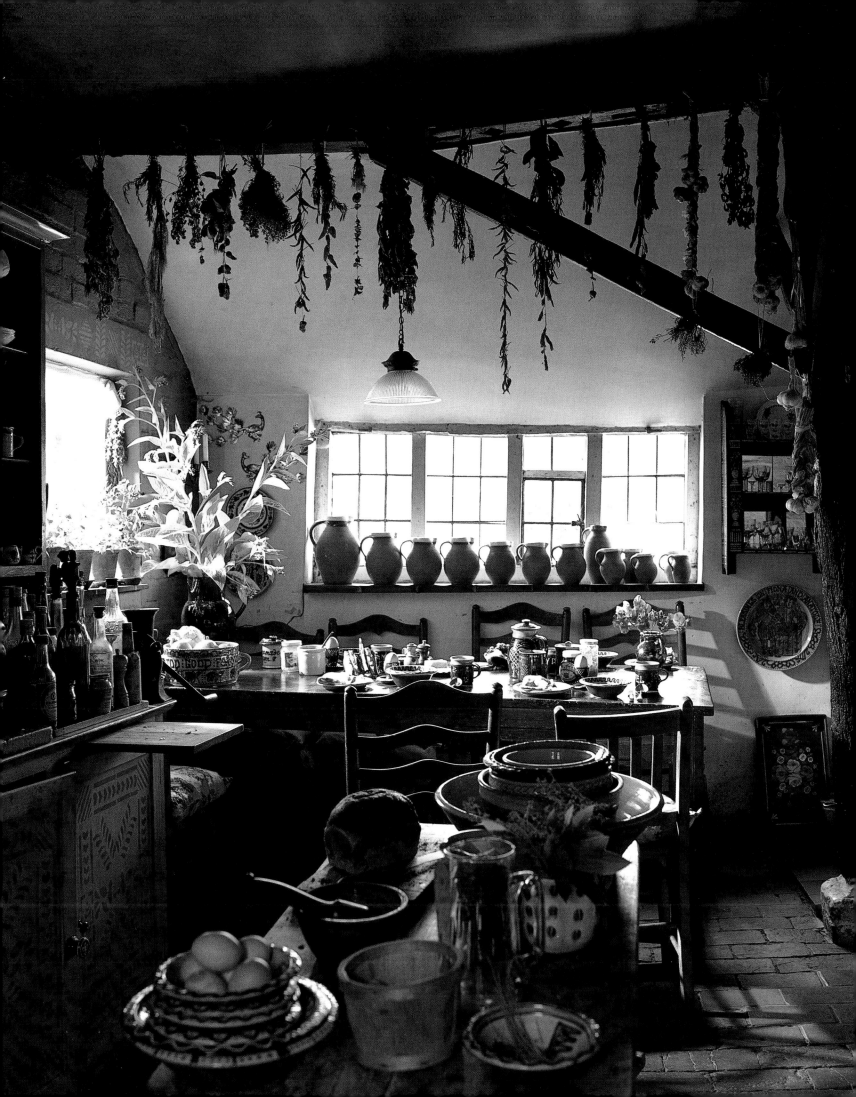

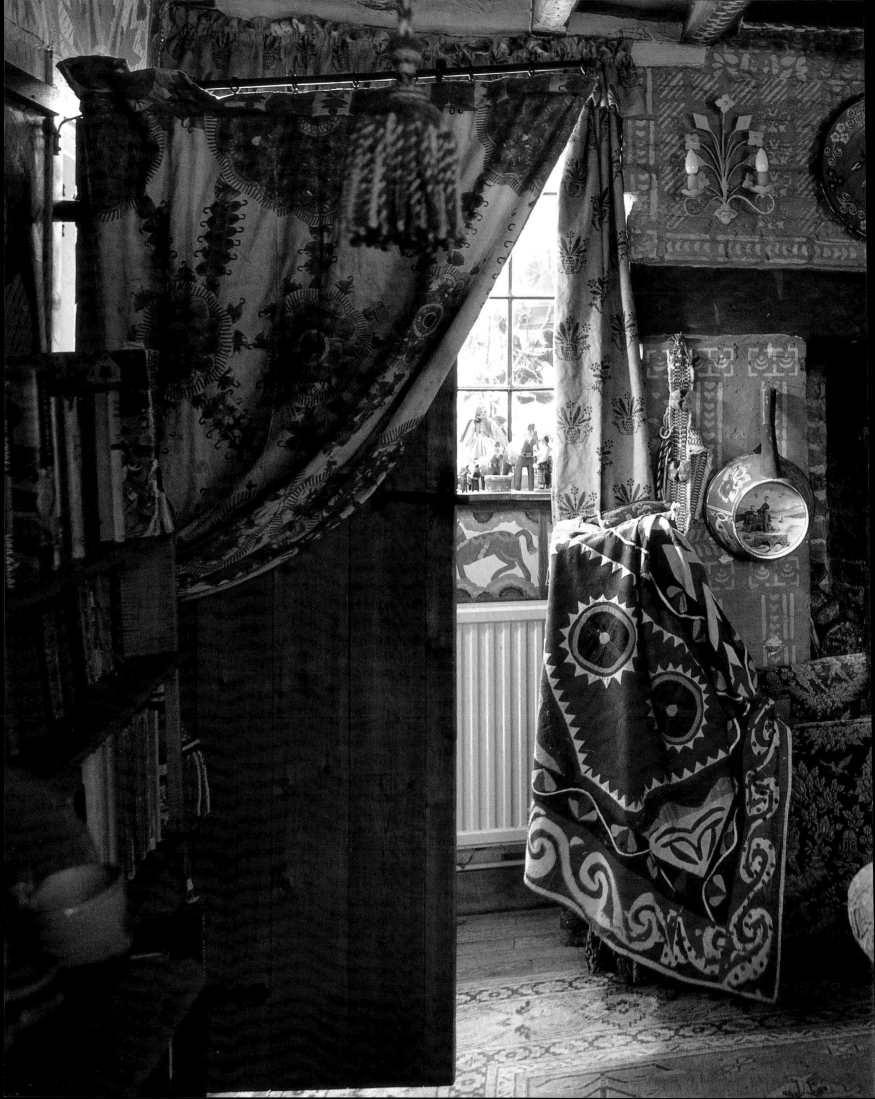

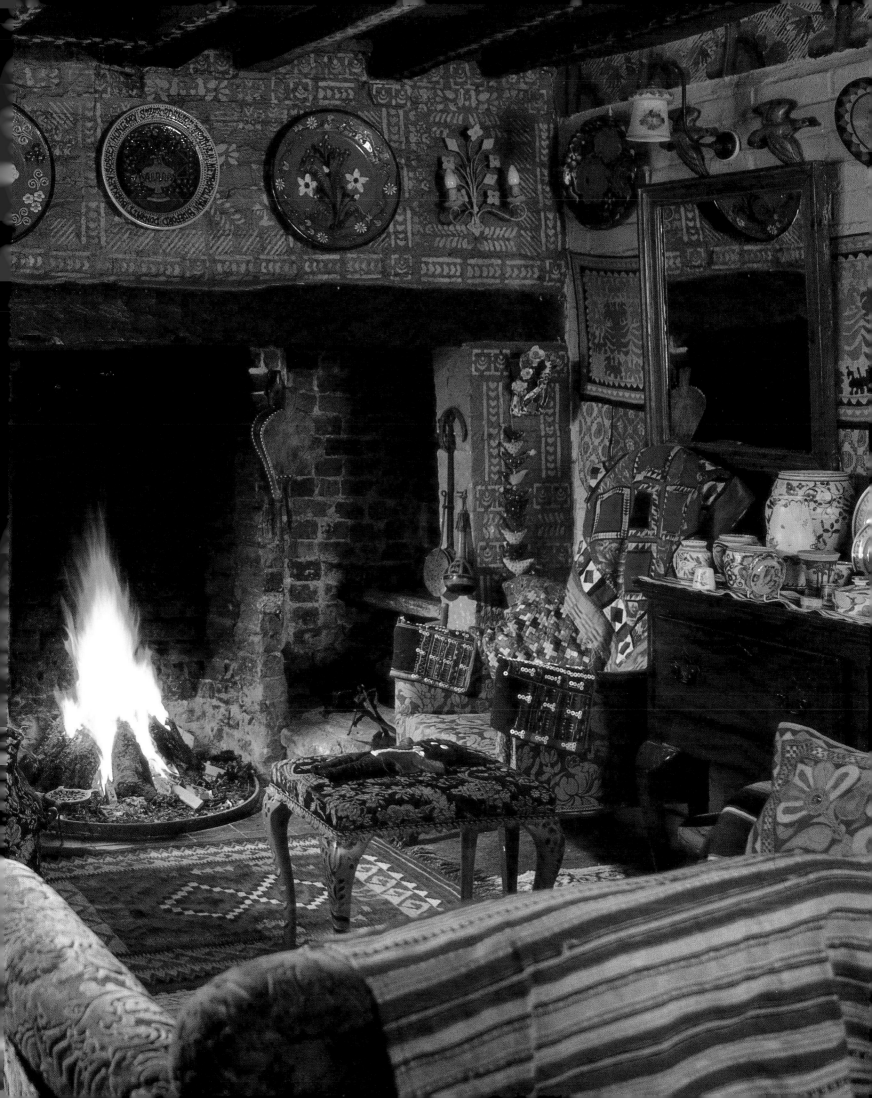

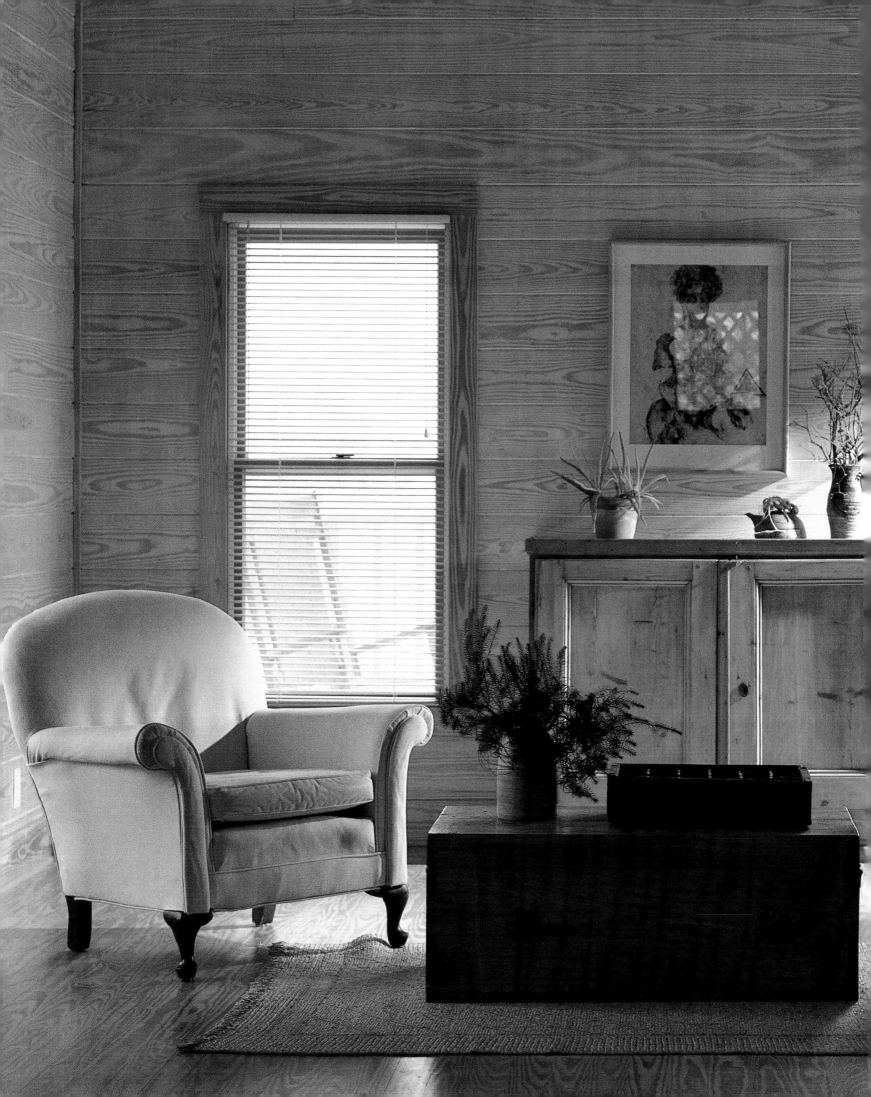

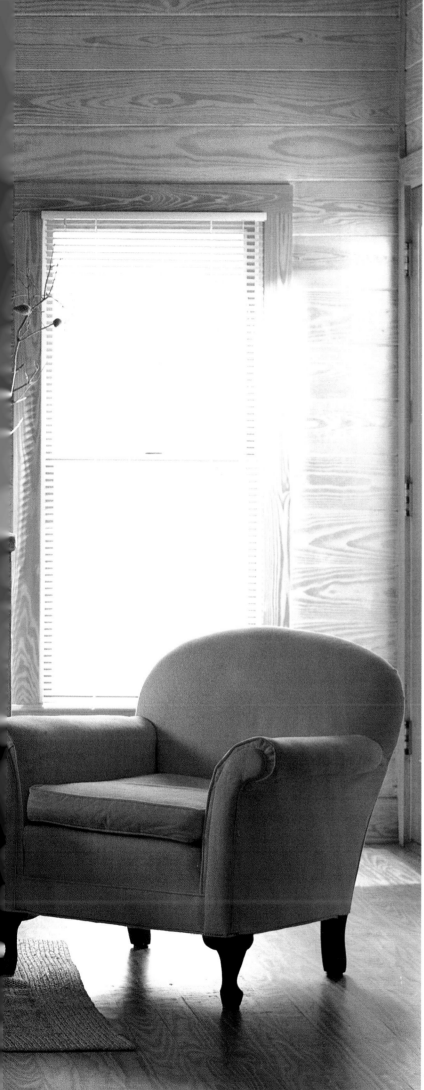

Simple lines

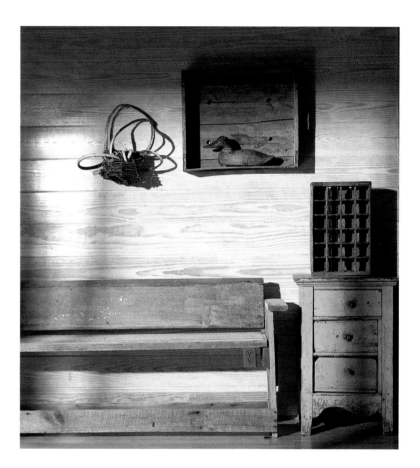

*C*ountry style does not necessarily dictate a cluttered environment. There is room for spare, peaceful settings. It is fundamental to this aspect of country style that the architectural elements of the house are kept clean and clear. For example, stair risers may be picked out with ceramic tiles or the treads lipped with smooth wood. There is little of the wrap-around, fitted-carpet style of many modern interiors.

Seaside in Florida, USA, is a modern development that draws on time-honoured vernacular traditions (see p. 158).

Left:
A single picture is the only ornament against the varying grain of the timber-clad walls. Furniture is generous in dimensions but small in amount – just a plain cupboard, a pair of comfortable armchairs upholstered in creamy cotton and a chest that doubles as a coffee table.

Above:
A seasoned plank bench stands next to a painted chest of drawers; above, a seed tray has been adapted to make a shelving unit.

Inland looks

The land is the starting point for most country style. Although labourers' cottages are small, the stock of buildings includes generously scaled farmhouses, converted barns, mills and presses. The architectural style will be dictated by the materials available to build homes from and the type of agriculture prevalent in the region. Because these buildings depend on the land around them, they seem to grow out of their surroundings and the colours used inside will often reflect the hues of the landscape. Soft, time-worn colours like clotted creams, leaf greens and washed browns are more common in cooler-climate farmhouses, while bright whites and deep hues abound in warmer climes.

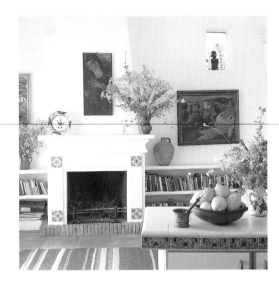

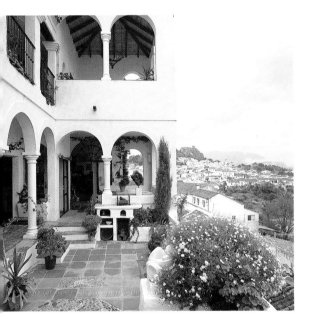

El Molino del Carmen *is a converted olive mill set in the Andalucian mountains inland from Estepona in Spain. It serves both as a home and a workspace for its artist owner. A terracotta-floored terrace overlooking pan-tiled village rooves has a romantic tranquility, enhanced by its view of kestrels entering the ruined convent on the slopes below and eagles circling the castle on the hill beyond.*

Top right:
Sculpted shelves filled with books, pottery and family treasures are sited either side of a plaster fireplace decorated with hand-painted tiles. A catholic collection of oil paintings and a profusion of wild flowers in assorted pots emphasizes the informal comfort of this room.

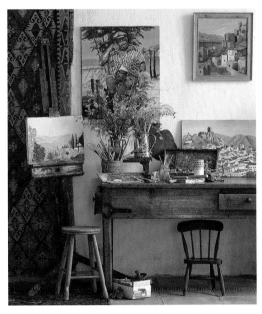

Middle right:
Colourful modern paintings inspired by local characters and scenes are clustered above a rustic table where palettes and paints jostle jugs filled with brushes and wild flowers.

Bottom right:
The curved and pierced staircase constructed in traditional Moorish materials – plaster, wood and tiles – is a dramatic counterpoint to the machinery retained from the days when this building was a working olive mill.

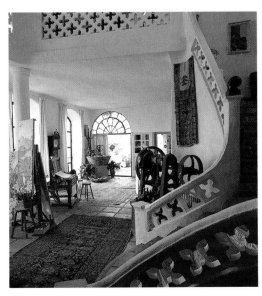

Far right:
The curve to this stairway is enhanced by the solidity of the studded, sun-bleached door. Local hand-decorated tiles have been used on the risers to counteract the severity of the line.

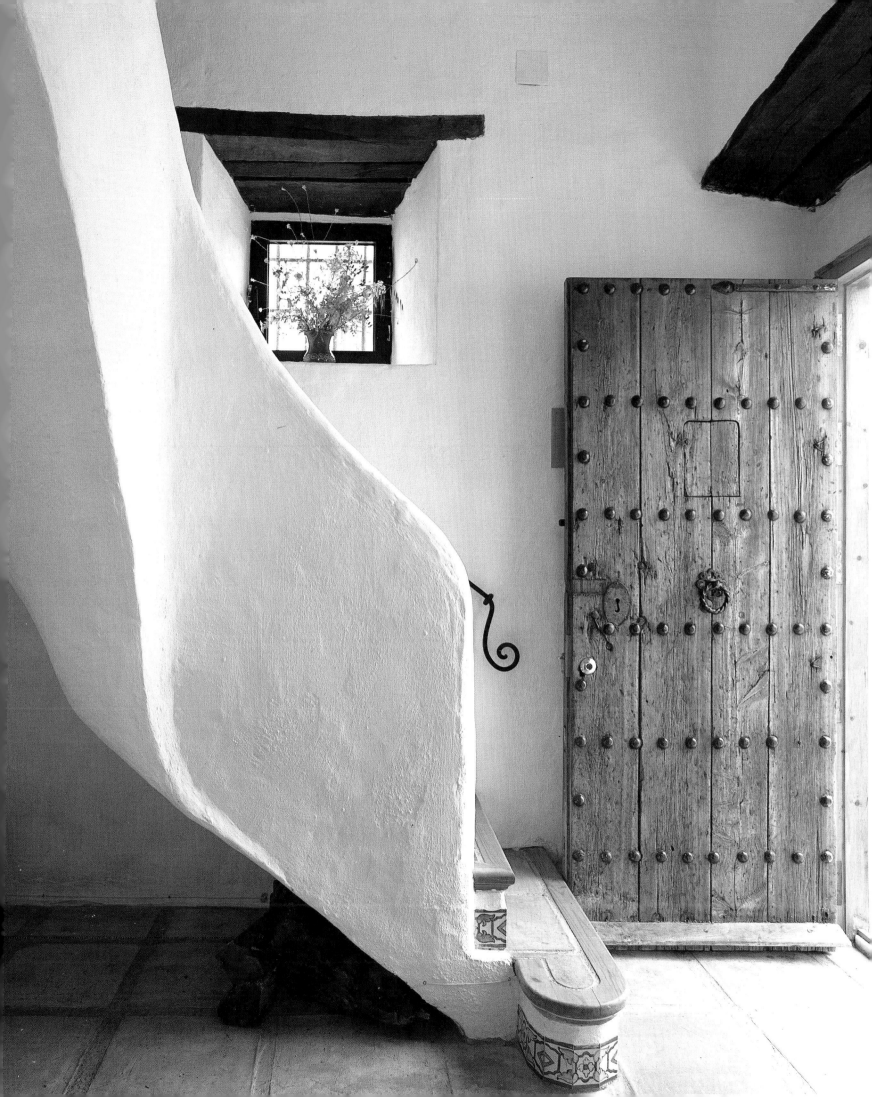

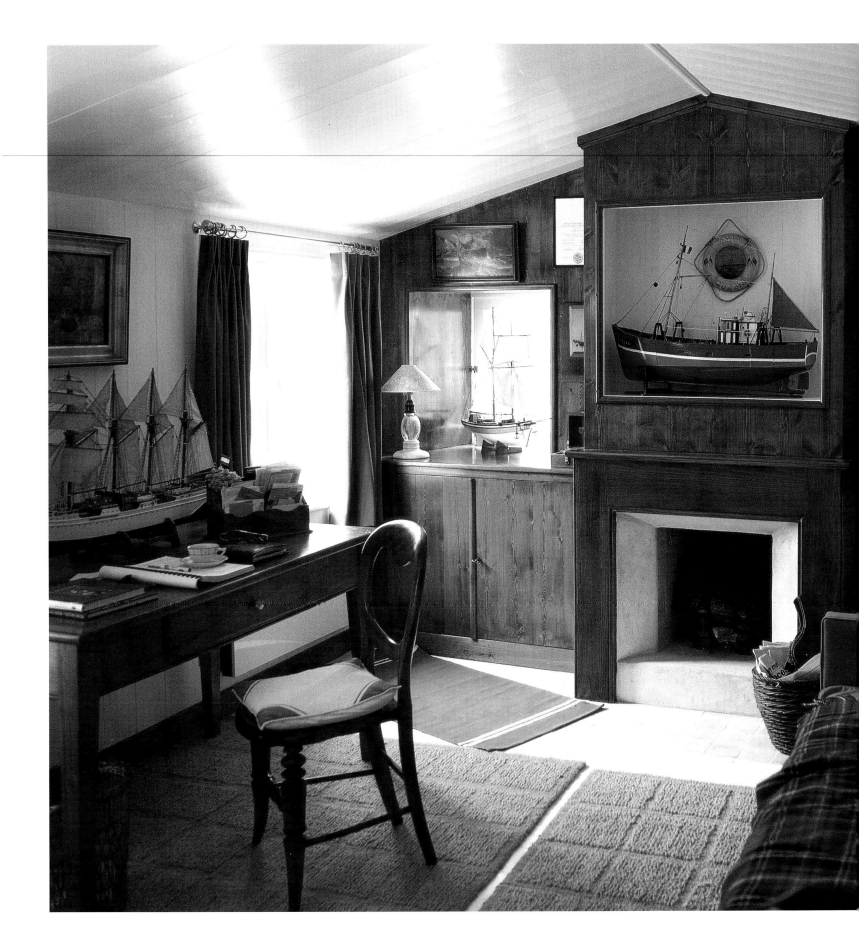

Coastal setting

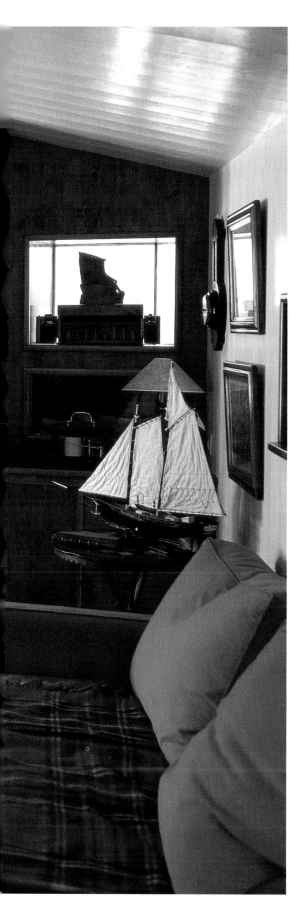

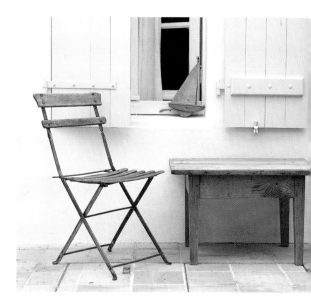

Maritime dwellers depended on the sea for their livelihood and their homes reflect this. Wood brought down to the coast for shipbuilding was used in the houses both as structural supports and to clad walls and ceilings. Often, it was painted in the colours of waves or driftwood. Houses were small, low-built and shuttered to keep out the biting winds that blow off the sea.

Where the land meets the sea, country style merges with maritime in this French seaside home, converted from a derelict hen-house, hut and fisherman's cottages on the Ile de Re off the west coast of France. The owners of this house have furnished it to fit in with the spirit of its location, buying unassuming furniture, blue and white fabrics and a collection of ornaments, old and new, that reflect the theme of the sea.

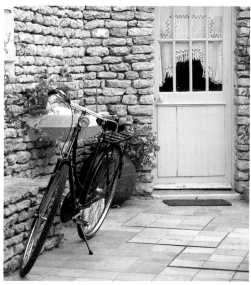

Left:
The dark-stained wooden units built into alcoves in this study are reminiscent of the panelling in old-time sailing ships – a mood enhanced by the models of masted schooners and yachts. A sturdy 19th century mahogany desk and chair add to the period feel. White-painted floorboards and rush matting lighten the room and prevent the captain's cabin theme becoming too serious or self-conscious.

Top right:
Pale blue-gray shutters, used to shut out harsh winds or baking sun, stand out against a whitewashed wall.

Middle right:
The crumbling exterior walls of the cottage were rebuilt from local Pisay stone.

Bottom right:
What was once a glass-roofed lean-to has become a sunny study area with the addition of a pine bureau and traditional French folding garden chairs. The floor is quarry-tiled for practicality. A row of pegs provides a convenient home for sturdy, windproof coats.

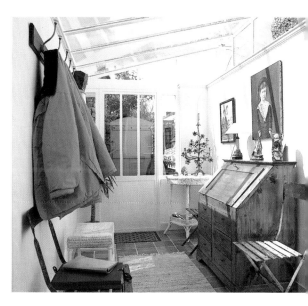

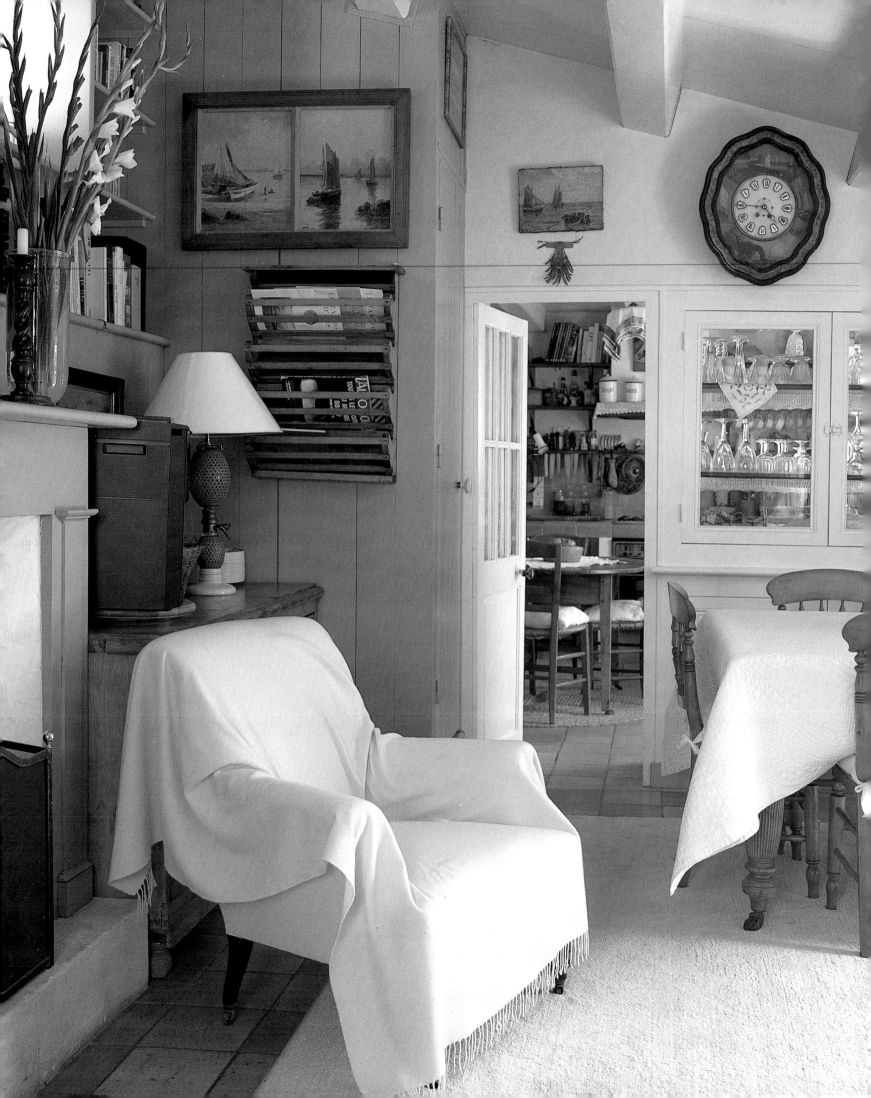

Coastal setting

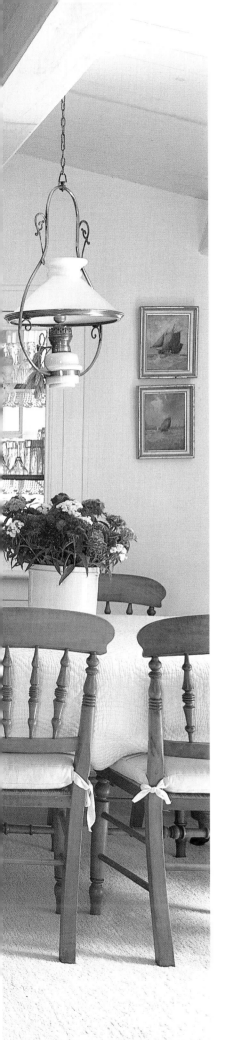

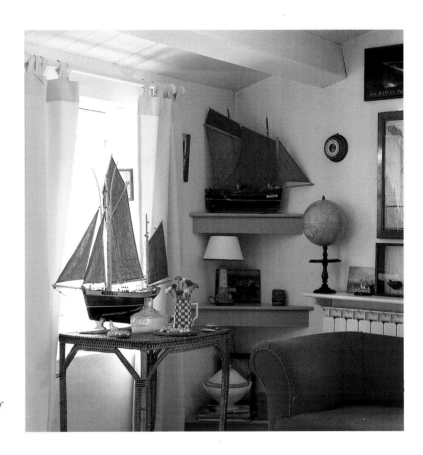

Left:
From the dining room the kitchen (see page 184) can be glimpsed through a window that acts as a hatch for serving food. Above the hatch hangs an ebony and maple late 19th century clock. Beech country chairs dating from the 19th century surround the large pine table. The creamy white of the sloping ceiling and beams is echoed in the soft furnishings. A white quilted cloth is draped over the table, a plain cream blanket shrouds the fireside chair and a textured white rug covers the terracotta tiles which have been laid throughout the ground floor of the house.

Below right:
Marine blue-greens dominate the sitting area. A subtle seascape framed in old pine is the focus of a collection of artefacts that lend a nautical ambience to this room.

Top right:
Painted wooden shelves make an attractive display area for a collection based on a nautical theme. The triangular design is an effective solution for a tricky corner. Skirting board was used to form a kickboard for the bottom shelf and to give substance to the higher shelves. Creamy yellow sailcloth curtains bring a natural warmth to the sea-coloured room and are a more original choice than the obvious nautical stripes.

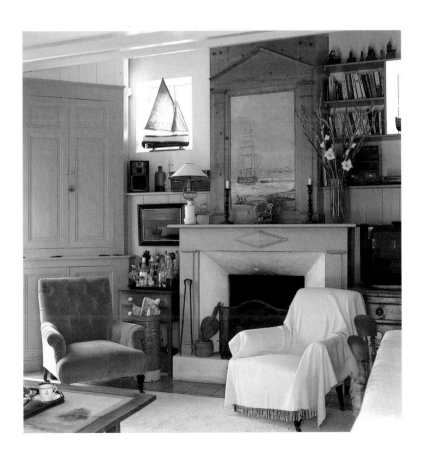

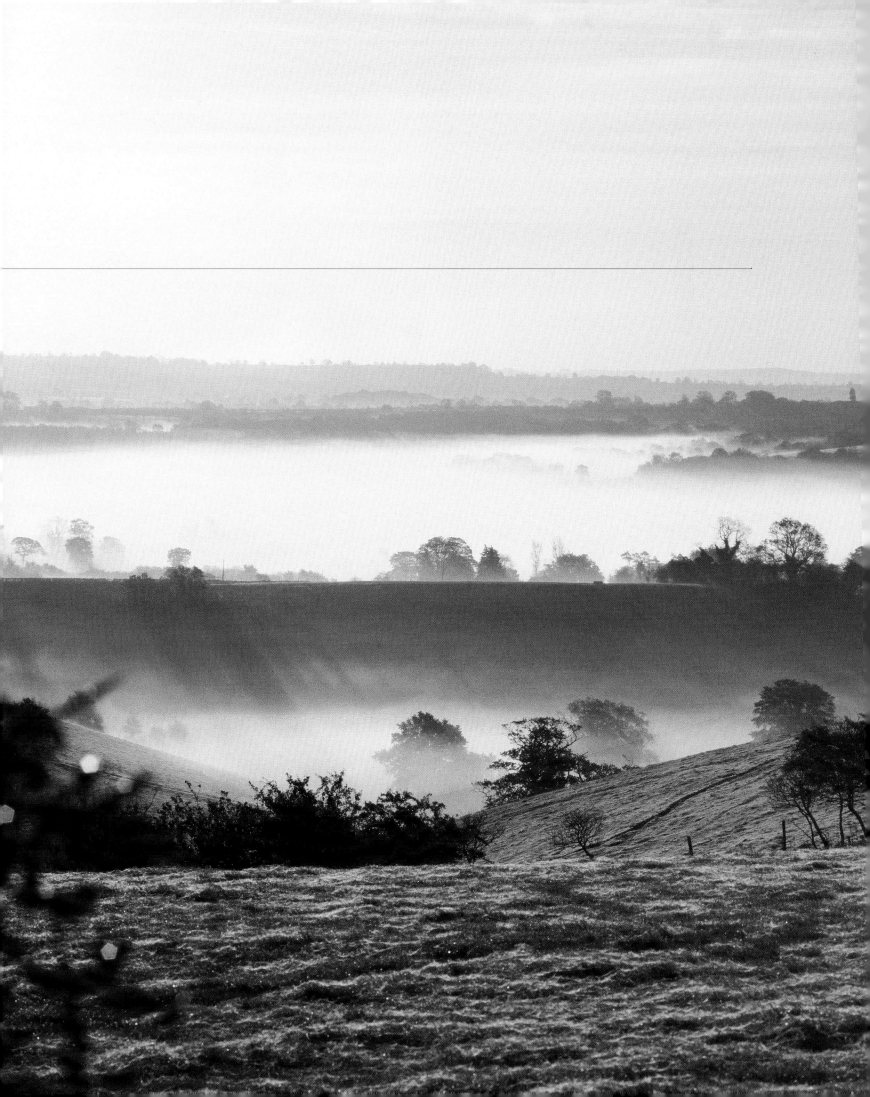

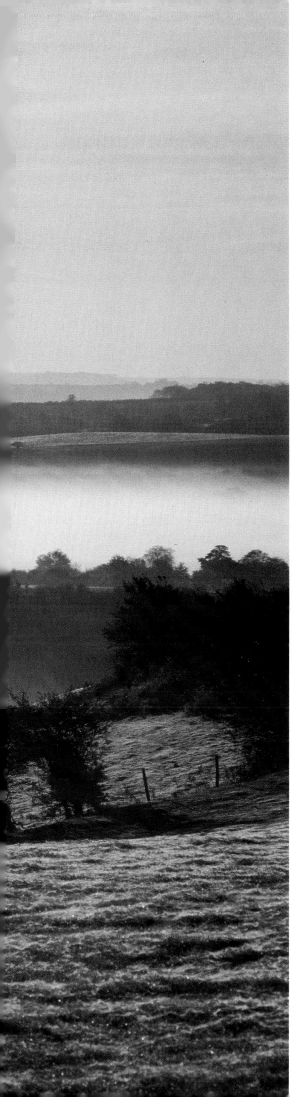

ENGLISH
Country Style

*I*f country style is the answer to the universal daydream of the simple life, then the English cottage is its precise location. Framed by hollyhocks, built of Cotswold stone the colour of vanilla fudge and roofed over with thatch or mossy tiles, the English cottage is the home of the romantic country idyll. Inside this idyllic interior the immediate impression is of clutter. It is as if the occupants once lived somewhere bigger. Elegant blue-and-white china for special occasions is now crammed onto the kitchen dresser next to rougher, salt-glazed pottery and wooden spoons. Books are heaped on side-tables because there is no room, or no wall smooth enough, for bookshelves. Oak chairs and tables are crowded near oversized fireplaces and seats are fitted under the windows in the deep recesses afforded by thick walls. It is the style of a comfortable confinement indoors, in rooms slightly smaller than had been expected.

Most cottages were purpose-built to serve as rural workers' homes. Many were constructed hastily between the 16th and 19th centuries to accomodate the rural poor near the lands of the gentry who needed their labour. The poor had been dispossessed by the rich when their old common lands were gathered into large estates. In some cases, the housing shortage was solved by converting vacated farmhouses into several cottages under one roof.

The cottage was always a minimal space, creating a clutter that would become one of the hallmarks of its style, along with the oversized look of beds in small rooms tucked under the eaves. Its best-loved architectural features developed in the same way, out of necessity. The front porch was originally built to help keep the entrance dry, but became exaggerated over the generations into a small lobby. The high dormer windows that give attic bedrooms their charm were a medieval invention to create headroom in the roof space.

Left:
The colours of the English landscape are softened by winter mists or summer haze. These muddy browns, faded greens and watery blues are echoed in country interiors.

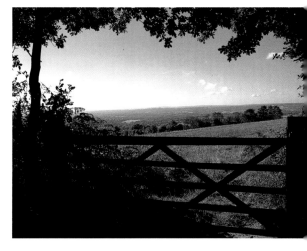

Above:
A traditional five-bar gate is witness to all the comings and goings of English agricultural life: the farmer collecting his cows for milking or sheep for shearing, harvesters bringing the grain home, and tractors tilling the fields.

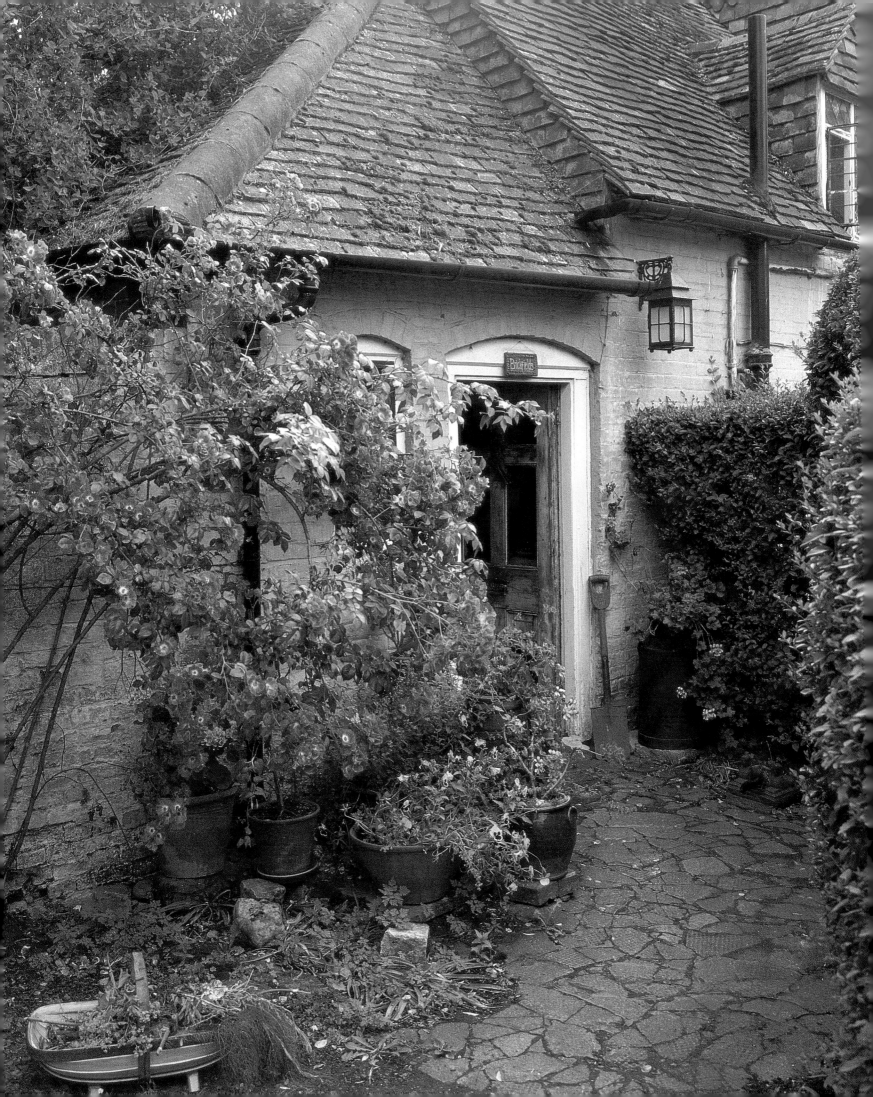

English country style

The unconverted farmhouse developed a more expansive style: although low-ceilinged attic bedrooms, similar to the cottage type, might be created upstairs, the living spaces below were more generous since the owners could afford to build out onto surrounding land and create several family rooms. The farmhouse kitchen tends to be large, with a long table set in the middle of it, while the cottage kitchen is a smaller, more ad hoc arrangement of cupboards in the corner of what was often the only living room in the house.

The cramped cottage became the epitome of all that is most romantic about England's countryside because it was cultivated as such by the 19th century romantics. To William Morris and the other leaders of the Arts and Crafts Movement the small, self-sufficient cottage represented a return to a wholesome way of life and a rejection of the grime and uniformity of industrialized Britain. As they fell in love with the rural style, they romanticized it and added little touches of their own imaginings. The Arts and Crafts architect, Charles Voysey, urged people to "Try the effect of a well-proportioned room with white-washed walls, plain carpet and simple oak furniture and nothing in it but necessary articles of use – and one pure ornament in the form of a simple vase of flowers." But Voysey, like Morris, made his living not from whitewash but from floral-patterned wallpapers, and so the romantic image of the cottage came to be papered over with flowers.

Not that a flowery, romantic idea of English country style is a complete fiction. The fact that many workers lived in "tied cottages" on their employer's estate meant that the English rural poor were physically near the rich. Decorative ideas from the Big House were quick to seed in the house of the poor man at his gate. The gentleman's parlour began to appear in farmhouses and wealthier cottages in the late 19th century. It was usually converted from an inner store-room, behind the kitchen and away from the drafts of the front door. Room

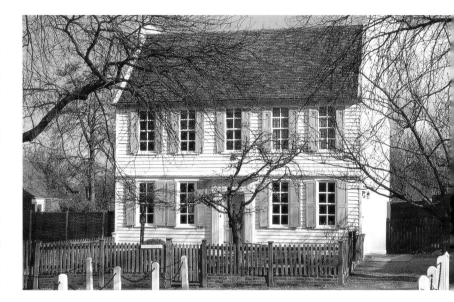

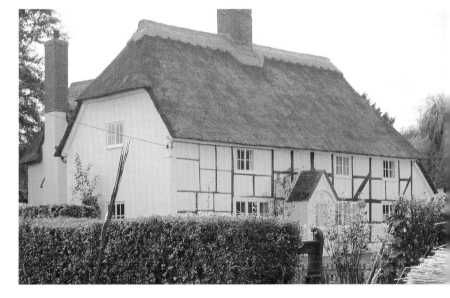

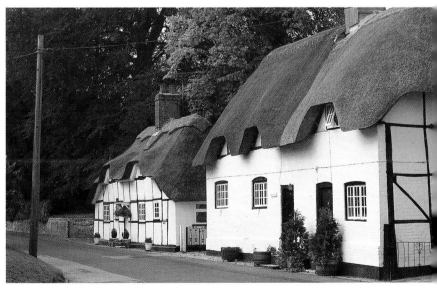

Right and left:
All over Britain, rural life is focussed around the village. The church, the local store and the public house, often grouped around a village green, are essential to the community spirit. Depending on the region, cottages may be constructed in stone, flint or cob; they may be brick-built, weatherboarded or the archetypal half-timbered type, with a thatched roof and roses growing around the door, that is everyone's English country idyll.

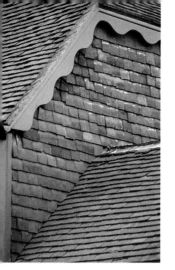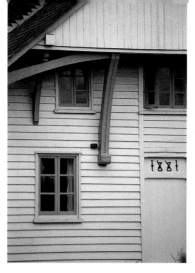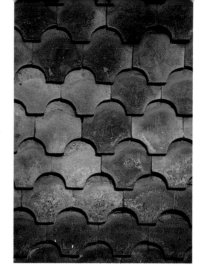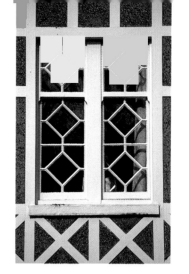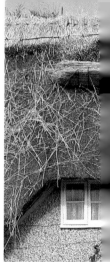

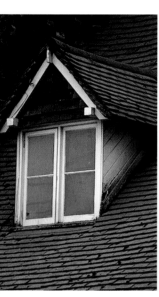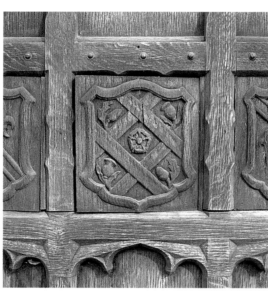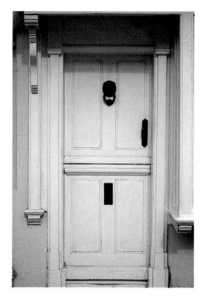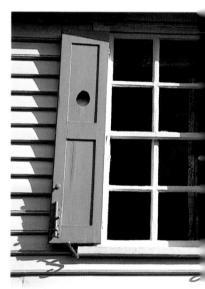

Above top:
English architecture, like its surrounding landscape, is shaped and coloured
by the weather. The steeply pitched roofs may shake off the rain, but its
insistent effect can't be ignored – building materials, whether wood, tile or
metal, are covered with a living green patina encouraged by the climate.

schemes and the odd piece of furniture were not the only hand-me-downs from the Big House. The glorious jumble of old-fashioned flowers that makes up the cottage garden as we now know it sprouted from cuttings taken from the plants of the rich. Originally a small strip of land in front of the cottage, used for growing vegetables, the garden was all that was remained for the cottager after the land he had farmed was enclosed by the lord of the manor. But as the estate owner planted and replanted his garden according to the latest trends, the old-fashioned flower varieties were passed by his head-gardener to the cottage dweller. Gradually, pansies, lupins, hollyhocks, and old roses appeared at random among the serried rows of cabbages, and the lovely rambling confusion that resulted in turn inspired the wallpapers and fabrics of the cottage interior.

The floral-patterned wallpapers of the English cottage are usually confined to the parlour and bedrooms, where the partition walls in the roof space are likely to be plastered wood and smooth enough to paper. In utilitarian rooms like the kitchen the walls are limewashed or painted pale buttermilks, egg-yolk yellows and thick creams to lighten rooms with small windows. Stencilled friezes might be applied high up on the walls to emulate cornices, their simple patterns repeated in block-printed fabrics for curtains. In the larger farmhouse, darker colours might be used: crimsons, deep greens and deep ochres that help contract rooms and warm them. And the generously sized fireplaces are often painted in contrasting colours to the walls.

The furniture of English country style is solid and plain, built by local craftsmen to age-old, purposeful designs. It tends

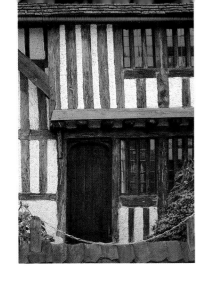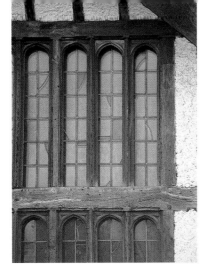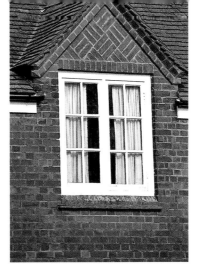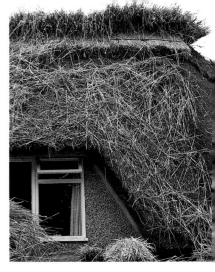

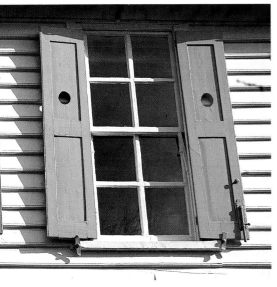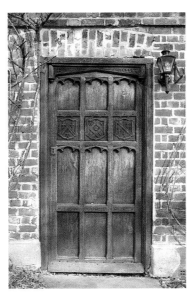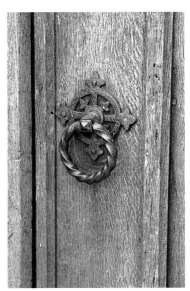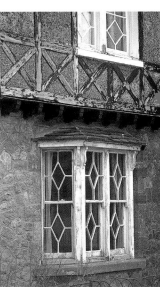

Above bottom:
The exteriors of English country homes are rich in decorative detail.
Dormer windows break up roof lines, glazing bars criss-cross windows,
carved wood and forged iron embellish doors and weathered timbers bisect
the faces of buildings.

to be used to break up spaces, particularly in the larger family rooms like kitchens, to create smaller, warmer areas. The pine or oak dresser, for instance, did not give way to the sideboard the way that it did in wealthier houses because it was often used to divide the cooking area from the dining part. There is a randomness to English country kitchens. The heights of the pieces of furniture are higgledy-piggledy, and painted wood is mixed with plain oak or scrubbed pine.

Country furniture was produced by local craftsmen and the designs they followed reflected the natural properties of the materials available. For example, the suppleness of beech was exploited for the graceful Windsor chair, whose distinctive spokes, set in a bowed-frame, were originally created by local wheelwrights.

Like the comb-backed Windsor chair – so-called because its curved top and spoked back repeated the shape of the haymaker's comb or rake – the whole of English country style depends on natural shapes. It revels in decorativeness, but in general patterns are used in small doses and are based on imagery familiar from outside. The blown roses on a hearth rug in front of the Aga range could be copied from the old-fashioned rambler just outside the front door, while the browns and reds of a kelim echo the tones of old brick. And the coach-and-horse scenes that decorate the ubiquitous blue-and-white china recreate a landscape still distinguished by its hedgerows and ploughed fields. The hedges themselves helped to generate English cottage style as they were created by the rich landowners to close off the old common lands of the poor, driving them into the small homes that spawned the most romantic country style of all.

43

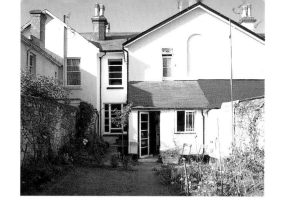

In an unexceptional early 20th century house on a busy main road in Devon Guimund Mounter, a dealer in antique country furniture, and Ana Simons have created a country home with the primitive feel of an earlier century.

Right:
A carved decoy duck sits on the mantel of this duck-egg blue fireplace, against the streaky limewashed walls. In many country bedrooms there is room for little more than a bed and a chest or cupboard. Here, however, space has been found for a simple chair and an attractive 18th century fruitwood wine table.

Below right:
Country furniture was often decorated and adapted to suit fashion or circumstance, rather than discarded. The previous owner of this 18th century Welsh press had whitewashed the whole piece, even the brass handles.

Below left:
In the bedrooms the walls have been papered and then limewashed, creating an uneven effect that increases as the colour slowly wears off.

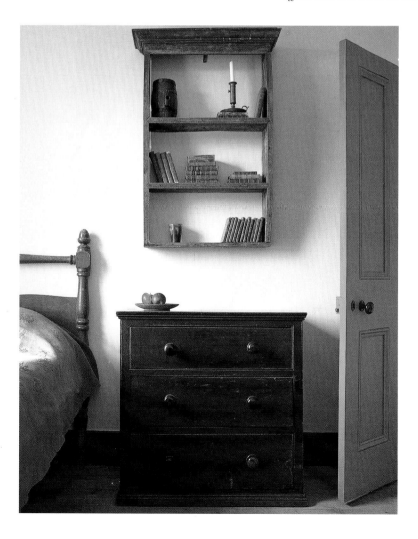

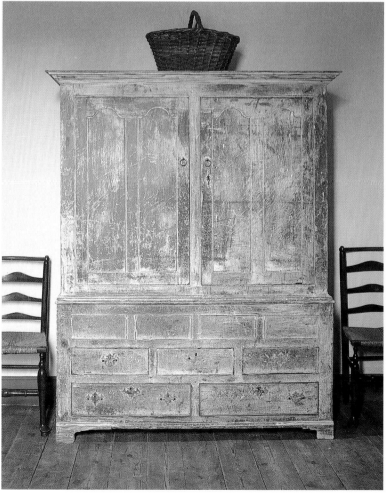

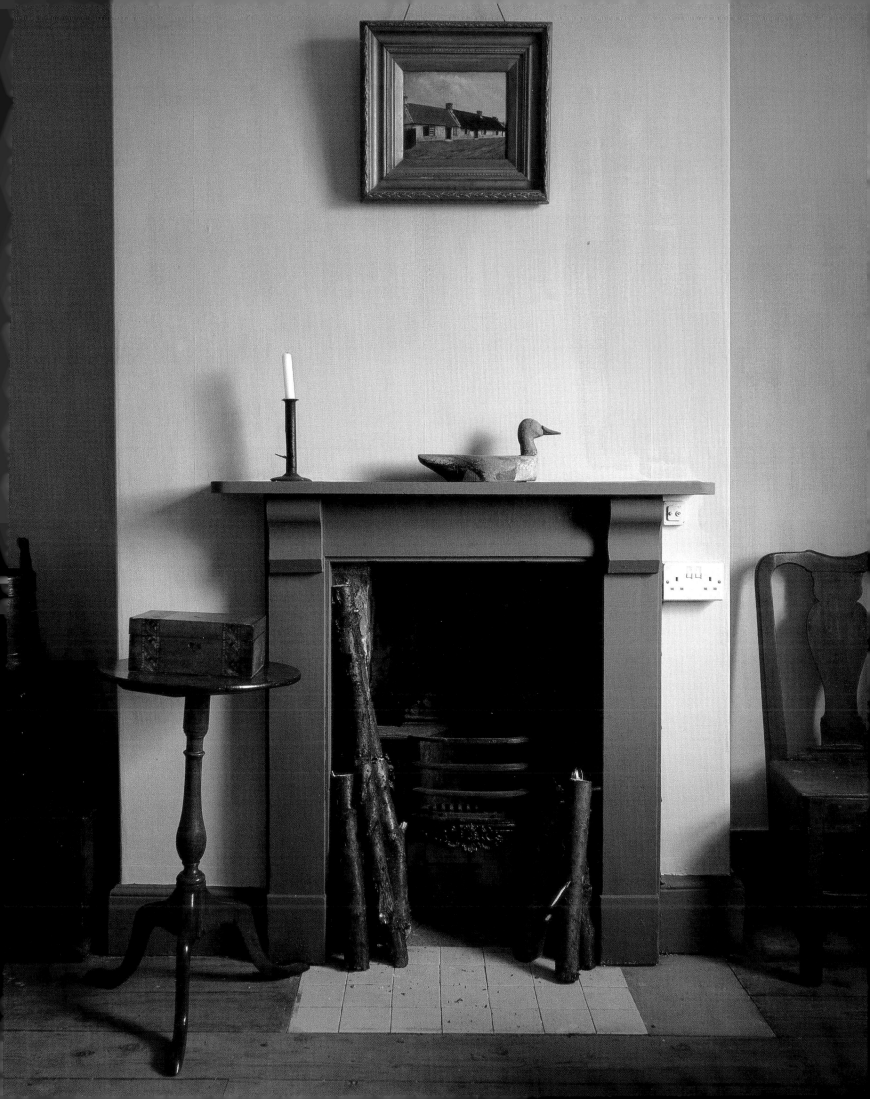

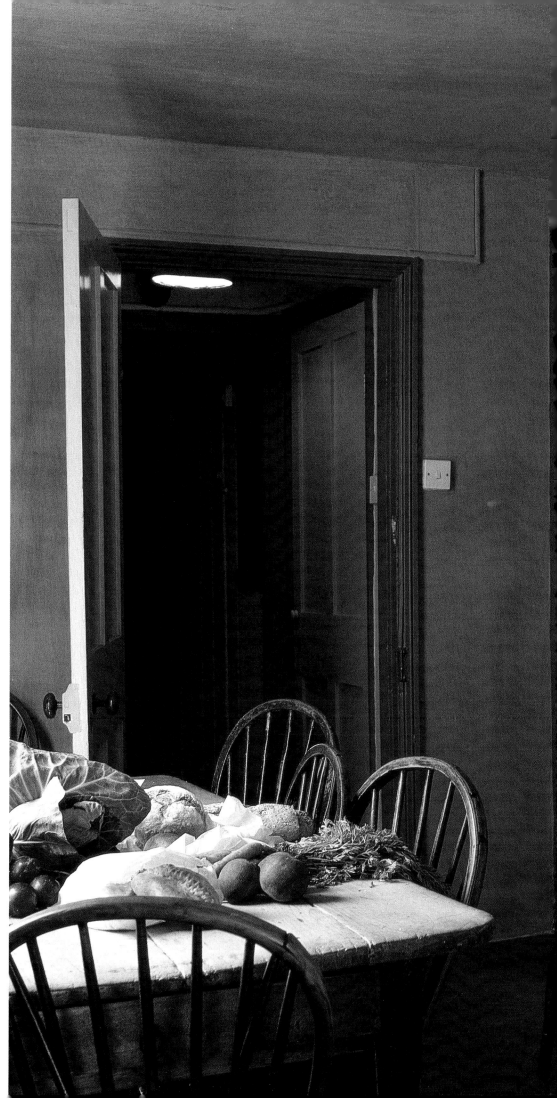

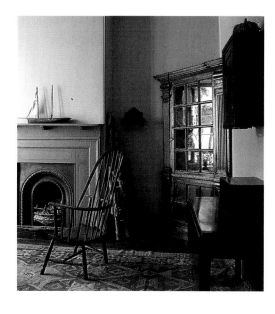

Above:
An early 19th century Cornish fruitwood Windsor chair sits in front of the cast iron fireplace, while a 19th century pond yacht, bringing to mind the West Country's close ties with the sea, adorns the mantelshelf. The 18th century corner cupboard, its bay-green paint dulled and worn by time, is a splendid country attempt at grandeur. Only the top is original; the base was designed, built and distressed to match by Guimund himself.

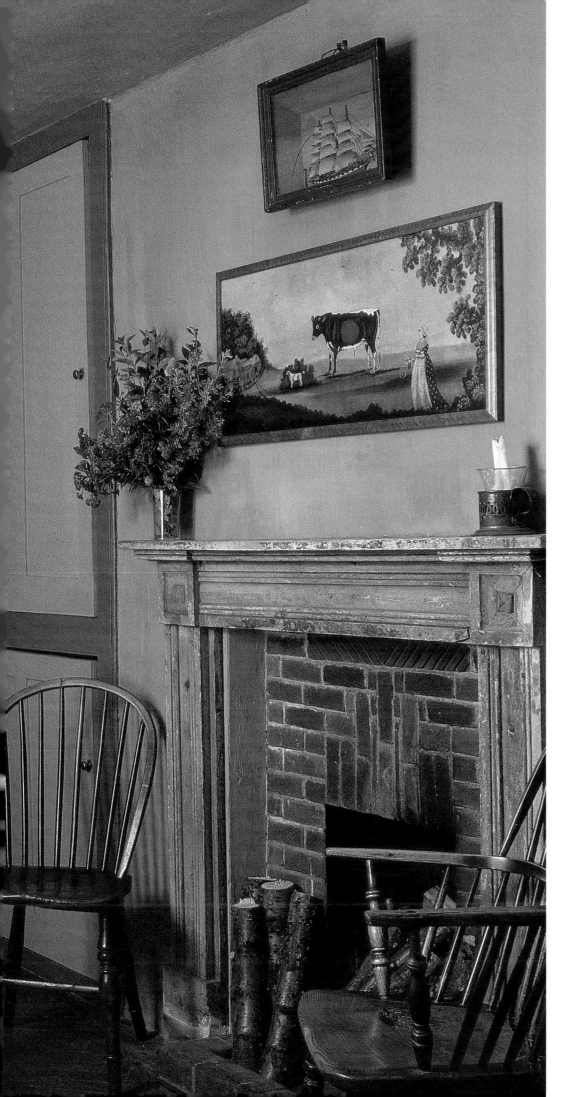

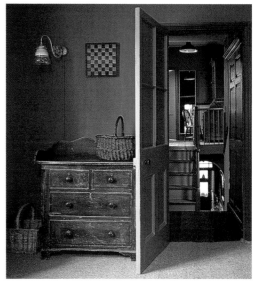

Above:
The essential ingredients of the primitive look
are sparse furnishings, bare boards or rush
matting, limewashed walls and woodwork in
natural earth colours, traditional duck-egg blue
or seaweed-green.

Left:
A sturdy wooden table and a set of chairs –
19th century fruitwood Windsors here – are an
essential central focus of any country kitchen.
The table is an interesting late 18th century
piece with an ash base and a reversible top
(scrubbed pine side for everyday use, polished
side for Sundays).

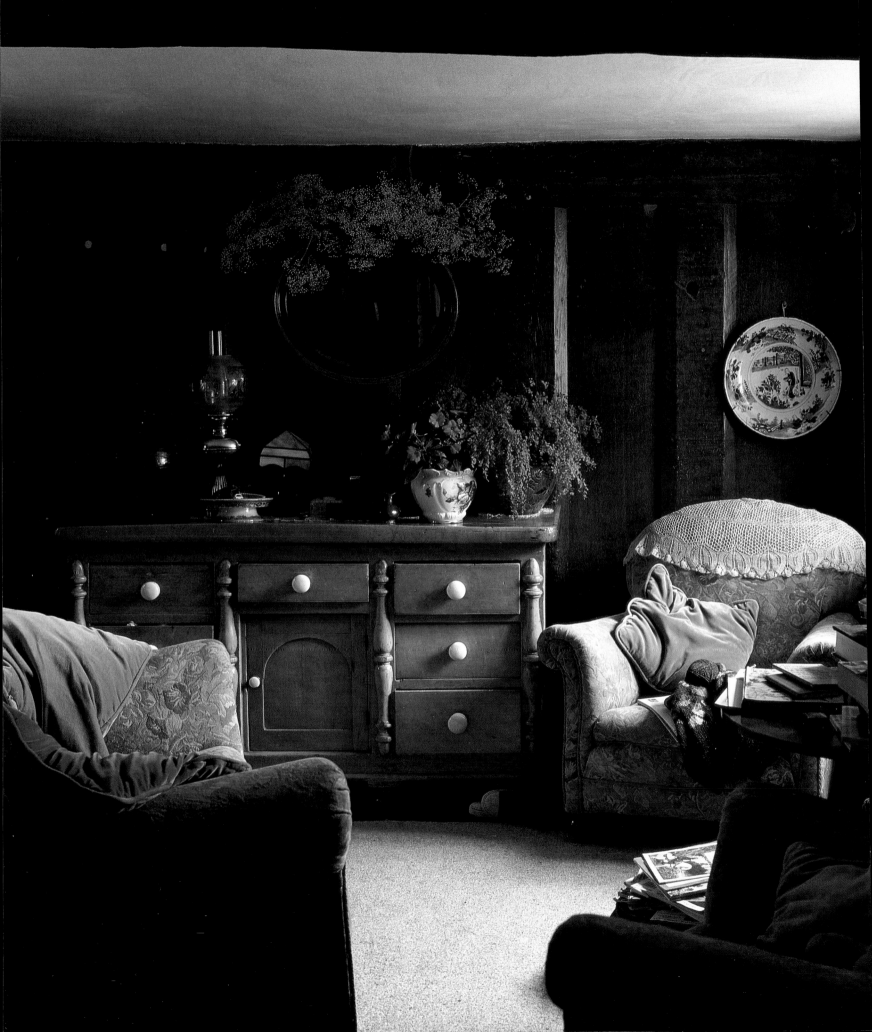

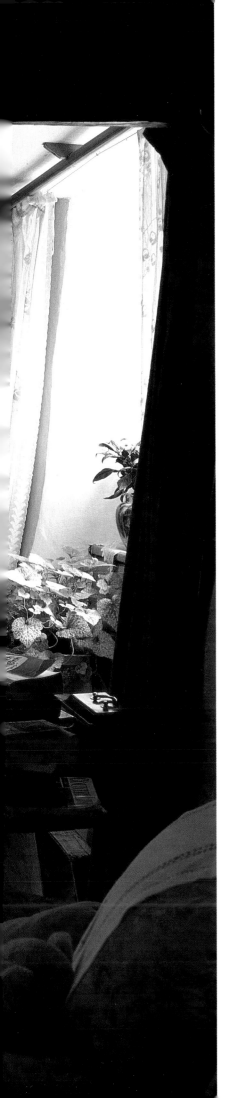

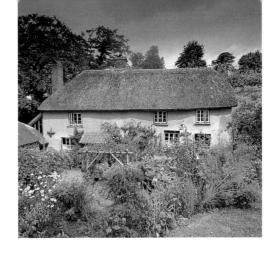

When Peter and Silvie Schofield found Huttswell Farm in North Devon it was almost derelict. Its traditional construction called for careful renovation. Built mainly of cob (a mixture of clay subsoil and chopped straw), the building can breathe only so long as no waterproof layer is applied inside or out. Traditional methods and materials were used to restore the house, including lime to make plaster, mortar and colourwashes.

Left:
The parlour is furnished in a comfortable, eclectic farmhouse style, with deep-cushioned armchairs covered in a faded English chintz. A 19th century pine sideboard stands in front of the loadbearing 16th century oak plank-and-muntin screen.

Below right:
The old plaster wall is limewashed in a soft shade of peach. Limewashing involves a certain amount of pot luck as, unlike modern paints where the required colour can be carefully selected from a chart, it is almost impossible to tell what colour the lime mixture will dry to.

Below left:
The electrical fittings have been painted with a modern paint to blend with the limewashed walls (limewash won't take to plastic).

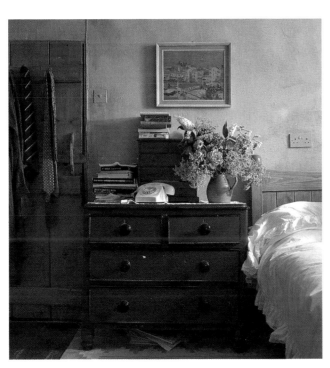

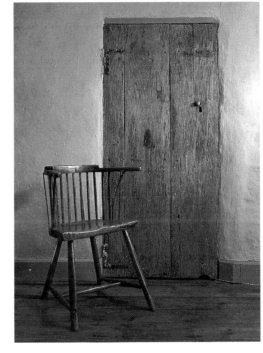

English country style

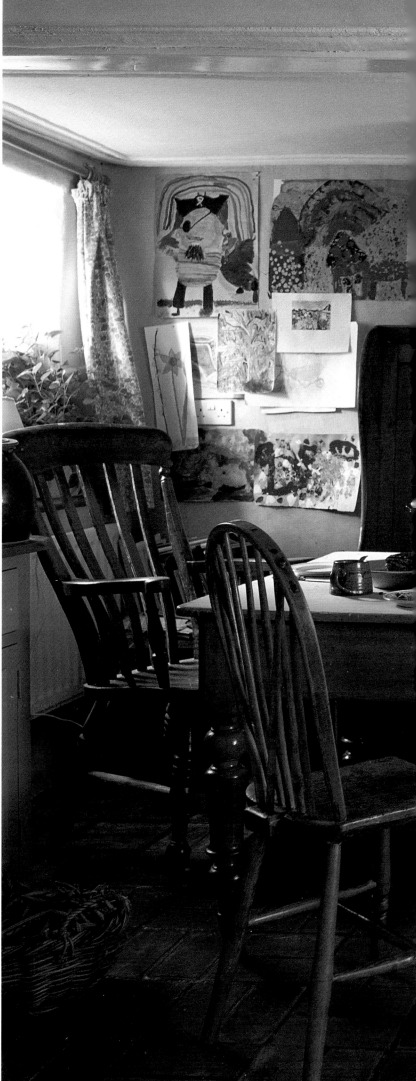

Right:
An old wooden settle and a variety of 19th century chairs surround a mellow pine table, creating an informal dining area in the kitchen. Children's paintings pinned to the walls give an air of unconsidered charm.

Below:
Cob walls will last indefinitely if protected from rising damp, so waterproof concrete has been used as an invisible sub-floor. Laid over it are old bricks which have been cut in half so that they are only 1¾ ins (4.4 cm) thick. An early 20th century latchhooked rug covers the floor in front of the coal-fired range.

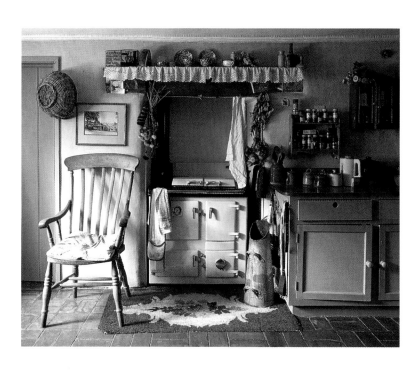

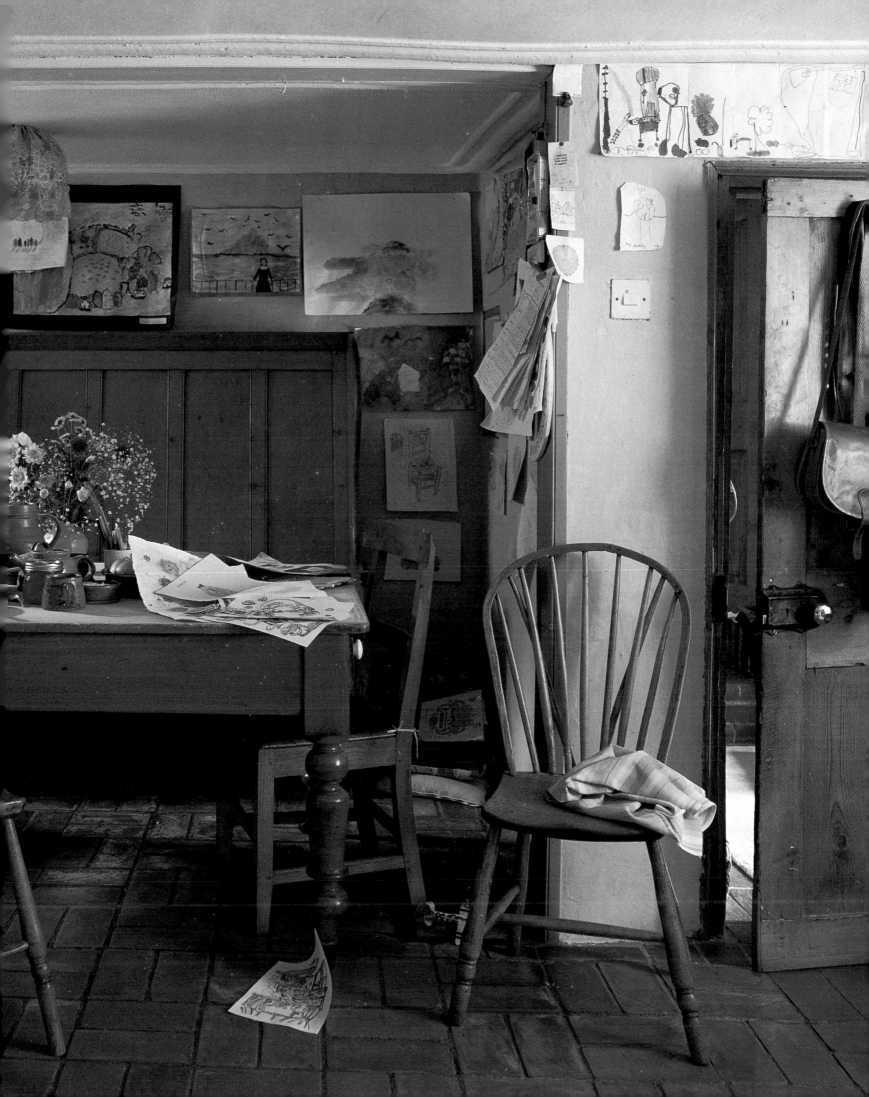

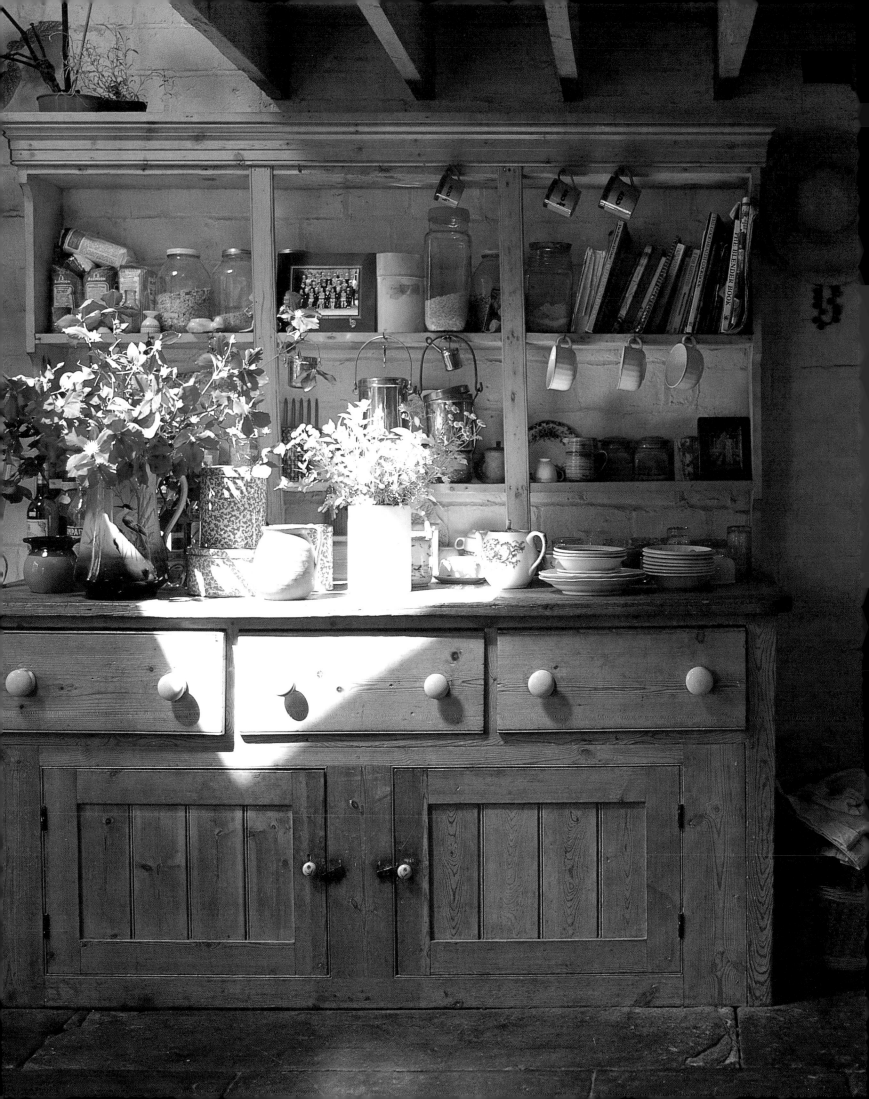

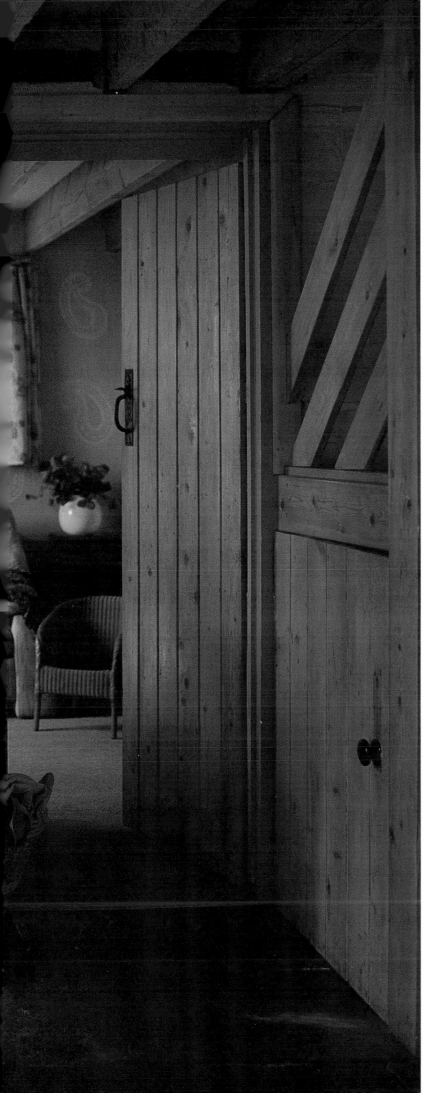

English country style

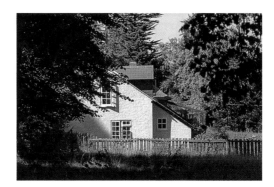

Jane and Terry Macey have transformed a once-derelict Edwardian lodge house in Somerset into a flexible family home and workshop for their clothing business, Jatz. The lodge house was originally a single-storeyed dwelling with extremely high ceilings, but the Maceys removed these to obtain enough height to accomodate two floors.

Left:
Natural materials are the theme of this home. Unadorned wood is on display in the solid lines of the old pine dresser. The walls have been stripped back to the brick and then painted cream. And concrete floors were carefully sledgehammered to reveal the original flagstones beneath.

Below:
The wooden armchairs and table were originally designed for garden use, but are an excellent choice indoors as they are robust enough to withstand the rigours of family life.

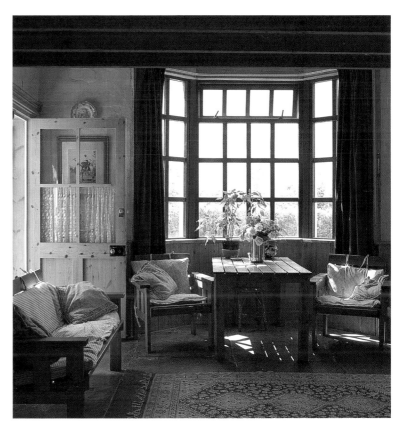

English country style

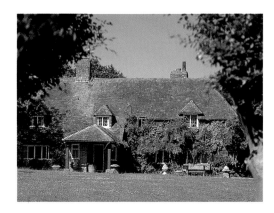

This beautiful building is part 16th century farmhouse, part 1930s country house. Located in the heart of Sussex, it is home to antique dealers Helen Linfield and Michael Wakelin. Inside, they have created a unique look through their confident use of colour and textiles and eclectic mix of styles.

Right:
A warm atmosphere is created with brick-red sponged and speckled walls, broken by a paper border, and a quarry-tiled floor. Against this background stands a curved 18th century fruitwood tavern table in front of a time-worn pine and sycamore late 18th century settle cushioned with Scandinavian textiles. The 18th century dresser is made of pine and walnut and houses a collection of 18th and 19th century artefacts (see page 203).

Below:
Folk art is the obvious complement to country style. This painted wooden seagull contrasts effectively with the speckled wall behind.

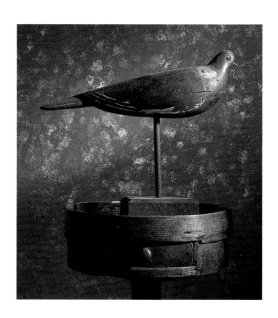

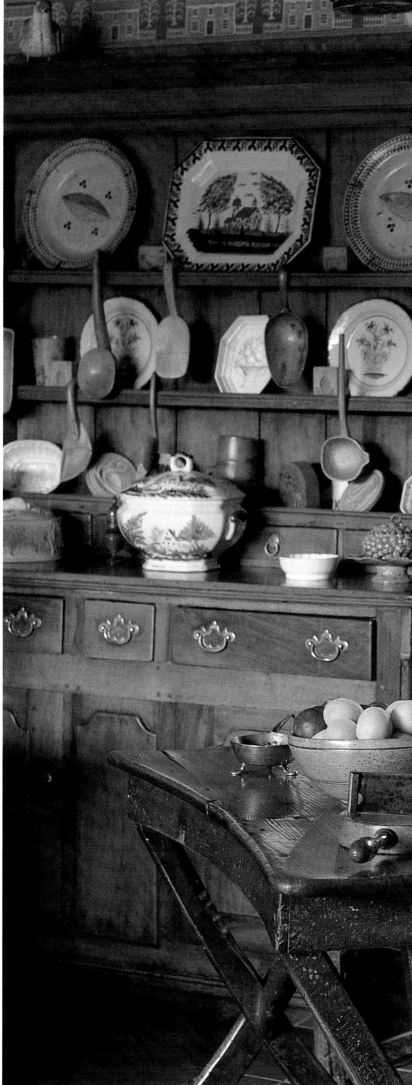

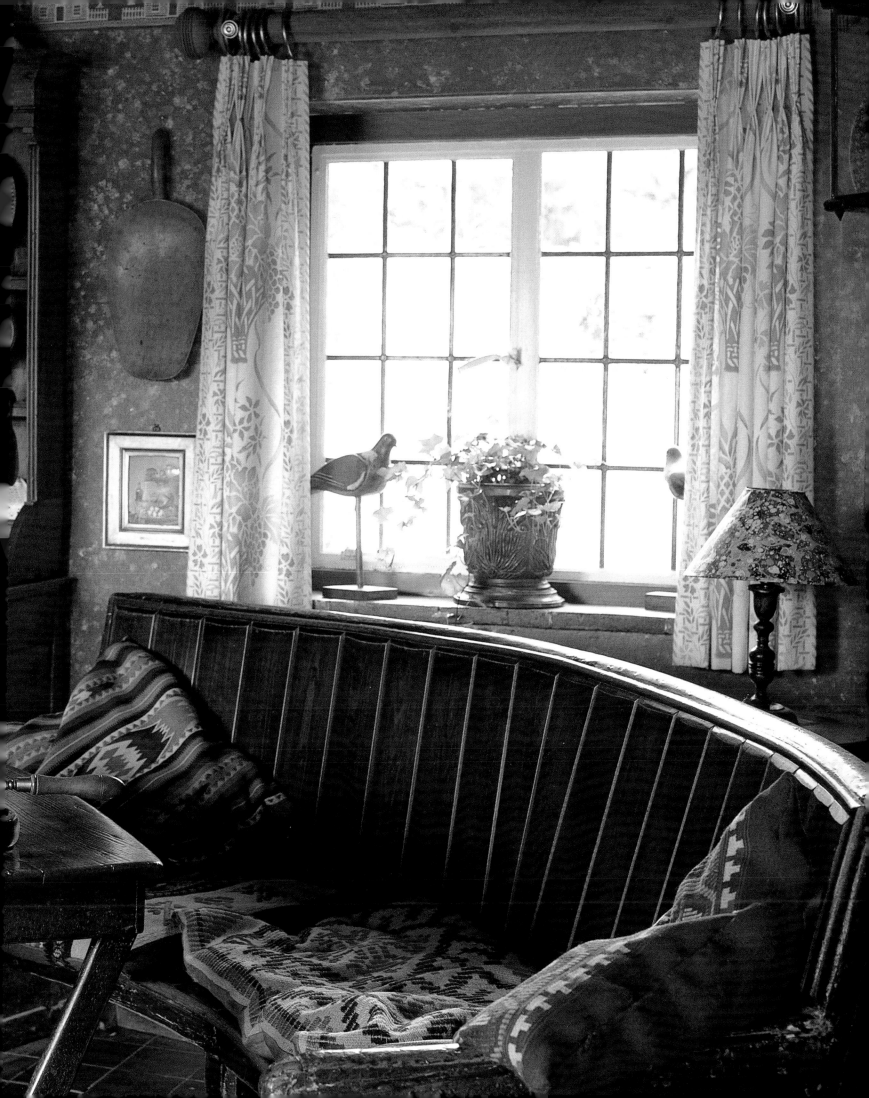

English country style

Throughout the house, the paint colours were specially mixed to achieve exactly the shades Helen wanted.

Right:
Rich use of paint colour is combined with textiles, folk art, painted primitive and country furniture to create a special ambience. The strong brick-red ceiling contrasts with the deep ink-blue beams, from which hangs a 17th century French iron chandelier. The table below it is the warm yellow of mature sycamore. It is surrounded with 18th century Windsor chairs, whose painted finish is battered with time, and four folding chairs with wicker seats and backs. Behind the table the wall is dominated by the huge inglenook fireplace, bracketed by two large brass candle sconces.
To the left of the inglenook stands an 18th century grandfather clock, painted in a deep green, with a faded green spice rack hanging next to it.

Below:
Notice how the proportions in which the blue and red are used on the units are the reverse of the proportions used on the ceiling. This, along with the careful selection of colours within the same tonal range, is the key to the success of such a strong and vibrant scheme. Even the quarry tiles and the Victorian rag rug on the floor harmonize perfectly.

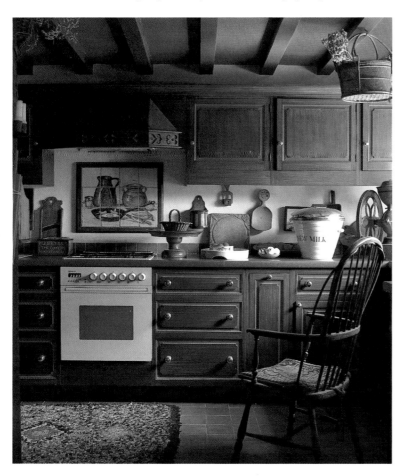

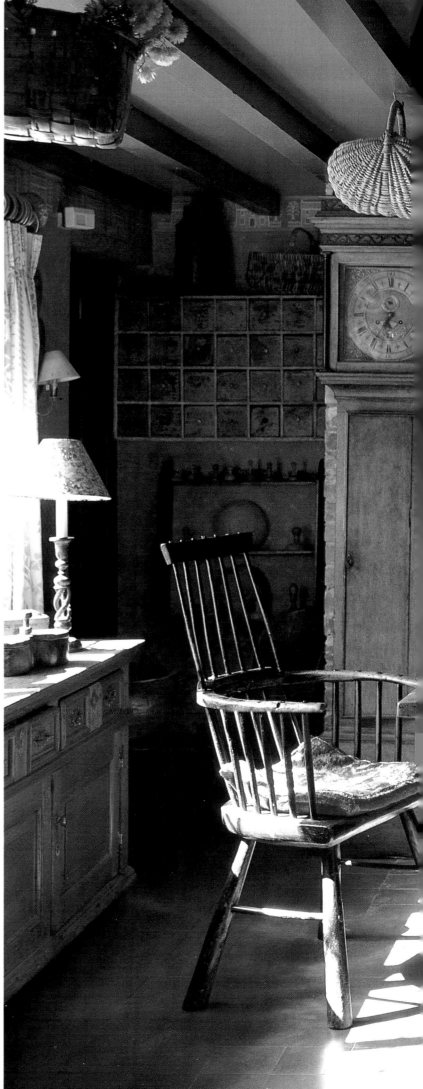

56

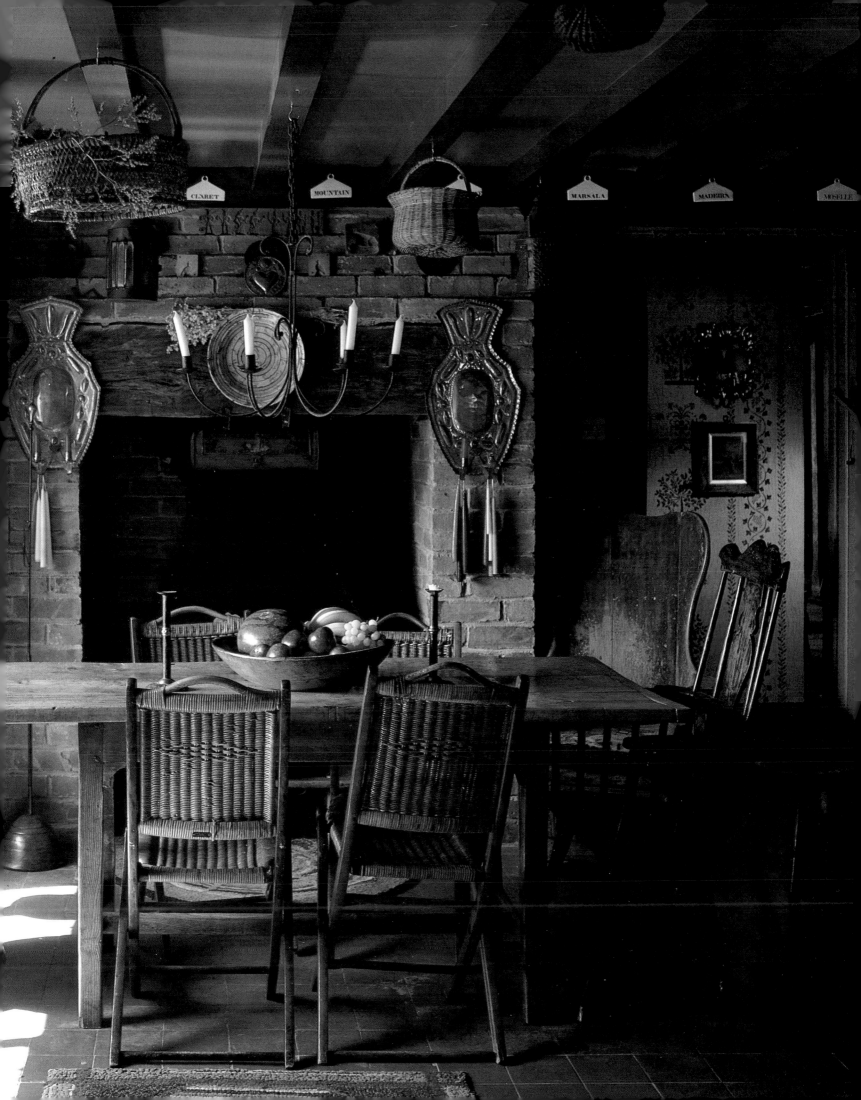

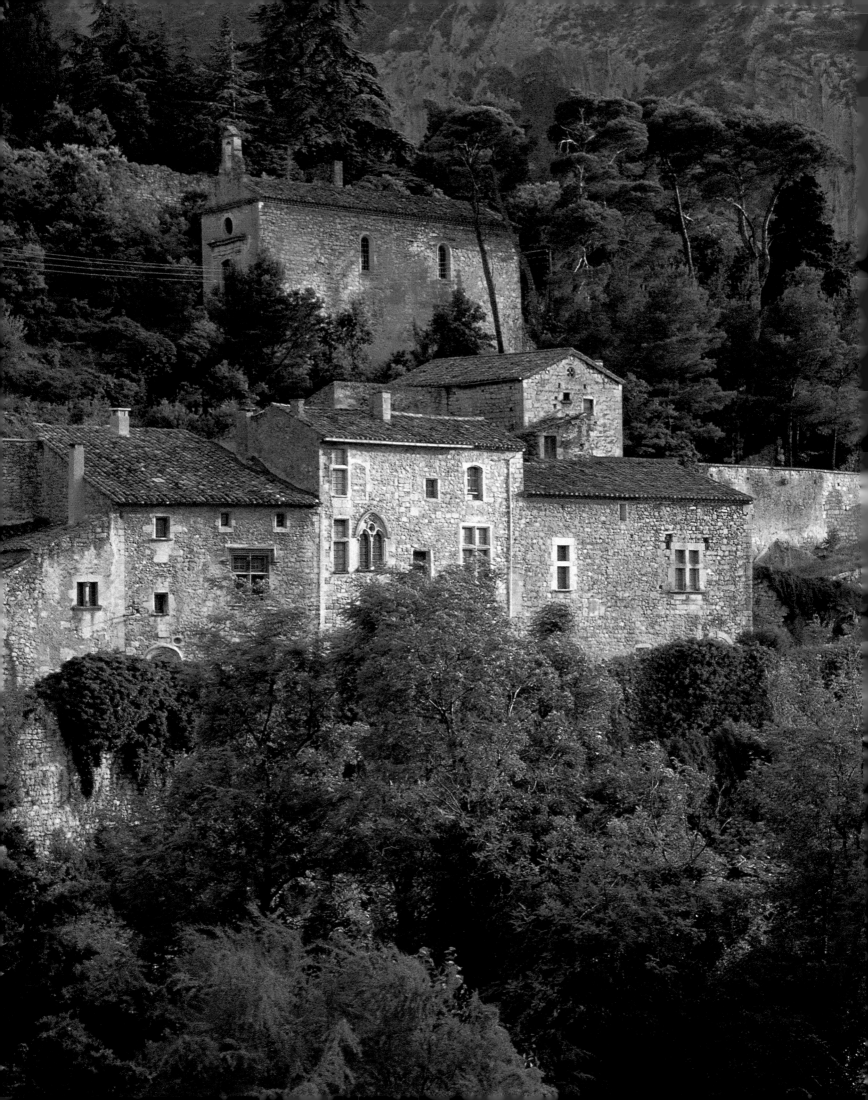

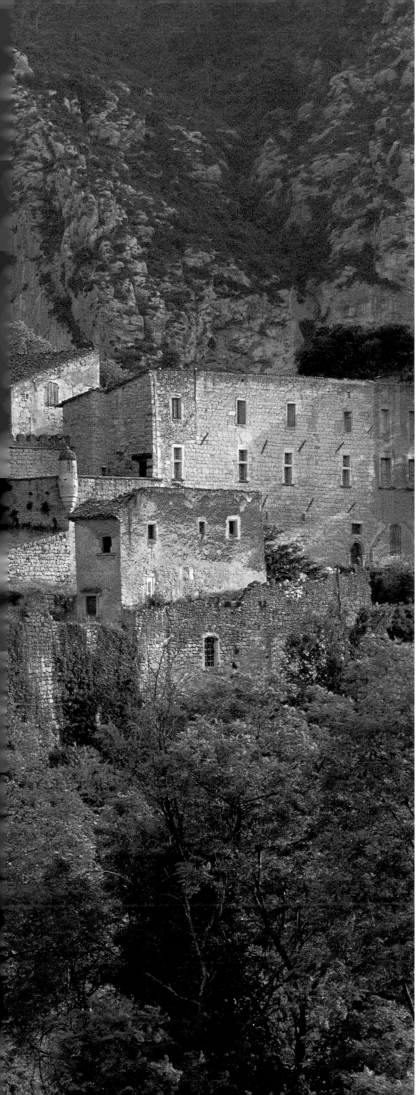

FRENCH
Country Style

The look that is labelled as French Country worldwide has been deeply influenced by the particular style of the region of Provence, France's deep south. Bordered on one side by the Rhône river and lapped by the Mediterranean sea, Provence fills the lower eastern corner of the map. The Provençal look is a farmhouse style but, under the influence of the *mistral* and the extraordinary colour range of the

Provençal landscape, the farmhouses look quite different from those in Italy. Instead of the tonal pinks and buffs of the Tuscan hills, the valley of Provence sizzles with contrasts under a brilliant blue sky. Swathes of lavender neighbour fields of sunflowers. Long files of cypresses, planted as wind-breaks, stand sentry around acres of golden corn. This is Van Gogh country. When the artist settled in the vibrant south and discovered its lusty combinations of burnt oranges, bitter lemons, cobalt blues and sunflower yellows, he wrote to his brother, exclaiming eagerly:

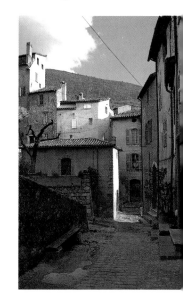

"I am using a tremendous lot of colours and canvases."

For the Provençal farmer, the canvas is a stone or clay-built *mas*, a small farmhouse whose appearance has been shaped as much by the need to keep the *mistral* out as to keep animals in. Its flat roof, built of round red clay tiles, is sandwiched several layers deep to resist the wind. The window shutters and oversized exterior doors, filling openings origand and oversized exterior doors, filling openings originally designed for cattle, are so many invitations for paint. The outside might be like Van Gogh's house – "fresh butter yellow with raw-green shutters" – or the walls might be

Left and above:
Provençal style takes its cue from the colours of the surrounding countryside – the ochres and russets of the earth are reflected in the mottled tawny-tiled roofs and warm stone walls. Here, the medieval village of Oppede-le-Vieux nestles into the wooded mountainside.

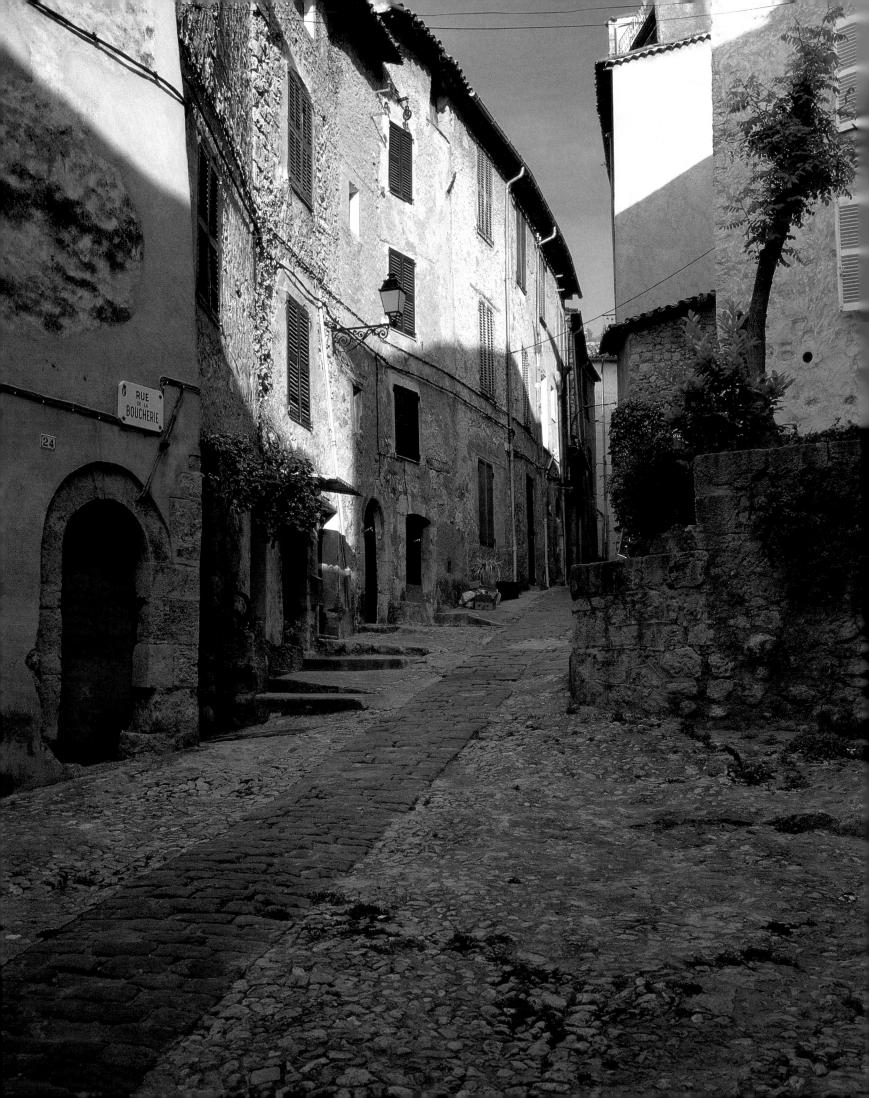

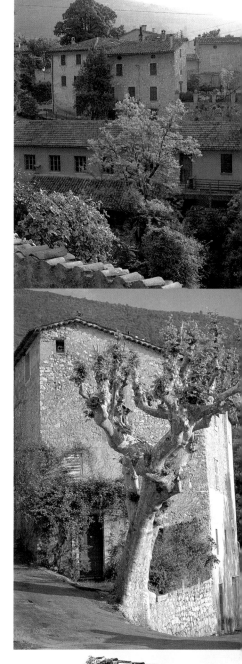

built from red clay and the shutters painted in a bright turquoise, which is said to repel flies.

The colours of the landscape are repeated indoors to bring in the view from behind the flaking shutters. The thick walls are whitewashed, or plastered and colourwashed in the tones natural to the local stone and clay, from buff to mustard yellow to dusky red.

In the furnishings and on painted furniture colours are grouped as they are outside, in contrasts of jangling intensity. Russet, yellow and green ceramic tiles might be set into a table top to create a glossy patchwork, while a bold checkerboard of red and white squares covers a kitchen floor. And a typical vista of whitewashed rooms is often interrupted by a splash of colour – an internal door painted the sky's baby blue or a high cupboard in citrus yellow.

Because the Provençal look is one of the most decorative of country styles, its houses have an air of informality, despite their lofty ceilings and large doors. The Provençal exhibition-ism of pattern and colour has made its prints world-famous. The bright fabrics were originally based on the East India Company's cottons, which arrived in bundles on the quayside of Provence's port, Marseilles, in the 17th century. Local weavers reworked the Indian designs in the Provençal colours, printing fruit, flowers and simple geometric patterns onto backgrounds of buff, mustard yellow, cherry red and the deep russet of the red clay hills.

The Provençal style owes much to the Mediterranean and its ports. Craftsmen and artists from all over France were attracted to the area in the 18th and 19th centuries to share in the trade of ideas and inspiration from over the sea. As a magnet for skill and talent, it was the rural equivalent of the court at Paris and as a result the furniture of Provençal homes was enhanced by skilled and imaginative work. Buffets, boxes, chairs and cupboards commissioned by wealthier farmers were often handsomely carved with sheaves of corn and knots of myrtle leaves or scrolls of music to symbolize a cultured household. The poorer smallholder could probably only pay for one embellished piece and it was likely to be a traditional general-purpose cupboard for food and clothes – the *armoire* – made of local walnut.

The rest of the furniture was built on the simplest lines:

Left:
The narrow, cobbled streets in many of the towns and villages of southern France have remained virtually unaltered since their medieval beginnings. Walls are washed in sunlight colours, broken by the faded blues, silver-greens or rusty reds of the shutters that are essential to close out the unrelenting sun and the piercing mistral *winds.*

Right:
The warm, intense colours of Provençal homes echo the rich, fertile landscape. The red earth and rugged hills are a backdrop for lush green foliage and fields of lavender, sunflowers and poppies, lit by a brilliant sun. Just as the vivid colours of each flower fades at the end of its season, so the sun and wind weather the vibrantly painted walls of the houses.

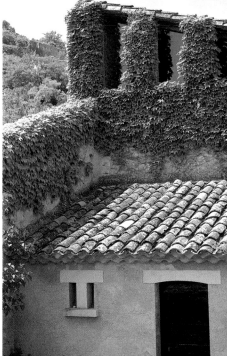

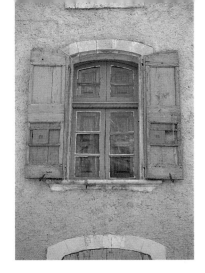 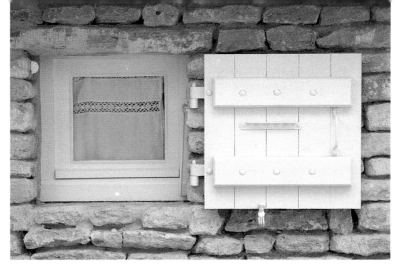 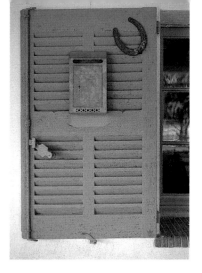

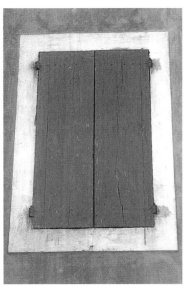 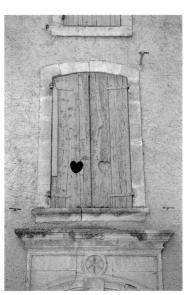 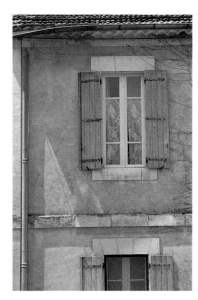 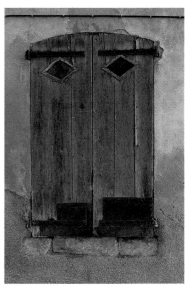

Above:
In France, windows are designed to protect the interiors from the elements.
They are often small, particularly on the north side of the house, and are
almost always shuttered. During hot summer days, the shutters are closed
or partly closed; they are opened during the evening to let in cool, fresh
air, and finally secured again when night falls.

box-framed beds, rush-seated benches, plain kitchen tables and the bentwood chair which, although invented by an Austrian, seems to stand for Provençal style because of its easy fluency. Decoration, when it could not be afforded in the form of carved wood, was painted on as ribbons of fruit and flowers on chest fronts or chair tops.

Modern versions of the old farmhouse style honour the tradition of simple furnishings by keeping complicated shapes and decorative patterns separate. A straight-sided sofa can tolerate a bright Provençal pattern, while a more curvaceous settee would best be upholstered in a plain colour – a ripe apricot or deep russet.

If there is one room that is associated with the Provençal style more than any other it is the farmhouse kitchen, as quintessentially French as the parlour is English. In England,

where class consciousness always ran deep, the parlour offered an escape from the kitchen and its associations with servility. The social levelling of the French Revolution saved the kitchen for the central position in the French house, which it retained even in the wealthier farmhouses with living-rooms *à l'anglaise*. In the Provençal kitchen are found the classics of French country furniture. They are, as the names of individual pieces show, simple and ingenious solutions for the storage and preservation of food. As well as the traditional *armoire*, the Provençal kitchen's famous pieces include the *salière*, a small, slope-lidded hinged box for salt, and the *panetière*, a decorative cage hung on the wall to hold baguettes. The deep, buffet-like *pétrin* was a chest designed for the kneading and rising of dough.

It is this Provençal tradition of purposeful kitchen

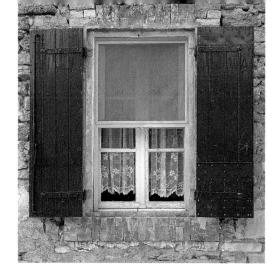
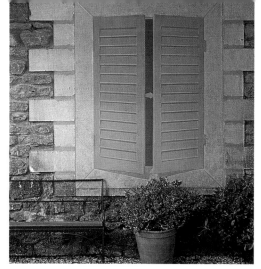
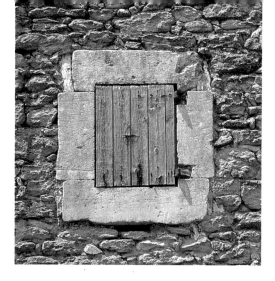
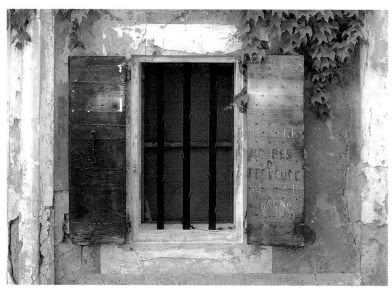
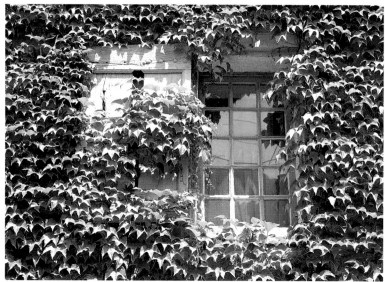

Above:
With pairs of shutters one side can be closed, the other left open to let in restricted light. Another way of allowing a little light to enter is cut-outs or louvres – these look decorative, but their primary purpose is functional. Not all shutters open and close – the pair shown top row, middle are a trompe l'oeil in paint.

furniture, down to the smallest salt box, that gives the French farmhouse kitchen its reputation as a cook's haven. The equipment (copper pans, carving knives and crockery) is placed where it is most practical: near at hand, rather than tucked away out of sight. The unconscious beauty of ordinary objects on display is one of the hallmarks of the French country kitchen and as important to its feel as its quarry-tiled floor, colourwashed walls and painted cupboards.

The picture painted of a typical Provençal kitchen would show a long table in the middle of the room covered with a bright-printed waxed cloth of red and yellow and surrounded by high-backed, rush-seated chairs. Behind it, a walnut buffet displays green glazed china and a bowl of lemons. Opposite, copper pots and a bunch of thyme hang above a giant stove, set into the old stone fireplace. The scene would be lit by a band of

sunshine, flecked by motes of dust, that slips through a casement window and runs down glazed yellow walls onto the flagged floor.

The kitchen, being the central, family room of the small farmhouse, is traditionally the room where colour is given its head. In the rooms beyond, through a brightly painted yellow door, the walls might be whitewashed and the accents cooler than in the kitchen, but there is the same seductive charm in the combination of beautiful wood, rough stone, glazed china and brilliant printed cottons. Perhaps the greatest appeal of the Provençal style is that it celebrates colour in one room and then offers a rest from it elsewhere in white-painted attic bedrooms or in the long, cool terraces, roofed with vines. The style of Provence, as the interiors revealed over the next pages show, is the most mercurial of country styles.

French country style

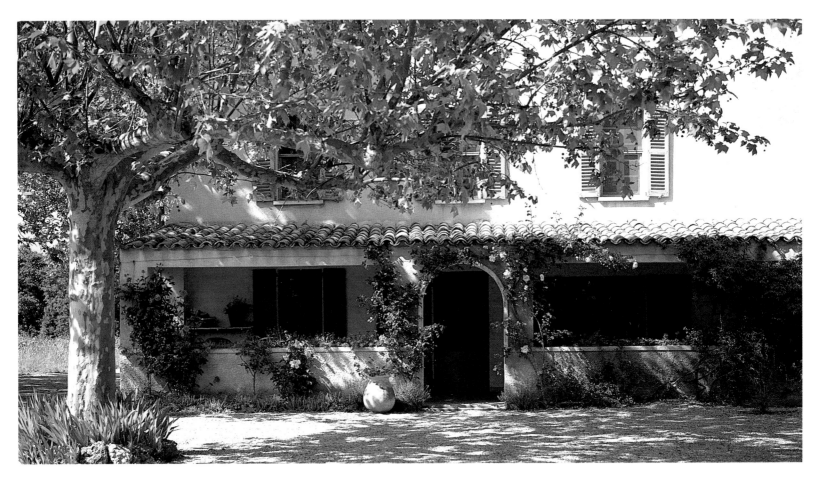

This converted 17th century silk mill is furnished in an eclectic country style. A spreading plane tree adds its shade to that of the terrace that runs the width of the house. The overlapping tiles are used on houses all over Provence.

Right:
Eating outside is an essential ingredient of French country living, whether on the terrace or under the dappled shade of olive and chestnut trees.

Far right:
Even indoors an outside view is important to French cooks. The shelf under the window is a typical feature of dark country kitchens. Placed for maximum light, it is used for food preparation and usually folds flat against the wall when not in use.

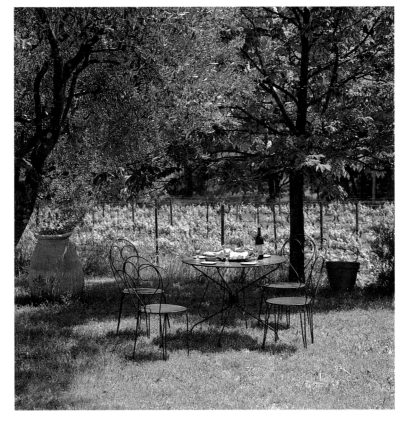

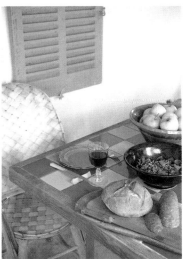

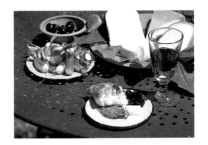

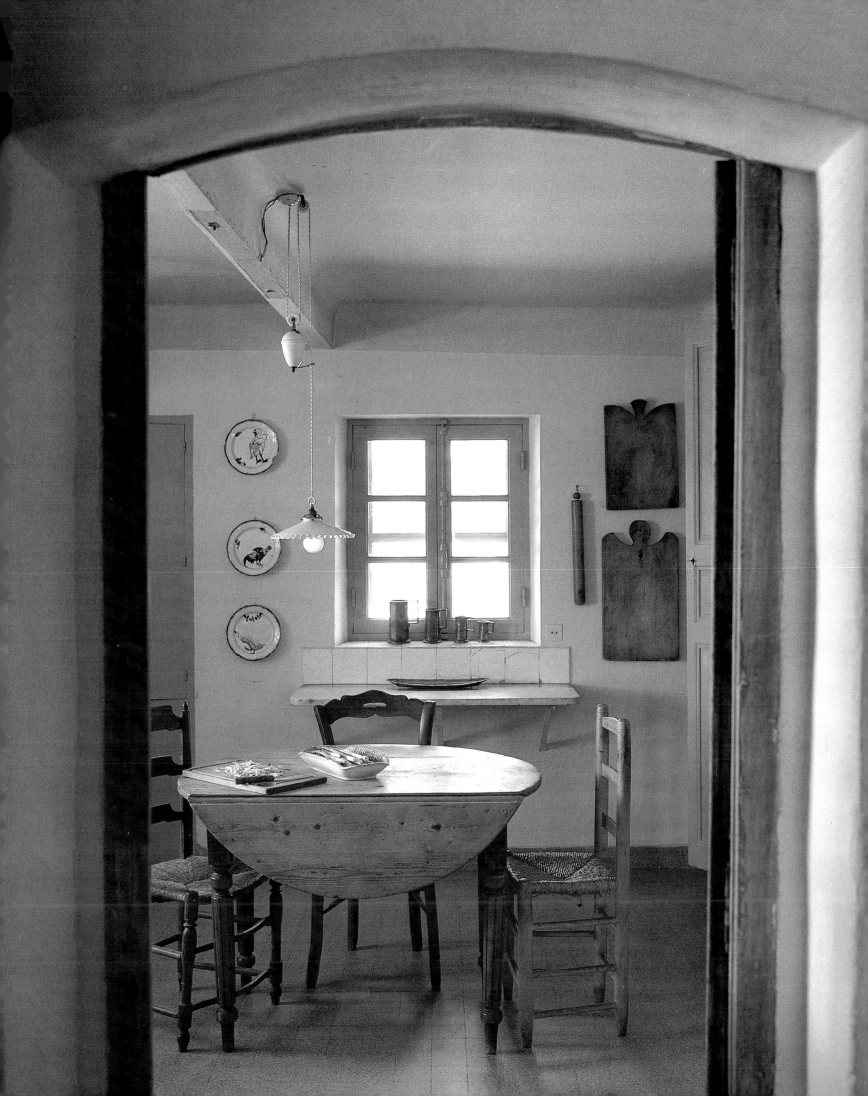

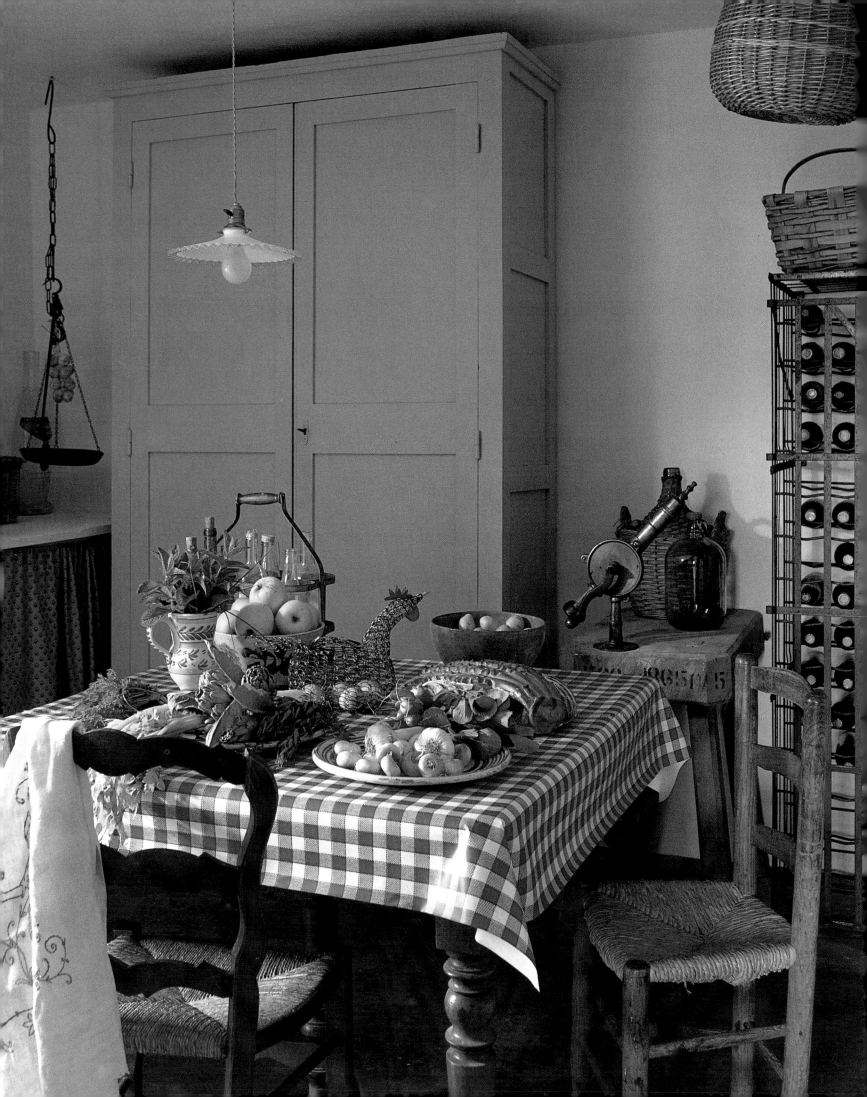

French country style

A larder or pantry to store food, usually home-
produced, is an important feature of many
country homes.

Left:
Wine is stored in typical Provençal wire racks
in this scullery, while summer fruit and
vegetables await attention on the practical red-
and-white checked oilcloth that tops the
sturdy table.

Below left:
Fruit and vegetables – the very essence of
country living – are bottled and preserved to fill
the shelves of the narrow wall cupboard. The
baskets piled up beneath were bought in
the local market.

Below right:
A traditional 19th century Provençal wire salad
basket holds mushrooms, while herbs and
onions stay cool on the marble-topped cupboard.
Freshly picked cherries look juicily appetizing
set against a yellow faience plate.

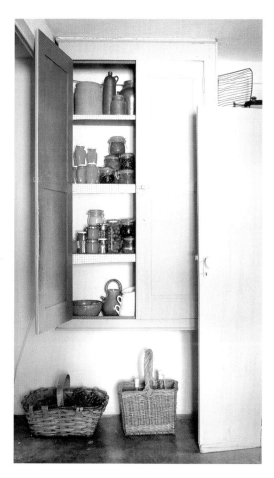

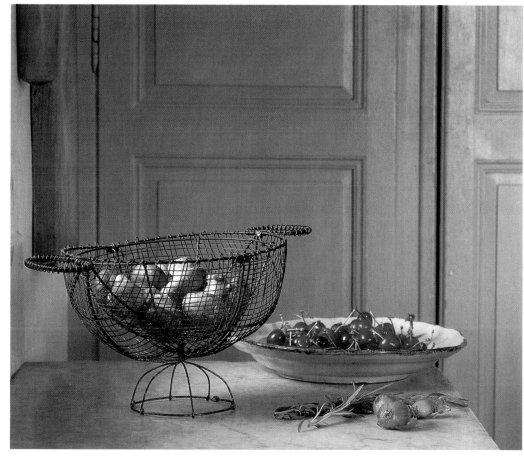

French country style

Le Muy's owner removed a false ceiling to
reveal the original oak beams, which she
waxed. She did not strip off all the old varnish
as totally stripped-back beams look new and
therefore won't work with the patina
of antique furniture.

Right:
Shafts of sunlight lend dimension to the gentle
curves of an 18th century beech ladderback chair
and highlight an 18th century Provençal
fruitwood buffet.

Below:
A rush-seated 18th century beech ladderback
chair harmonizes well with a 19th century
chestnut desk.

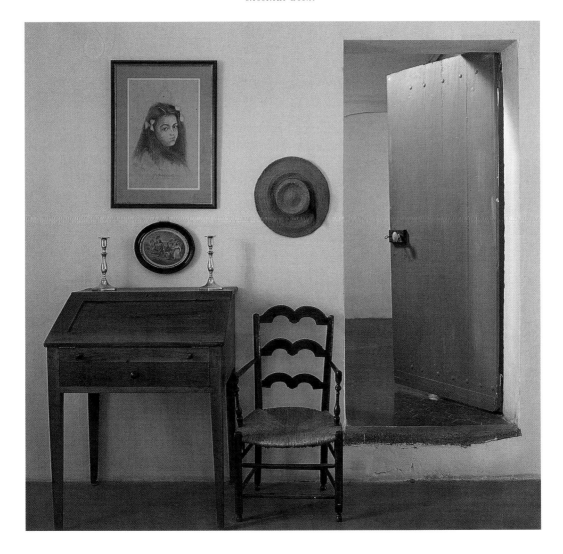

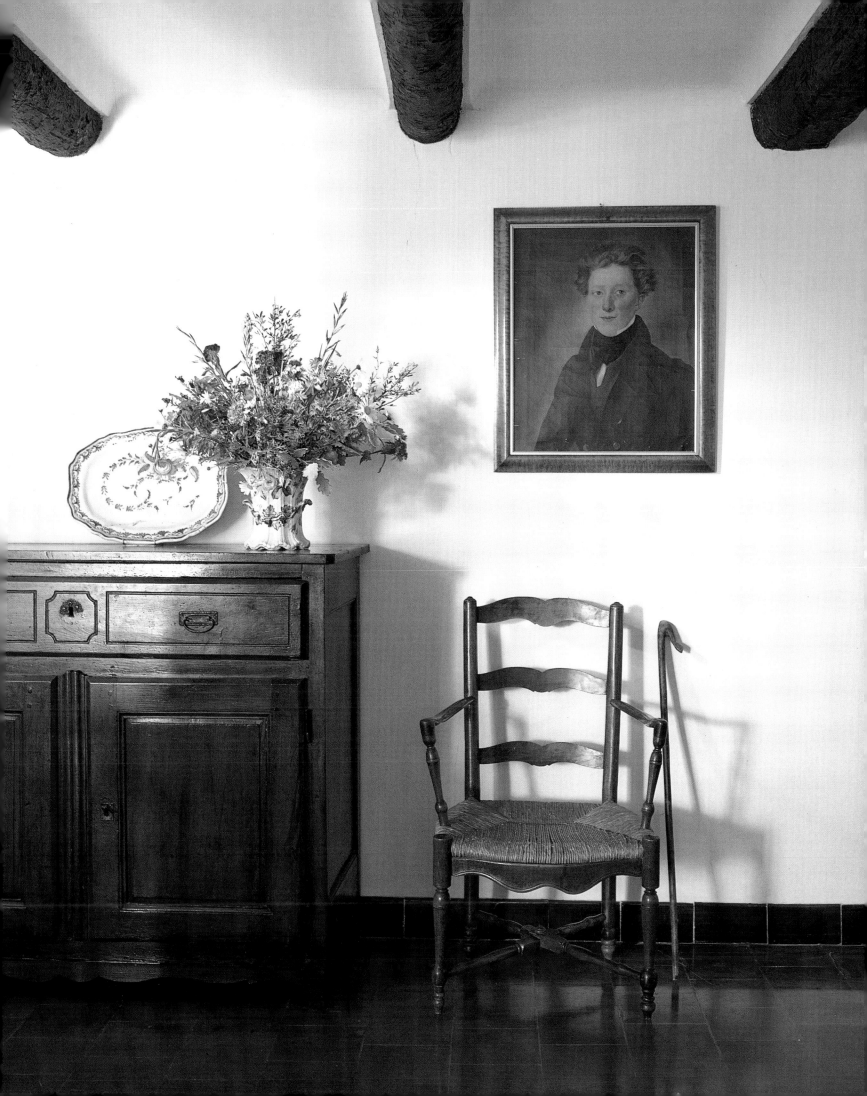

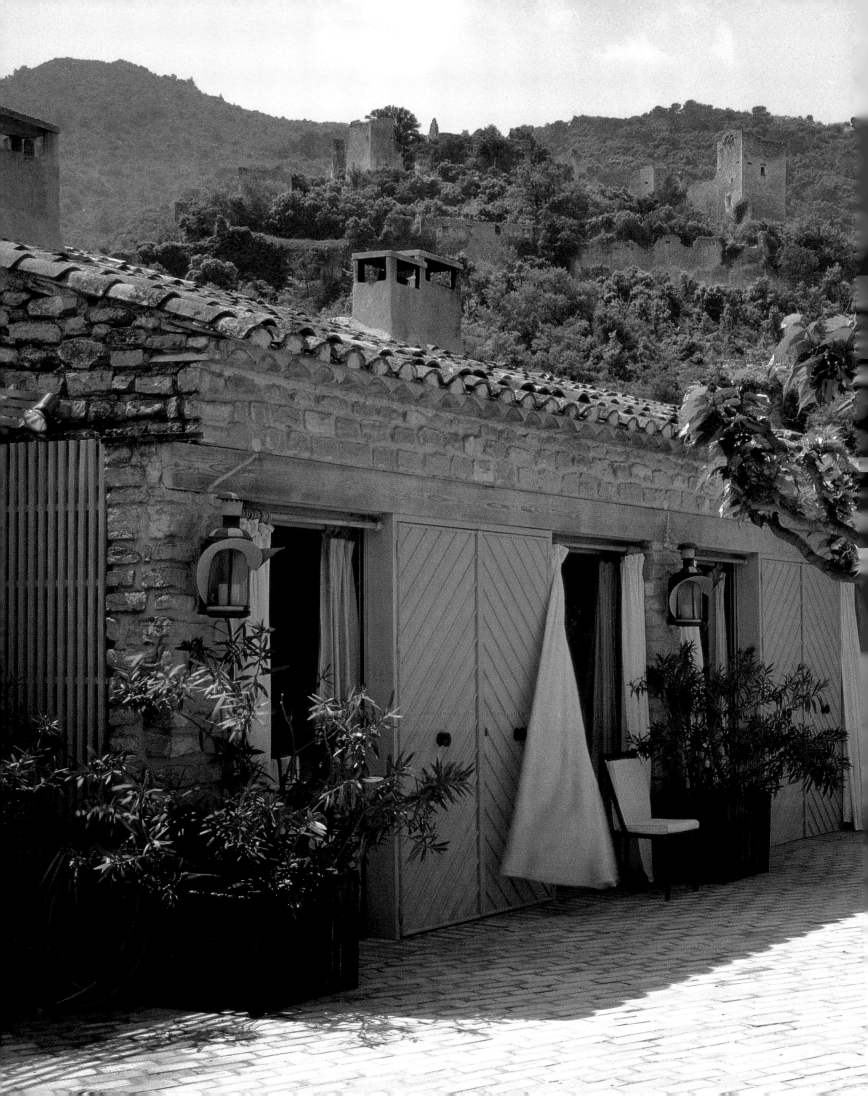

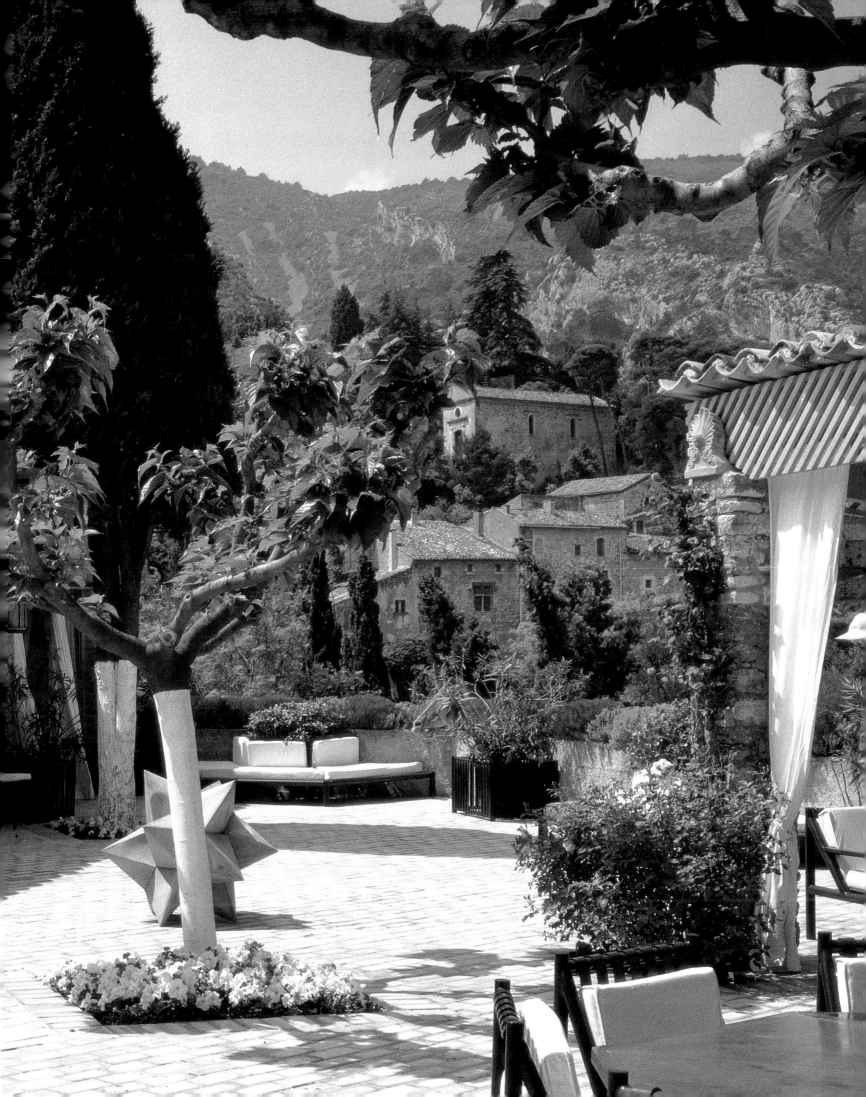

Interior designer Dick Dumas converted this house in Provence from a roadside diner, selecting it in preference to an original farmhouse because it has wonderful views over the unspoilt 12th century stone-built village of Oppede-le-Vieux. He added decorative beige slatting to cover the ugly cement brick exterior walls.

Previous page and right:
Paved with local bricks, the terrace serves as a big open-air drawing room. Luxurious outdoor sofas, modern versions of traditional French garden benches, were designed by Dick Dumas. The pool is made less obtrusive by painting its interior a muted lapis lazuli, rather than the usual bright turquoise. Beige-painted doors fold back to reveal two sets of natural cotton curtains, each on their own wooden pole, that serve to keep the sun off the house. The tree trunks are painted with white limewash (a local remedy against bugs) and underplanted with white petunias.

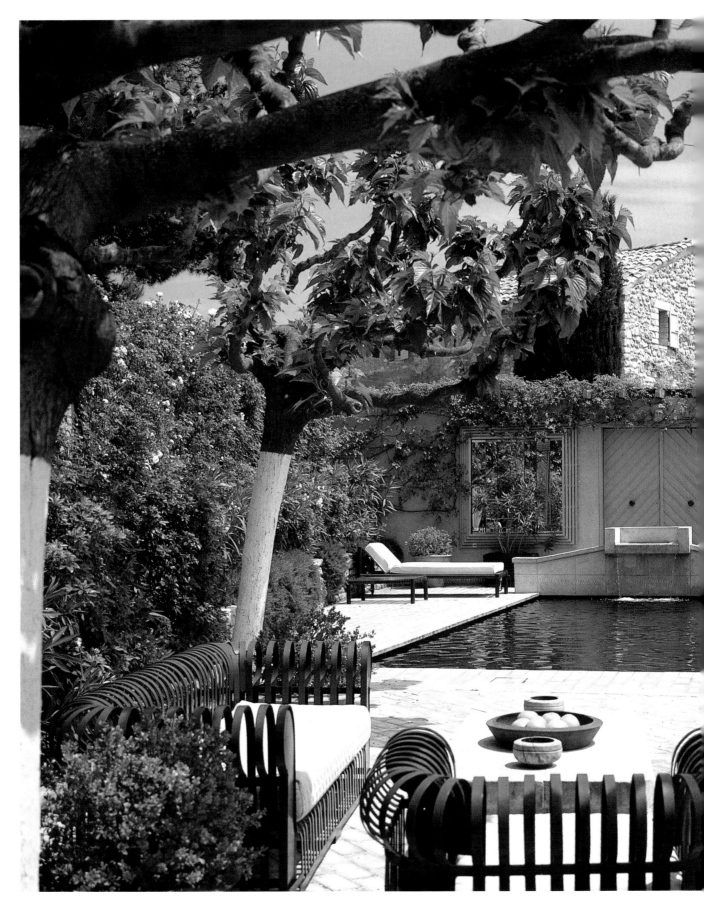

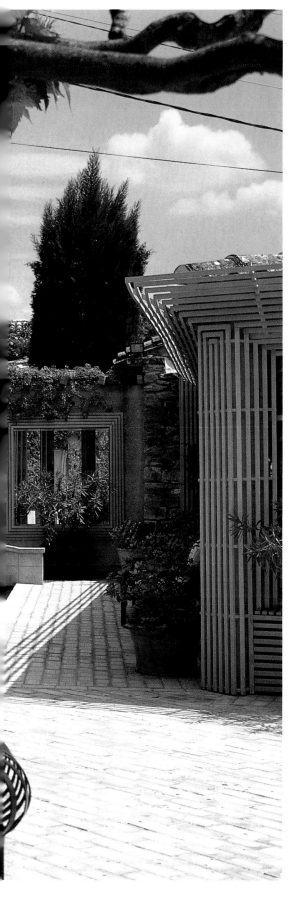

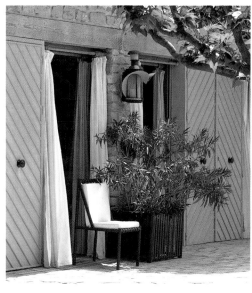

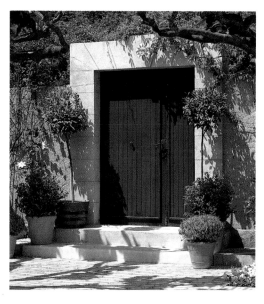

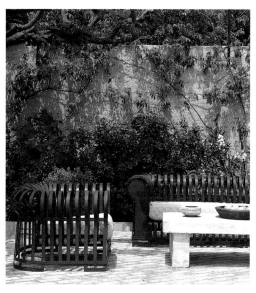

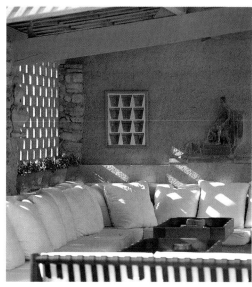

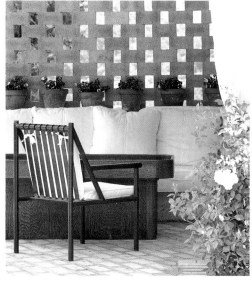

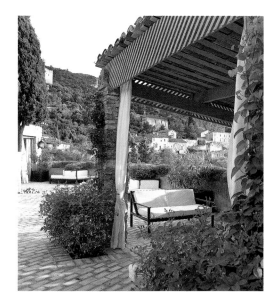

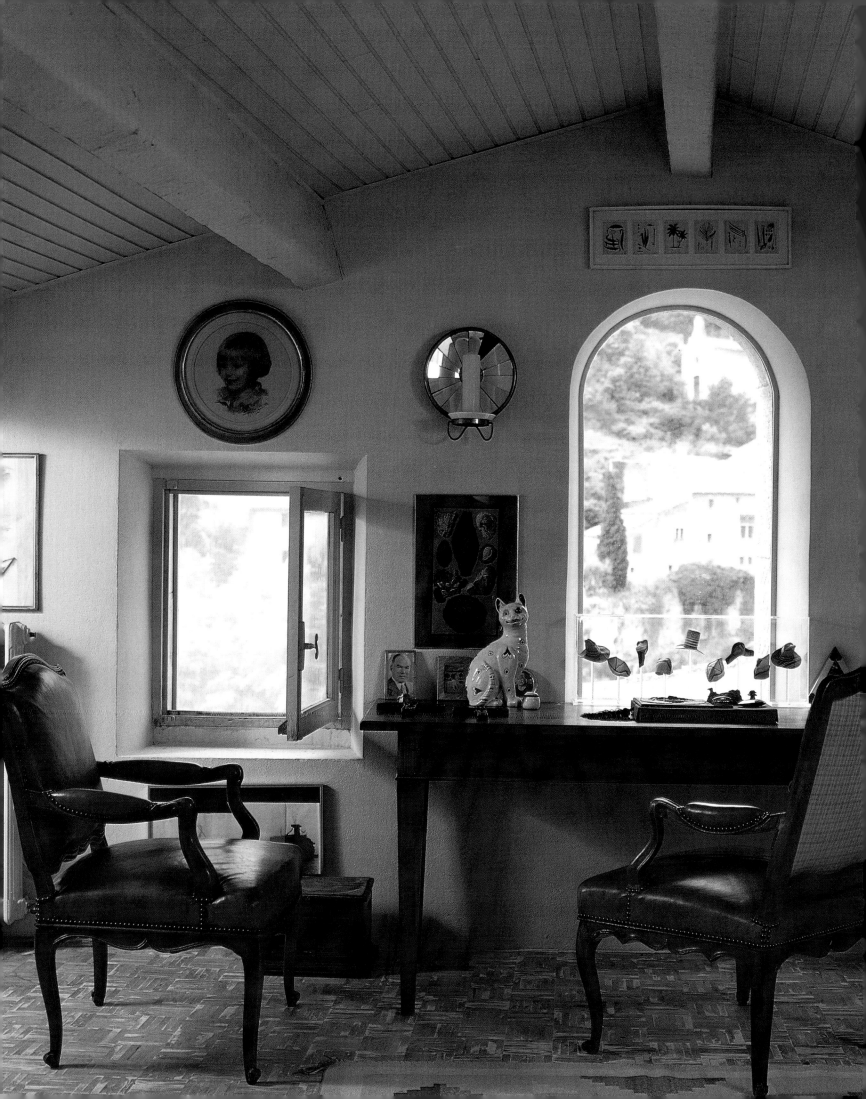

French country style

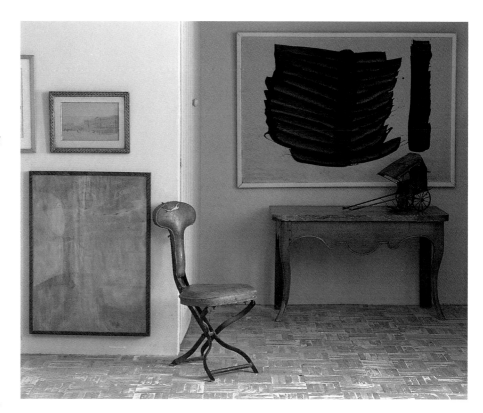

In this study-guest room urban and country antiques are mixed with modern art to create a look that is typical of a sophisticated French country home. Dick Dumas gave the wooden parquet floor – an unusual feature in Provence – a more rustic feel by rubbing in white paint.

Left:
On the Louis XVI mahogany bureau plat *sits a Gallé faience cat alongside a collection of World War 1 miniature hats. The walnut* fauteuils *are Louis XV; their simple lines and leather upholstery suit a country style. The view through the arched window to Oppede-le-Vieux and beyond is quite beautiful, as if a painting of a medieval French Provençal hill village was contained within the window frame.*

Top right:
A jump seat from an old motor car co-exists happily with modern paintings.

Bottom right:
Natural, muted colours and textures create a soothing ambience. Books for browsing are stacked on an English 18th century miniature oak dining room table.

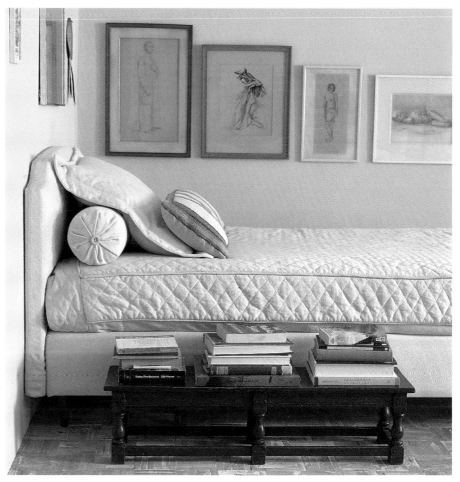

French country style

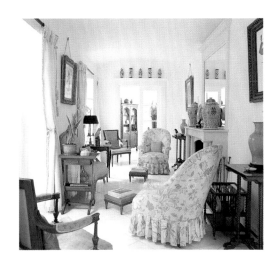

Caretaker's accommodation and six vaulted coalholes beneath André de Cacqueray's central London home have been transformed into a guest apartment suffused with the atmosphere of Provence.

Right and far right: The small dining room is furnished with an 18th century English mahogany table and country style Louis XVI rush-seated walnut dining chairs. An 18th century style French armoire contains a concealed bed. The room looks out over the tiny basement garden which is "grassed" with green glass chippings and lit by strip lighting to compensate for the lack of natural light in this underground world.

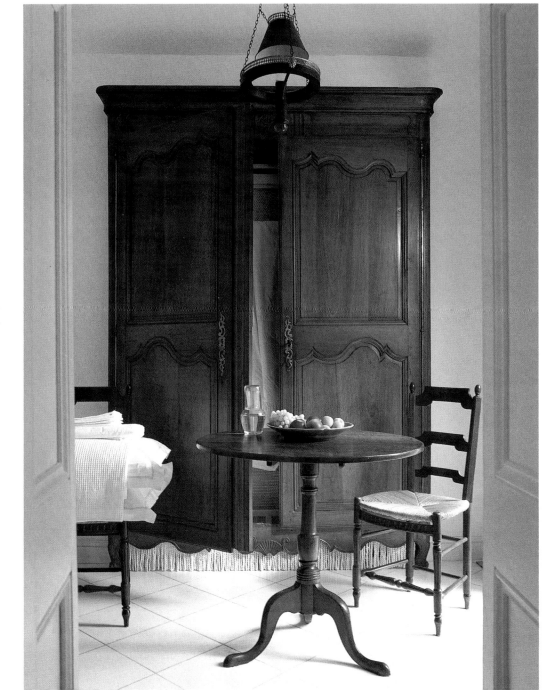

Above left: A white, sunshine yellow and blue colour scheme brings shades of southern France, the sea and sky, to an urban English living room. French provincial furniture adds further authenticity. The 19th century French stone fireplace has a low mantelshelf that is deep enough to display impressive artefacts such as these Chinese blue and white ginger jars. Behind, an overmantel mirror doubles the light filtering into this basement room. The floor is tiled in pure white marble, a practical continental touch adapted for the cooler British climate with the installation of underfloor heating.

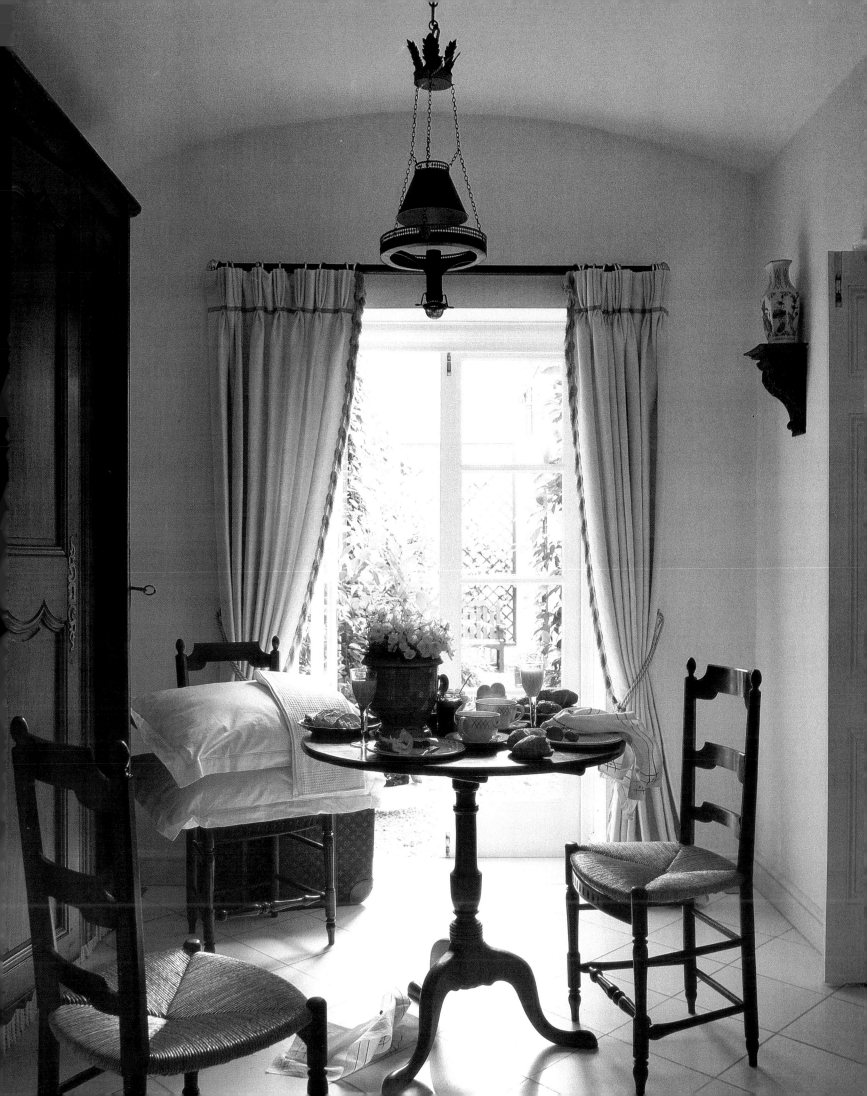

ITALIAN
Country Style

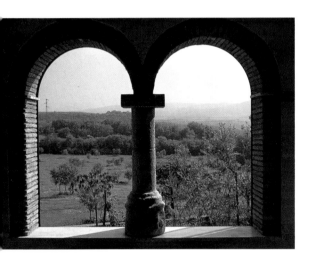

*T*he country style that is universally accepted as typically Italian has its true home in a small area of rustic Italy: the provinces of Tuscany and Umbria, whose rolling, vine-clad hills cover the knee-cap of the Italian boot. The appeal of Tuscan style has spread beyond its region, and beyond Italy itself, because it is generous while remaining simple. The houses are built big, to be cool, with high, beamed ceilings and thick walls. Although they are paved with glossy expanses of ceramic or marble and equipped with terraces that suggest a life of leisure, the rooms are roughly plastered and the colours are weather-beaten. This is the style of a temperate region, where the sun is treated as a benediction not an affliction, brought in through shutters to lie in slats on the floor and stored in the warm terracotta hues of the rooms inside. By contrast, in the arid, sun-scorched south the architecture appears to be hunched against the glare. Here, homes are extraordinary bright-white *trulli* – blind-looking buildings whose round exteriors are unrelieved by balconies and their windows narrowed to slits.

The typical Tuscan house is low, stone-built and stuccoed over in a faded pink or golden ochre, its entrance flanked by a pair of lemon trees in giant terracotta pots. A roof of fluted terracotta tiles echoes the pattern of terraced vineyards in the surrounding Chianti country. Originally built on its hilltop as a farmhouse, it was probably converted into a country home by city-dwellers soon after farms were divided up by the redistribution of agricultural land in the 1950s. Once-separate buildings that housed animals are now joined to the main house and old granaries and olive stores have become the big, bare rooms characteristic of Tuscan style.

Inside, the colours are borrowed from the landscape's palette: burnt sienna, named after the red clay hills surrounding Siena, terracotta and yellow ochre. Like storage heating, the warmth of these colours absorbs the daytime heat and gives it back to the rooms after sunset. Cooler tints, for rooms that

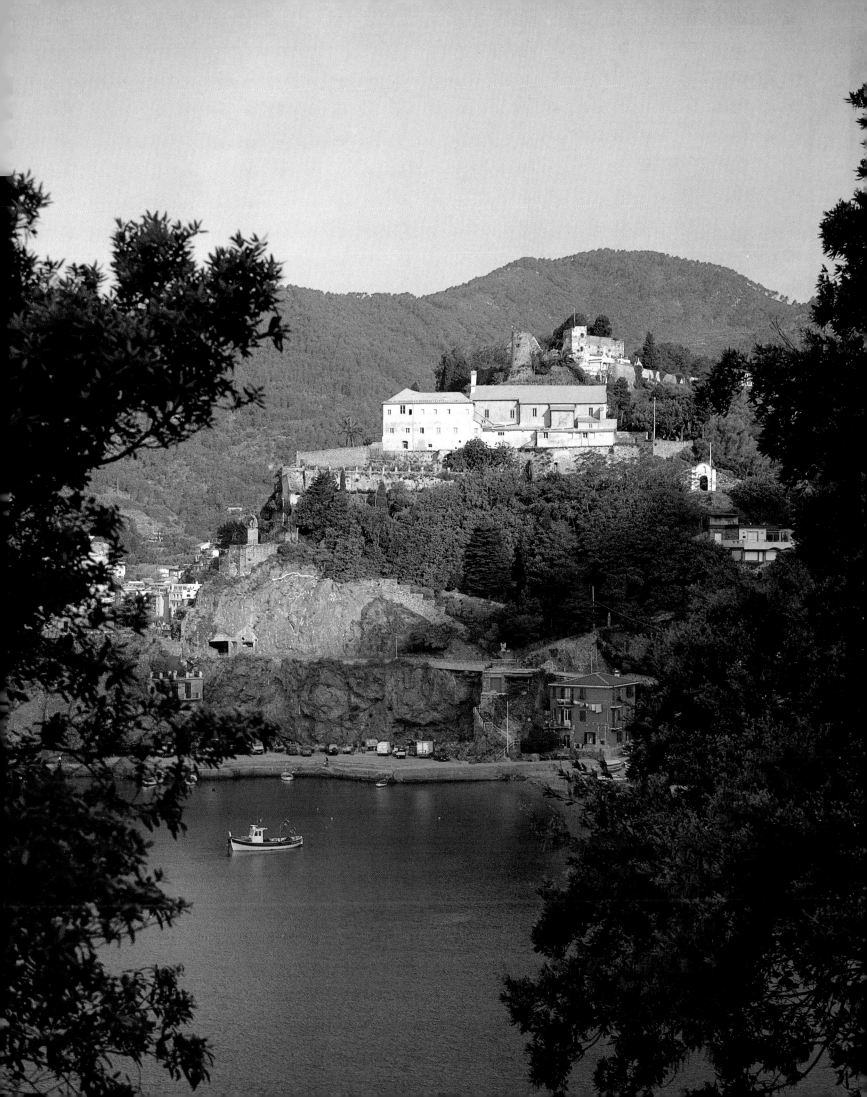

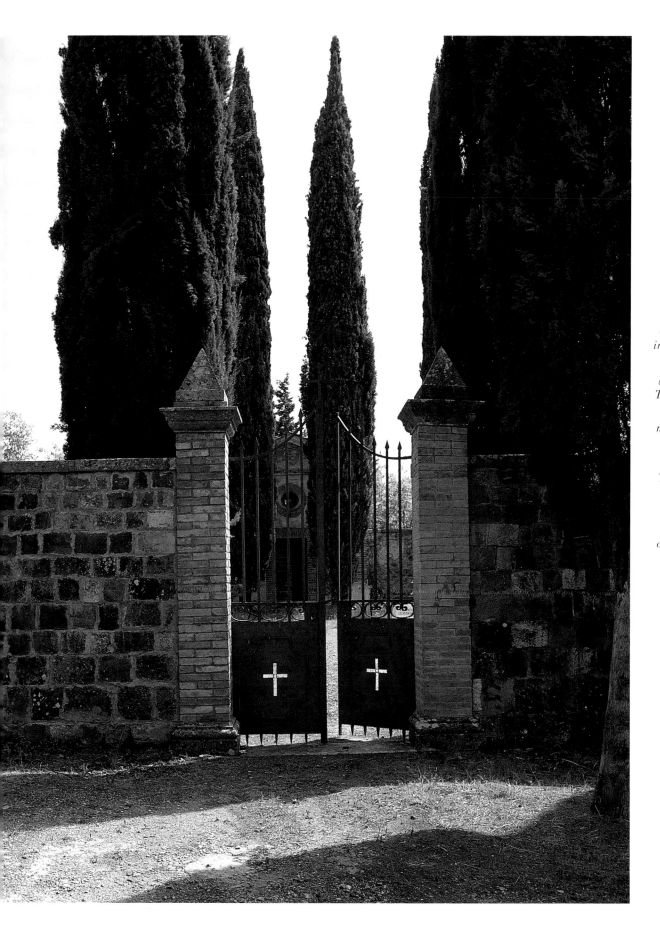

Left:
In rural Italy religion has a very important place in community life; the local church is often the grandest building in the village. These imposing gates, echoing the heavenward-soaring cypresses, mark the entrance to a graveyard.

Right:
The rolling hills of Tuscany and Umbria are clothed in vines and cypress trees; their formal rows broken up by small clusters of dwellings, like the hill village of Labro, top.

are needed during the day for siestas, are copied from the herbs that grow in hazy drifts across the Tuscan countryside: the old green of thyme, the gray-blue of lavender. Colours are used generously, not as hints here and there but as solid blocks of flat paint covering walls and ceilings. Where there are single splashes of a different hue, they might come from a row of terracotta pots filled with bright pink geraniums, a clutch of tomatoes ripening in an olive-wood bowl or the acid yellows of lemons and glossy greens of olives taken up in the kitchen's thick-glazed china.

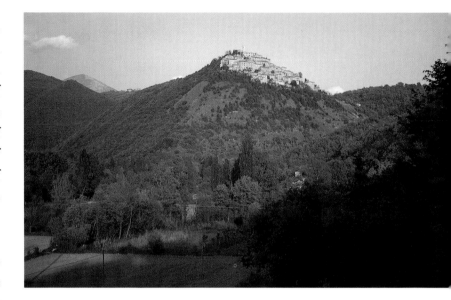

If Italian country style has one colour, it is terracotta. The influence of the tonal landscape of Tuscany and Umbria is so direct that this is a style that does not easily tolerate discordant notes. However, as a style that elevates simple forms into sculptural silhouettes it is more tolerant than most of modern shapes. It can accomodate an articulated chrome desk lamp alongside a storm lantern, a glass-topped table as much as a chestnut-wood one.

The traditional furniture of a Tuscan house is simple, but the plainest lines are dramatized when offset against the rough, granular walls and battered paint. The richness of that contrast can lend a sculptural quality to the most ordinary chair and turn an elaborate piece of furniture into one that looks theatrical and ungainly. Wooden chests and dressers, made from local chestnut, are left unpainted, but furniture isn't always plain. Inferior wood is often disguised in the *arte povera* tradition, where flowers and landscapes are painted in a thin, flat watercolour to emulate the ornate inlays of richer men's furniture. Decorative detail is also provided by wrought iron, shaped into curly bedheads and ornate window grilles. A Tuscan home doesn't house much built-in furniture, except where shelves or small cupboards are fitted into the deep recesses afforded by thick walls. The niche is one of those style elements of the modern urban home originally inspired by the thickness of a rustic wall!

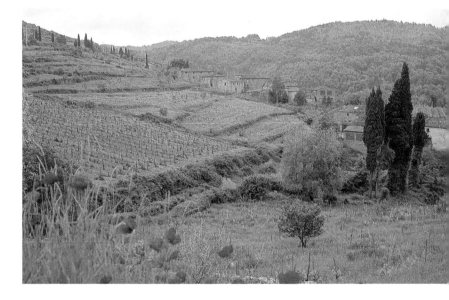

Furnishings are also fairly plain: the fabrics are more often striped than floral, in bold combinations of yellow and blue, or red with green, like medieval pennants. There are creamy, loose-woven covers for beds, gauzes to hang around them and few, if any, curtains. The faded colours of the walls might be repeated in roughly woven tapestries, embroidered

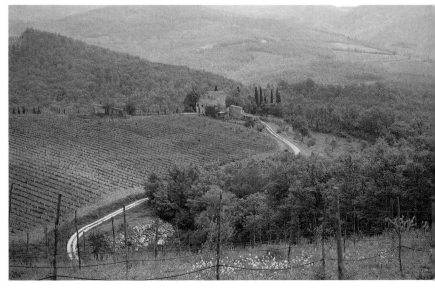

Italian country style

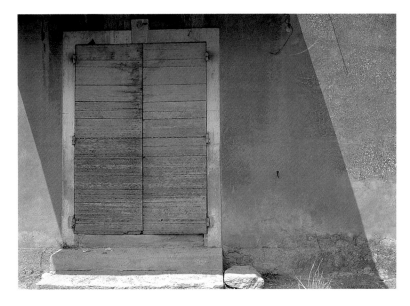 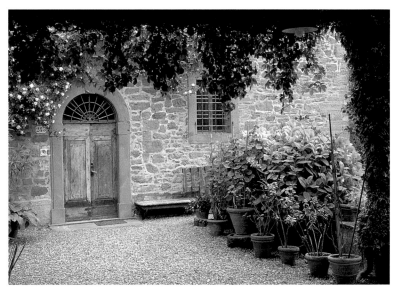

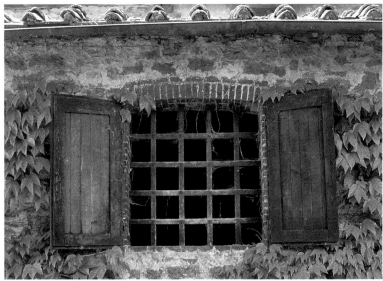 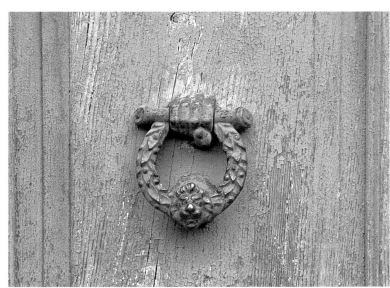

Above:
Italian country architecture may borrow some elements from grand
classical style, like the door knocker bottom right, but the materials and
workmanship have a rough honesty that signals their rural origins.
Weathered wood, stone and faded ochre plasterwork give the buildings a
uniquely Tuscan texture.

cushions or pillows and hand-worked kelims.

The generous scale of Tuscan houses has created a style that is less cosy than English country interiors (see pages 38–57) and more formal-looking than French Provençal ones (see pages 58–77). The formality comes from the way that the furniture is placed around the outside of rooms rather than scattered around the middle. It is a practical arrangement that has grown into one of the recognizable elements of the style: the Tuscan house tends to flow from room to room, through wide arches and generous doorways, and from inside to

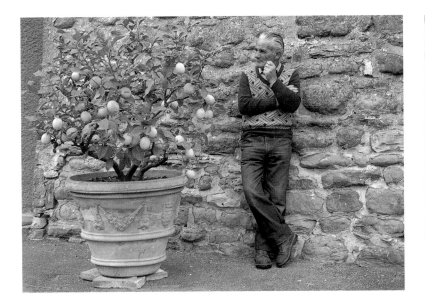

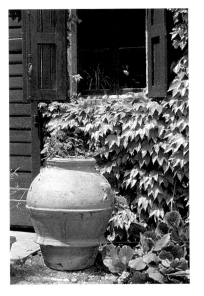

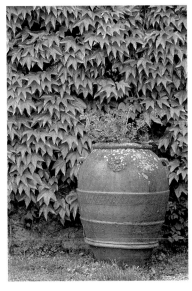

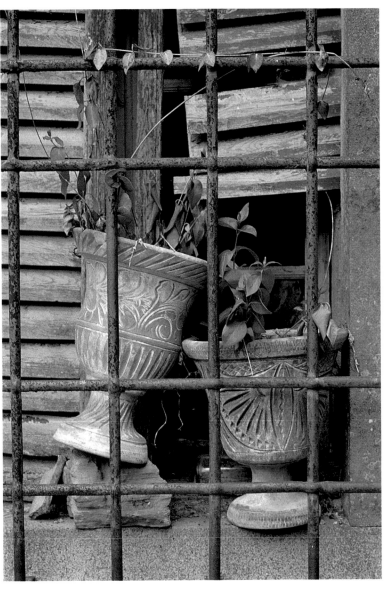

Above:
The local clay of Tuscany is terra cotta; *the Italian for baked earth.*
Today, its name is applied to the unglazed earthenware made from it, and
to its characteristic reddish-brown colour. These terracotta urns, moulded
from the Tuscan earth, are paired with greenery, colourful flowers or shiny-
leaved lemon trees rooted in Tuscan soil.

outside. It is perhaps this slightly formal aspect of Italian country style that has made it easy to translate into modern apartments, where the same proportion of space to relatively little furniture can be used on a smaller scale.

The following pages reveal a selection of homes, from a modern Etruscan-style apartment in London, England, to a Tuscan house that was once the home of the local priest, which share the same country mood. They all celebrate the beautiful terracotta and ochre hues, the granular walls and bare rooms that characterize Italian country style.

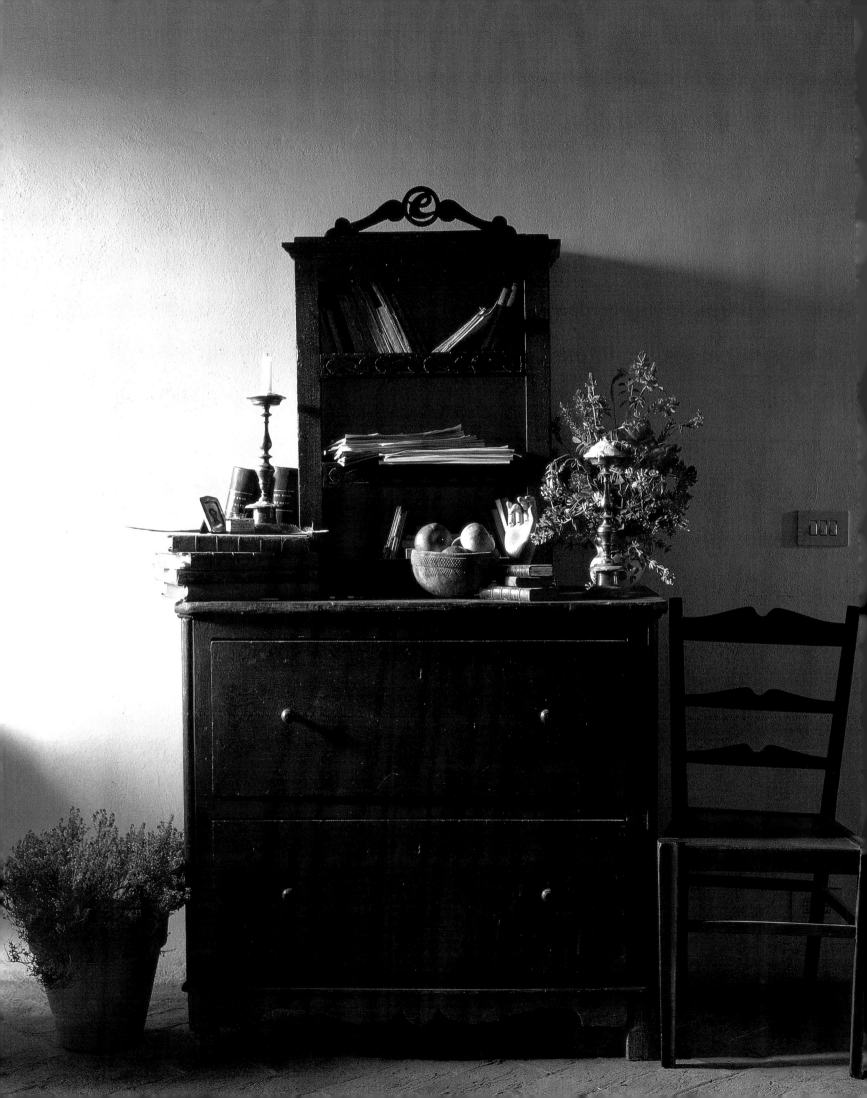

Italian country style

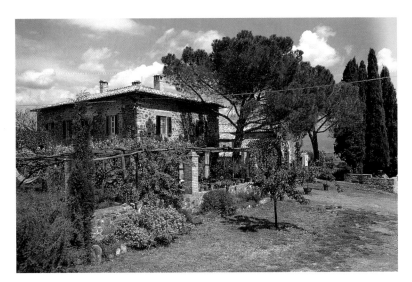

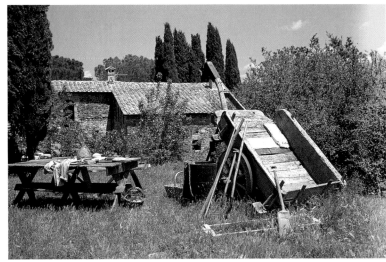

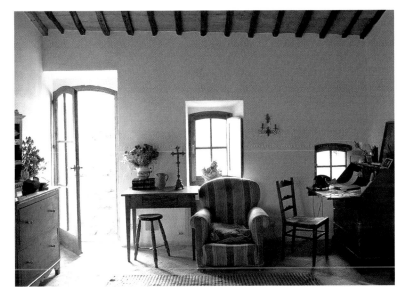

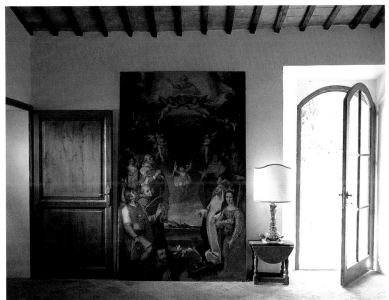

This low-built stone house near Montalchino in Tuscany was built in 1798 for the local priest, and is situated next to the 16th century church. It has been renovated with local materials – marble, chestnut and terracotta – which have much in sympathy with the "soul" of the environment.

The garden and outbuildings were provided for practical, not decorative purposes – food supplies for the priest and his household came from his own plot. Beyond the stone outbuildings stands a workman's table laden with delicious local produce. Preparing and eating food out of doors is an essential part of Tuscan country living. Nearby, an old cart displays a collection of antique agricultural implements. This was put together inexpensively, with many items found discarded in the outbuildings. The cart and collection serve to emphasize the proximity a country meal once had to its source – no juggernaut or supermarket intervened between tilth and table.

Three views of this most successful Italian sitting room show an interesting blend of country styles.

Far left:
A 19th century painted chest and simple rustic chair, classic Italian country pieces, are enhanced by mellow brass candlesticks and bunches of flowering thyme.

Top left:
A local 19th century chest, table and chair mix well with the 18th century English mahogany bureau when set against cool, fresh white walls, a warm wooden ceiling and brick floor.

Bottom left:
A large oil painting is left unframed so that it fits into the country setting. The strength of the architecture ensures that the Tuscan mood triumphs.

Italian country style

When planning colour schemes take inspiration from the soft, warm shades of the countryside; the hard, bright shine of urban style will seem intrusive.

Right:
The gentle sheen of waxed wooden furniture is a perfect complement to the warm glow of the well-trodden brick floor. The bedspread is Indian-made. The earthy tones of vegetable-dyed textiles from the third world are better suited to a country setting than the vivid hues of chemical-dyed European fabrics.

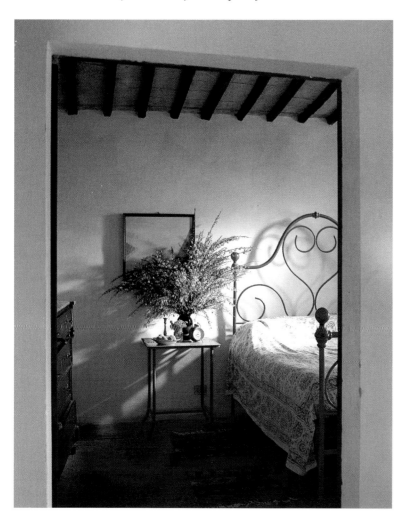

Above:
A 19th century iron bed found rusting away in ruined outbuildings has been revived with a coat of earth-coloured paint.

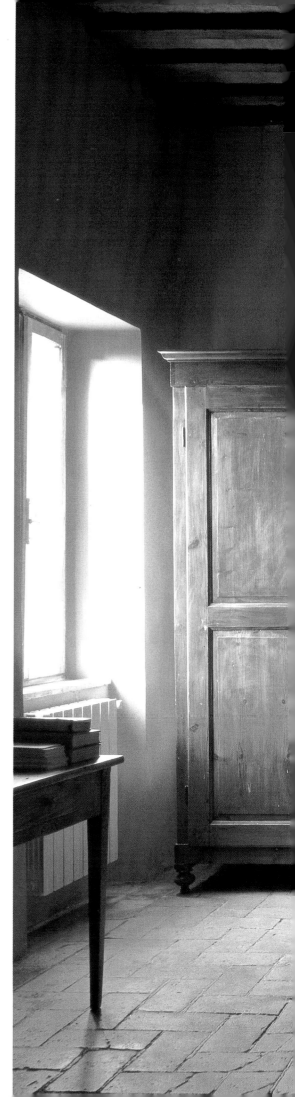

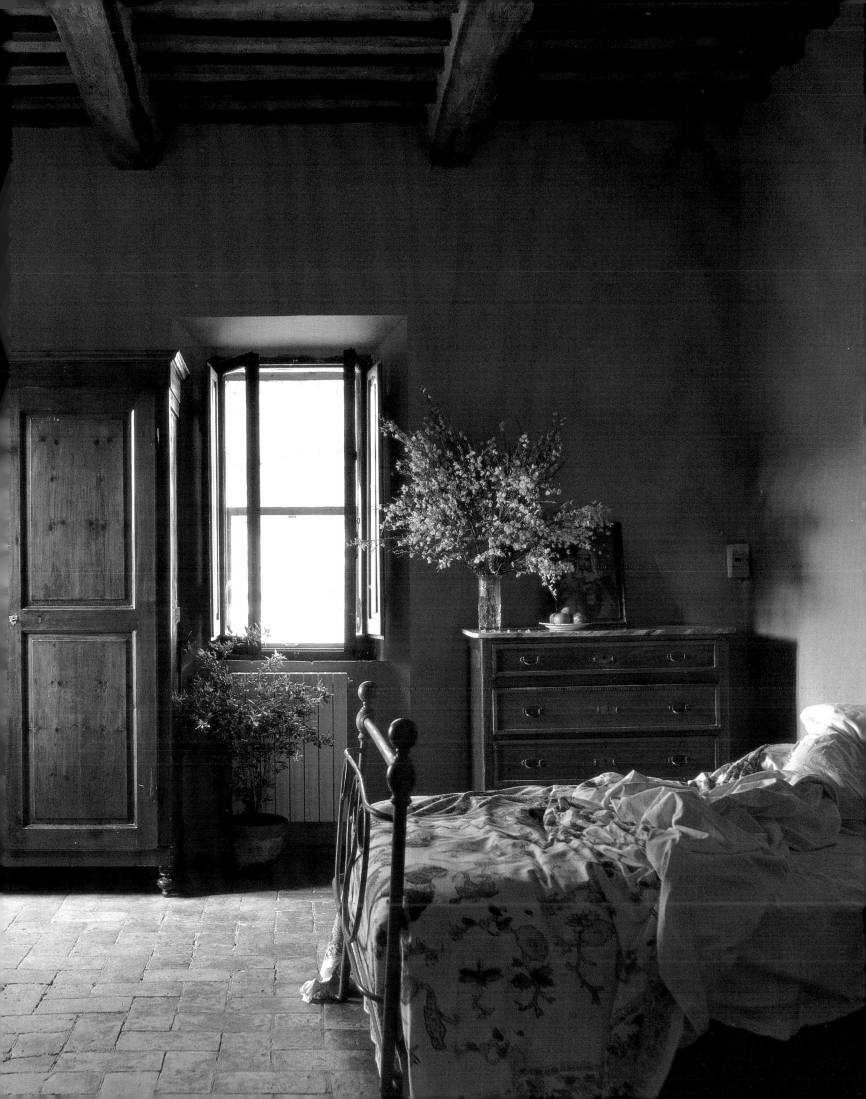

Italian country style

**The Italian region of Siena was the inspirational starting point for this
Tuscan-style home. Though country in mood, it is set in London, England.**

Below:
*The marble tabletop's reds, greens and yellows echo the colours used in the
paint effects on the wall, which create the illusion of dusty frescoes. The
design of the metal-framed chairs is reminiscent of traditional Italian
wrought-iron furniture.*

Right:
*Dry, earthy colours – ochre and terracotta – on the walls and soft
furnishings bring the sun-baked flavour of Tuscany to this dining room.
Large terracotta tiles, aged by stamping dirt and linseed oil into them,
cover the floor.*

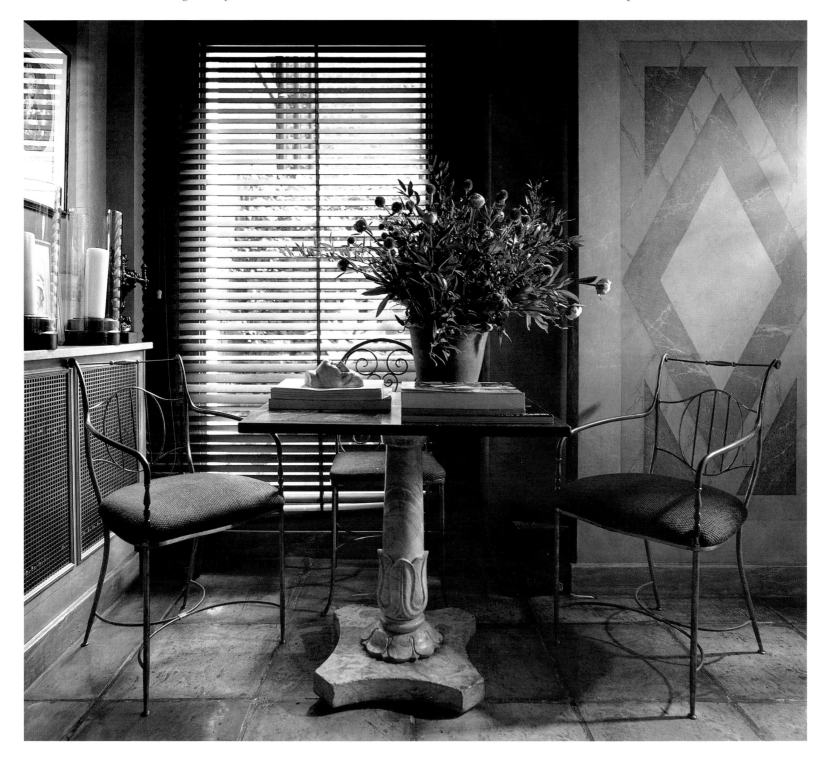

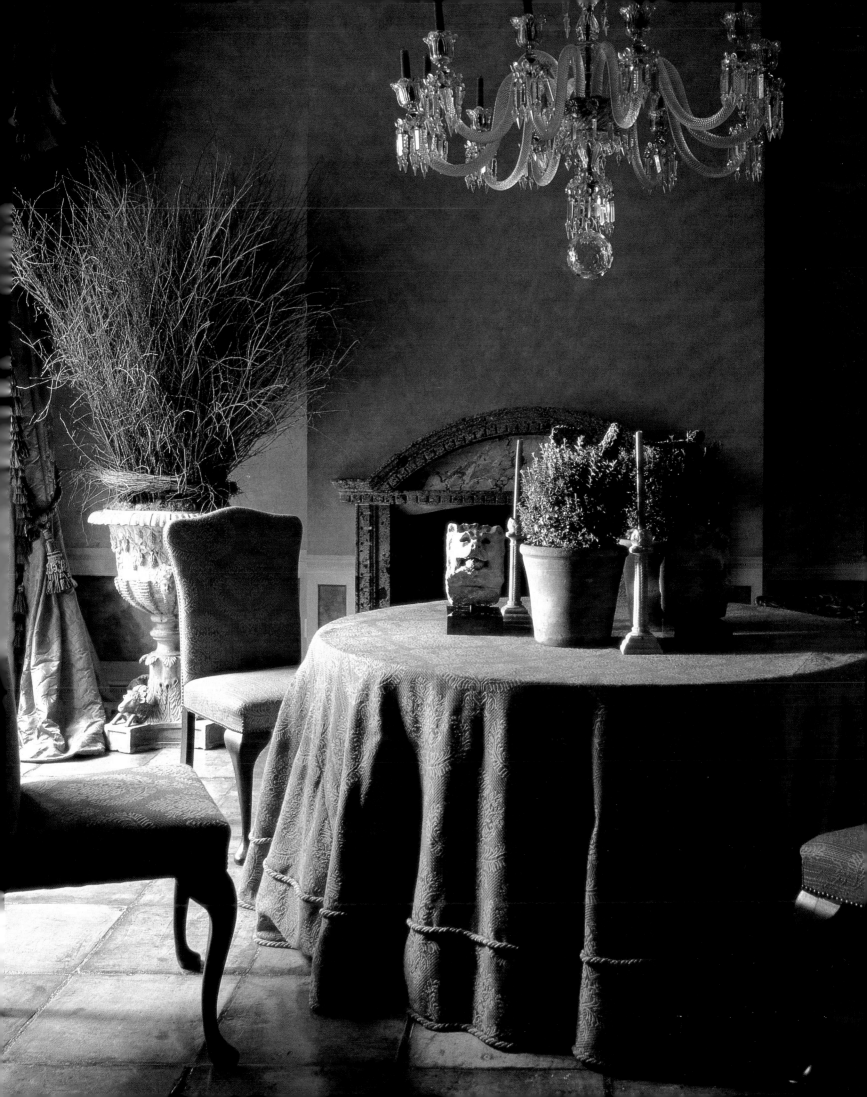

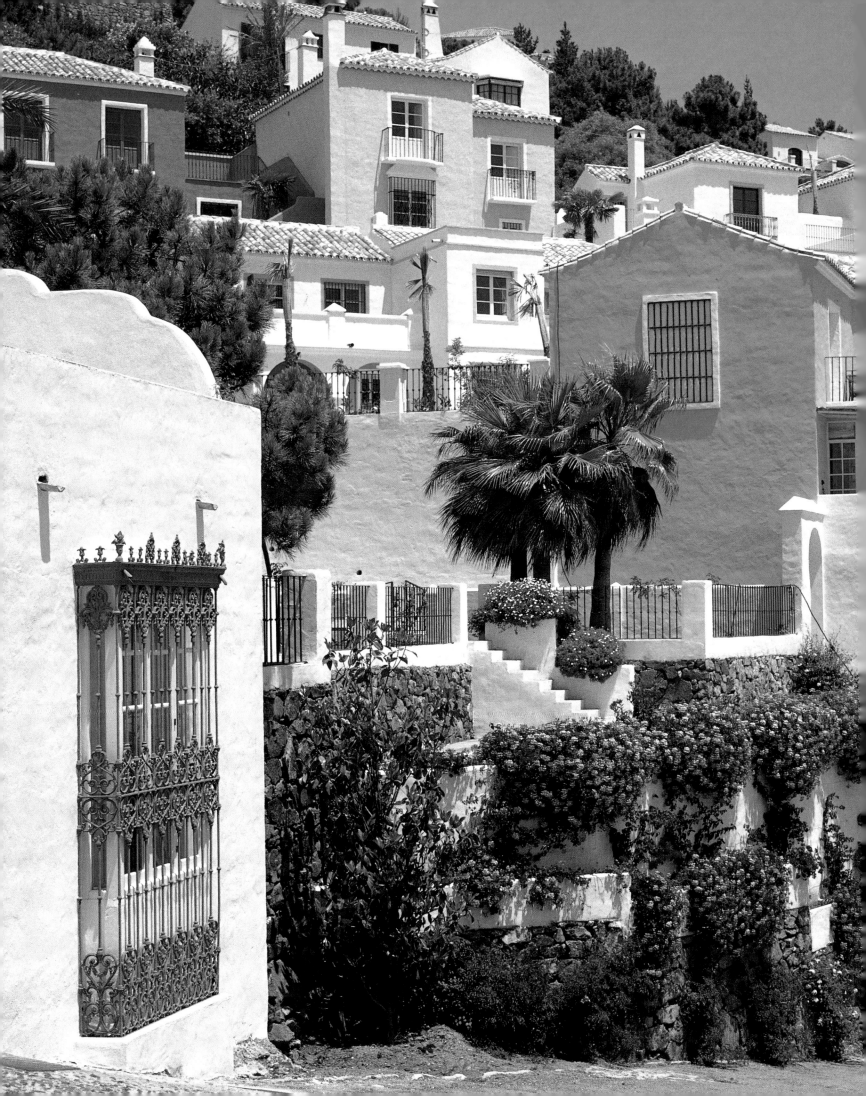

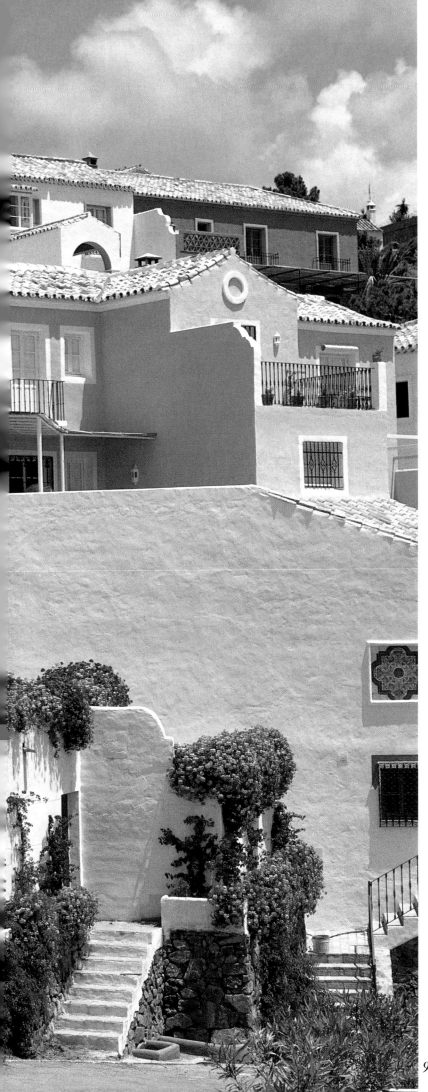

SPANISH
Country Style

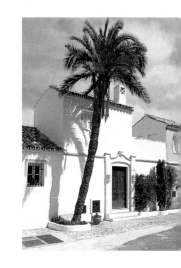

*E*veryone has an image of the Spanish country villa: a mini-citadel of high, whitewashed walls which seem to pulse in the heat under the burnt crust of a red-tiled roof. An almost neon-pink bougainvillea shoots up the side of the house and vies with brilliant turquoise shutters. Through the ornate window grilles there are glimpses of flagged floors, plain wooden furniture and bright glazed pottery. This broad vision fits the universal idea of a Mediterranean house, but when the details are filled in the mood becomes essentially Spanish. The interior looks as if it has been sculpted from plaster, with flowing staircases and elaborately shaped arches. There is a profusion of curtaining, of hangings and screens which turn large rooms into a series of private compartments. The patterns are bold geometrics in brilliant colours. The Spanish country style looks away from Europe and toward Africa, only 20 miles off its southern coast, over the Straits of Gibraltar. Its dramatic curves and wealth of weaves and hangings are the exotic gifts of the Moors – the tribe of Arabs, Egyptians, Berbers and Syrians who invaded Spain in the 8th century and ruled it for 700 years.

Andalusia, the province stretching across the southern coast of Spain, was the capital – *al-Andalus* – of the Moors' Spanish kingdom and the last bastion of their rule before it fell to the Christian armies from the north. In the south, the Arab influence on Spanish homes went deepest and gave Spanish

Above and left:
The hillside village of Heredia near Malaga in Southern Spain was built by architect Paco Parlade in the 1980s, following the traditional building methods of the region. This modern development is designed to avoid the soulless atmosphere of most new estates. It encapsulates the age-old style of the country communities found throughout the rural hills of the southern Mediterranean, where brightly painted village houses cluster together as if for protection against the blazing sun. (Further views of Heredia are shown on pages 102–3).

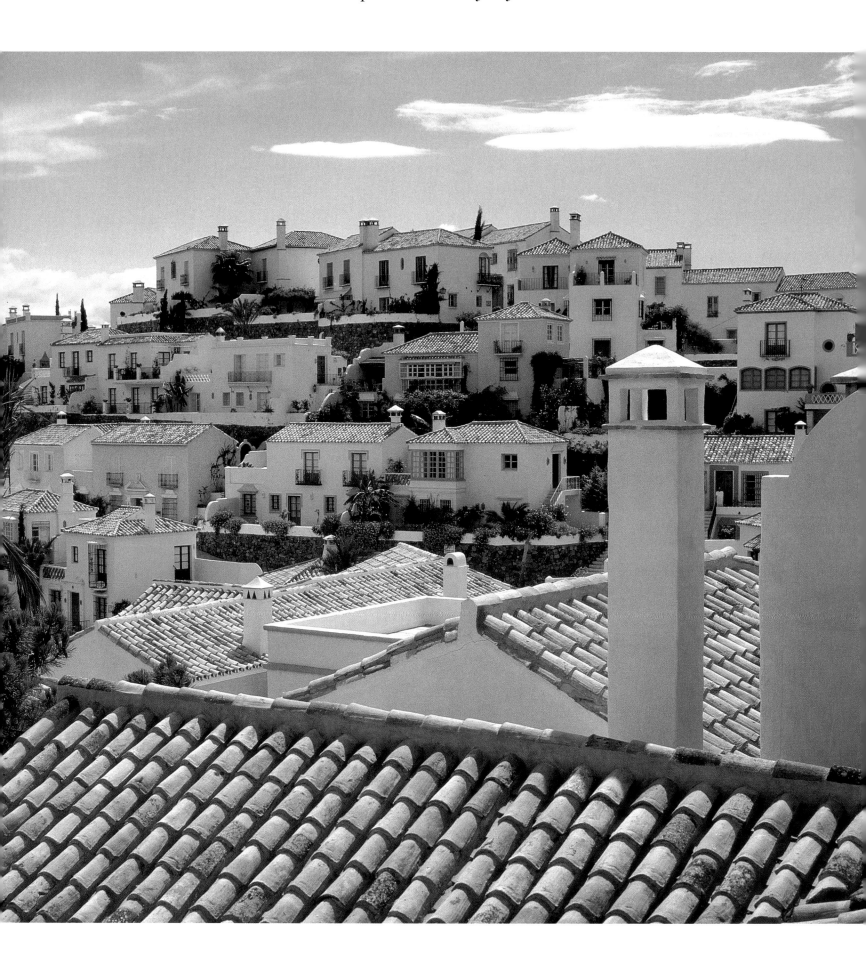

country style its exotic flavour. The words in Spanish for builder and architect are Arabic, as are the words for alcove, portico and terrace.

The south is the most fertile part of Spain, but it is still a harsh landscape, where the desert palm and the prickly pear grow alongside groves of oranges and lemons. The rural Spanish were some of the poorest people in Europe, very few of them even enjoying the smallholdings of French peasants. Spanish country style belongs instead to the wealthier farmers of the south, whose farms often developed into the huge *laitifundo* estates as they encroached on the common lands. The farmhouses were built of plastered mud or, for the better-off, of stone, with ceilings and some furniture built of another rare commodity – wood.

The style of the south was shaped by the searingly hot land and by the social traditions of the Arab rulers. On the outside, heavy doors and shutters shut the sun out, but also kept the women within hidden from view. Indoors, women were often separated from the men by hangings and curtains, which helped darken rooms. Everything inside conspired toward coolness and ventilation. Floors were laid with flagstones which could be sprinkled with water to keep down the heat and dust. A style of cut-out patterns evolved so that some light could be admitted into the heavily shaded rooms. Shutters were carved with curly filigrees or windows screened with lattice-work. Internal plaster walls and staircases might be pierced with simple geometric motifs.

Left:
A view over the sun-baked rooftops of Heredia, displaying the pan-tiled roofs and decorative plasterwork chimneys that are typical of southern Mediterranean villages.

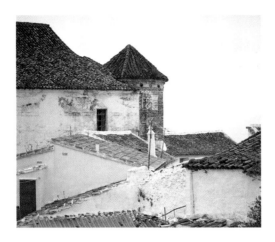

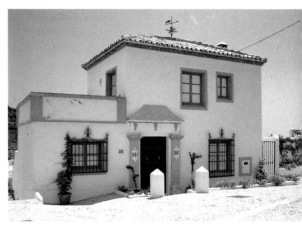

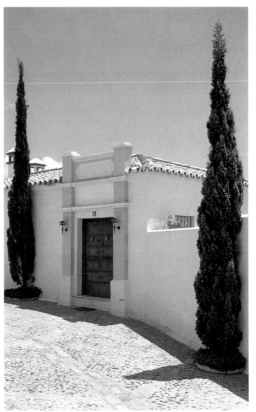

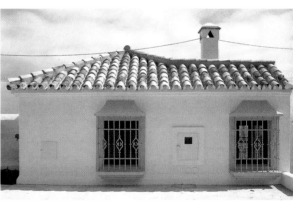

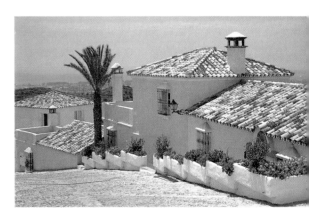

Above:
The shutters and grilles of these houses reveal the Moorish influence on this region of Spain, which created an architecture that ensured the Islamic preference of privacy for the women of the house.

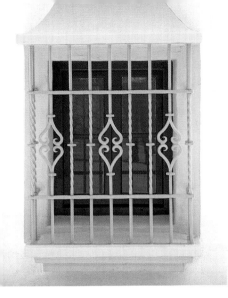
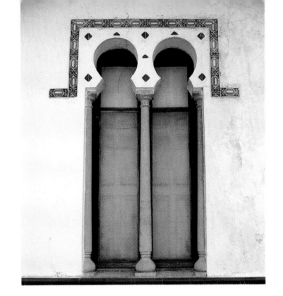
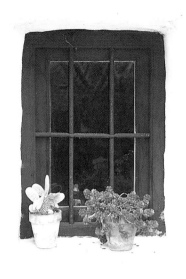
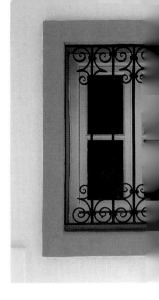

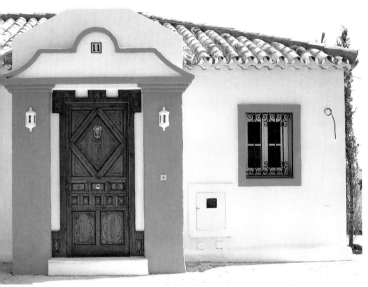
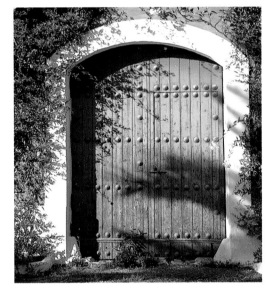
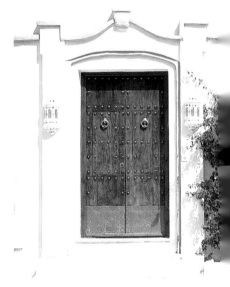

Above top:
Windows vary from exuberant Arabic-influenced designs to the traditional
small window (third from the right) that kept out the heat of the day.
Decorative grilles and pierced shutters keep interiors private and cool.

The Spanish style arranges rooms quite differently from the French and Italian, again because of the combination of practical necessity in a hot land and the influence of Arab traditions. Furniture is noticeably low-built and the floor is given special attention, being both the coolest part of a room and the place where women were expected to sit. Under the rules of Arab society only men were given chairs or benches, the women making themselves comfortable on rugs and cushions or on a *tarina* – a dais strewn with carpets. Daily life was lived in the one large central room, whether it was an enclosed foyer or a double-height internal courtyard. Bedrooms were tucked into alcoves off the side, or put above on a mezzanine floor. Traditional Spanish houses rarely had separate dining rooms: meals were taken instead off small tables in the main room, which was divided up into a series of distinct areas using curtains and screens. The modern Spanish country interior might preserve a feeling of the style by using rugs to mark out different areas in one room, while its kitchen might be fitted into a small, tiled alcove or simply installed in one corner, screened off by a brightly woven curtain.

The rural Spanish interior revels in geometric patterns and brilliant contrasts of colour. Floral decorations are rare, though occasionally a rose might appear as the emblem of the Knights Templar and symbol of the Christian reconquest. But the Moorish influence wins out with bold geometric patterns – circles and semi-circles, four-cornered stars, diamonds, octagons and triangles decorating the surfaces of tiles or inspiring inlaid floors. The famous horseshoe outline of the Arab arch is often used as a pattern. The love of strong shapes encourages walls to be treated as exhibition spaces for brightly coloured plates, delicately wrought *torchères* and wall-mounted braziers, once used to burn olive stones for warmth at night.

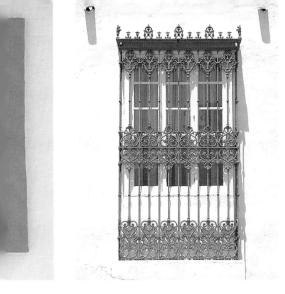
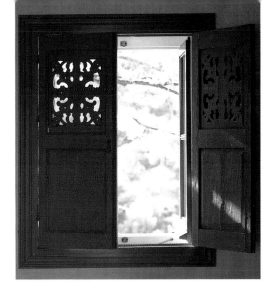
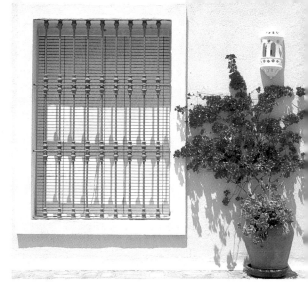
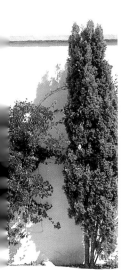
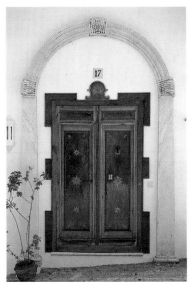
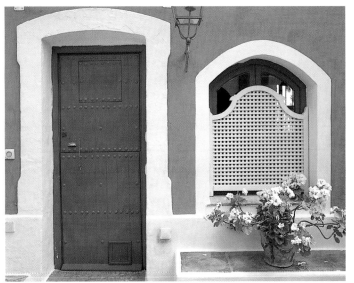
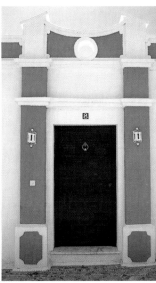

Above bottom:
Spanish house builders generally install massive studded wooden doors set
in elaborate frameworks. Moorish-influenced, this reflects the Islamic
demand for privacy.

The colours are those of a landscape which is lush, but scorched. The crimson and green of Spanish peppers, or perhaps of the red earth and the southern cypress, might be used in a boldly patterned pelmet hanging around a bed. A band of Andalusia's deep blue-glazed *azulejo* tiles along a wall makes a vivid contrast with the acid-yellow faience plates hung up for decoration.

Spanish country furniture is extremely simple: sofas are often no more than daybeds and benches might be built out from the wall in slabs of cool stone faced with brightly patterned tiles. Chairs are rush-seated, four-square designs in unpainted pine or yew. The traditional Spanish meal, which consists of a series of small courses called *tapas*, has inspired a profusion of small side tables and buffets. The modern coffee table, which might jar in a French farmhouse, has a particular appropriateness in the setting of Spanish country style. So do rich woods like mahogany, whose dark patina, when set against the backdrop of brilliant whitewash, fits into a style of contrasts.

The *chiaroscuro* of light and dark is a hallmark of the Spanish country style. Just as tickets to a bullfight in Spain are divided between *sol* or *sombra*, so the Spanish house makes no halfway deal with the sun. Instead of the sun-warmed tones of the Italian farmhouse, the colours of Spanish style tend to be either fiery or very cool. White is a constant foil to the dark furniture, richly coloured rugs and brightly glazed tiles. The contrasts are multiplied when solid walls are punctuated with open-work patterns, shutters pierced with filigree and hard floors softened with kelims.

The geographical accident that fixed Spain to Europe but separated it from Africa by only 20 miles of sea led to the development in the south of a Spanish country style that combines Mediterranean and Moorish, familiar and exotic.

Spanish country style

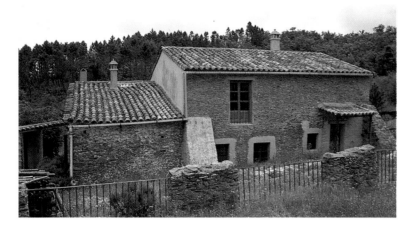

El Parrero, a simple vineyard-maker's dwelling, is used by its owner as a refuge from modern Spain. It is not just a romantic haven, for a stay here takes you back to genuine basics. The owner has not installed electricity: candles, a gas cooktop and a wood-burning stove provide heat and light.

Below and right:
The living room is furnished with simply carved local furniture. Because the original slat-and-pole ceiling is low, it is painted white to reflect more light into the room.

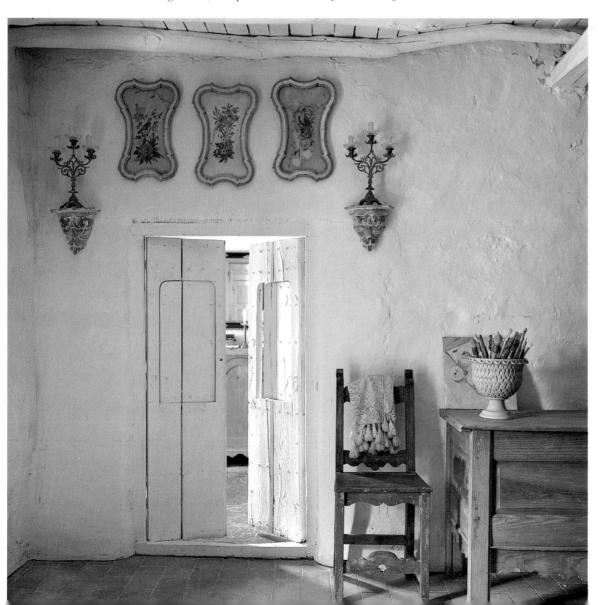

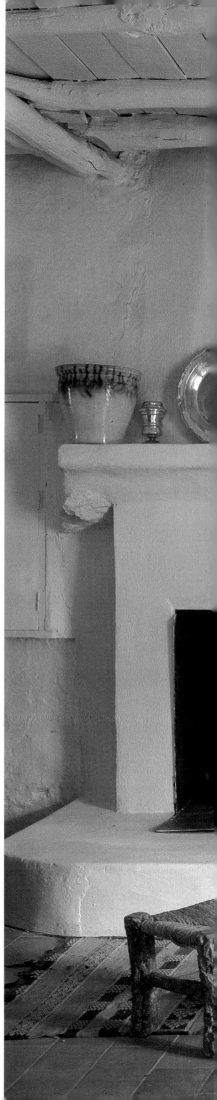

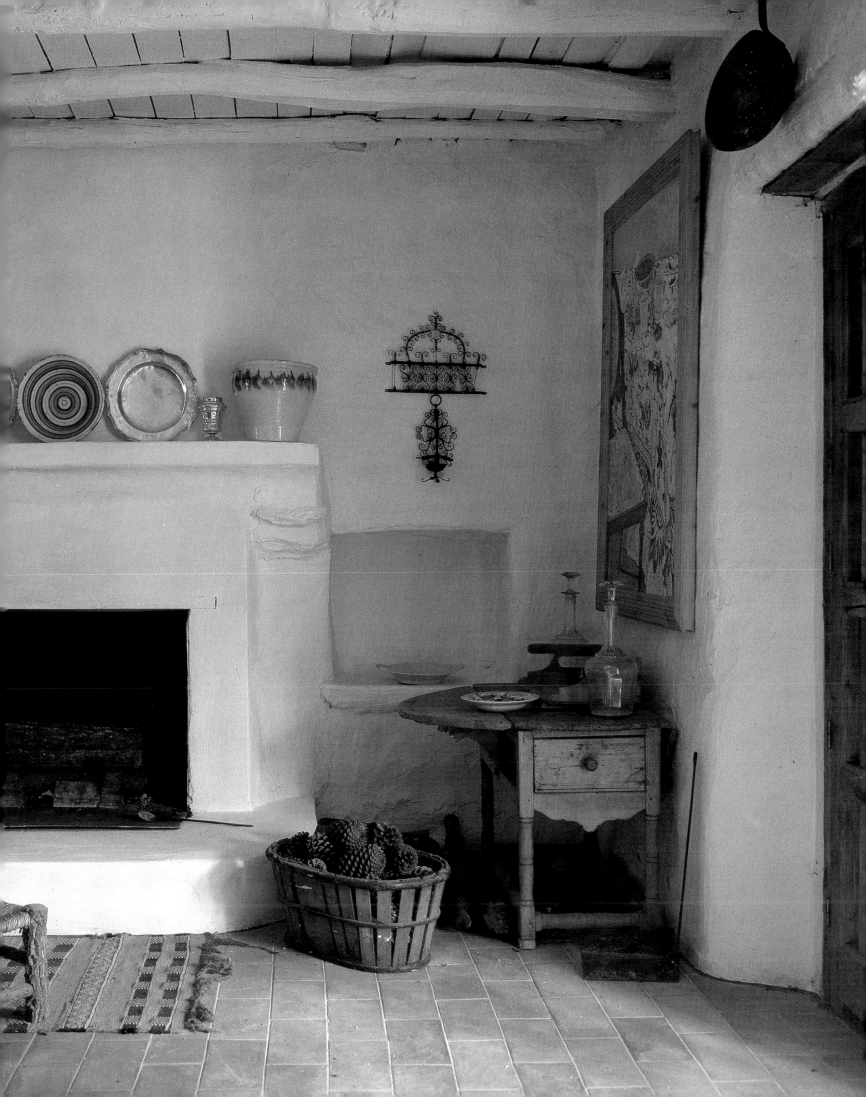

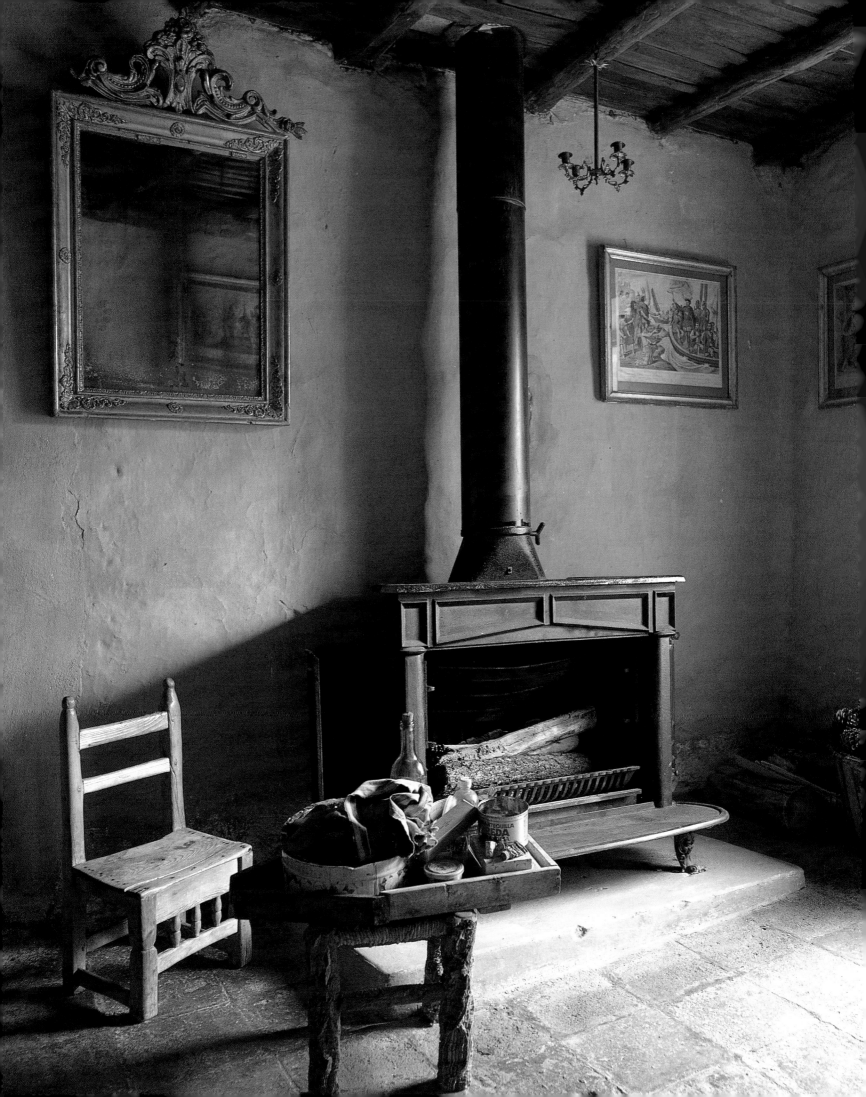

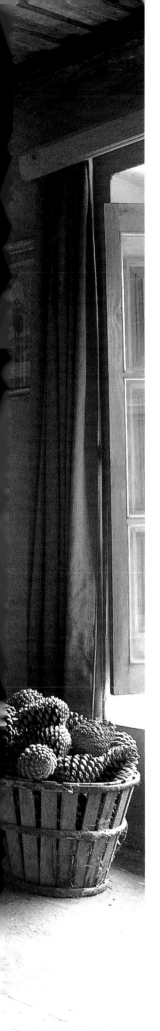

Spanish country style

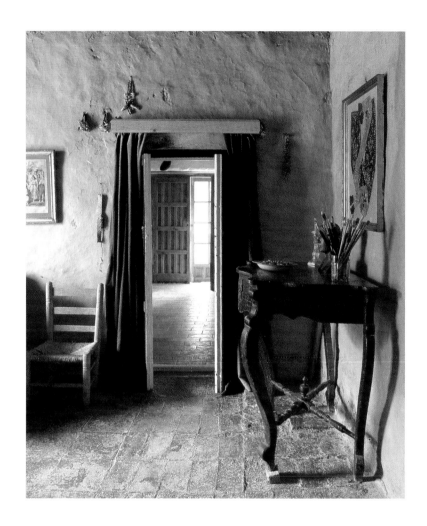

Above:
A well-worn brick floor, natural beamed and boarded ceiling and deep-toned rough plaster walls provide the simple, strong architectural framework that is essential to an honest country style. The walls display prints of the Spanish conquest of South America, a reminder of Spain's colonial heritage.

Left:
Thick, sturdy walls keep the interior cool even in the heat of the Iberian sun, so this wood-burning Bilbao stove is essential to dispense with the chill of evening. Nearby stands a rustic stool, its legs made from local cork trees, laden with the tools of the artist owner's trade.

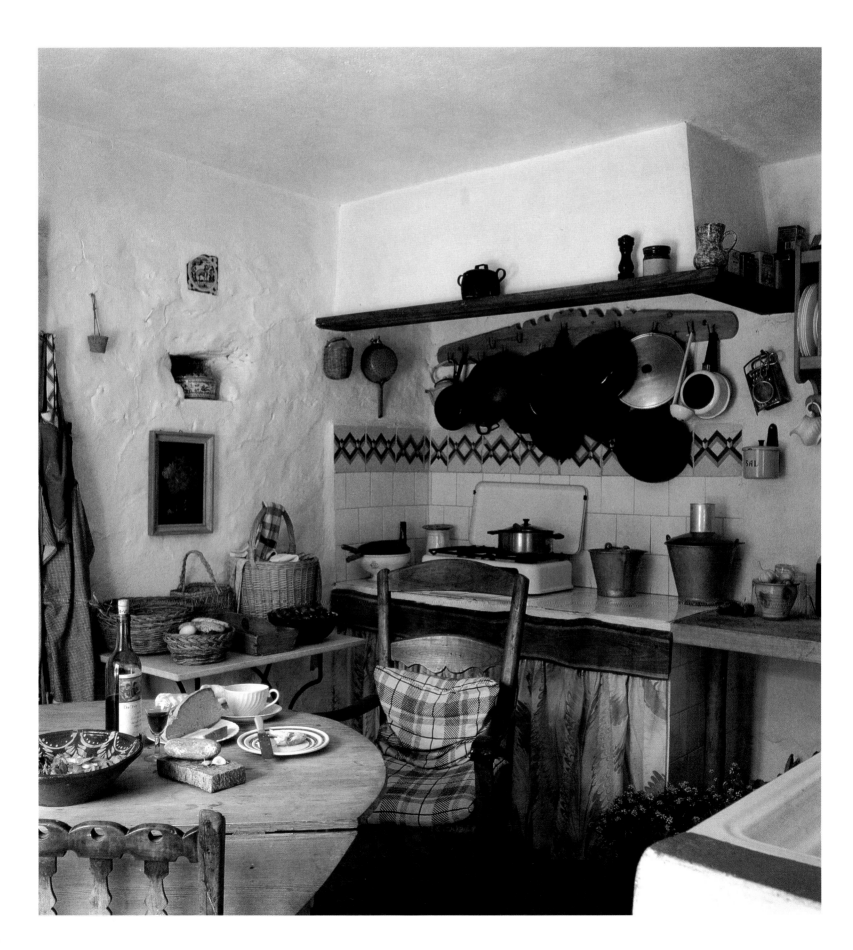

Spanish country style

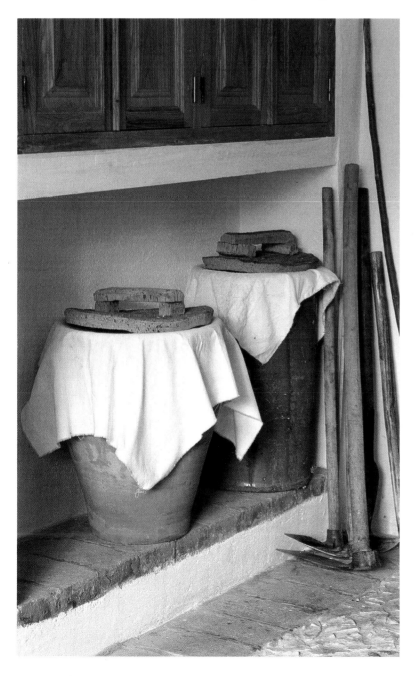

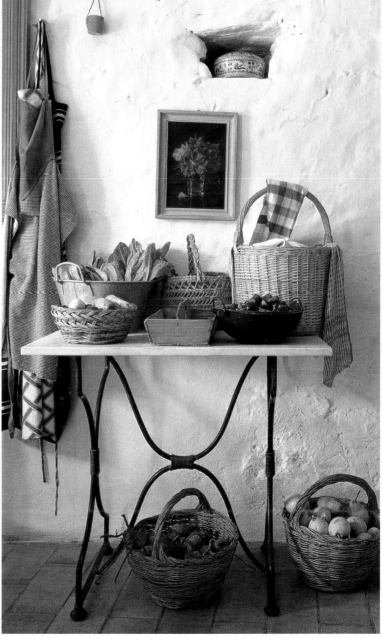

La Heredia *is a village in Southern Spain built by architect Paco Perlade during the 1980s. Like William Clough Ellis's Portmerion in North Wales, built early in the 20th century, and Seaside in Florida (see p. 160), also constructed in the 1980s, this purpose-built village is an attempt to recreate the community atmosphere most modern developments lack.*

Right:
This room is an excellent example of a quite exceptional attention to detail that has produced an uncluttered, timeless Spanish country look in a modern development. The architect has designed shutters and ironwork which are practical as well as aesthetically pleasing, and a simple curtain pole from which hang basic checked cotton drapes. Any lingering "newness" in the building is dispelled by good Andalucian 19th century pine country furniture and a traditional quarry-tiled floor strewn with local rush matting decorated in a stitched terracotta design.

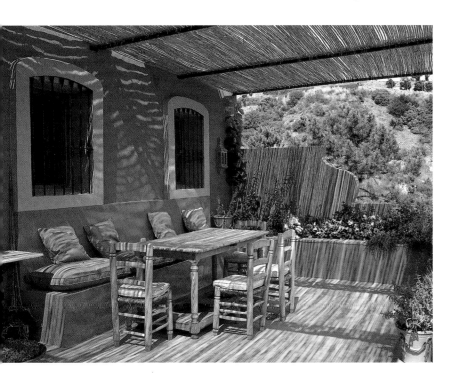

Above:
Traditional terracotta and green decorates the outside of this house, and proves an effective foil to the sun-bleached wooden furniture. The built-in bench is an echo of the North African influence on Spanish style.

Far right:
A characteristic arch, local quarry tiles and a fine 18th century Andalucian food cupboard give this hallway an immediate Southern Mediterranean feel.

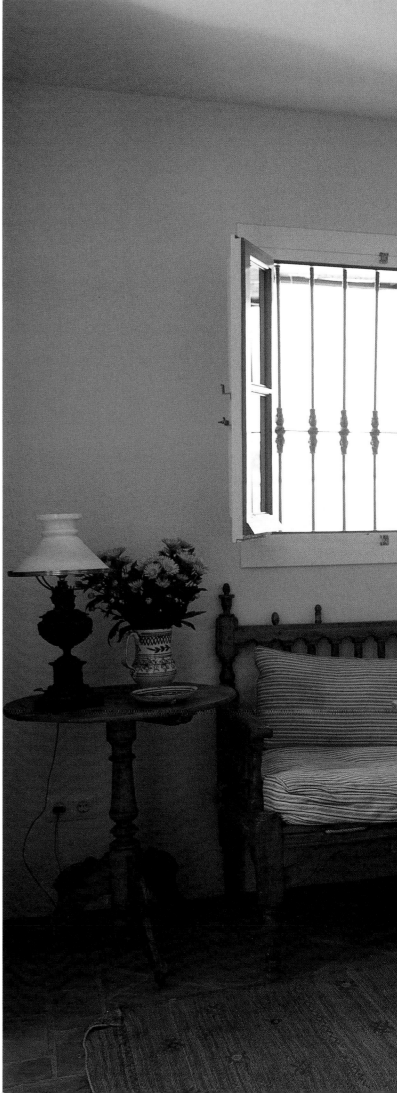

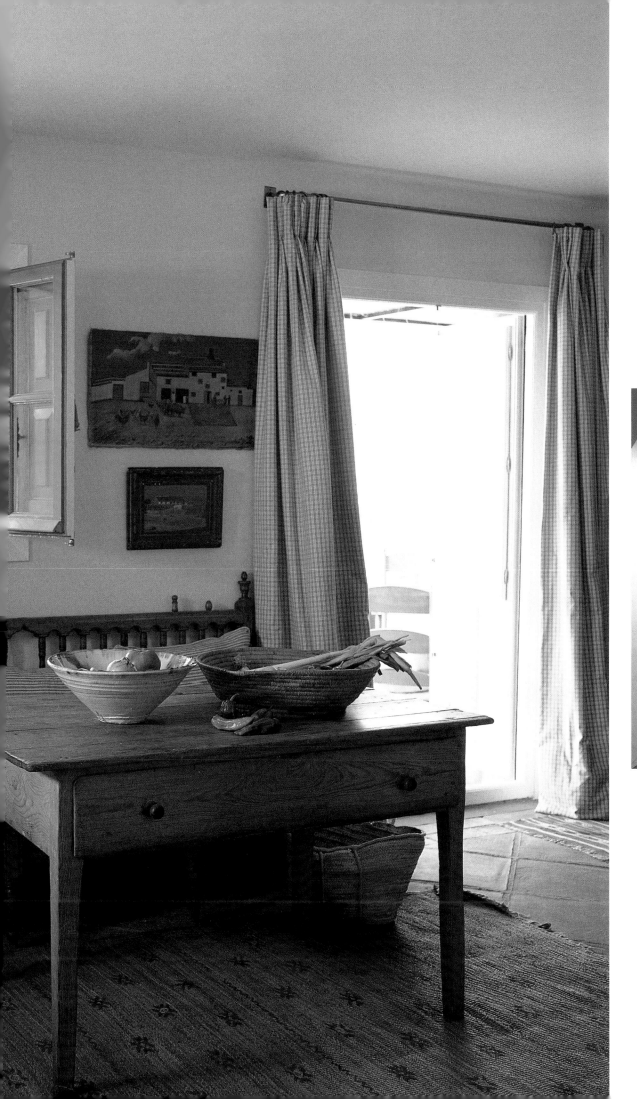
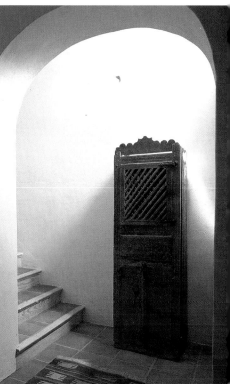

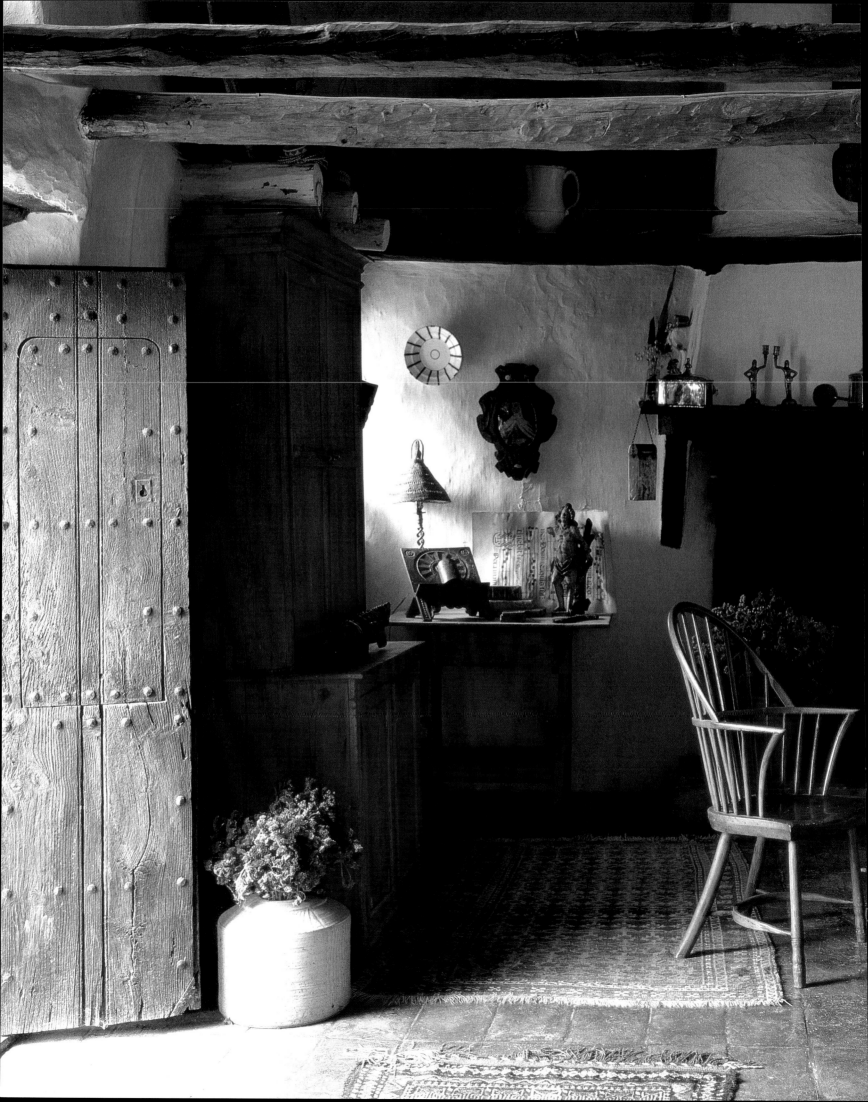

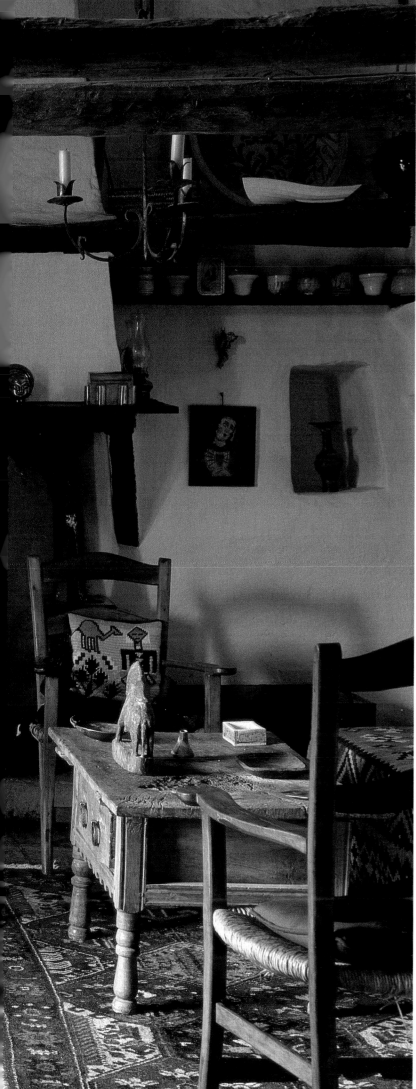

Local stonemasons built this rustic finca in Southern Spain in the early years of the 19th century. Abandoned at the time of the Spanish Civil War and completely untouched when owner Stephen Andrews discovered it, the house was replete with authentic features – unglazed windows protected by wooden shutters, heavy wooden doors and beams and a tiled roof.

Left and below:
A window high above the door lights the beams in the roof of this whitewashed room. With the exception of an English Windsor chair, all the 19th century pieces are Spanish. Other artefacts are culled from around the world, yet because they are hand-crafted none seem out of place.

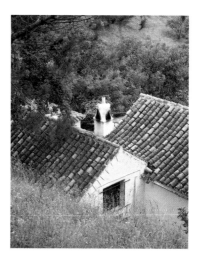 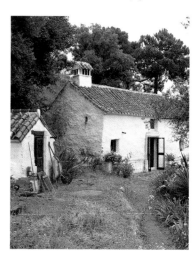

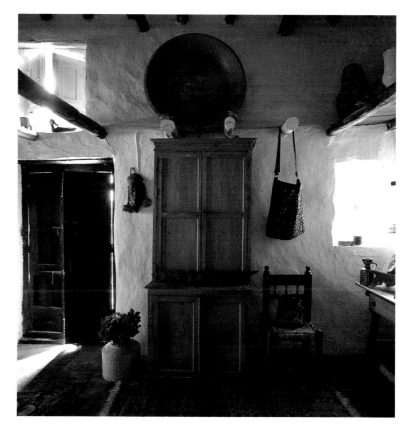

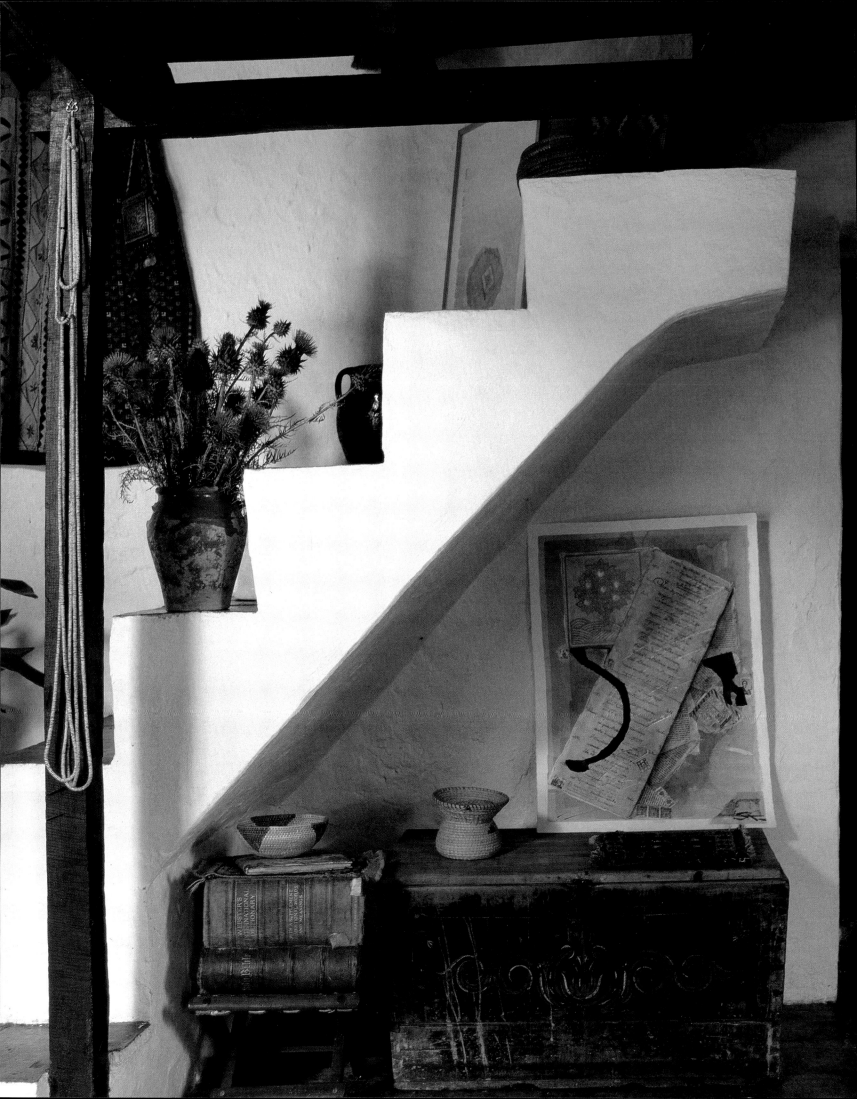

Spanish country style

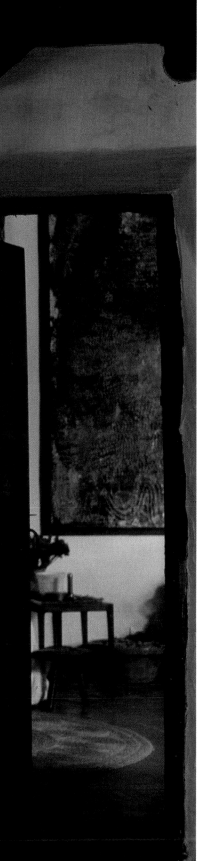

An eclectic display of hand-crafted objects gathered on the owner's travels furnish this house.

Top right:
A 19th century gateleg table houses boxes, pots, and vases, all dominated by a 19th century South Indian painted wooden figure.

Below right:
A Spanish table and crucifix share a corner with a Hindu Sun temple (in the small niche) and modern artwork – a jardiniere by Jo Lydia Craven and a picture – "Tree Drawing" – by Martin Bloch. On the windowsill stands a hand-thrown pot by Lucie Rie. A single shelf, with chains and pendants hanging from the brackets, is crammed with well-thumbed poetry books and piled with yet more objects.

Left:
Purple thistles are pushed into a locally potted vase perched on a step of the white-painted stairway that leads up to the sleeping area. Underneath, a collage by the artist-owner stands on a South African chest, known as a kis, next to a tiny stool piled with antique leather-bound volumes.

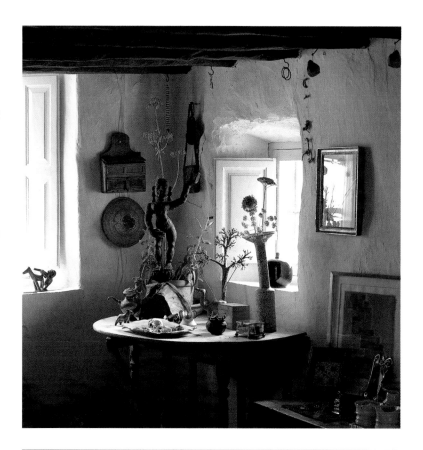

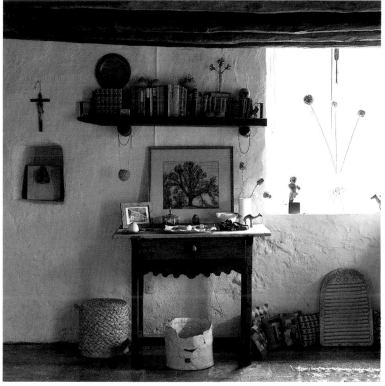

Spanish country style

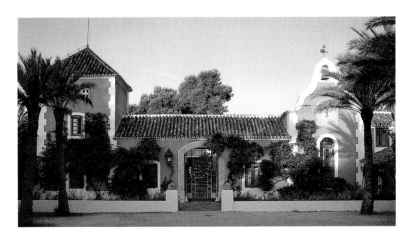

The architect Jaime Parlade converted a simple 19th century farmhouse, rebuilt from a fire-damaged ruin in the 1950s, into this traditionally inspired family home. The house is entered through a filigree gate set into a white-painted wrought-iron grille.

Below:
The filigree gate leads into a pebble-floored central courtyard, where raised flower beds overflow with an abundance of daturas hung with white and pink trumpets.

Right:
The style of this terrace has its roots in the Moorish tradition in Spain, where Europe met Africa. The terrace floor is paved with local terracotta tiles, while Greek columns frame views to Gibraltar and Africa beyond. The simple wicker furniture is covered with cushions and pillows made from kelims and African blankets.

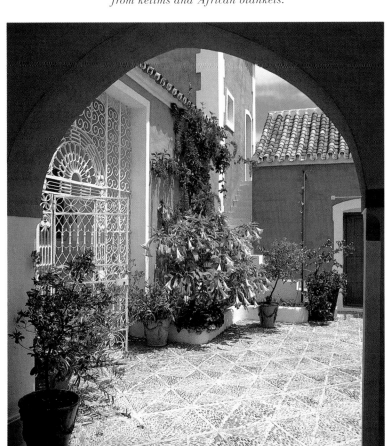

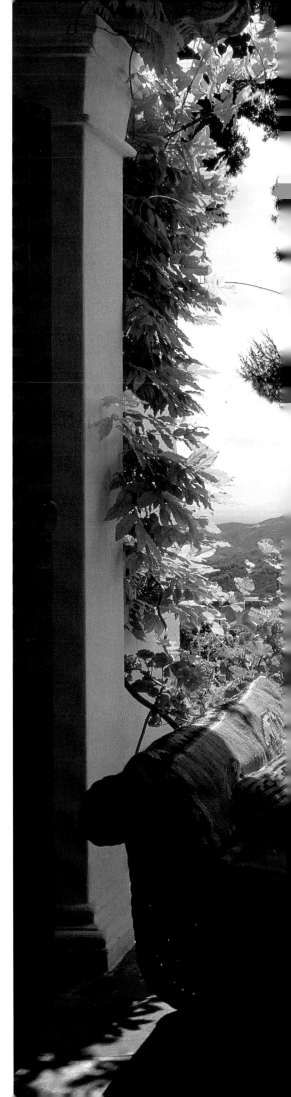

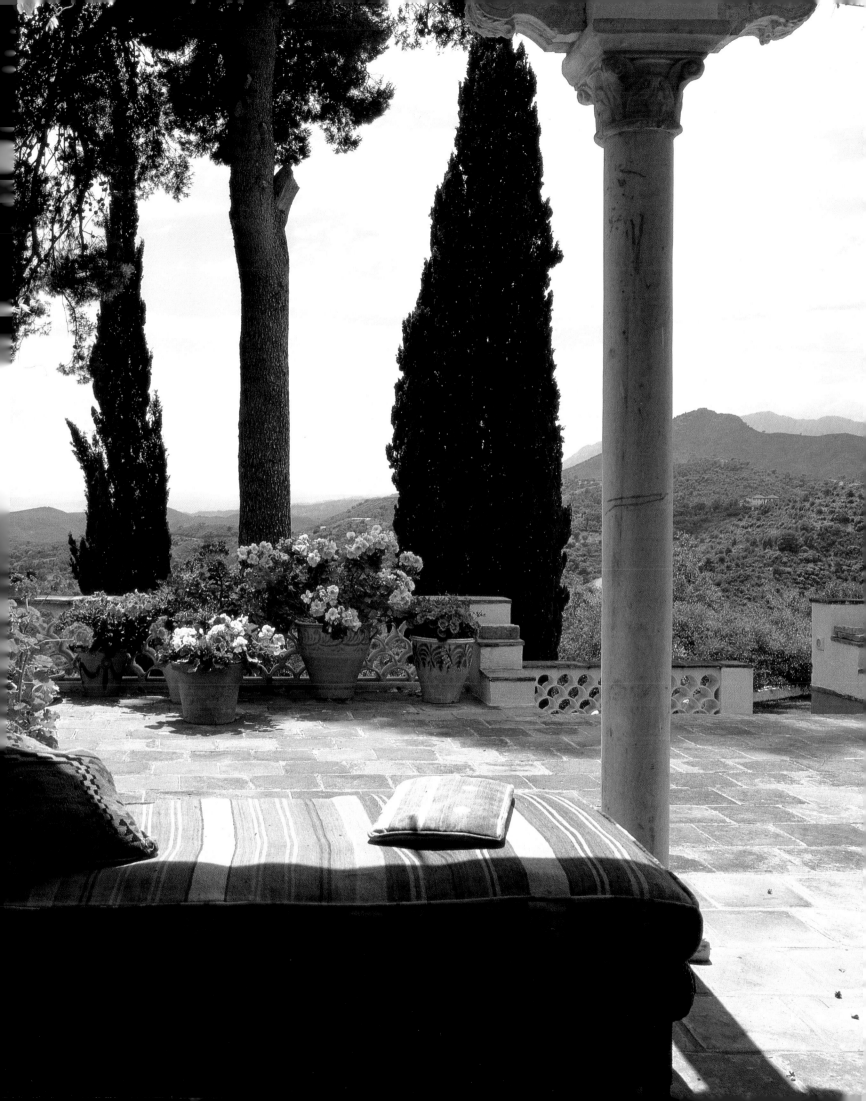

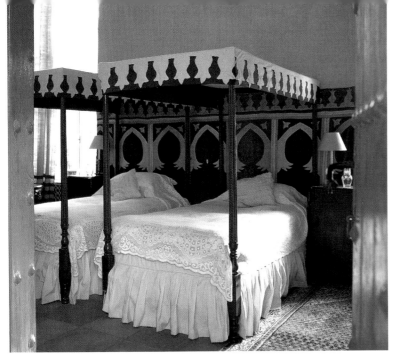

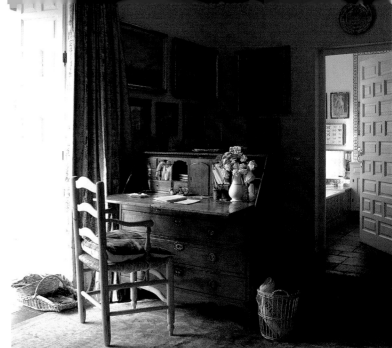

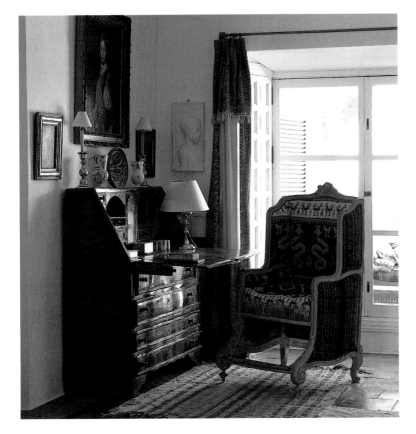

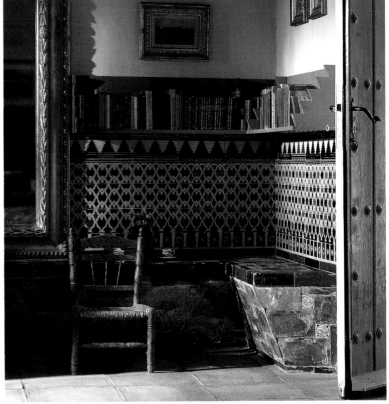

A genuine Spanish feeling, with a thread of Moorish influence, pervades this house.

Top left:
Moorish-styled pelmets and wall-hangings in green, white and maroon make a pair of 18th century English four-poster beds suitable for Spanish nights.

Above left:
Country style does not have to stick to the rustic. Here simple white walls and a quarry-tiled floor are enriched by elegant but not sumptuous furnishings: an 18th century bureau, Moorish throne chair, Kashmiri curtain, pale-coloured kelims, dark Spanish oil paintings and local faience.

Top right:
An early 19th century walnut bureau and modern ladder-backed chair give a period feel to this comfortable writing area. The multi-panelled doors and shutters are typically Spanish.

Above right:
Glazed and unglazed tiles have been used to create a Moorish bench, built to a traditional design used in the retreats of North African menfolk.

Right: This entrance hall opens off the internal courtyard (see page 108). A flamboyantly Spanish arch surrounds the coat rack, while diagonally laid terracotta tiles, 18th and 19th century oils in heavy gilded frames, large 18th century faience dishes and a 17th century torchère all add to the Iberian atmosphere.

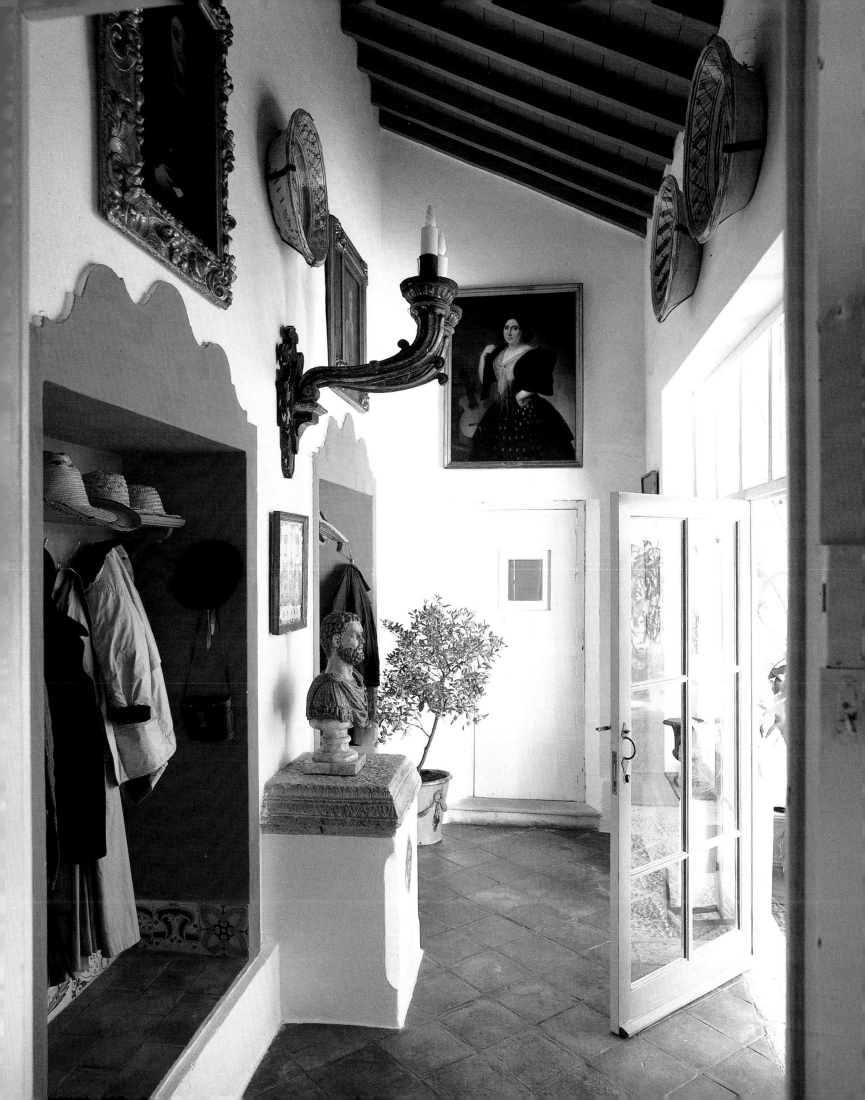

Spanish country style

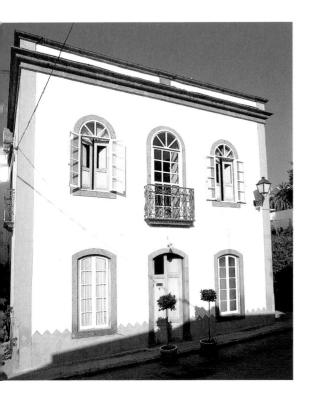

Interior designer Christophe Gollut's village house is an authentic copy of the Museo de Colion in Verqueta, Gran Canaria, a building which was originally home to Christopher Columbus.

Right:
The traditional stone-flagged inner courtyard is open to the sky, its walls painted rich blue to contrast with the faux stone doorways. Hardwood pillars support the first floor. The twisted brass candlesticks are 19th century pieces. The banisters of the stairway to the roof terrace are carved in a traditional island design. Also locally made is the refectory table. The director's chairs have been magically transformed by recovering their seats and backs with pieces from a distressed Arabian carpet.

Below left.
Drinking water is acquired in the age-old island way by being filtered through a thick porous stone basin called a pila, set in a niche in the blue walls of the open-to-the-sky central courtyard. The pila is filled from a tap directly above it and sweet, pure water drips through the stone into frosted glass wine bottles which store filtered water until it is required for drinking and cooking.

Below right:
A locally made pot and a Moroccan lantern bought in the nearby market fill an empty corner.

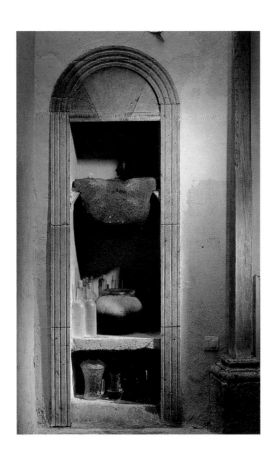

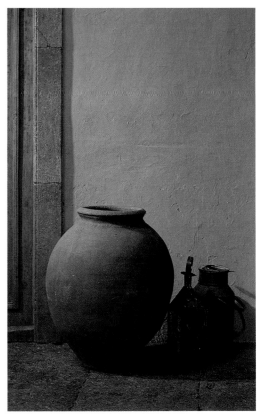

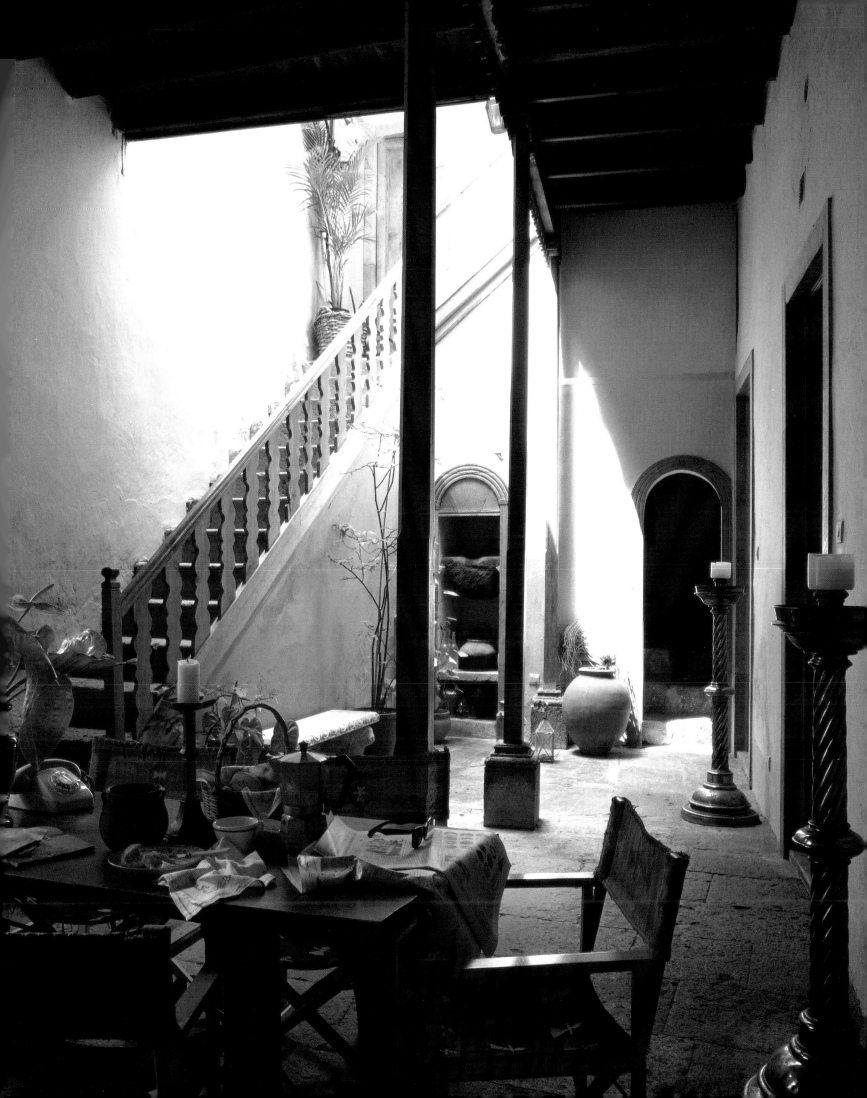

Spanish country style

Below left:
The entrance hall walls are a triumph of trompe l'oeil, *painted to look like crumbling stone slabs. The hand-operated door bell sited over the green entrance doors eschews modern technology – it is operated by pulling on a rope from outside.*

Right:
Double doors, screened by simple checked cotton curtains secured top and bottom, lead through from the entrance hall to a guest bedroom.

Below right:
A 19th century console table, flanked by two chairs, stands opposite the landing window on the upper floor, which overlooks the courtyard below.

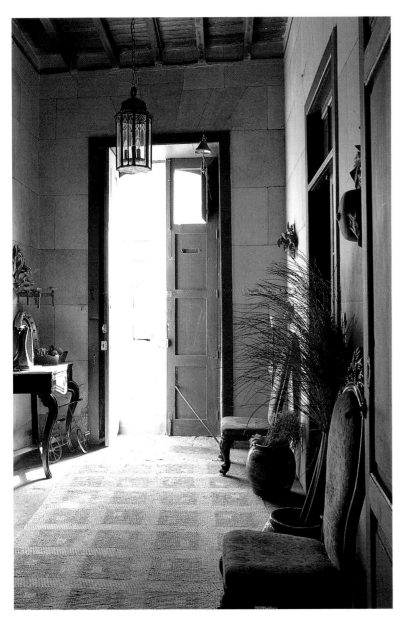 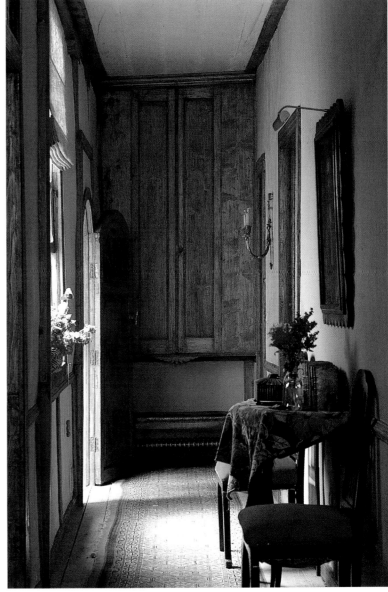

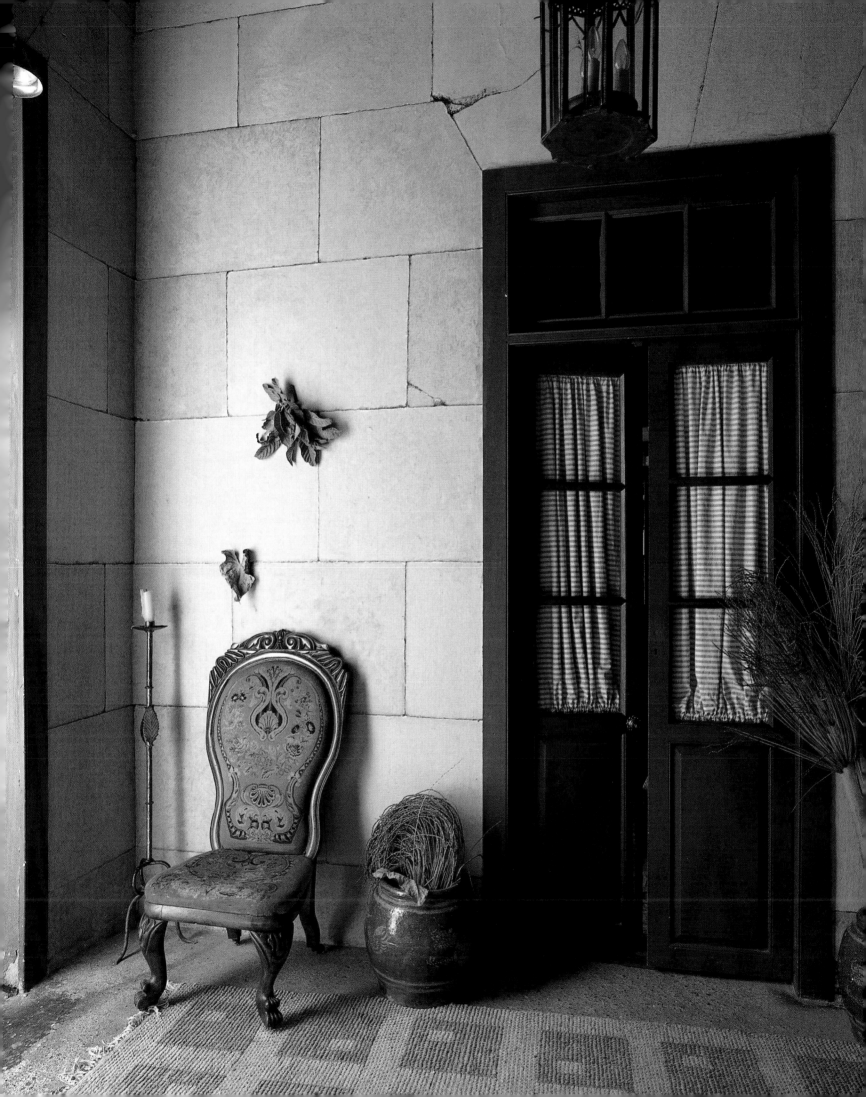

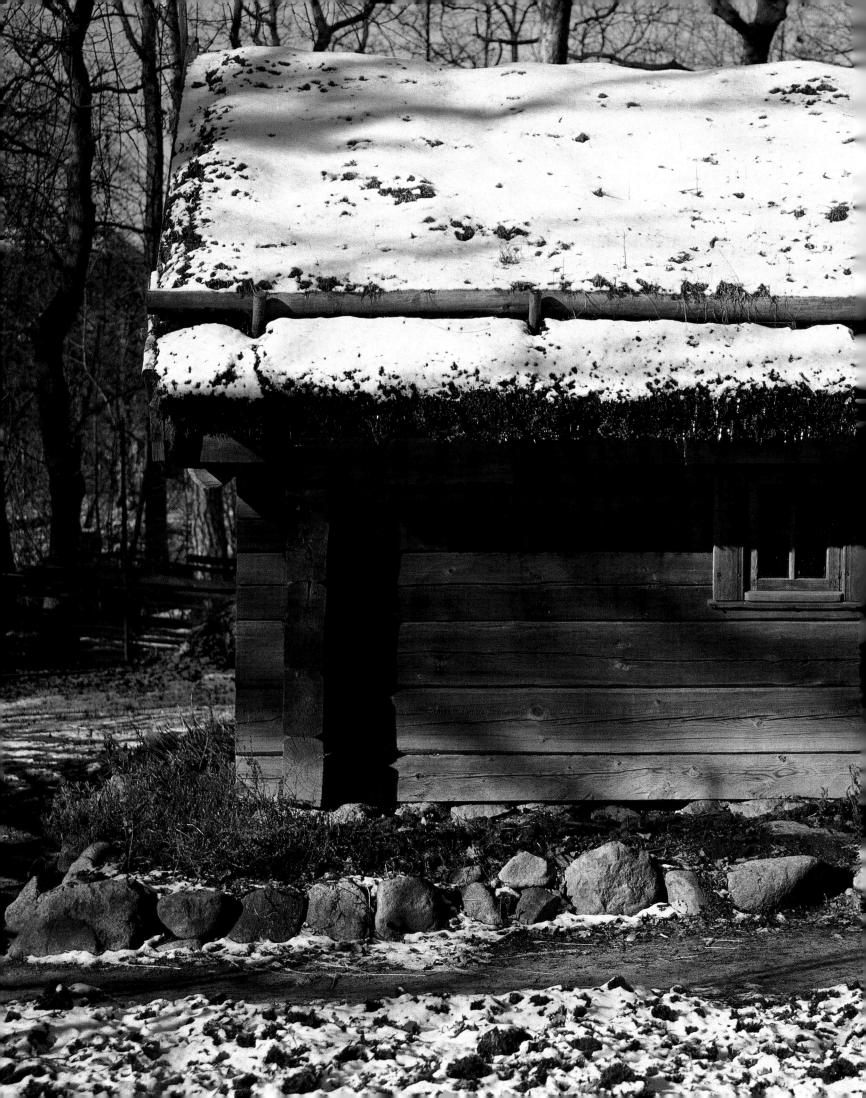

SCANDINAVIAN
Country Style

The style the world knows as Scandinavian country is the style of farmhouses in Sweden's provinces. The rural communities that live there are among the most isolated in Europe, separated by a landscape of lakes and forest and by the ferocity of the long winters.

There is much in the traditional Scandinavian farmhouse that is familiar from the pioneer homes of early America. Wood predominates inside and out, from the shingled or split-log roofs to the raftered ceilings and pale pine floors. The colours – ox-blood red, deep blue and sea-green – are those of New England homes. And Scandinavian wooden furniture is often carved and fretted with the same simple folk motifs loved by the Pennsylvanian Dutch. Built on a larger scale than the American settlers' homes, Scandinavian farmhouses often accommodated two generations of a family together and might have to house many more when far-flung communities came together for festivals. Many buildings

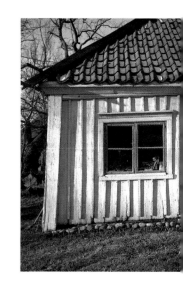

were double-storeyed, with extra bedrooms fitted under the roof. Rural Scandinavia took the seasonal changes seriously. Some farms had separate summer houses where the family would move at the end of the winter to be nearer their pastureland. Others transferred daily life to lighter, cool-tiled outhouses when summer came.

Despite Scandinavia's isolation from Europe, European tastes took hold and shaped its native style. From the 17th

Above and left:
The rigours of climate and geography have shaped Scandinavian homes. The great forests which served as sources of building materials (and fuel to provide warmth in frozen winters), also contributed to the isolation of the small farming communities. Farmsteads grew up on cleared patches of land, and had to be completely self-sufficient. Buildings and furnishings were hand-crafted from raw materials gathered nearby.

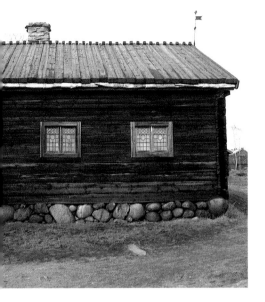
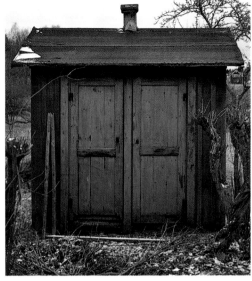
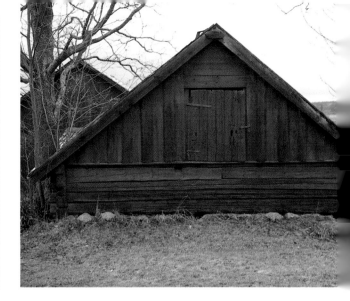
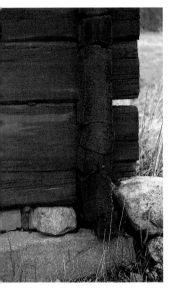
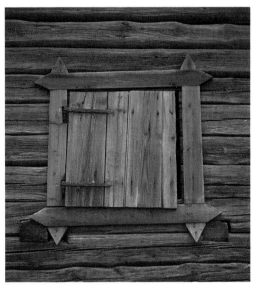
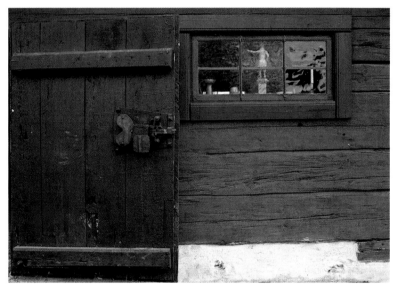

century, Sweden had a long love-affair with France, nurtured by its culturally conscious king, Gustav III, who sent artists out from Stockholm to plunder the Rococo and neo-classical styles of France. The love-affair turned into a marriage when Napoleon's marshal, Jean-Baptiste-Jules Bernadotte, became ruler of Sweden in 1818. Slowly, the borrowings from France made their way from the houses of the nobility into those of the farmers, staying there long after the aristocracy had adopted the fashions of the 19th century.

The French influence in Sweden created rural interiors that combine decorativeness with simplicity. Rococo came to the isolated farmhouses in small steps, brought by travelling painters who might decorate the family's wardrobe or one wall facing the fire with garlands of fruit and flowers. As the timber trade brought economic prosperity to the countryside in the 19th century, interiors became more embellished. Wealthier farmers employed painters to decorate the walls to look as if they were hung with framed pictures, and dining furniture made its way from town to country. While traditional stools, built on three legs to stabilize them on uneven floors, remained by the fireside, grander pieces were arranged around the walls. Fixed benches gave way to delicate chairs, often these were

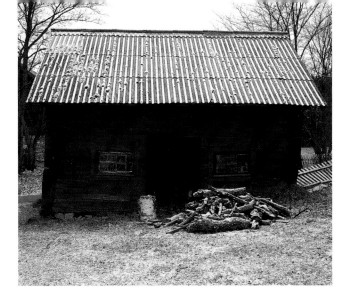
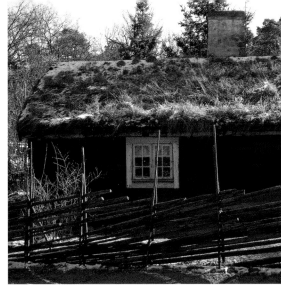
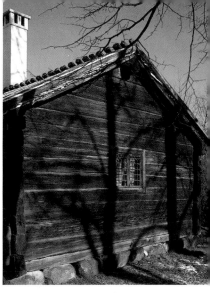

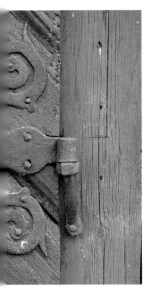
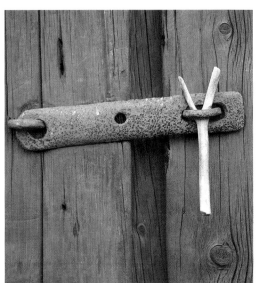
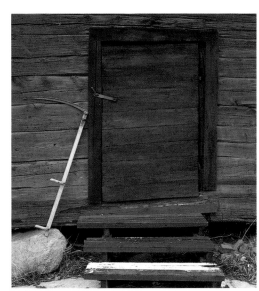
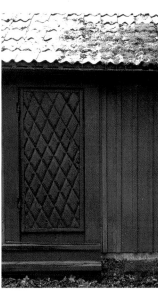

Bottom row:
Scandinavian homes are built to survive biting Northern winters. The heavy log walls absorb daytime heat from the well-stocked fireplaces and radiate it back at night. The logs are carefully notched and dovetailed to shut out drafts, and gaps are plugged with moss or turf. Windows, situated on the south side of houses, are kept small, their frames tight-fitting, to fend off the cold.

made locally but based on the neo-classical shapes popular in France, such as the Greek *klismos* chair, with its gently swayed back and tapered legs.

The French style did not displace Scandinavian country pieces, it supplemented them. The original simpler furniture survived because it was often built-in or ingeniously designed to save space, particularly in the coveted area around the fire. Traditional chairs had folding backs or wide seats to convert them into small fireside tables for meals. Some had boxes underneath for storage. Cupboards and beds were built into the walls. Awkward spaces were exploited: stoves and cupboards were fitted into corners, plates were displayed in racks on walls. Displays of pewter and copper were a measure of a farmer's wealth and treen a measure of the long evenings. Both treen and grandfather clock cases were produced by farmers to supplement their incomes over the winter.

Scandinavian style is a style of contrasts that reflects the extremes of northern seasons and the marriage of isolation with French influence. It resides as much in a graceful rococo chair as in a solid three-legged stool, in a delicately painted *armoire* or a plain pine cupboard. It can be light and dark, polished and raw, summer and winter at the same time.

The **Mora** farm was built in an area that mainly consists of uninhabited woods, mountains, swamps and small lakes. In a region that lacked arable lands, the forest was an important source of income. A rich tradition of handicrafts developed, notably treen and decorated grandfather clocks. These were always called Mora clocks, although only the works of the clocks were actually made in Mora – the cases were made and painted elsewhere.

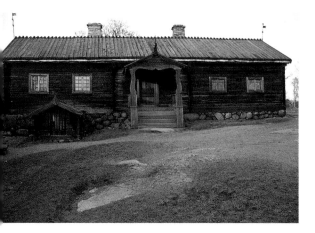

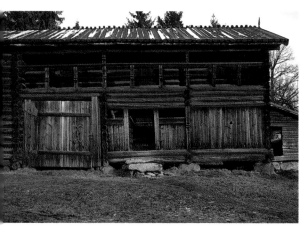

Far top right:
In front of two tiers of built-in beds, decorated with woven woolen hangings, stand stools which double as storage boxes.

Far bottom right:
Plate racks on the wall display the family's wealth of dishes.

Right:
This carved and painted 19th century bed has a cupboard built-in at the foot.

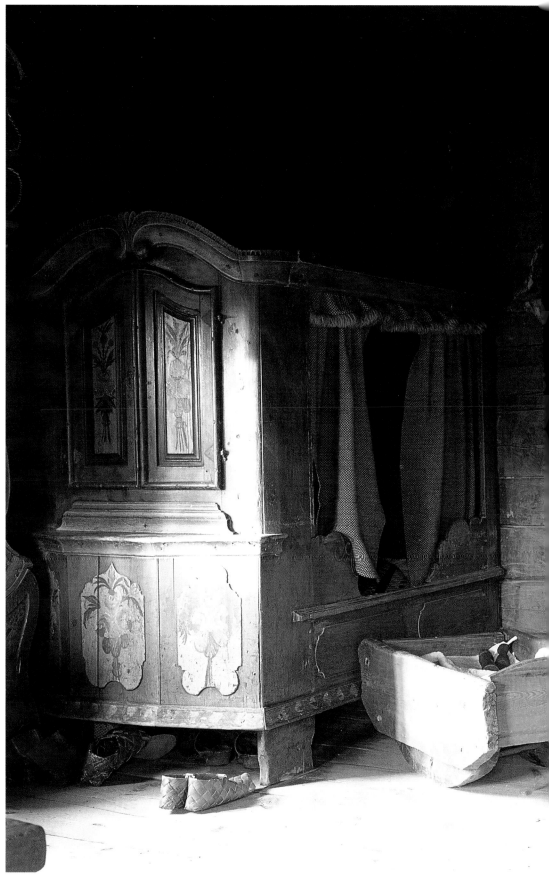

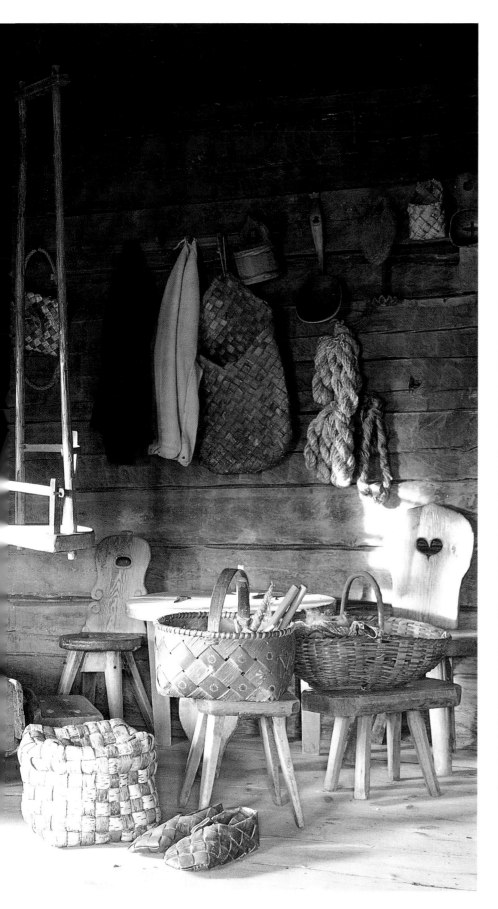

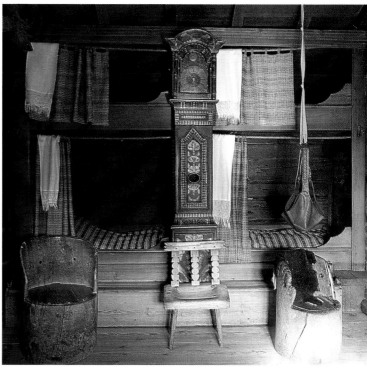

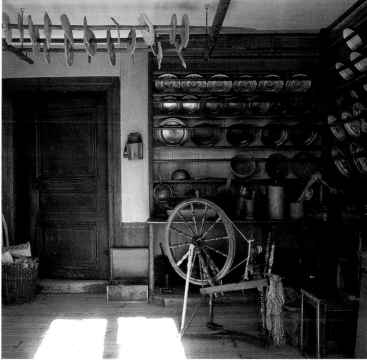

Scandinavian country style

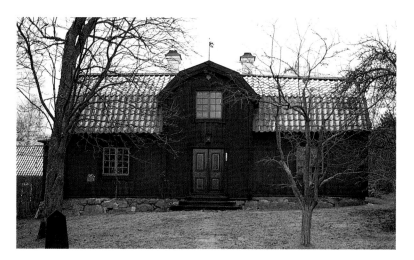

Lars Olsson's home in Vaksala, Sweden, comprises an outhouse converted from a small corn store and mill built around 1800 and a main house built in the late 18th century. Before the early 19th century all Swedish country houses were left unpainted in the natural wood, but around the mid-19th century a painted finish – often red, yellow or gray – became fashionable.

Right:
Rustic Swedish furniture fills this dining room: early 19th century farmer's chairs and a painted pot cupboard stand below an earlier painted cupboard that dates from circa 1790.

Below:
A 19th century Swedish pine milking stool stands in front of the open fire. The wooden container for logs to the left of the hearth was originally used to store corn.

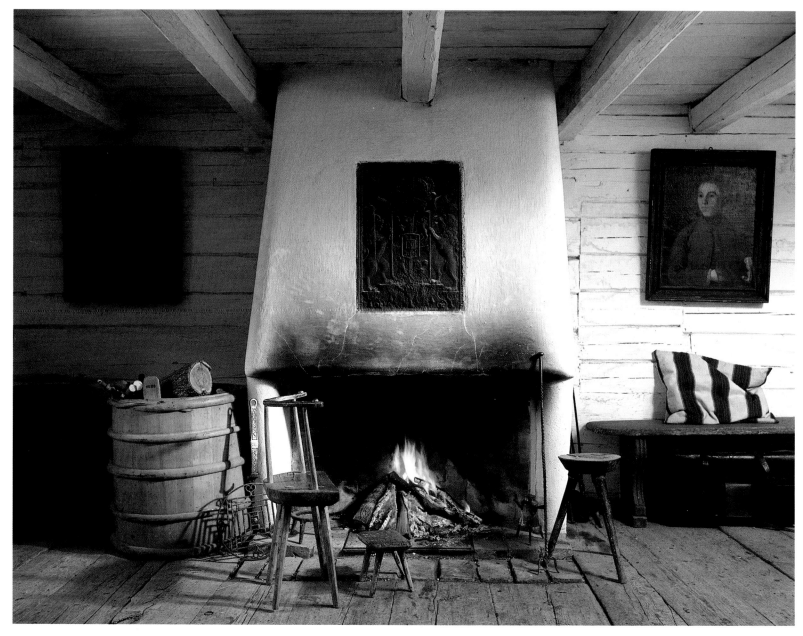

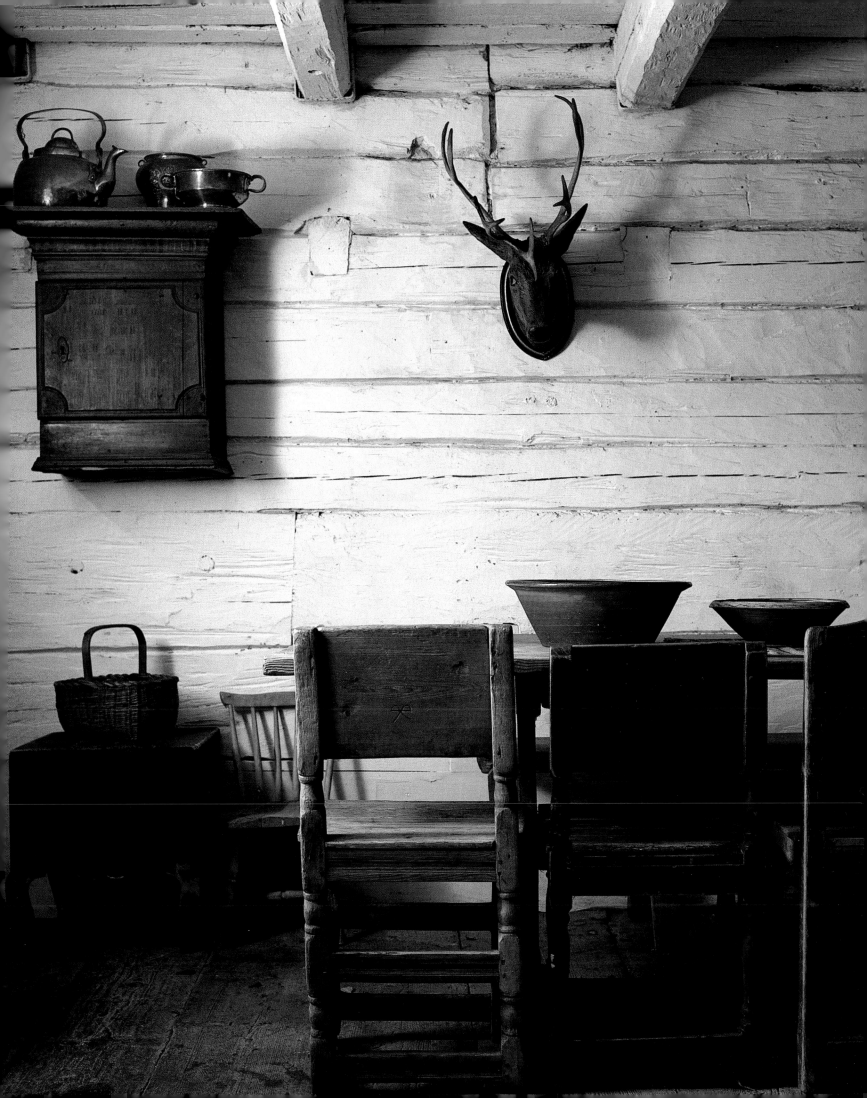

Top right:
An early 19th century pine desk and an adjustable mid-19th century painted chair stand beside a rare Swedish painted cupboard dating from 1762. Painted cupboards were traditional in the Uppland area of Sweden, but unfortunately so many of them were stripped during the 1960s that it is now very hard to find one like this, with its original paint still intact. The carved and painted box standing on the desk dates from 1776.

Bottom right:
This part of the house originally served as a corn store and had very low ceilings. Lars Olsson increased the height of this room by 2 ft (60 cm). The original position of the beam can be seen just above the new window. The frame has been painted and then rubbed back to the wood, leaving traces of paint behind, to blend the window into the surrounding wall. In front of the window stands a 19th century painted cupboard.

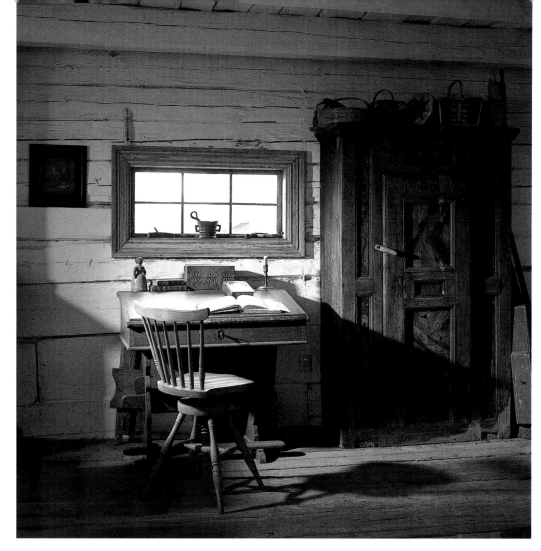

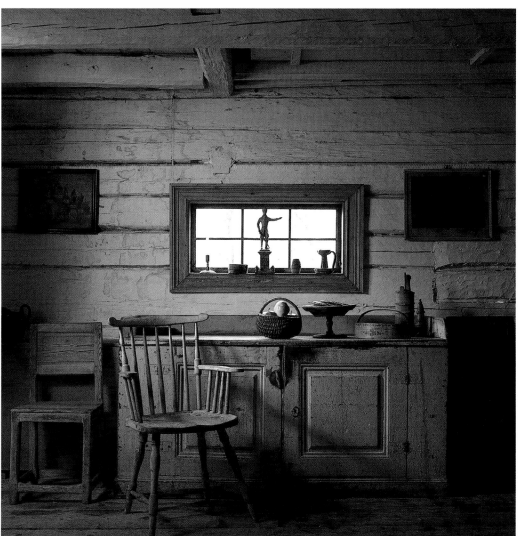

Right:
A very fine Swedish cupboard from Uppland, that dates from 1774, dominates one end of the large kitchen. In pine painted with flowers, the cupboard's scale is in keeping with the massive 19th century pine trestle table. The table is surrounded by early 19th century roughly painted rustic farmer's chairs. The 18th and 19th century Scandinavian treen bowls provide a pleasing contrast of natural colour against the painted wood.

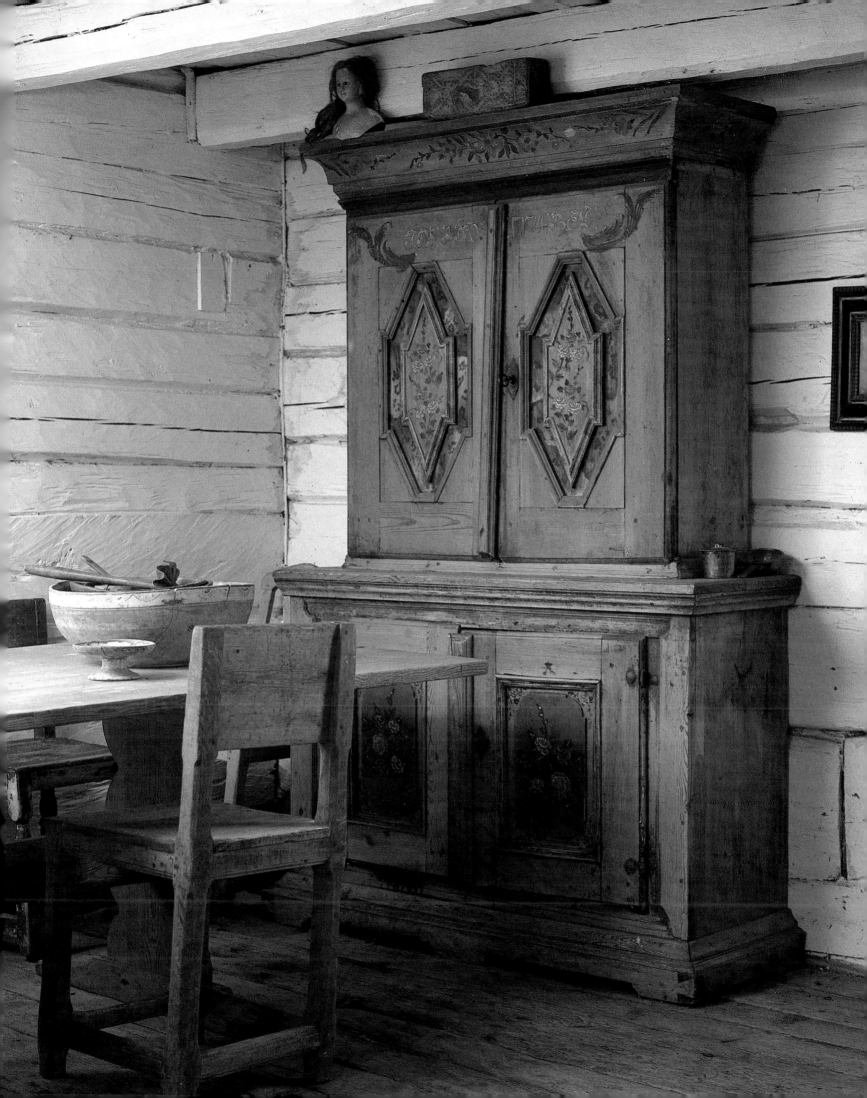

Lars Sjoberg's home at Odenslunda was rebuilt in 1770 after the original late 17th century house burned down. Lars has researched the house carefully to restore it to its 18th century appearance. Distressed paintwork has been left and even recreated to make the house feel authentic, though it is an interesting point that, when the house was rebuilt in 1770, the paintwork would have looked new. Odenslunda has a friendly, lived-in atmosphere and a true country lack of self-consciousness.

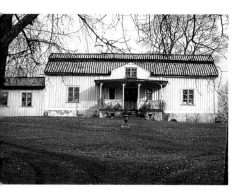

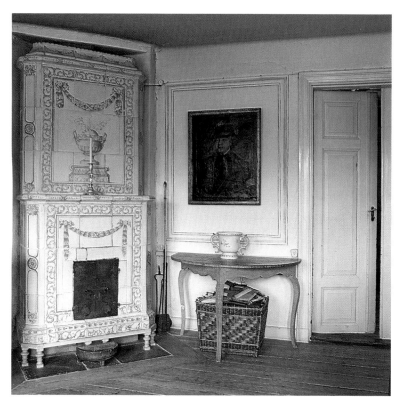

Top right:
Next to an 18th century Stockholm Swedish stove that still retains its fine original tiles stands an 18th century side table which bears some original paint.

Far right:
The curtains and hangings around the canopied Gustavian-style bed were hand-printed from an original pattern. The rococo chairs date from the 1770s.

Below right:
A plain 19th century stove warms the bedroom. Simple painted wall boards are outlined in blue, in traditional Gustavian style.

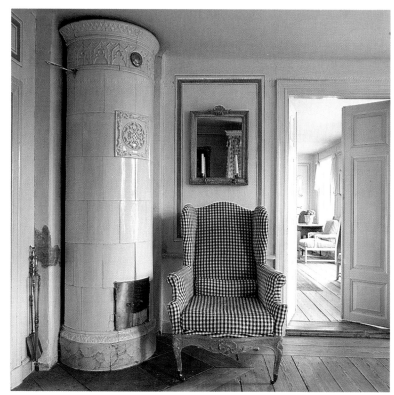

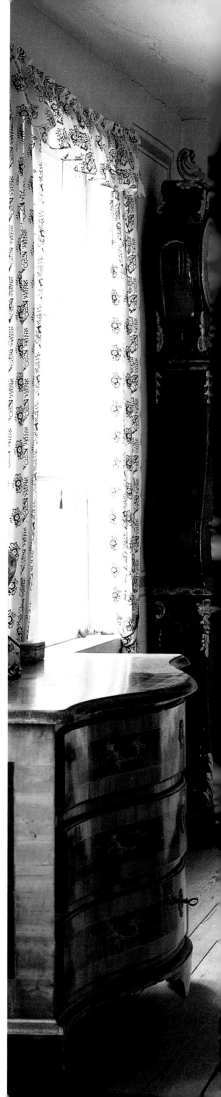

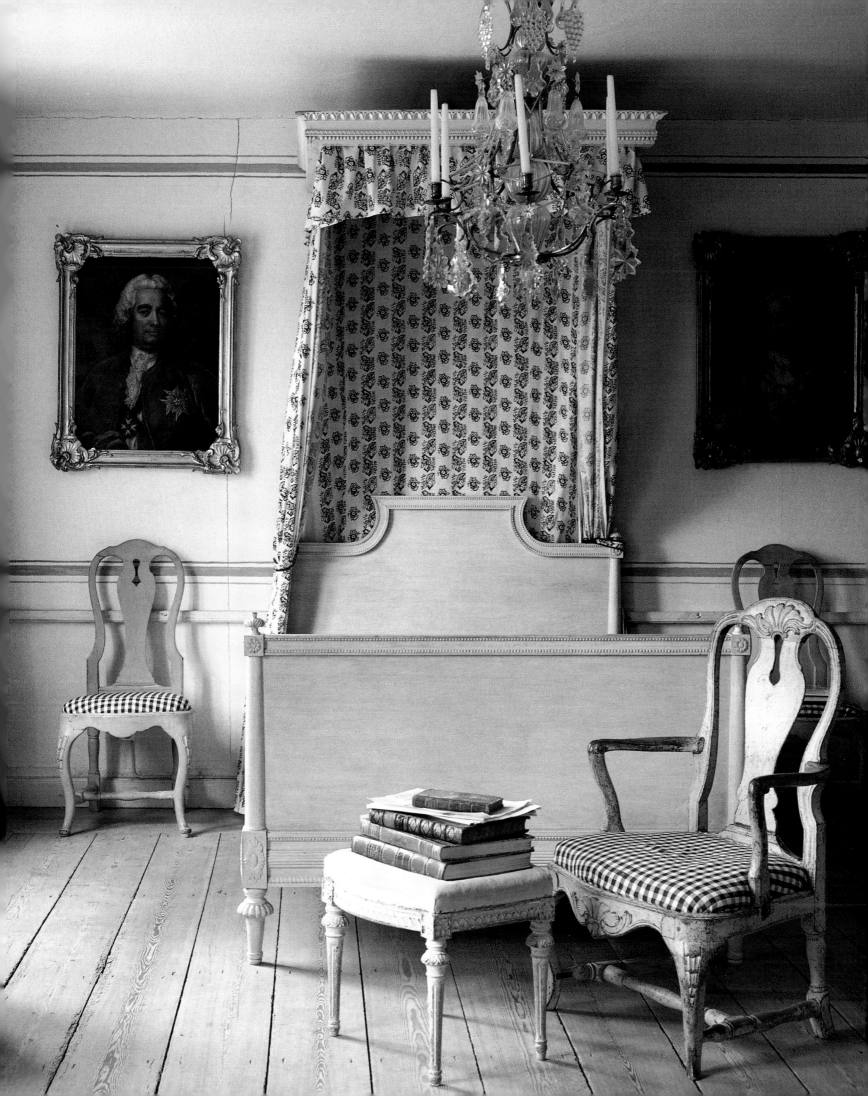

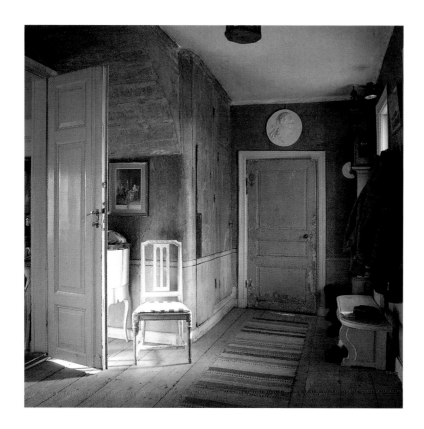

Right:
Spring greens and yellows that help to banish Sweden's winter gray have been used to upholster a Gustavian chair and 18th century painted Trog sofa in this living room.

Above:
In the hallway, Lars has carefully preserved the traces of original paint found under layers of paper. The doors have been deliberately stripped back to their 18th century layer of paint and then left.

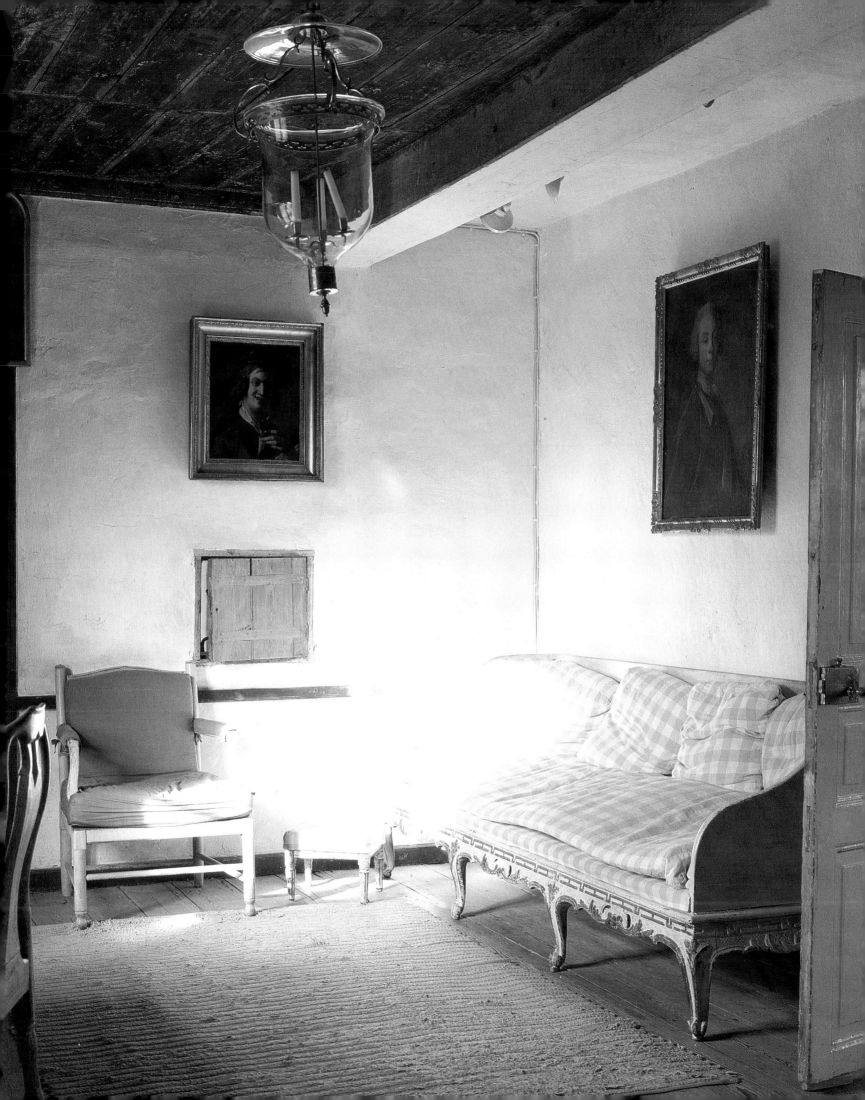

AMERICAN
Country Style

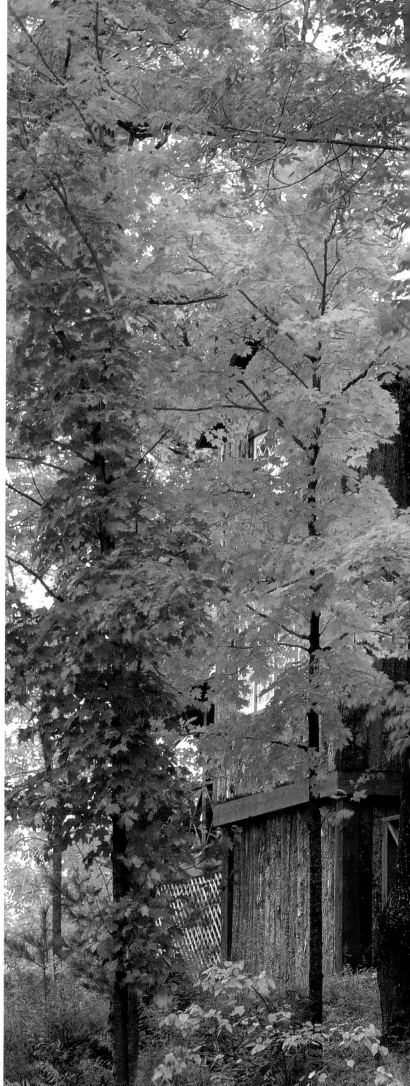

*I*n 1850, an American architect called A. J. Downing
compared one of his designs for a traditional American
farmhouse with a similar one in the English rural style. He
wrote: "There is perhaps in this house a little more independence and a little less lowliness manifested, both being
expressed in the higher stories and the greater space from the
ground to the eaves in this design." It would appeal to
American farmers, he added, because they "love independence above all things, and
hence instinctively and un-
consciously lay hold of anything that manifests it."
American country style is the
style of an independent people. Its most-loved features
are those created by the early
settlers, as they set up home
away from home up and
down the Atlantic coast in
the 17th century. Independence meant not just the spirit of an
independent America, but of independent communities
within it. Some were closed from the outside world because of
the exclusivity of their religious beliefs, others because the
world outside was hostile or isolated by a rough terrain.

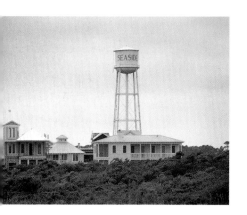

The isolation of the pioneering communities from each
other produced a variety of strong regional styles, from that of
the Ohio farmhouse set among the mid-West's rolling plains to
the Cape Cod cottage perched by the sea. American country
style embraces the homes of the Shakers, the Amish, the
Pennsylvanian Dutch and the New Englanders, as well as

Right and above:
American country style developed from native Indian ingredients blended
with a rich seam of traditions and skills imported from Europe by the
early pioneers, who constructed homes with whatever materials came to
hand. This melting pot of old and new was stirred until a style evolved
that was distinctively American yet evocative of its pioneer roots.
From coast to coast, the new continent's abundance of wood was used to
build country homes.

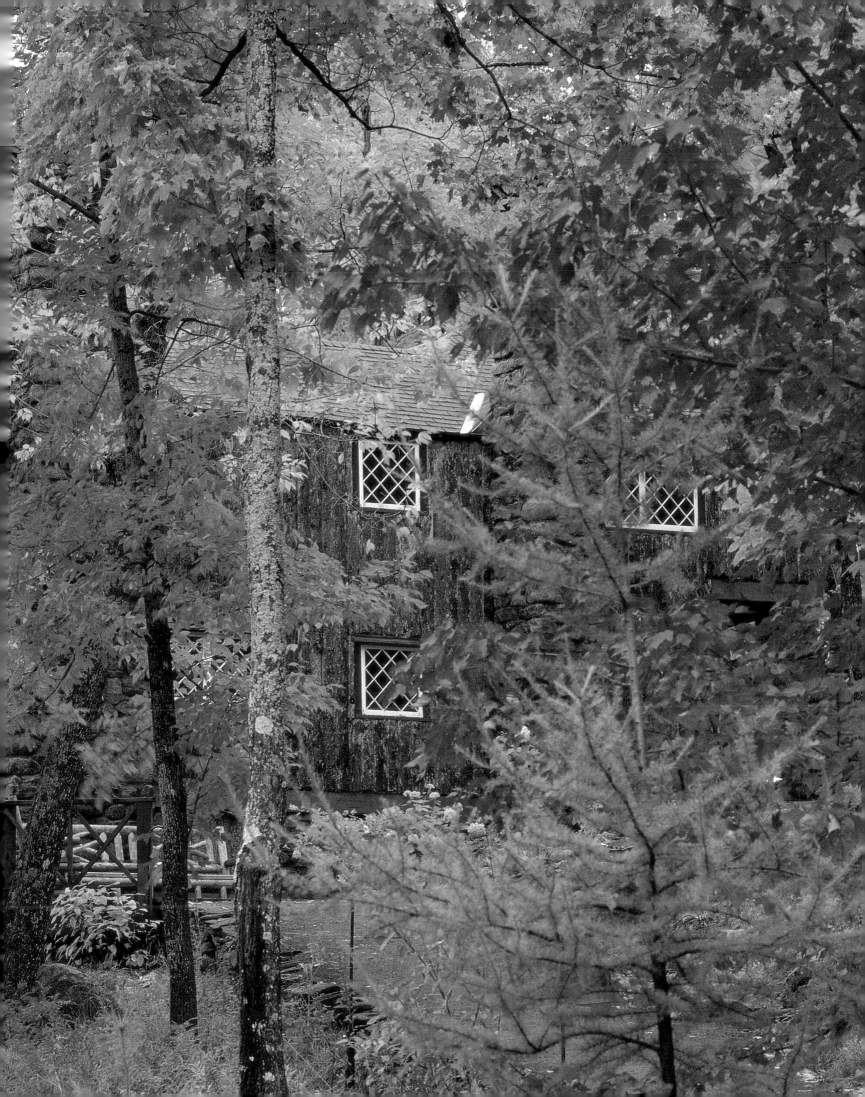

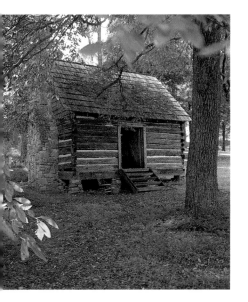

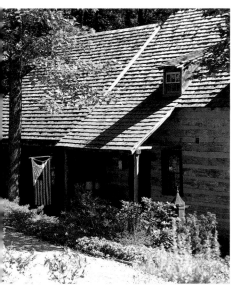

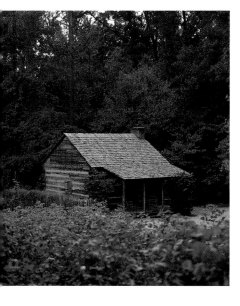

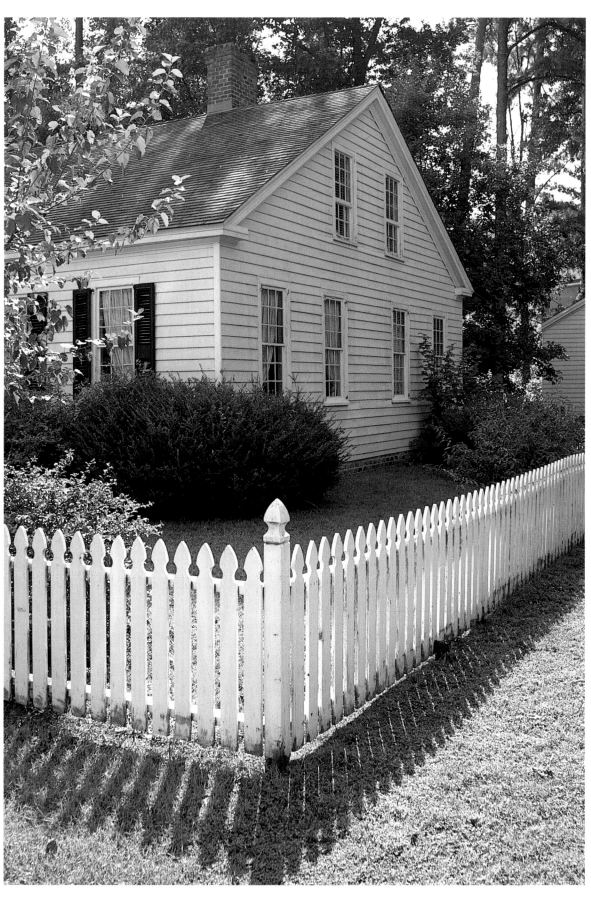

rustic-looking Adirondack log cabins which, ironically, are not authentic rural homes, although inspired by the country. The Adirondack camps were created at the end of the last century as weekend retreats for wealthy New Yorkers. The designers took the original furnishings of real log cabins – basic shapes made from bent boughs and notched woods – to an extreme to create a look of exaggerated rusticity.

What American country styles do have in common is an abundance of wood, from the Atlantic's white cedar to the cypress of the deep south, as well as cherry, hickory, maple and elm. It might be crudely worked for the structures of houses – logs were often split into wide planks and then placed, in what was known as *puncheon* flooring, so that the flat sides formed the floor of one room and the round sides the ceiling of the one below. But as the tools and skills developed, America's wood was turned, planed, polished and fretted to produce pieces of furniture whose decorativeness is often a surprising contrast to the severity of the rooms around them. Wood gave the interiors a surface for paintwork that gleamed softly in deep, full colours like bottle-green, teal and reddish-brick. The colours were used in counterpoint to each other – the matchboarding on the walls perhaps painted blue-green, the door a deep brick and a small cupboard a vivid turquoise. This geometry of colours is a hallmark of American rural interiors, inspired by the wealth of wood and the cheapness of paints which were home-made from milk and pigments.

Like farmers all over the world, the settlers built houses using the materials they found, but with the difference that, as transposed people, they were influenced by the traditions of their original countries or of the religions that they carried with them like baggage. The Dutch and Germans who came to Pennsylvania brought with them memories of their folk art traditions and cast about for the materials from which to conjure them. Iron was hand-forged into decorative latches and trivets to protect table-tops. Tin was cheap and easy to cut and pattern with punched designs of hearts and songbirds. Squares of pierced tin were used for the fronts of food cupboards, with the holes serving as ventilation. Stencilling provided a cheap way of imitating the elaborate interiors of wealthy houses and was used to decorate chairs, chests, walls and floors. Brightly coloured traditional cloths were recreated

Far left top: This modest cabin is a typical pioneer home. The dimensions of such a cabin were largely determined by the height of the trees – and therefore the length of the logs they yielded – in the vicinity. These dwellings were often constructed without windows and with small gaps between the logs. In summer these were open to bring light and cooling breezes inside; in winter they were draftproofed with mud.

Far left middle: An Amish log house.

Far left bottom: A field of cotton surrounds a Southern pioneer cabin.

Left: A farmhouse in Dekalb, Atlanta.

Top right: A New England barn.

Middle right: These wooden houses in Madison, Georgia once housed slaves.

Below right: An Amish log house set in beech and poplar woods that provide a convenient source of fuel for the winter.

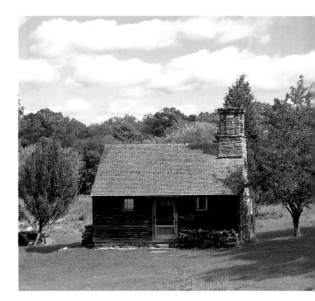

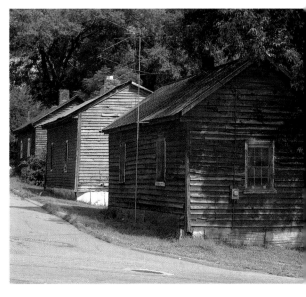

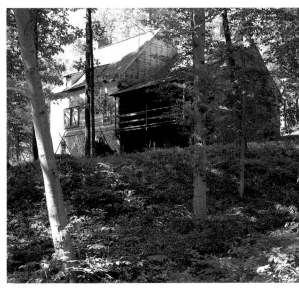

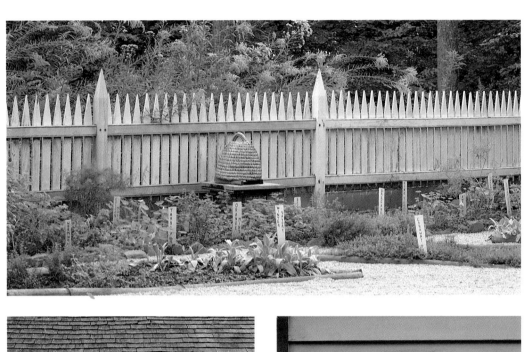
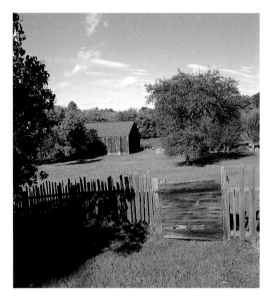
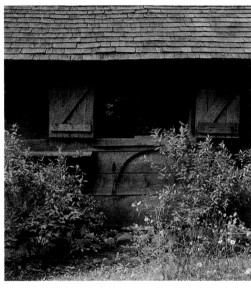
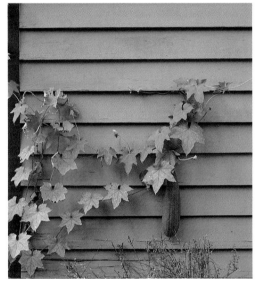
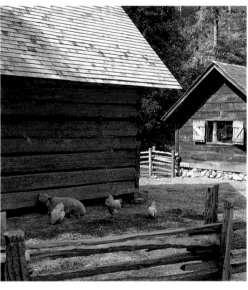
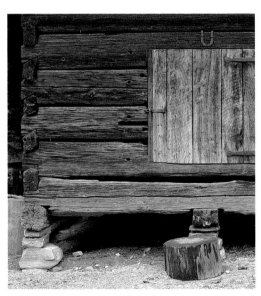
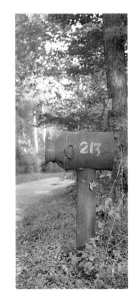
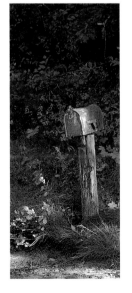
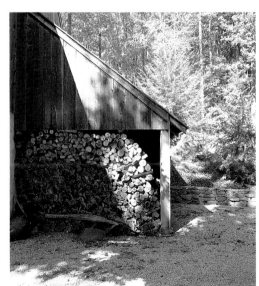

communities surrounding them and set a style across the South of languorous porches, roofs of tin to deflect the heat and large, open rooms with sleek floors, glossed to a reflective finish in whites and creams. Cooling interior colours of brilliant white, ice blue, pale yellow and peppermint green are the trademark of the south and have been reproduced in the modern Seaside development at Miami Beach, Florida.

Even the furniture of the great Southern house made its way, slowly, into the rural community. English pieces were brought in the holds of the trade ships that stopped on the Atlantic coast for America's cargoes of tobacco and wheat, and so rustic versions of Chippendale and Hepplewhite Georgian designs gradually appeared in Southern rural homes in the 18th and 19th centuries. By the same route furniture designed for ships, like the lightweight rattan steamer chair, made its way into southerners' homes. Alongside these pieces there would be simpler American furniture, like the

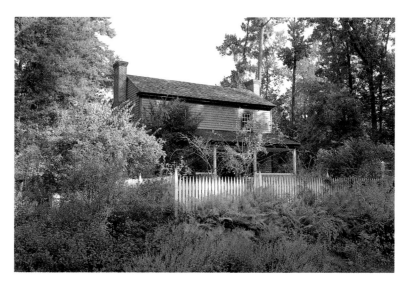

rocking chair, which was invented in the 19th century south to lullaby its occupant to sleep in the afternoon heat.

But it is the far more modest interiors of the religious communities that have created the most famous and most-loved of rural styles from America. The strict creeds of the Amish, the Shakers and Quakers governed their houses as much as their hearts and created a strong style that is so utterly simple that it looks almost modern.

Since a Shaker interior often doubled as a meeting place, it needed to be as uncluttered as possible. Small objects were packed away in round wooden boxes, painted in light reds, blues, yellows and greens to colour-code their contents. Cupboards and drawers were built in and wooden settles might be fitted with hinged flaps to convert them into tables. The ladderback chair, with a seat woven from rush or fabric tapes, was the Shaker solution to the need for seating that was sturdy yet light enough to be hung up out of the way, on pegs fixed to battens that ran around the room. These thoughtful, carefully arranged interiors are the epitome of American rural style.

The Tullie Smith house is a plain 1840s plantation farmhouse with a typically Southern front verandah. Situated in Atlanta, it has been preserved by the Atlanta Historic Society.

Right:
The Hall Room was the main living area for the house and is furnished with a collection of 19th century painted and stripped wooden furniture from the Southern states. The doors of the 18th century style corner cupboard are open to reveal a display of pottery decorated with American scenes.

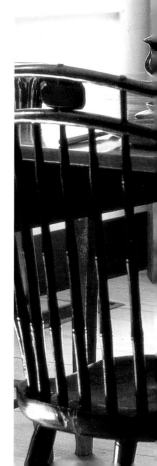

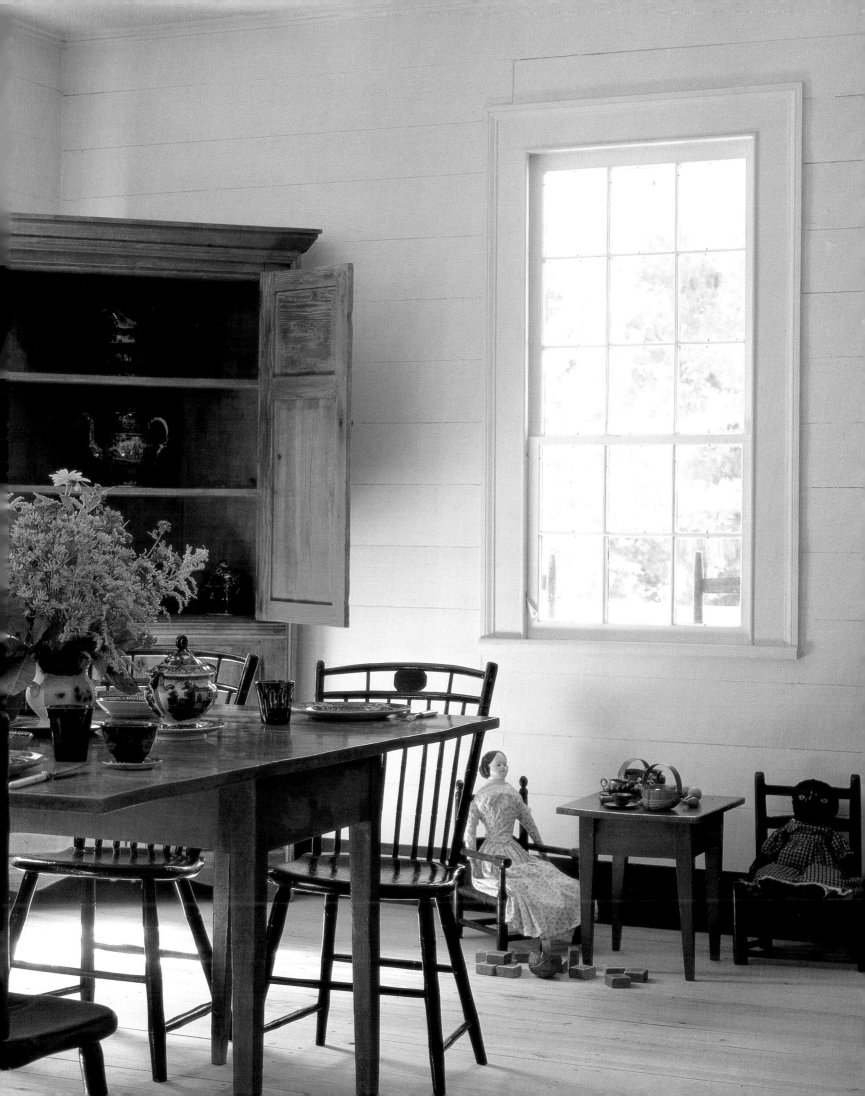

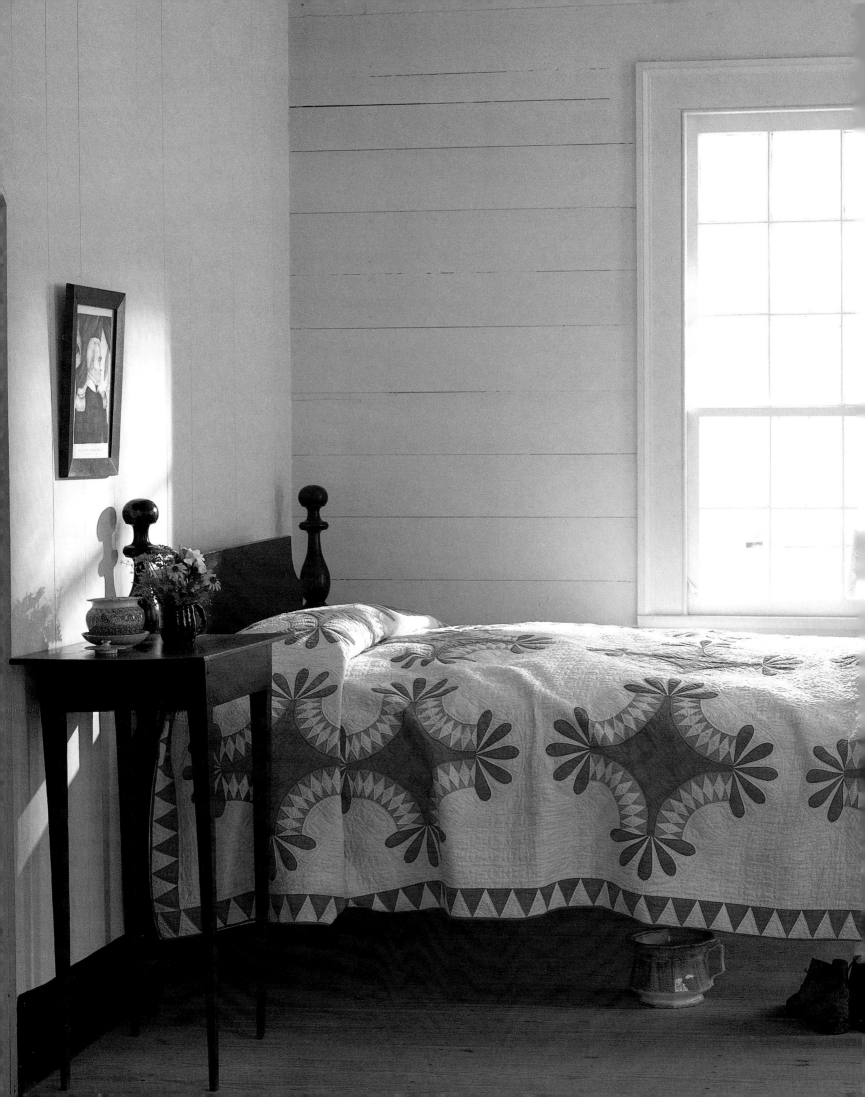

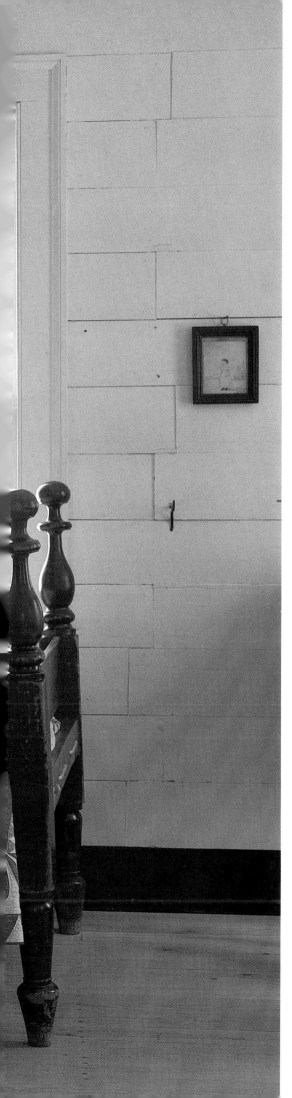

American country style

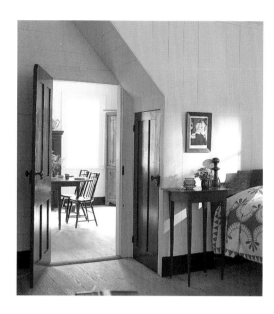

Top right and left:
The bedding – one straw and two feather mattresses and a "turkey track" pattern quilt – on this traditional cannonball bed rests on ropes which can be tightened by turning pegs. This is the origin of the saying "Night, night, sleep tight." The wooden furniture is stained with buttermilk mixed with Georgia red clay.

Middle right:
Typical of a colonial interior, this house is simply decorated, with function and economy to the fore. Here, clothes hang from utilitarian pegs on the wall, above a capacious green-painted blanket chest.

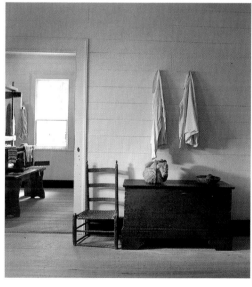

Bottom right:
This 19th century clothes press has been decorated with a stain which has been streaked and grained while still wet.

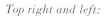

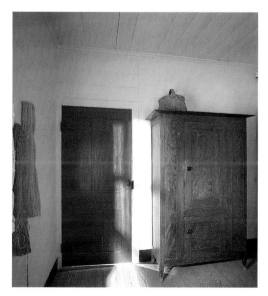

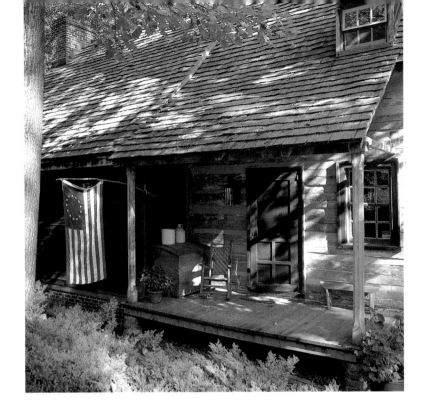

Jim and Liz Cherry found this 1737 Amish farmer's log house in Lancaster
County and moved it to this beautiful site near French Creek in Chester
County, Pennsylvania. Unlike the early settlers' log cabins, brought to the
Delaware Valley in the 1660s by Swedish immigrants, this house is
constructed on proper foundations. The back of the building is banked to
compensate for the sloping site.

Right:
Originally four rooms, the great room contains the kitchen, living and
dining areas. At the end of the living area a two-board pegged, yellow
pine tavern table, dating from circa 1740, is flanked by a pair of
ladderback chairs from circa 1830 that retain their original brown paint.
Table and chairs originated from the Shenandoah Valley, Virginia. The
sofa is new, in the country Chippendale style, and has been covered with a
checked Delft-colour fabric.

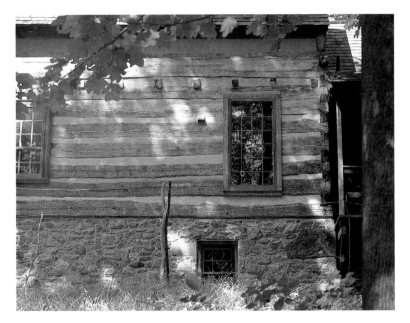

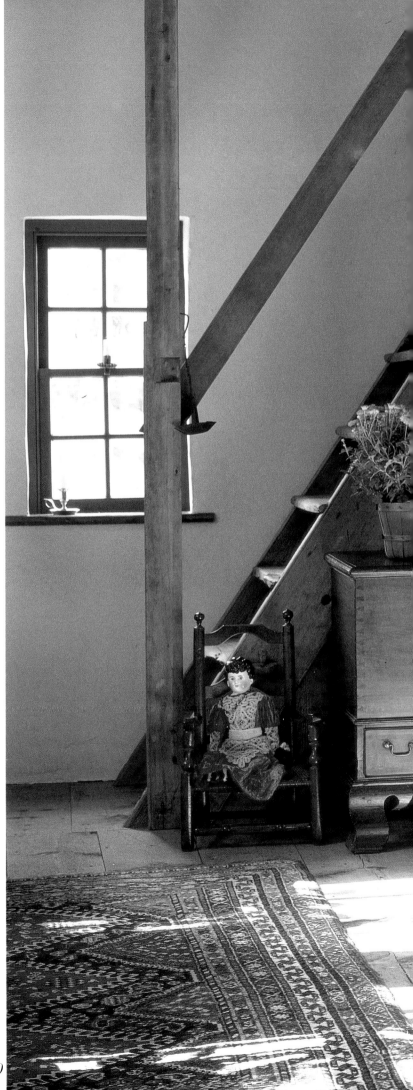

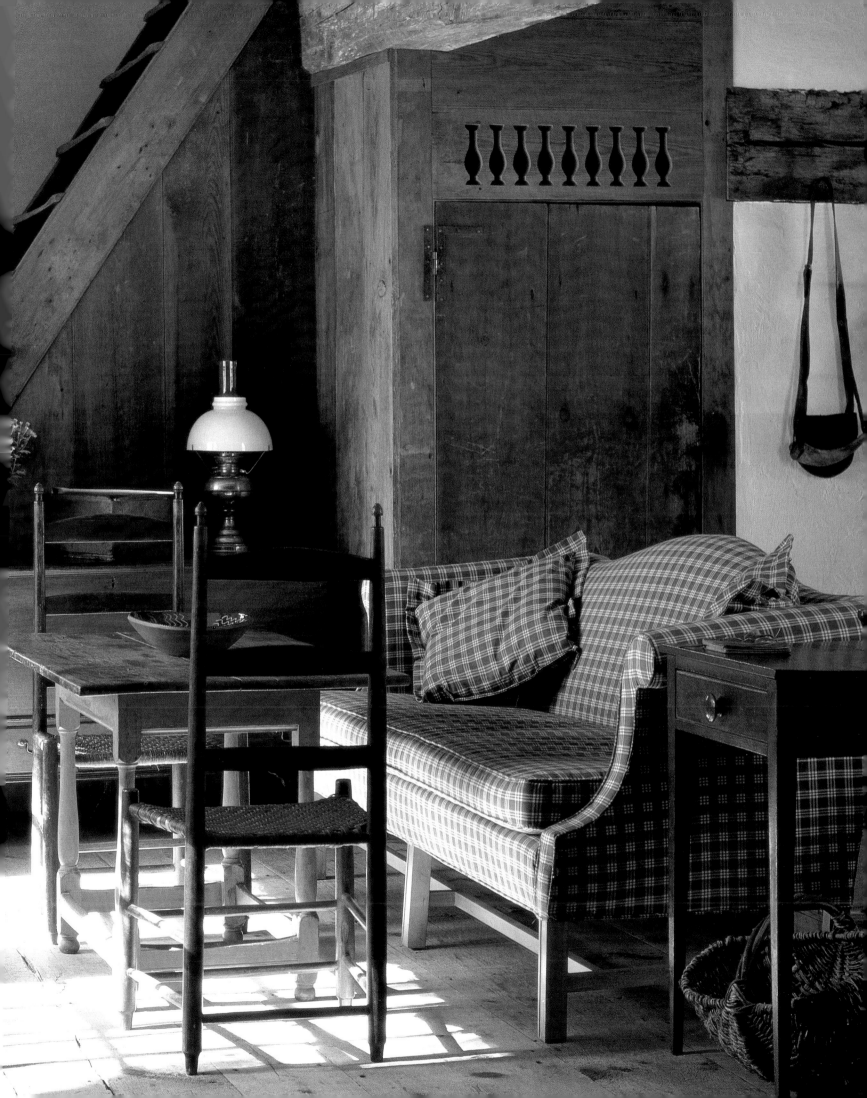

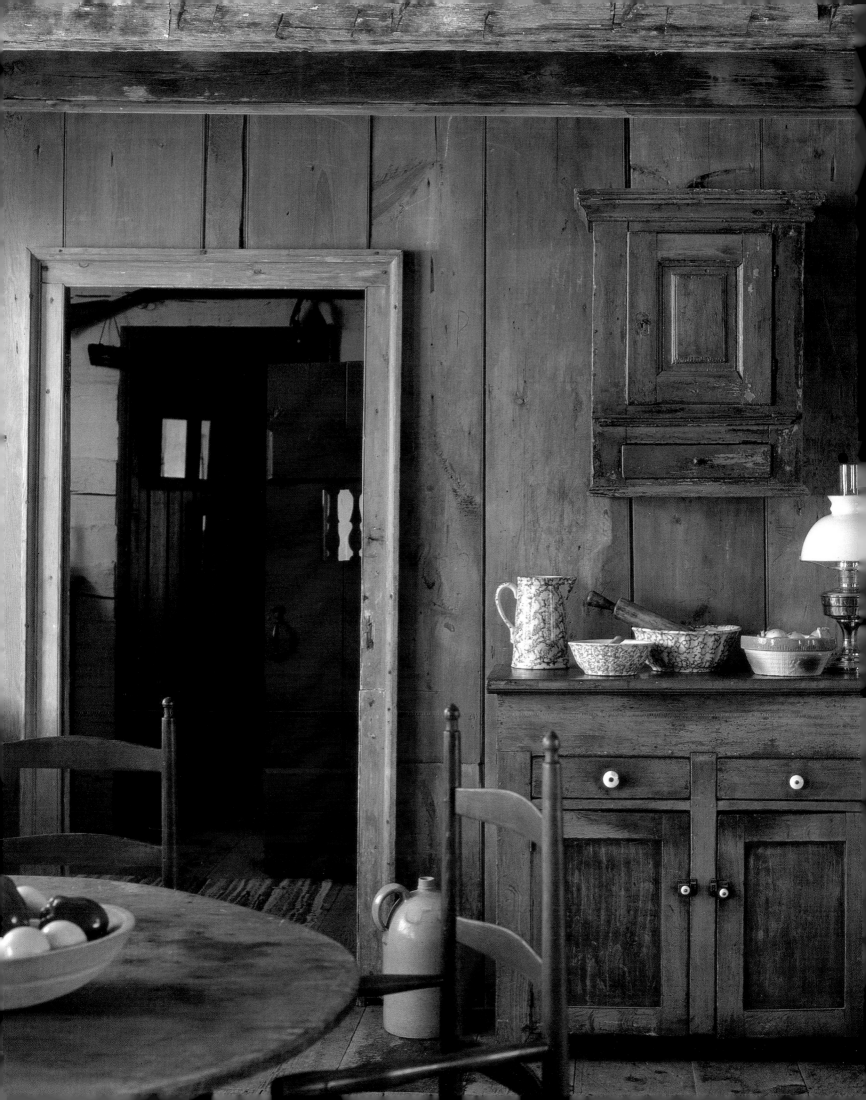

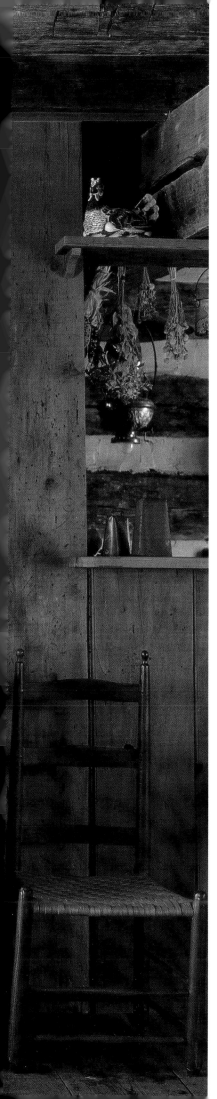

American country style

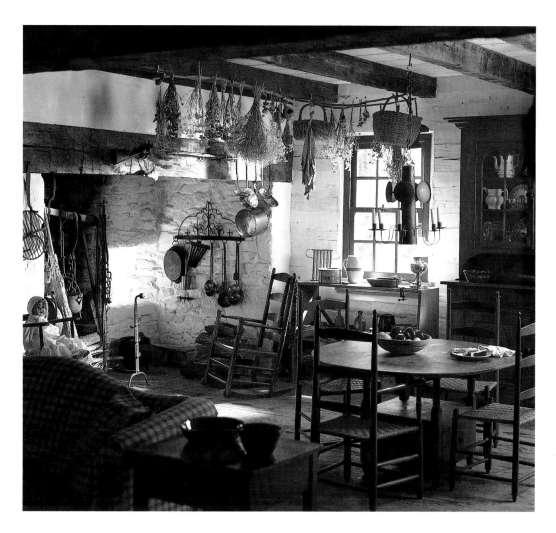

Above:

This rooms evokes a flavour of old America. Herbs and flowers dry from a hazel switch suspended between ceiling beams above an open fire. To one side hangs a fine collection of old cooking pots and implements – country cookware changes very little through the centuries. To the right of the fire is a tiny window, set deep into the thick chimney wall, installed by Jim to provide extra light. Close by the hearth is a maple slat-back rocking chair, dating from circa 1790, that manifests a distinct Shaker influence. Its entire mushroom-topped front post is turned from a single piece of wood. In the foreground is a round pine table dating from circa 1800. A New Hampshire chair table, it swivels around and down to convert from a table to a chair. Originally painted red, the top has long since worn down to the natural scrubbed wood, although traces of the original paint can be seen in knots and crevices. Above the table hangs a tin chandelier copied from an old one by a tinsmith.

Left:

Plank walls are a wonderful background for painted country furniture. The hanging Pennsylvania pie cupboard dates from circa 1750. Below it stands a poplar dry sink with an opening lid, dating from circa 1810, which was painted with milk paint many years ago. This paint has worn away, leaving the merest hint of colour in the crevices and cracks and along the grain. Today, many people try to reproduce the aged paint look. To achieve a successful result you must closely examine old paintwork so that you become familiar with the patterns of genuine wear.

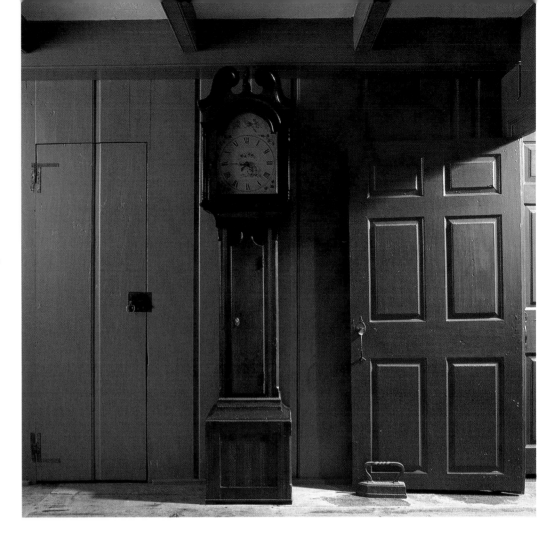

Far right:
Against the vibrant red walls in the hallway of this log house are set simple country pieces – a 19th century painted chair, wooden bucket and flat iron – while the floor is brightened with a rag rug. On the wall a row of pegs is home to plaid and denim jackets and a straw hat, the traditional workwear for American farmhands.

Above right:
This beautiful Pennsylvania tall clock was cut down to size long ago. Made in pine and cherrywood circa 1810, it is signed Abraham Birkey, Norristown (which is in Montgomery County). The cupboard door was cut from the panelling and all but disappears into it when it is closed.

Below right:
The master bedroom is situated in the timber-framed addition to the log house. Its panelled woodwork and ceiling beams are painted a restful gray-green and the flooring is mellow pine boards softened with 19th century rag rugs.
The focal point of the room is the bird's eye maple Sheraton high post bed dating from circa 1800. Although this is not a country piece, it is typical of the grand urban style hand-me-downs found in many rural homes. Its white and ochre draperies are piped in red to complement the colourful applique marriage quilt. This was made to celebrate a wedding and is embroidered with the date of the ceremony and the names of the bride and groom – John Kachel and Elizabeth Seidal, 1851. Next to the bed stands a tiger maple table dating from circa 1800 and through the doorway can be glimpsed an original brown-painted ladderback chair that dates from circa 1830 and originates from the Shenandoah valley, Virginia.

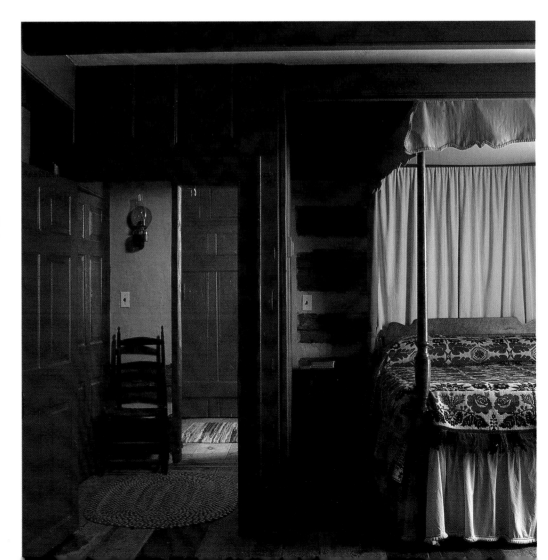

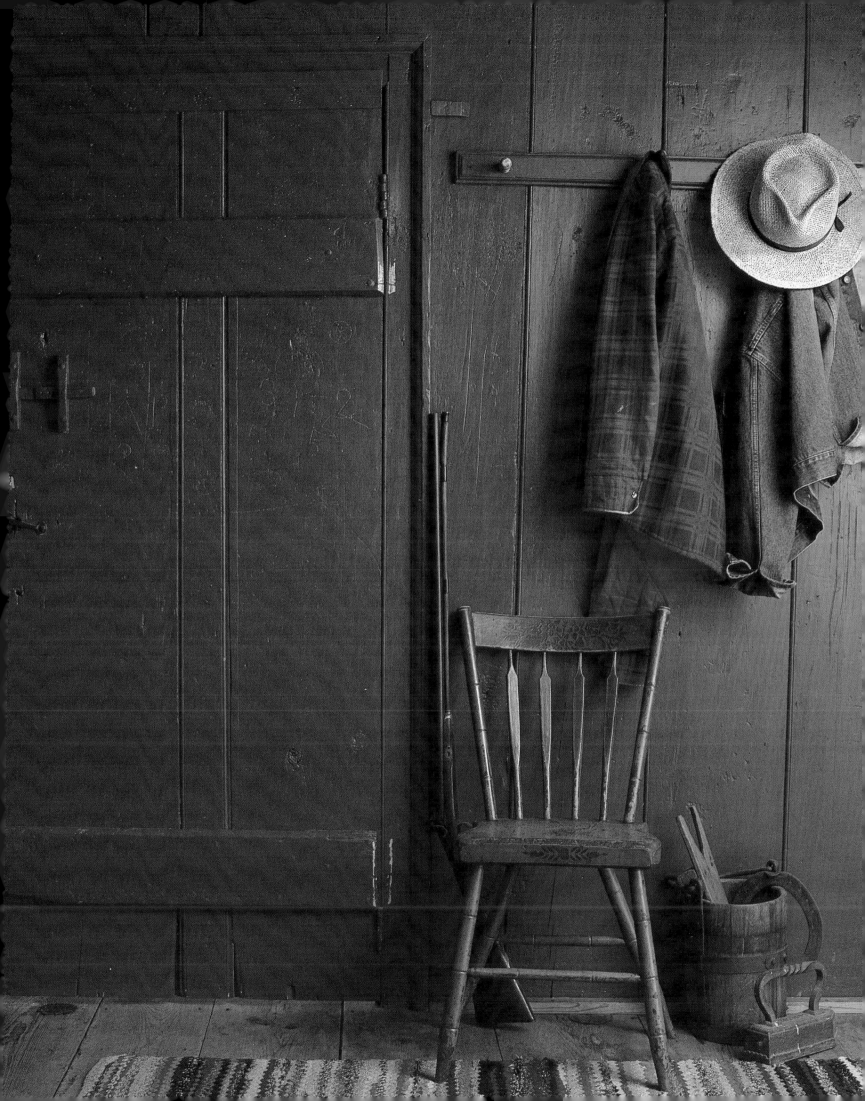

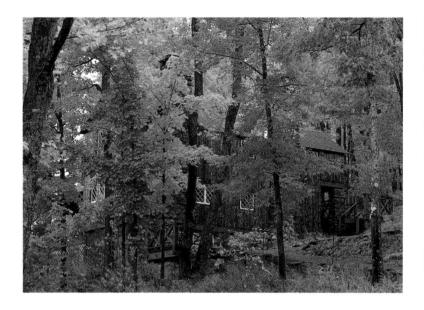

Bull Cottage at Blue Mountain Lake forms part of the Adirondack Museum. In the late 19th century, as a reaction to urbanization, a back-to-nature movement grew up in America that sought to fulfill the yearning for a return to pioneer roots. This influenced the development of the summer lodges of the Adirondacks, in the far north of New York State. The rough-hewn rustic furniture, made by local craftspeople and incorporating the natural forms and irregular shapes of the raw material, is the ideal complement to the exposed wooden ceilings, peeling log beams and stone fireplaces of the traditional pioneer-style dwelling.

Right:
The doors of this corner dresser are decorated with mosaic flower baskets made from ten different woods. Wood was not just applied, but woven too. The pair of yellow birch rocking chairs have woven ash splint backs and seats.

Below:
The living room features furniture made by Ernest Stowe, a carpenter to whom rustic furniture was a sideline. He used decorative elements – like the inlaid white birch bark and split whole yellow birch rods on the dresser shown right – that were more usually associated with high-style cabinet work. The late 19th century silver plate and brass cooler on the table is German in origin, and is decorated with ornate reliefwork depicting stags' heads and hunting scenes.

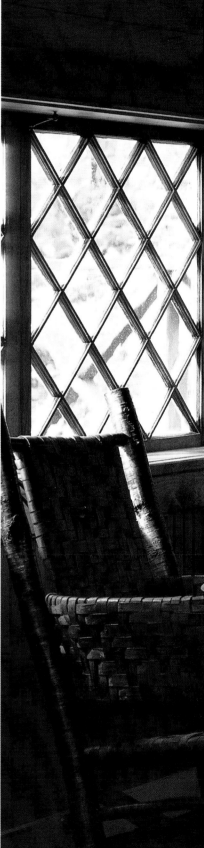

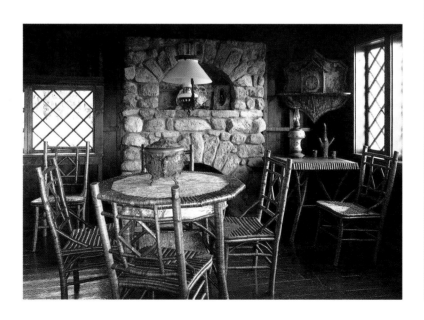

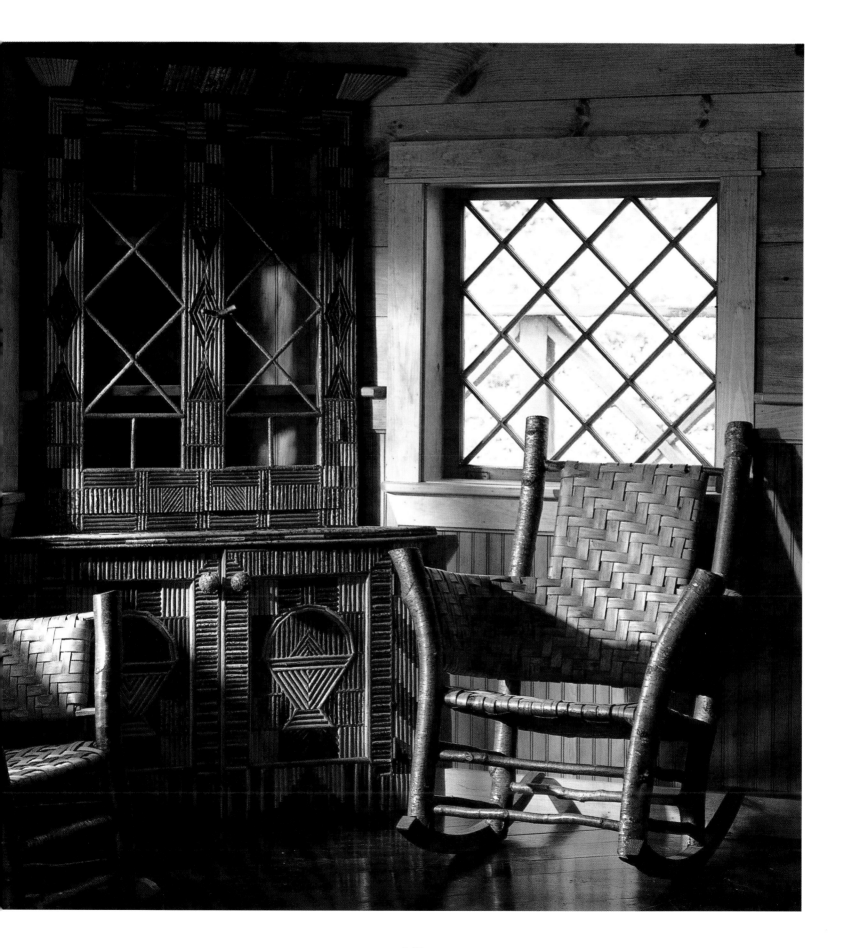

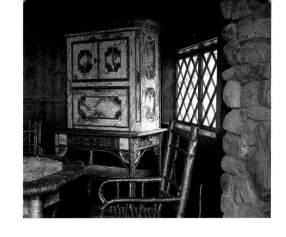

Below:
The decorative qualities of bark are enormous –
sometimes as many as ten types are used in a
single piece of furniture.

Right:
American style often marries old-world
techniques with new-world materials, like the
bark marquetry work on this cabinet.

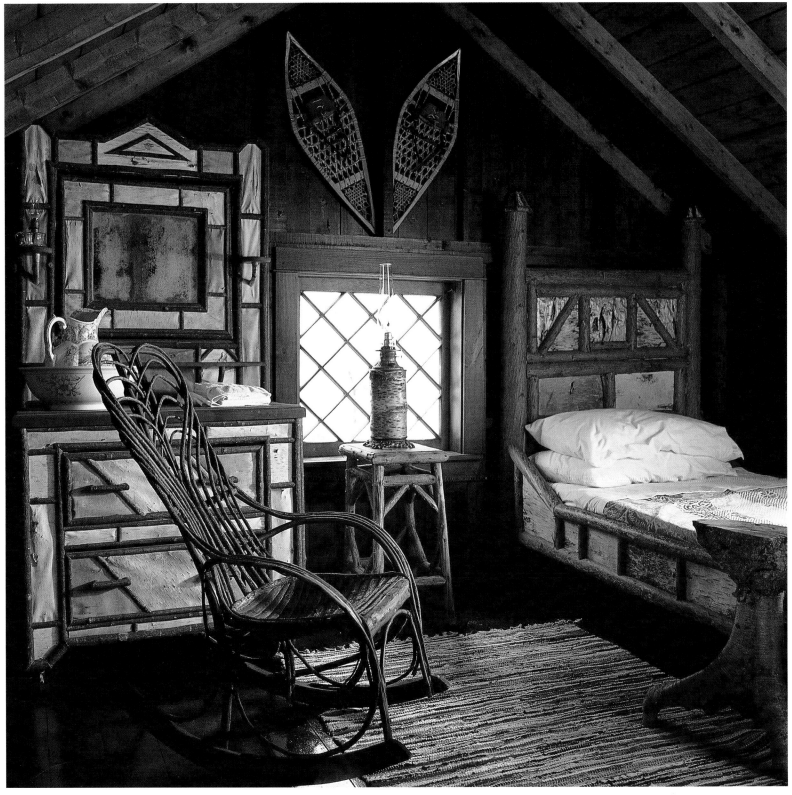

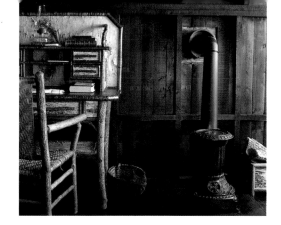

American country style

Left:
A desk decorated in twig and bark and a rustic chair stand next to the cast iron coal stove that warms the room.

Below:
Forest materials furnish this room: a bed with a headboard of applied bark, a woven hickory rocker and a deer hoof footstool.

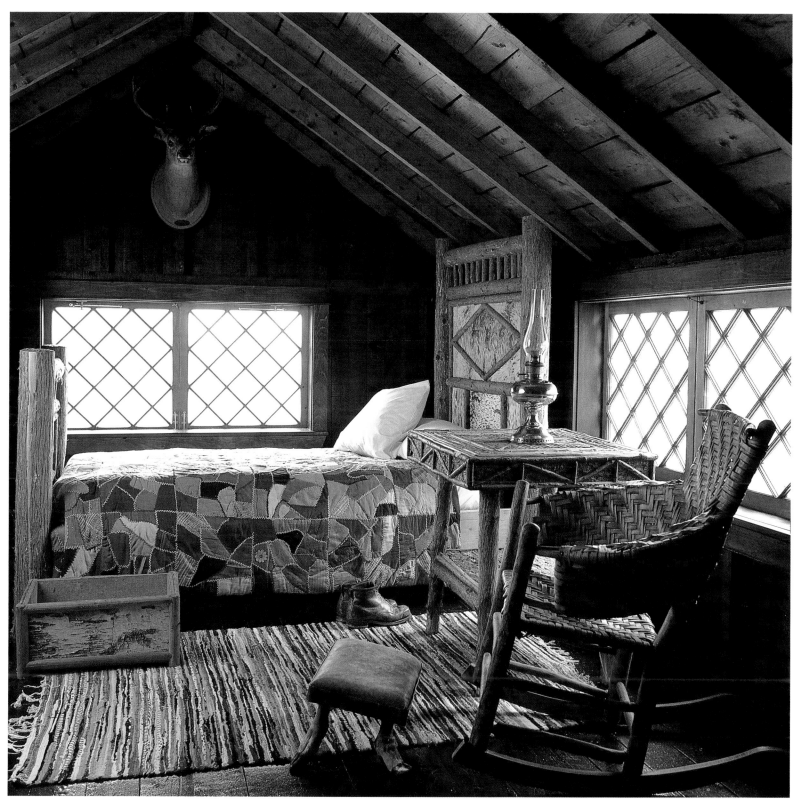

149

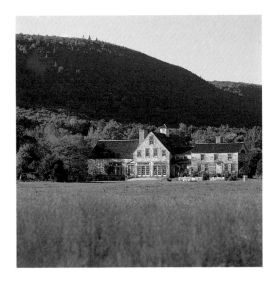

The Maine connected farmhouse consists of big
house, little house, back house and barn all
joined together. Inspired by this, Sally Spillane
and Robinson Leech gathered together a
farmhouse from Connecticut and an 18th
century barn from New York State and re-
assembled them, sandwiching them either side
of a modern reconstruction of a burned-out
18th century Massachusetts barn.

Right:
*The walls are hung with some of Sally and
Robin's collection of architectural stars, fleur de
lys and tie rods, along with eel spears. The
period painted furniture has been collected from
all over North America. Each painted cupboard
has a differing origin – Canada to the left, New
Hampshire to the right and Pennsylvania in the
middle. And the decoy duck sits on a brown-
stained table from New York State, while the
dull-green ladderback chair originates
from New England.*

Far right top:
*A cluster of objects – stars, signs, boxes, painted
cupboards – fill the room behind an 18th century
Canadian settle.*

Far right bottom:
*Barns can be made cosy with bright textiles and
open fires. Here, a substantial log fire is laid in
the stone hearth, while a Mexican blanket
warms a summery wicker chair.*

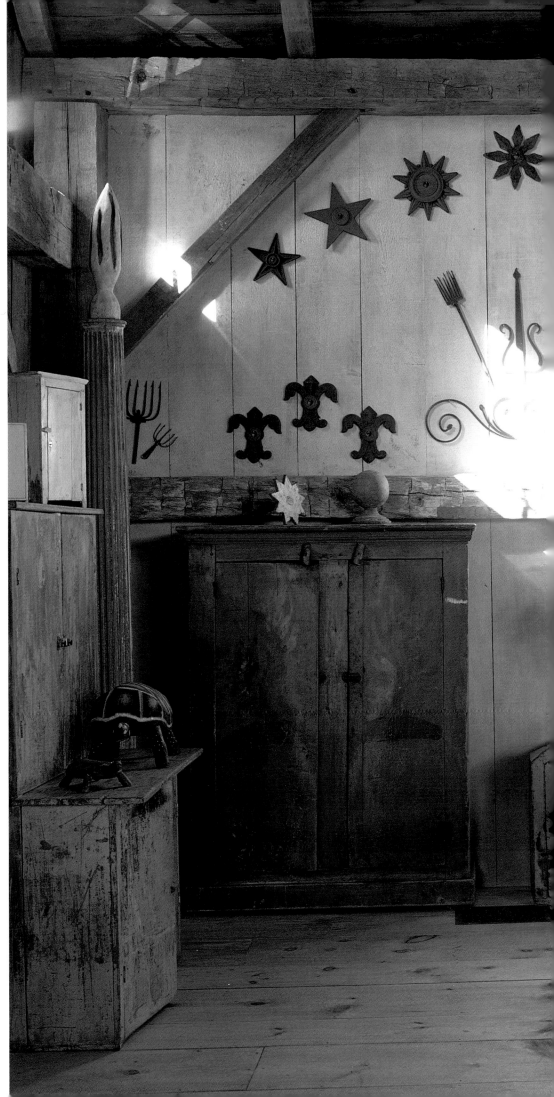

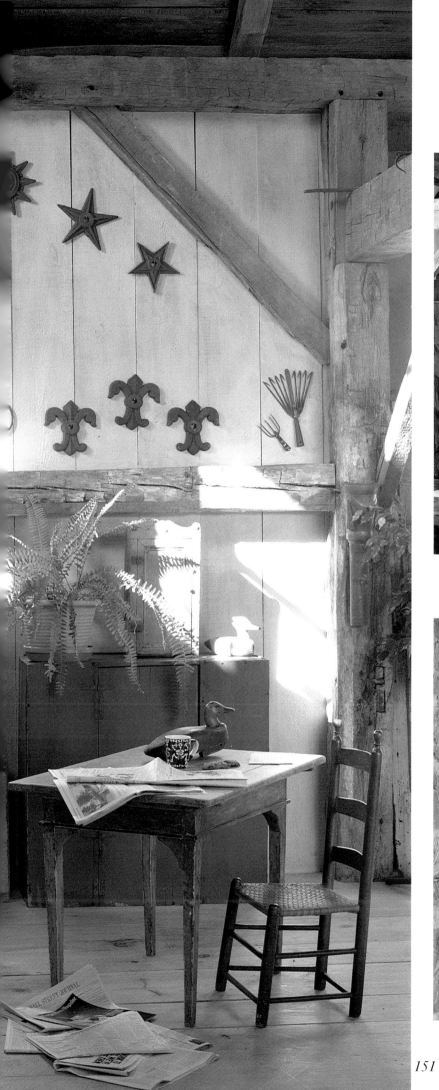

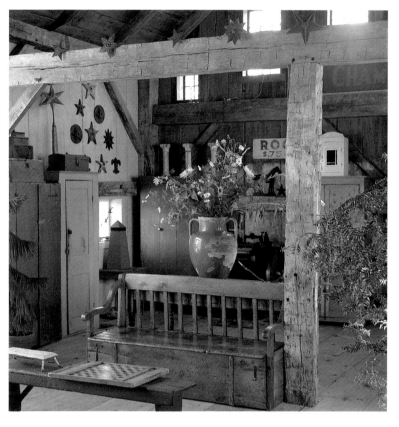

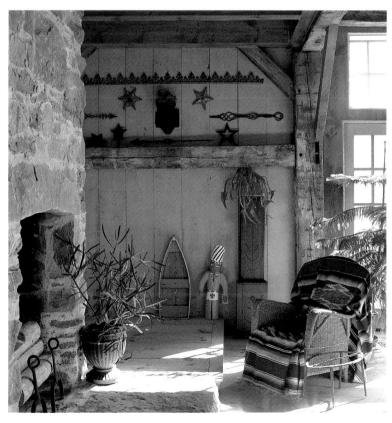

American country style

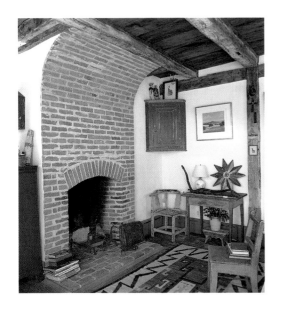

Right:
This dual aspect bedroom is filled with sunshine filtered through windows curtained with green foliage. Bright colours inspired by New Mexico decorate the room. The stencils are adapted from examples found at an 18th century Spanish colonial village near Santa Fe.

Below:
Time-worn painted furniture combined with bright colours on walls and floors produces a look that is unusual, yet easy to live with.

Left:
A vast brick chimney stack with an arched lintel curves toward the wooden ceiling formed by the floorboards of the room above.

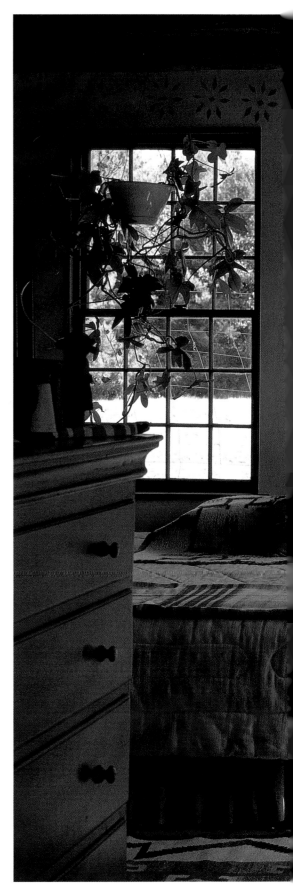

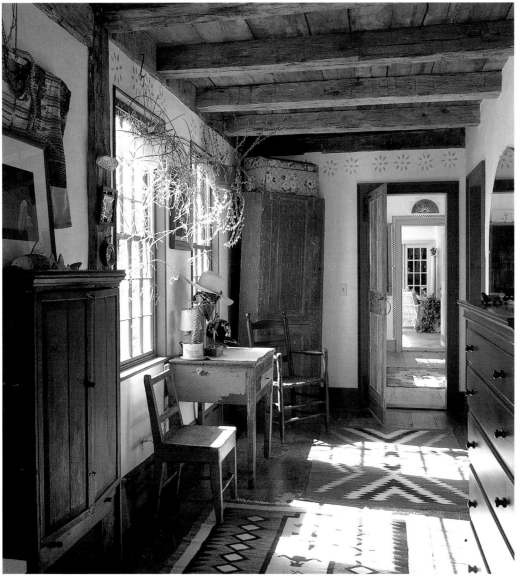

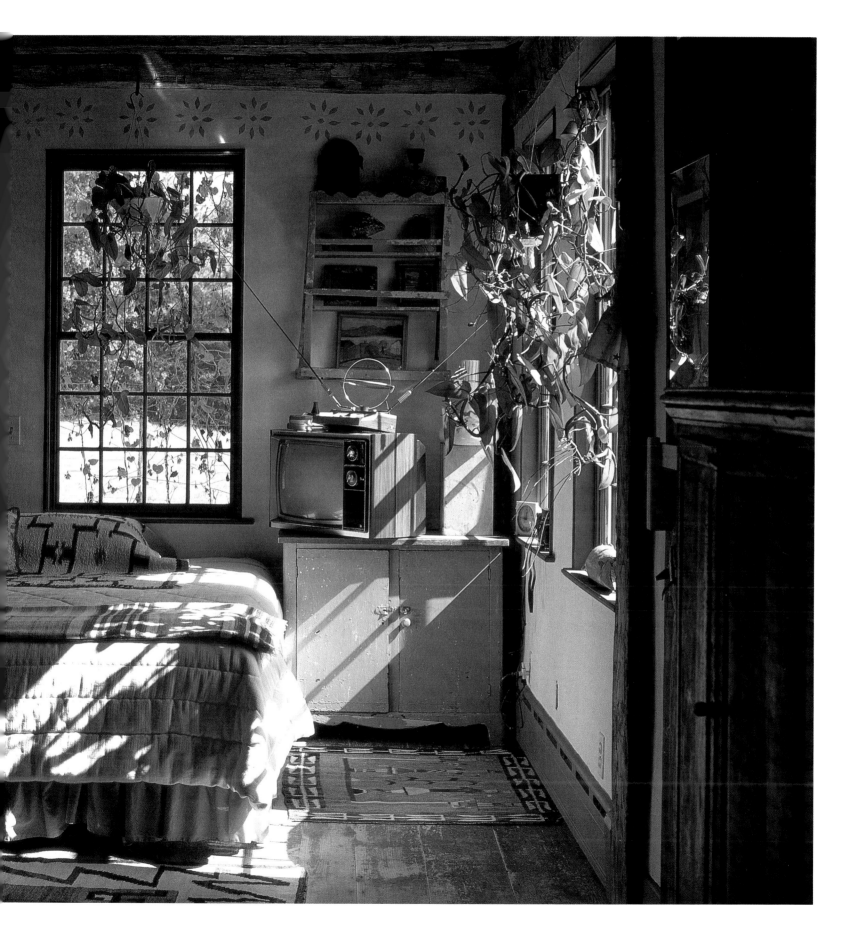

American country style

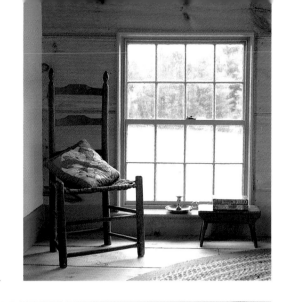

Right:
Electric turquoise and white paintwork, bright furniture and rugs echo Mexican style.

Below:
Against a background of black and white, a colourful naive painting and a collection of cactuses introduce a Mexican mood.

Far right:
A bright green door gives a South American feel to this Connecticut home. A Seth Thomas clock stands on the 19th century Canadian desk.

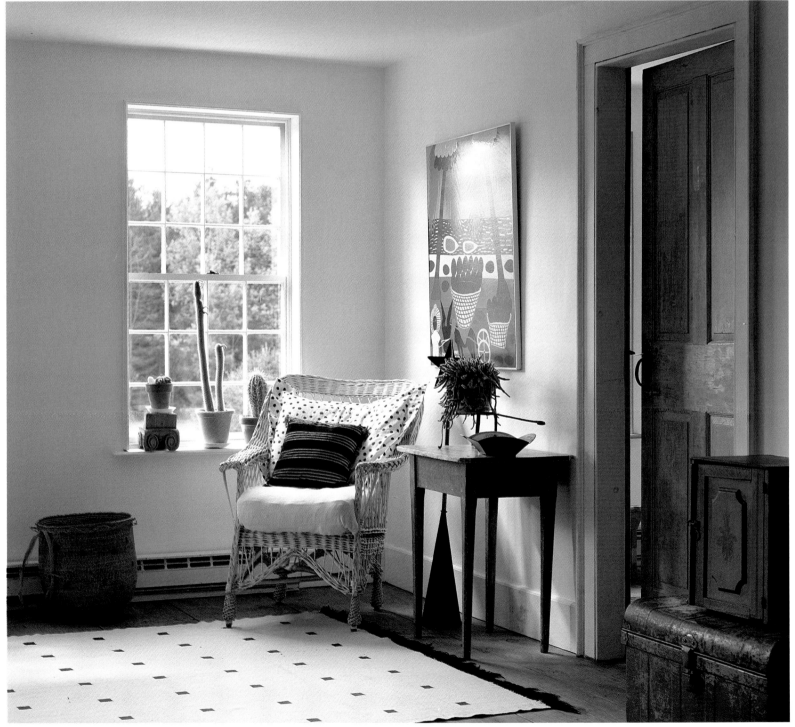

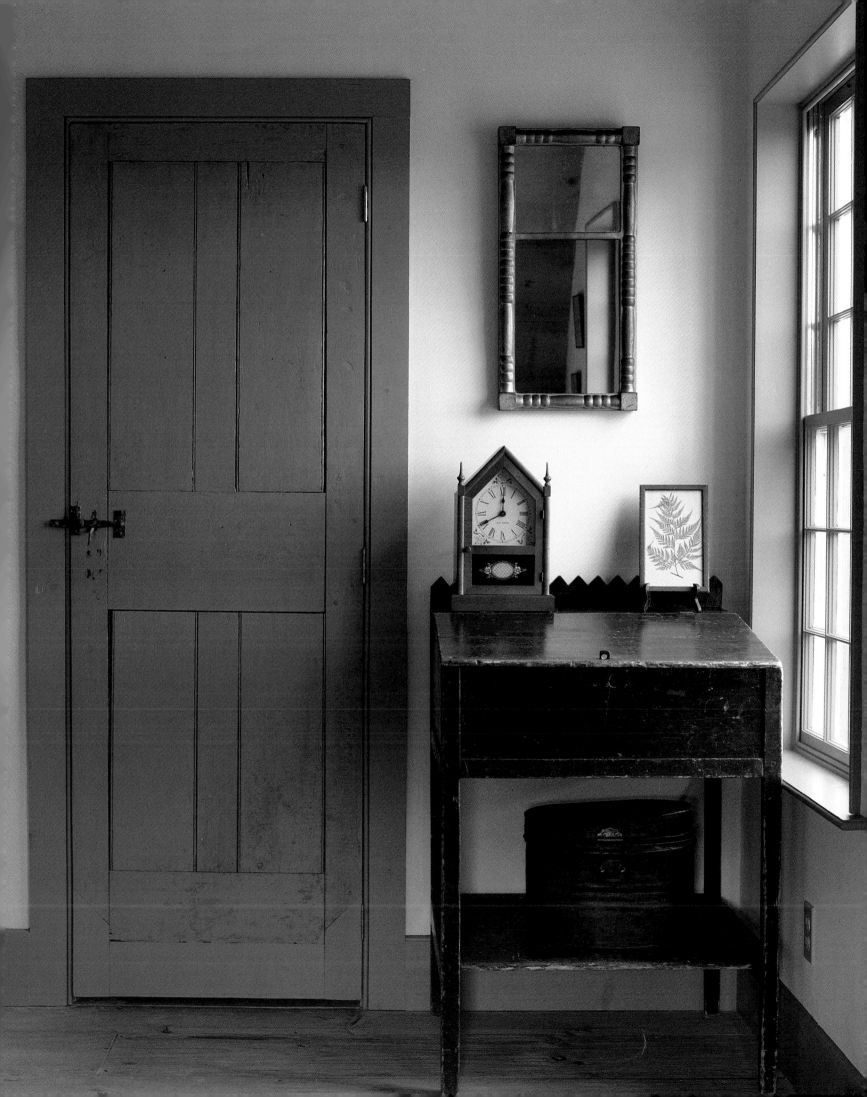

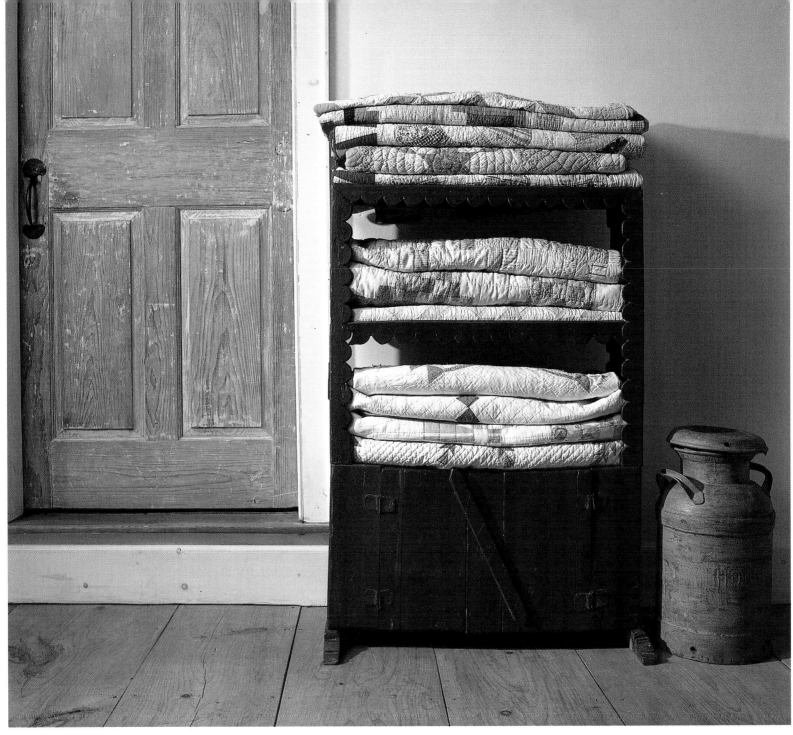

Home-made textiles, particularly quilts, are a principal ingredient of
American country style.

Above:
A Canadian "shoefoot" cupboard holds a collection of patchwork quilts.

Right:
The quilt hanging on the wall is a "rolling star" design. On the floor, in
front of the vinegar-grained six-board chest, is a brightly coloured hooked
rug, salvaged from a dump. Sally cleans her rugs by laying them upside
down on very dry, cold snow and brushing more snow across the back. She
leaves them there for about an hour.

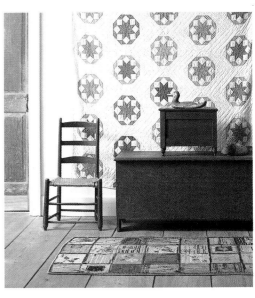

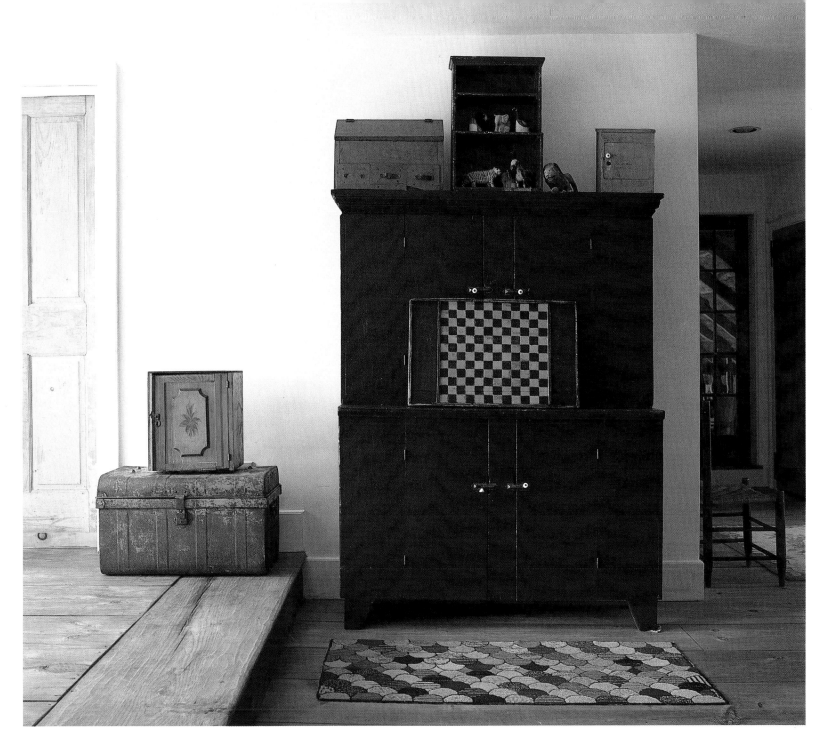

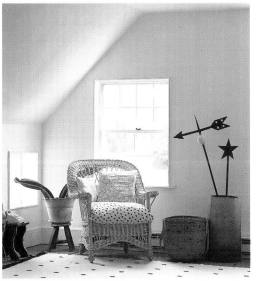

Above:
*A rusting, ochre-painted trunk stands next to an ox-blood coloured
cupboard that is topped with a stack of painted boxes, including an old
ballot box (right).*

Left:
The spiky star and arrow are cut-tin lightning rods.

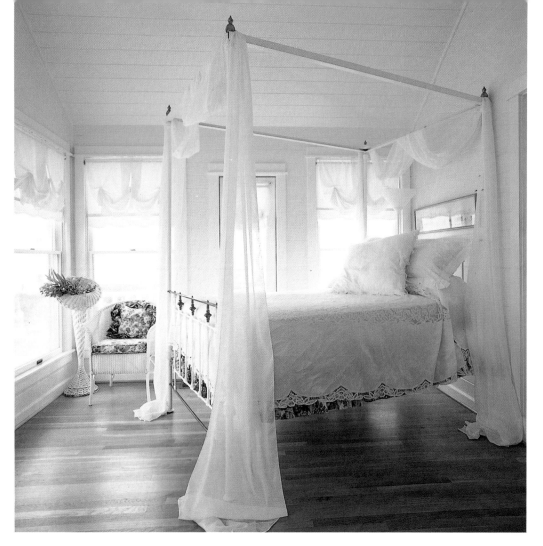

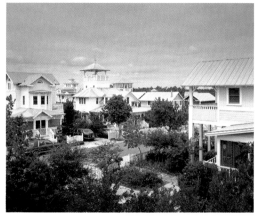

Seaside in Florida is an new 80-acre development by Robert Davis, built with the aim of reproducing the community spirit of a country town. A model of social architecture, all the houses have porches to sit out on and converse with strolling neighbours. The white picket fences and the designs of the houses are based on Charleston and Savannah Southern states vernacular.

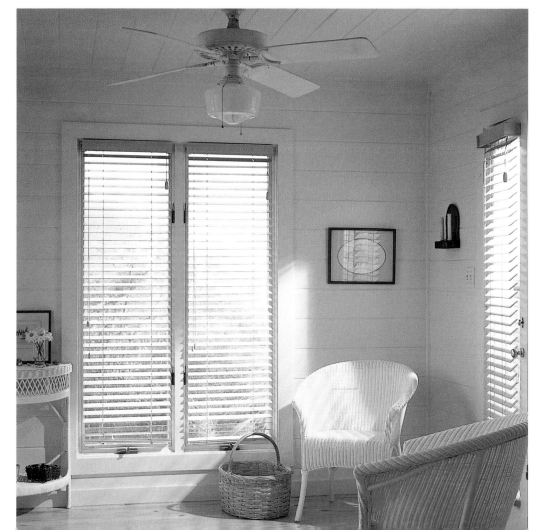

Right:
Like the houses constructed in the region from the 1800s through to the 1940s, homes at Seaside are built to be comfortable without air conditioning. Ceiling fans provide a refreshing down draft, while the beldevere in the roof, a traditional feature of Southern architecture, allows heat to rise up through the interior and escape outside through its windows.

Top left:
White walls, lacy bedlinen and mosquito netting draped over the traditional brass and iron four-poster bed keep a hot-climate bedroom crisp and cool.

Below left:
This house is designed to let the sun's light in without its accompanying heat. A ceiling fan, windows screened by wooden slatted blinds painted in virginal white and airy Lloyd Loom chairs all combine to produce a cool freshness.

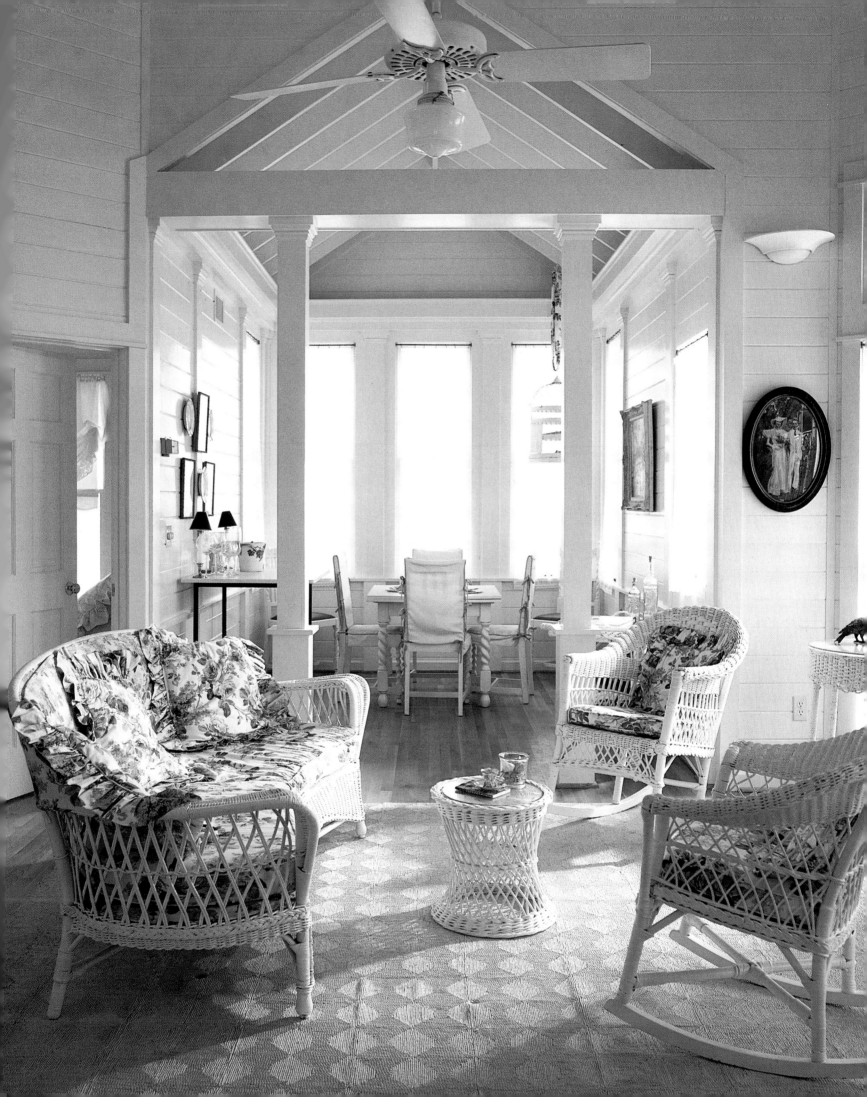

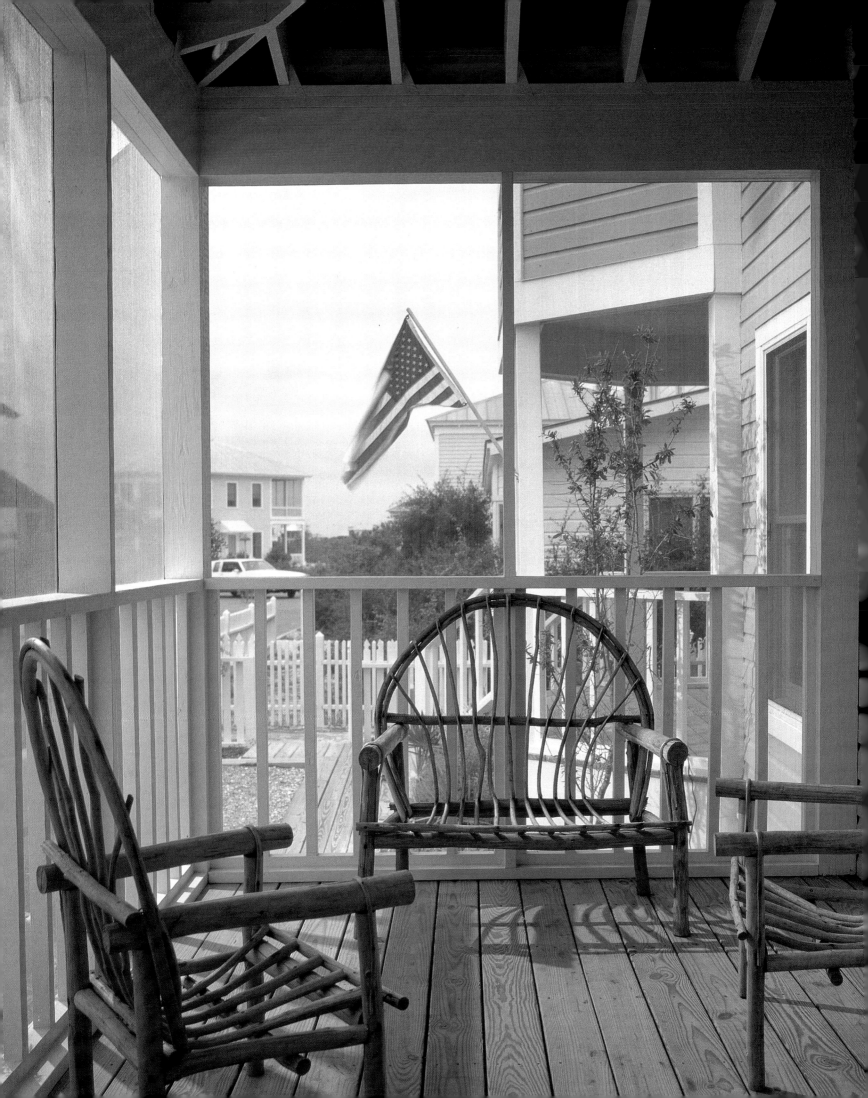

American country style

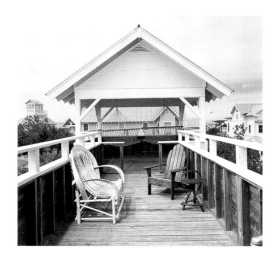

Left:
A verandah, built within easy hailing distance of the street, is the traditional place to relax in the late afternoon sun.

Below:
The guest-room bed has an Adirondack-style (see page 146) twig headboard. Its honeycomb patchwork quilt provides a pool of colour against white walls. Baskets and a period box are used for storage – an informal idea that is suited to country style rooms.

Below:
Though modern and well-equipped, the kitchen's simple lines, with neat white-painted cupboards beneath the work surface and open shelving above, give it a country feel. Natural furnishings – a 19th century drop-leaf table flanked by wicker chairs – add to this mood.

Left:
The sunbleached deck is furnished with rustic and Adirondack-style chairs, while at its far end hammocks swing in the breeze.

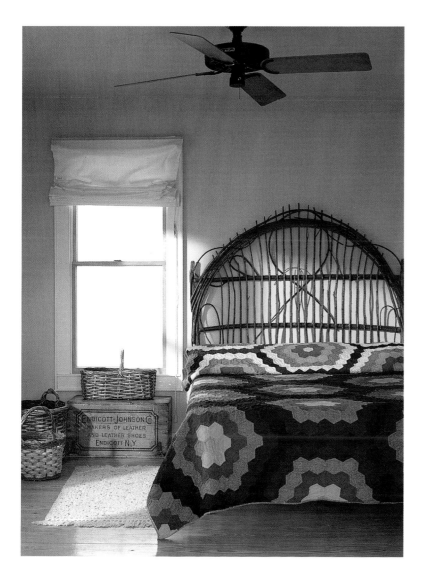

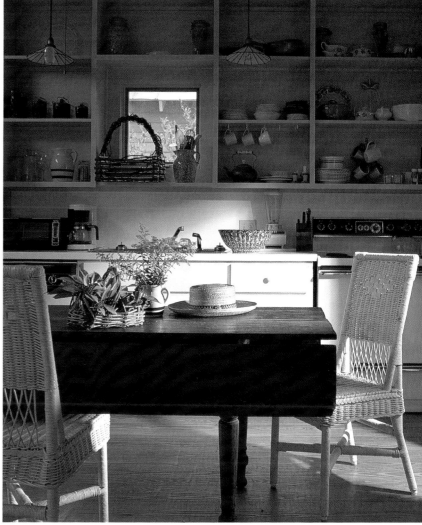

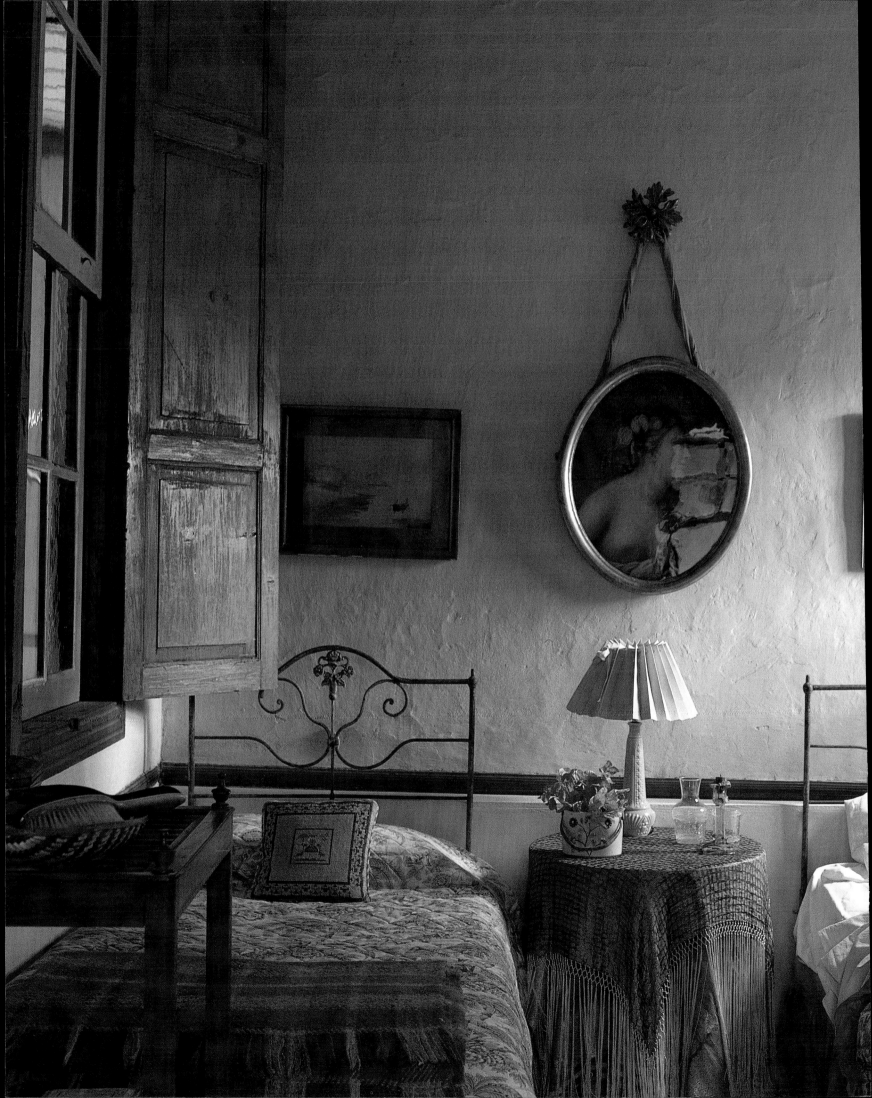

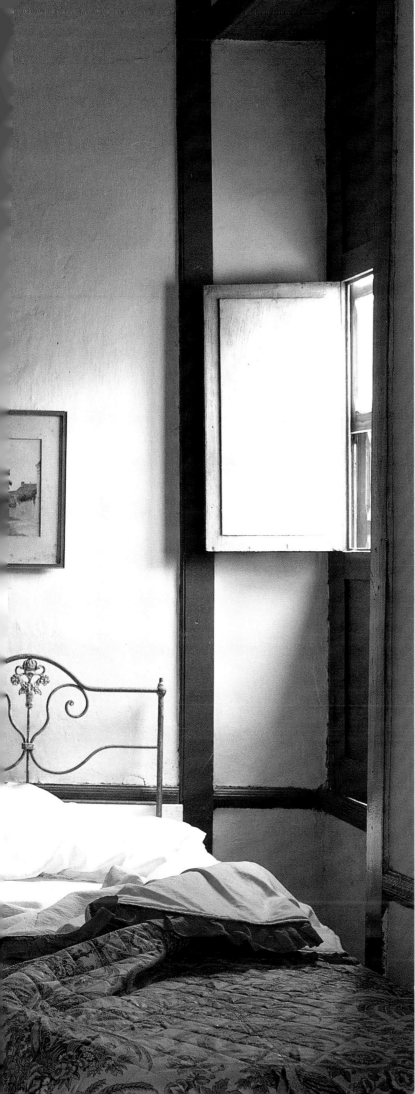

ROOM BY ROOM
in Country Style

*T*he country room is ageless and timeless. Climate and landscape dictate its framework, while its furnishings are governed by the practicalities of rural life rather than by fashion. Evolving through the centuries, the country room is a living environment. It absorbs ideas from other cultures, reinterpreting and incorporating them until they are part of the rich fabric that consti-

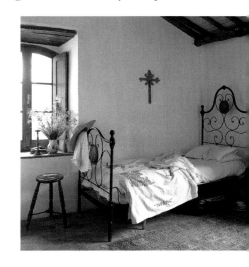

tutes each country's particular style. For example, a French bedroom may contain a carved walnut or fruit-wood *armoire* lined with one of the distinctive Provençal cotton prints that originally drew their inspiration from textiles imported into Marseilles from India in the 17th century. America, naturally, has the most eclectic rooms of all. The influence of the European countries from which the first settlers came is overlaid with the distinctive American style that originated from the need to improvize. The diversity of style which has developed from the mingling of cultures and traditions is heartening confirmation that country style continues to grow and evolve over the centuries, while remaining true to its rural beginnings.

Left:
A Canary Islands bedroom with soft furnishings from many nations: the floral bedspreads are English chintz, the embroidered shawl draped over the table Moroccan, the bedlinen local and the iron bedsteads were bought in Portugal. To restore such beds use a matte black or dull gloss paint on the ironwork and clean up any brass with lemon juice. Too much gloss and polish will look out of place.

Above:
A Renaissance wooden crucifix is perfectly at home on the whitewashed walls of this former Tuscan priest's house, creating an air of almost monastic simplicity.

Living rooms

Comfort is the principal ingredient of the country living room. In cool climates this means a warm cocoon created from overstuffed seating, squashy cushions, warm rugs and a roaring open fire. In hotter regions, a cool, fresh retreat is called for, with white walls, ceiling fans, tiled floors and shuttered windows. Nothing should be too precious or studied, for country living rooms are, above all else, for living in. They take their cue from the original one-room country home where living room meant just that – part kitchen, part living room, part bedroom, with all domestic activity revolving around the hearth. This was the nearest most country people came to a reception room.

Right and below:
In this sunny New England room well-worn painted furniture is mixed with generous armchairs to give an impression of relaxed, informal comfort.

Overleaf:
Pieces from different dates and traditions can be blended together easily in a country home. Here, an 18th century New England pine tavern table with a breadboard end complements the William and Mary walnut armchair to its right, which dates from circa 1690. On the left stands an early 18th century Pennsylvanian corner cupboard.

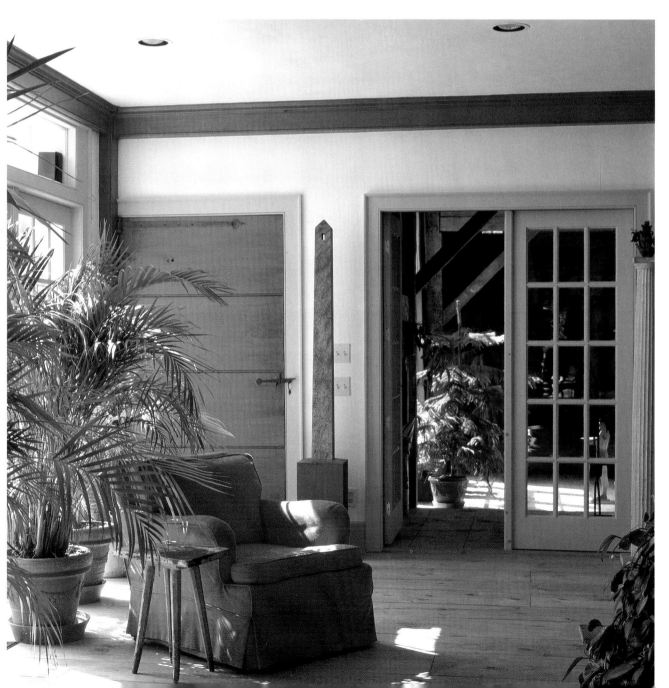

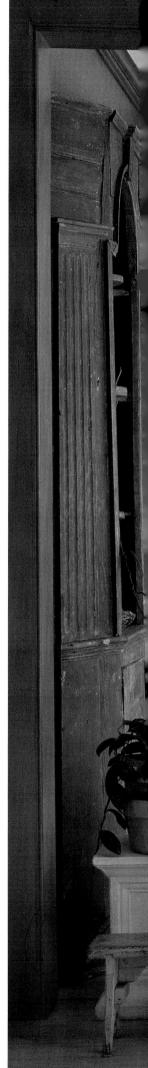

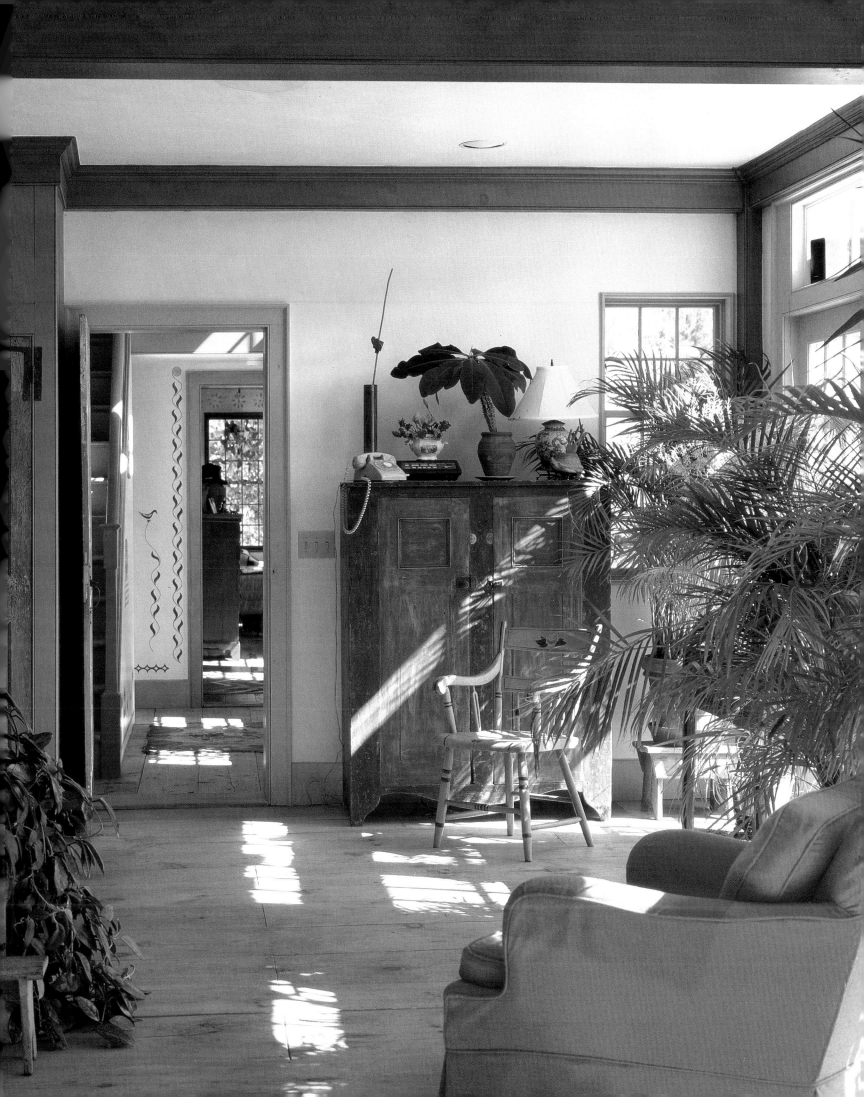

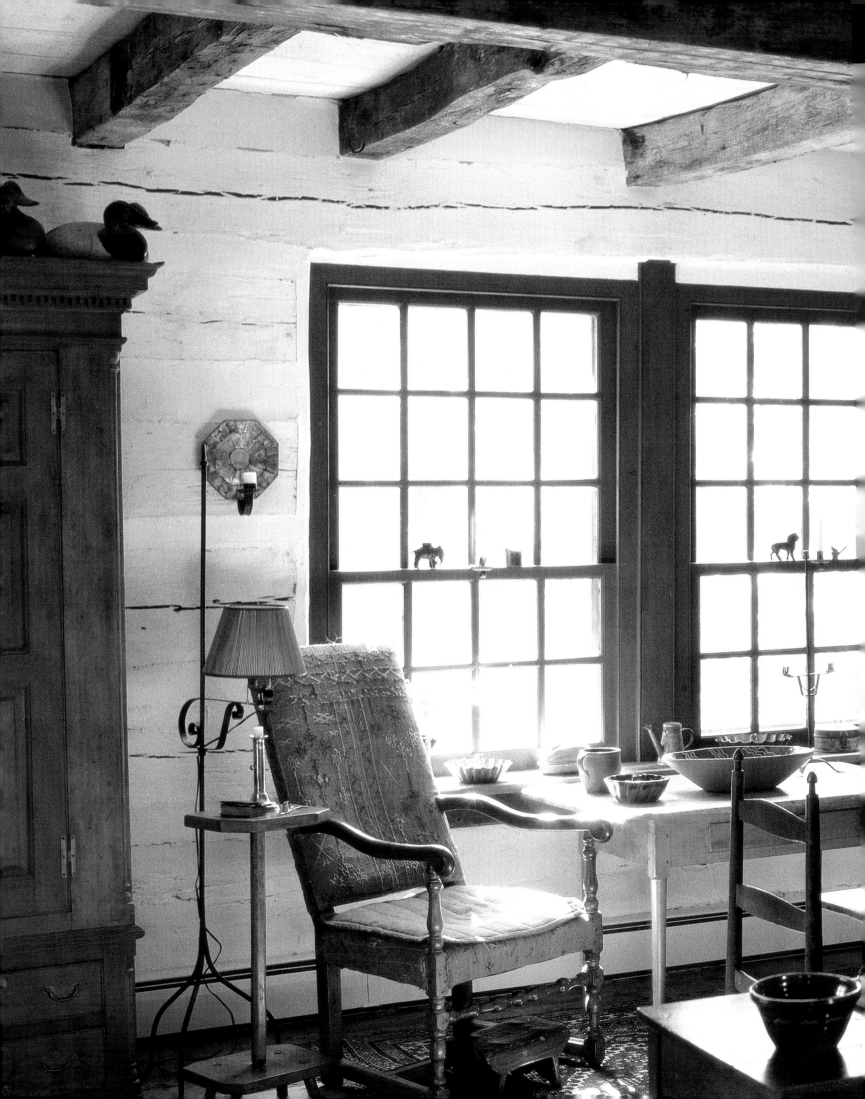

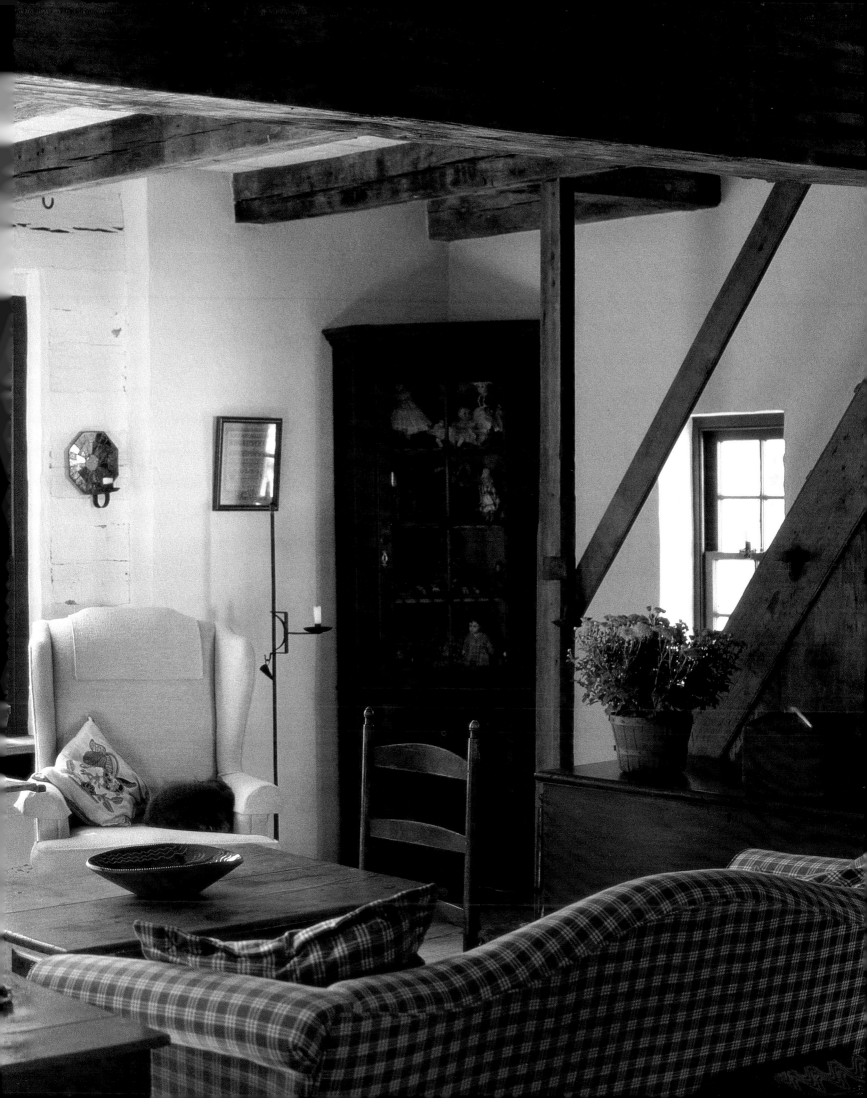

Living rooms

Right and below:
Neutral-coloured upholstery, parquet or brick flooring, stone fireplaces and
rough plaster or slatted wooden ceilings add rustic texture to these modern
French rooms.

Bottom:
A vaulted ceiling, traditional fireplace and quarry-tiled floor create a
strong Spanish framework for the green and white ticking-covered chairs
and modern wooden coffee table.

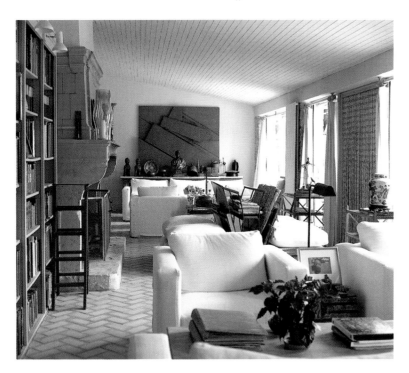

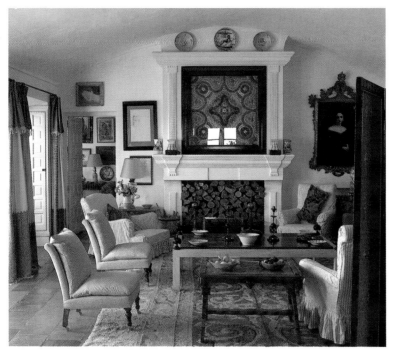

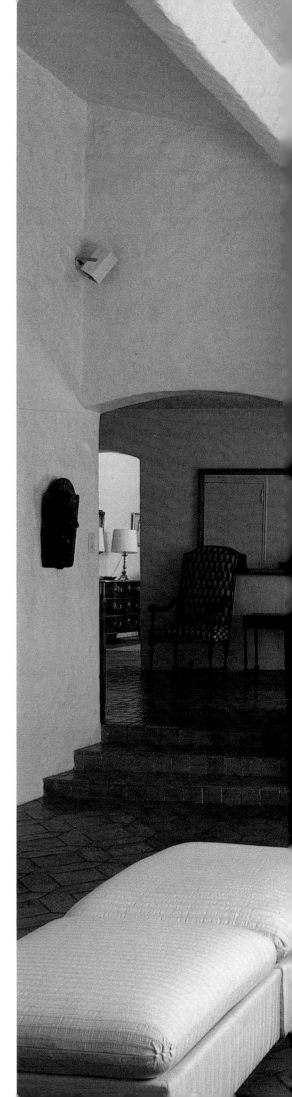

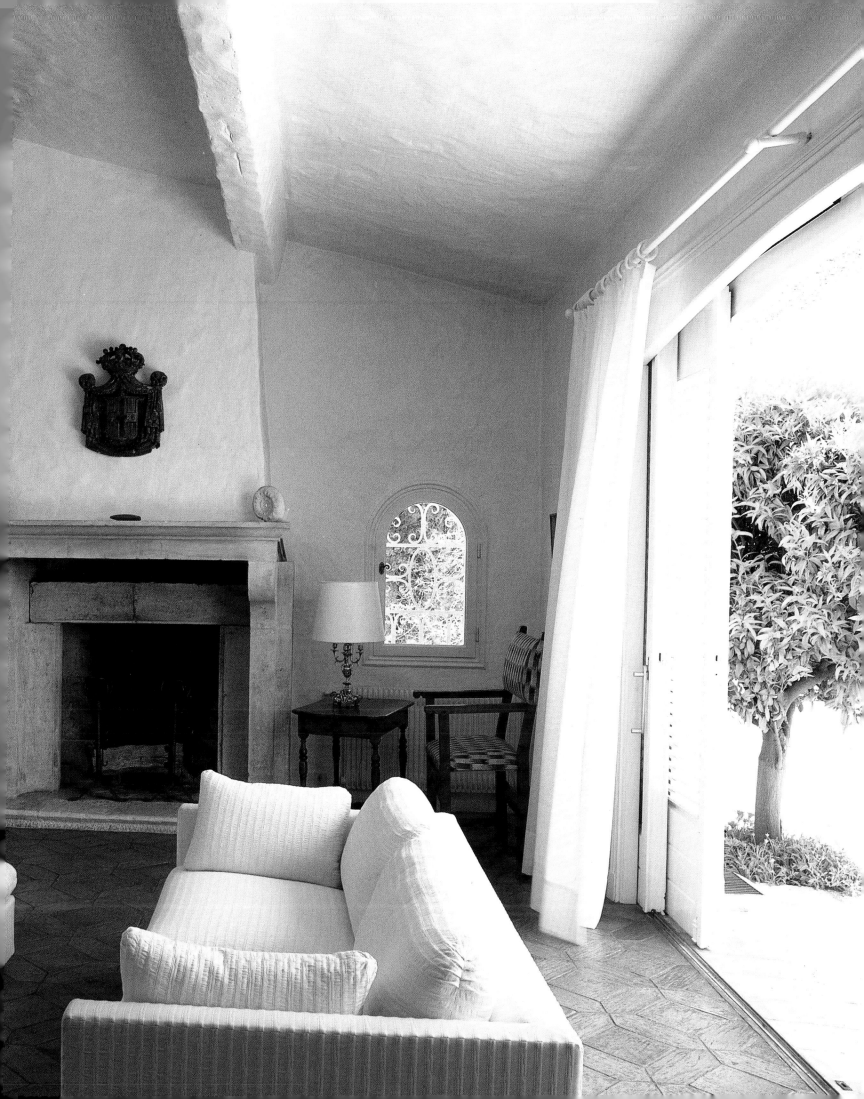

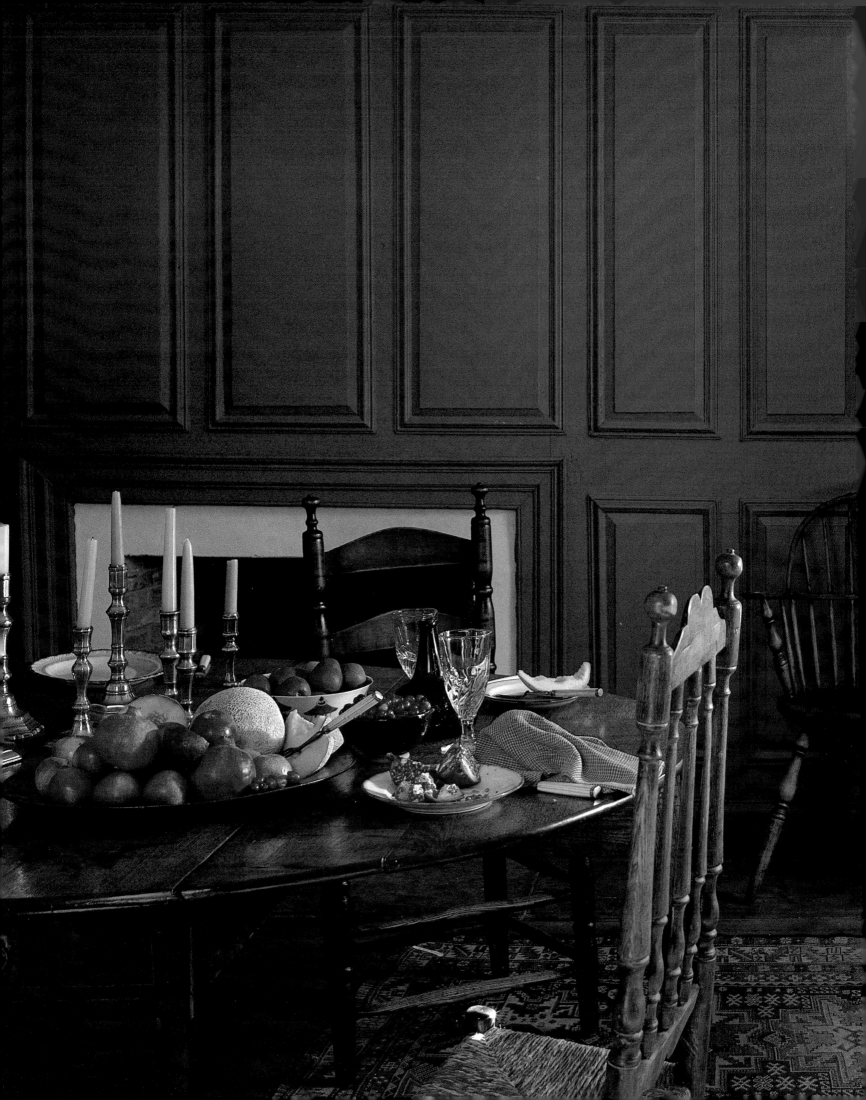

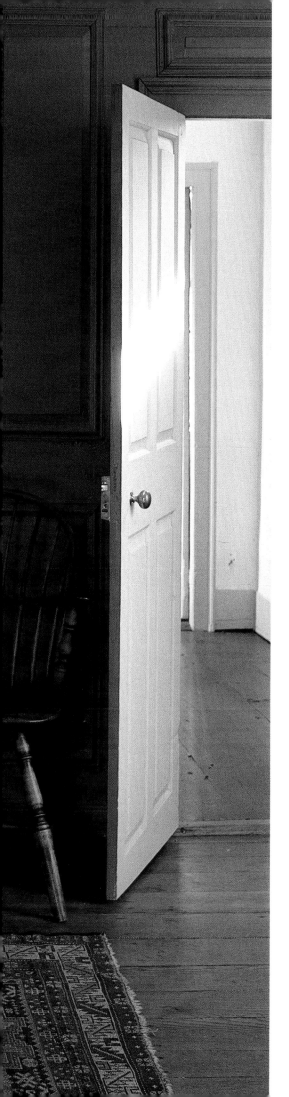

Dining rooms

*I*n most country homes the dining room was – and is – part of a multi-purpose kitchen-cum-living area (see page 165). England was the first European country to design a room especially for eating, and that not until the 18th century. While the gentry dined in stylish splendour, the rest of the population continued to eat in the kitchen until well into the 19th century. During this period, in the homes of the growing middle classes in Europe and America, comfortable dining rooms evolved, furnished with an easy combination of 18th century antiques, rural and contemporary pieces.

Today's country dining room draws on this style to create a relaxed setting where the table dominates. Furniture is often simple: sturdy pine tables surrounded by rush-seated chairs that have migrated from the farmhouse kitchen. The country mood calls for homely pottery tableware. There is no need for anything to match – a unifying theme is more authentic than a dainty dinner service. Chairs, too, can be a collection of different country styles or woods – mix Windsors and ladderbacks, oak and yew. Harsh electric lighting should be forsaken for the warm, atmospheric effect of candles (see page 232). And table decorations should have a simple honesty that is in harmony with nature: casual arrangements of wild flowers and grasses (see pages 226-7) and bowls filled with berries, pinecones or shiny apples.

Left and below: The country feel in this colonial American dining room is created by the furniture – rush-seated 18th century spindlebacks and a Windsor chair – and the soft natural green paintwork on the wooden panelling and doors. The green is the original mellow milk paint colour – the owner Stephen Mack scraped off five coats of paint to reveal it. Milk paint has none of the harshness of modern formulations because it colours the wood itself, while today's paints merely coat it.

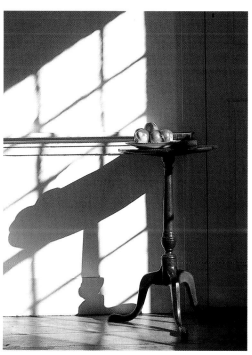

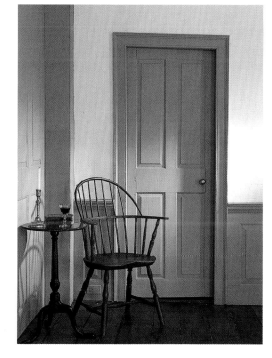

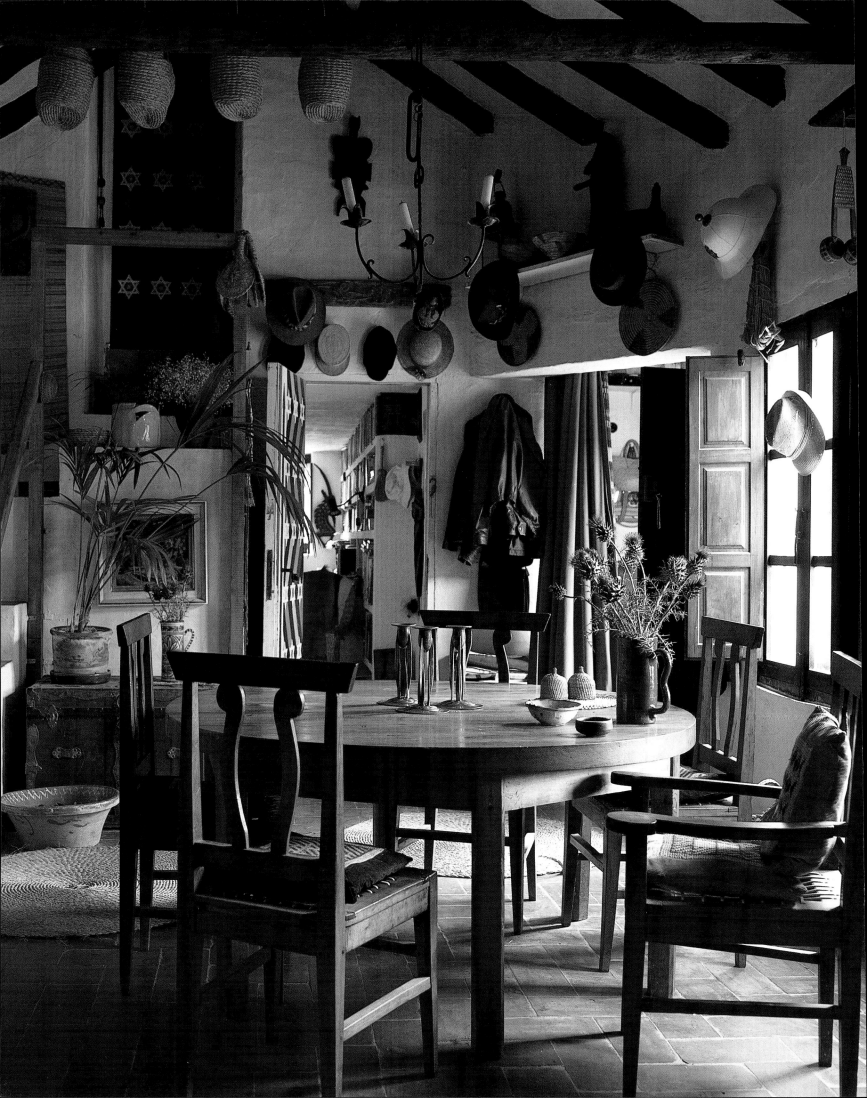

Dining rooms

Left:
Ironwood chairs from Africa and a locally made pine table are the focus of this informal dining area in a Spanish finca. Appropriately, the stitched matting's original purpose was to strain wine.

Top right:
Antique pewter and fine leather-bound books adorn an 18th century carved walnut buffet in a French dining room.

Far top right:
Modern craft pieces like this table by Richard LaTrobe Bateman blend well with country style because contemporary craftspeople usually work with natural materials and adapt traditional designs and techniques.

Middle right:
An 18th century corner display buffet is filled with French and English china. The burnished copper ornament on the wall hides a light fitting – an ingenious solution to the problems of harmonizing technology with country style.

Far middle right:
Rugged beams contrast with whitewashed walls in this French dining room. The chairs and tables are 18th century oak pieces.

Bottom right:
Gingham-covered Gustavian-style chairs, light paintwork and a 19th century pine cupboard decorate this Swedish country breakfast room.

Far bottom right:
In the Mediterranean, dining rooms are often outdoors (see page 199), and meals are eaten al fresco on quarry-tiled or stone-flagged terraces. Here, swathes of white sailcloth shade tables dressed in flower-sprigged cotton.

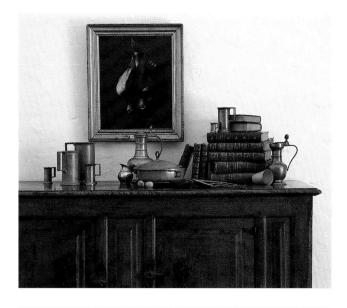
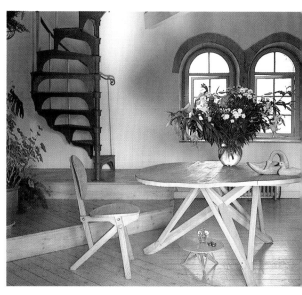
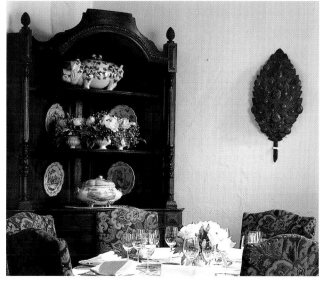
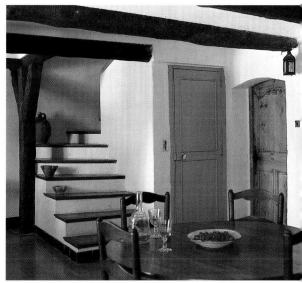
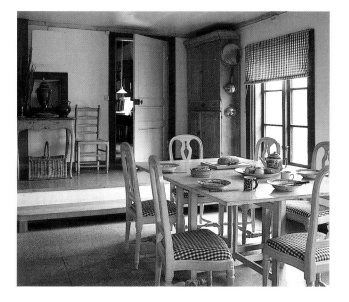
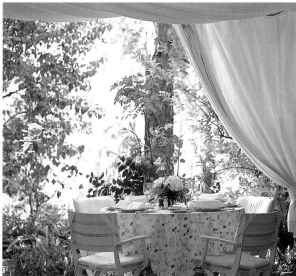

Kitchens

The fundamental appeal of the country kitchen is far more than a nostalgic yearning for the past. It is an acknowledgment of the kitchen as the hub of the household, the place where families are nourished and where family and friends gather to work or relax.

The importance of the kitchen as the heart of the home can be traced right back through the centuries to the time when meals were cooked on open fires in the middle of the same room in which everyone lived, ate and slept. Furnishings were rudimentary – at mealtimes roughly made stools or benches were pulled up to planks laid over trestles for the duration of the meal. And rammed earth or stone floors were covered with rushes which were changed only once a year.

Few would want to recreate that level of authenticity. Nonetheless, a distaste for soulless 20th century laminate and steel food preparation laboratories has sparked a move back to kitchens for living in, rooms that reflect those country kitchens that were for centuries at the heart of peasant life. For most of us, this is necessarily a 20th century interpretation of rural reality. Modern benefits like piped water, which have dispensed with the need to pump water from the well, should not be eschewed. Operating a pump was no simple matter: 30 minutes or so of muscle-aching work several times a day was needed to keep a household supplied with water.

To reconcile the past with a contemporary lifestyle needs careful planning. Certain practical features from the past like a sturdy central table, hard floors and a walk-in pantry have been joyfully rediscovered by contemporary country dwellers. And traditional kitchen implements such as copper cookware and wooden bowls are visually appealing as well as useful. However, modern tools like mixers and microwaves can pose a decorative problem. Placed alongside the time-honoured *batterie de cuisine*, such gadgetry detracts from the authentic country mood unless care is taken to conceal them discreetly. Pie safes and dressers will swallow up smaller items, while larger pieces like washing machines and dishwashers can be plumbed in behind cupboard doors, or if there is space, relegated to a separate utility room.

Right:
Water from the well or pump serviced centuries of country kitchens. Although installing a pump is not practical today, it is important to choose fittings, like those in the picture opposite, that echo the earlier technology.

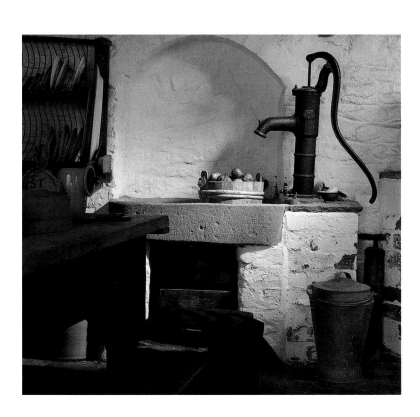

Right:
A simple stone sink set in solid wooden cupboards provides the perfect period look in this American kitchen. Above, open shelves are lined with serving dishes, pots and plates.

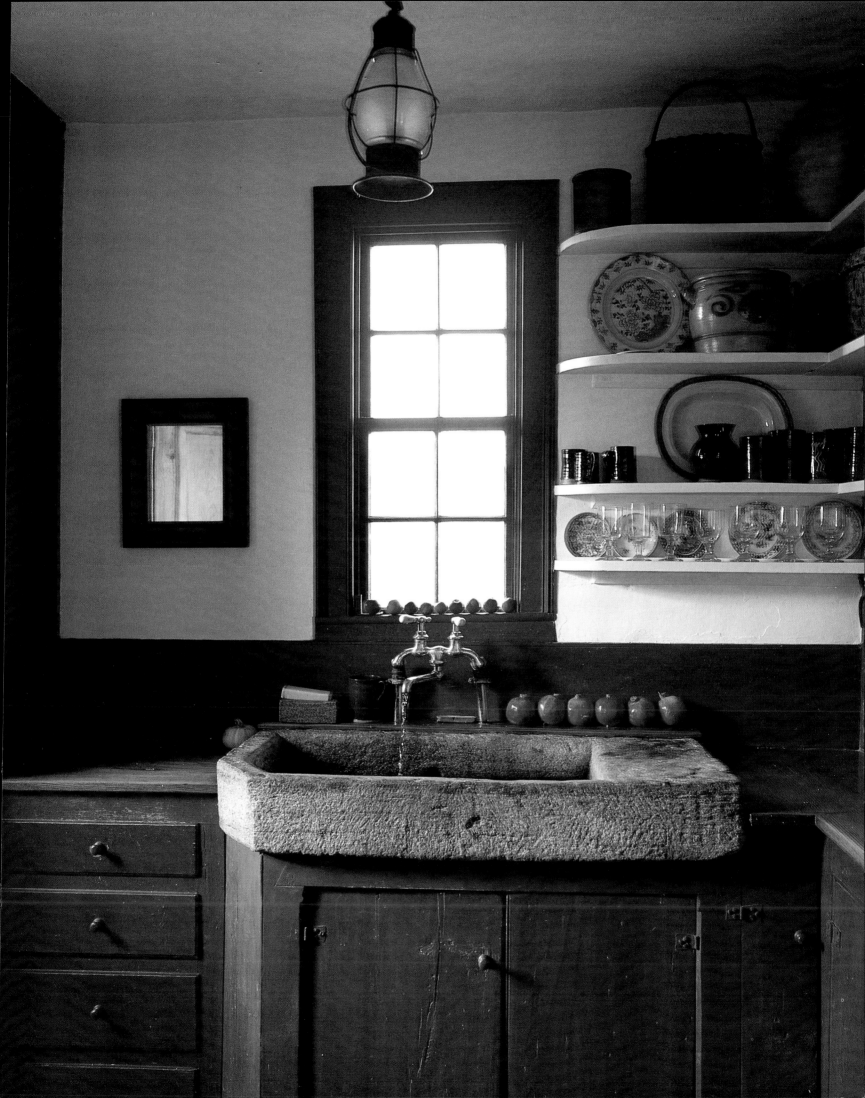

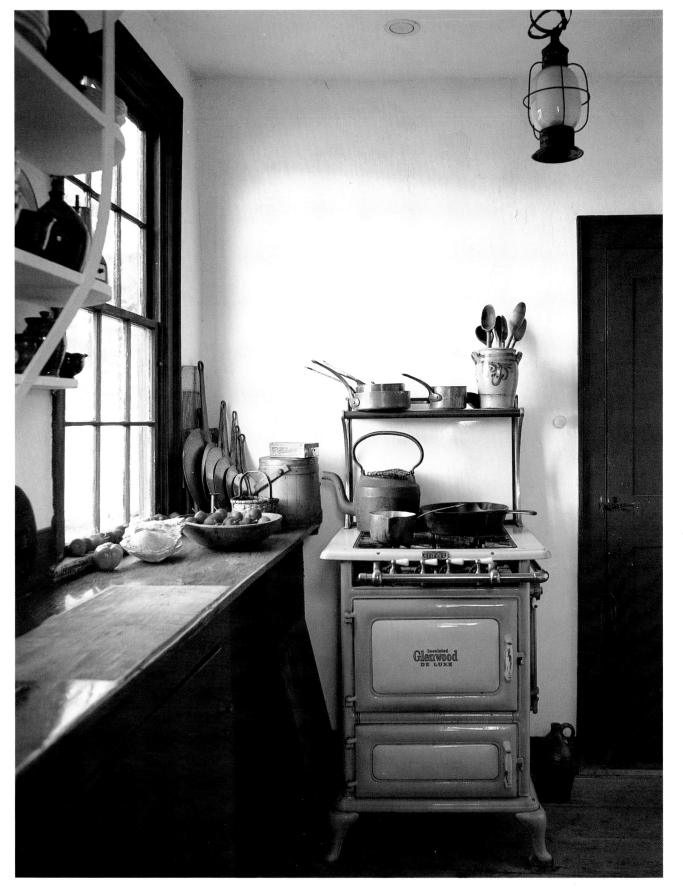

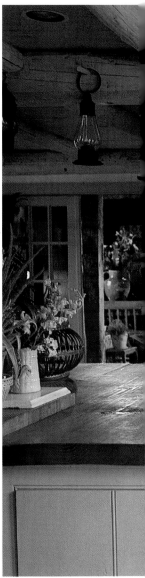

Kitchens

Below:
In this New England kitchen solid pine counters top cabinets painted to blend with the old Canadian cupboard set against the far wall.

Bottom right:
In early American wooden houses, as in Scandinavia, the kitchen was often housed in a separate cabin to minimize the risk of fire.

Middle right:
A traditional open stove heats this Scandinavian kitchen.

Right:
Country texture on show: shiny copper jelly moulds on a rough-painted brick wall above a well-worn wooden butcher's block.

Left:
Homely-looking ranges are ideal for country kitchens.

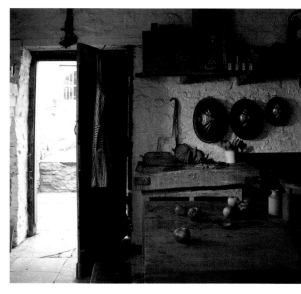

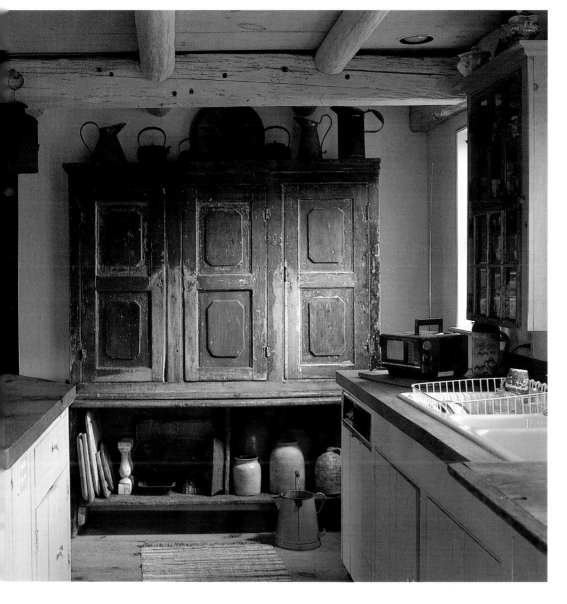

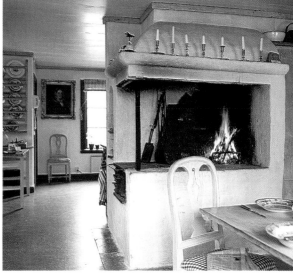

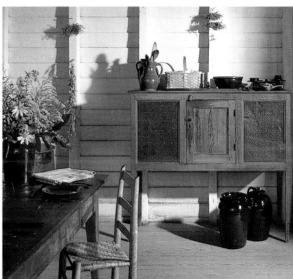

Kitchens

Top row, right:
A walk-in larder or pantry is a traditional feature of English country kitchens. Here, the food stays cool on Bath stone shelves and the walls are painted in an earthy terracotta.

Top row, far right:
A rich use of colour brightens this stone-flagged Spanish scullery.

Middle row, right:
Hand-painted 18th century faience tiles add a note of colour to the working area of this Spanish kitchen. Practical wooden spoon racks and decorative local pottery are Spanish elements that could easily be transported to a farmhouse in Sussex, England or an apartment on Park Avenue, New York.

Middle row, far right:
The return of the freestanding kitchen of earlier generations has revived the fortunes of many practical kitchen pieces like this 19th century Andalucian pine display cupboard.

Bottom row, right:
In country homes food preparation is often carried out seated at a sturdy table. The oil lamp illuminating the work surface is essential in Swedish winters, when daylight lasts no more than a few hours.

Bottom row, far right:
Thick-walled country houses have broad windowsills, as in this English pantry, which make good resting places for food stores.

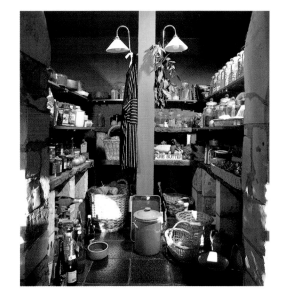
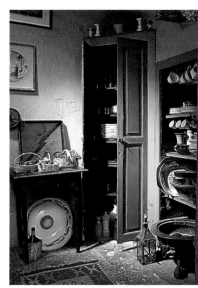
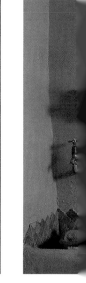

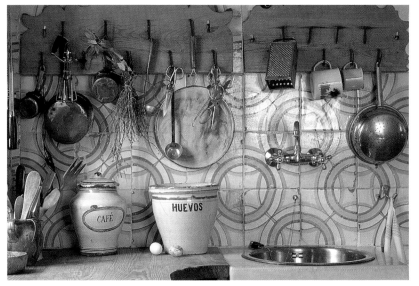
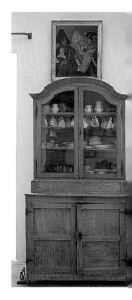

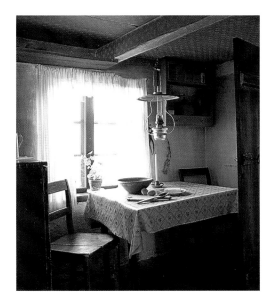
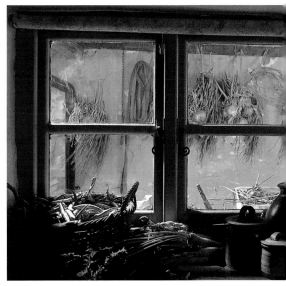

Kitchens

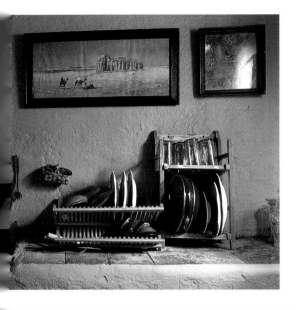

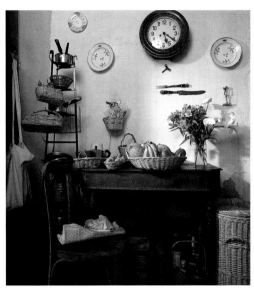

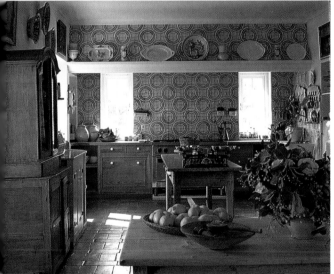

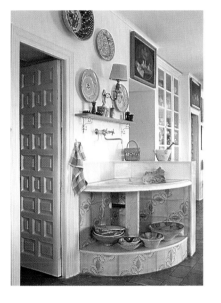

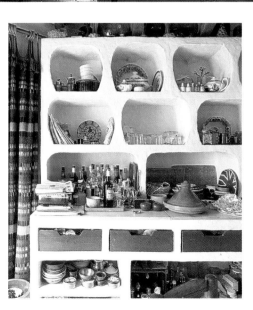

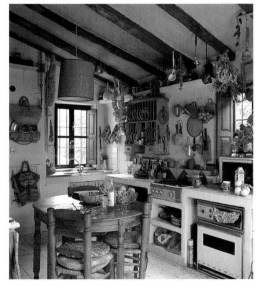

Top row, far left:
Much-loved pictures have laid the foundations for a rich colour scheme. Original fittings like this sink and tiled drainer are often removed because they seem uneven or just not up to date, but it is far better to accentuate their charm.

Top row, left:
Practical decorative items adorn the walls of this kitchen in the Canary Islands. Everything is conveniently to hand, even the key to wind the kitchen clock.

Middle row, far left:
This Spanish kitchen has been designed so that the attractive period elements – the pine furniture, faience tiles and brick floor – are not overshadowed by modern cooking equipment.

Middle row, left:
A clean, bright white used on walls and woodwork and set against the warm red brick floor gives a Mediterranean feel to this kitchen. A custom-built sink unit, incorporating display storage for bowls, is ideal for preparing a summer's worth of salads from the fresh produce in the garden.

Bottom row, far left:
Almost sculptural, this Spanish kitchen shelving has a strong Moorish influence. The curtain next to it, which divides the kitchen from the living area, is a Xhosa blanket transported from Africa.

Bottom row, left:
Function is on display in this eclectic Spanish kitchen hung with culinary paraphernalia. Counters are marble, but this is no indulgent luxury, simply an economical use of local material as marble is cheaper than wood in this part of Spain.

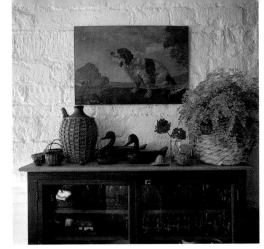

Kitchens

Left:
A wooden display cabinet used to store glasses is set against a rough-textured painted stone wall and topped with rustic baskets and carved decoy ducks.

Below:
Textured tiles, once used to dry the malt in this malthouse, have been relaid on the ground floor to provide a practical floorcovering in rooms that lead straight off the garden.

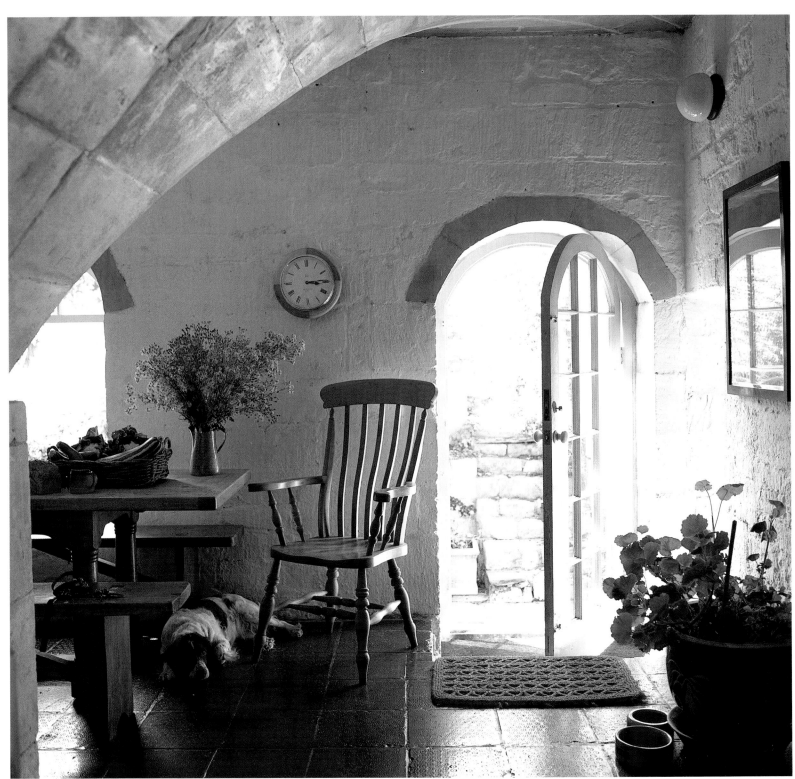

Kitchens

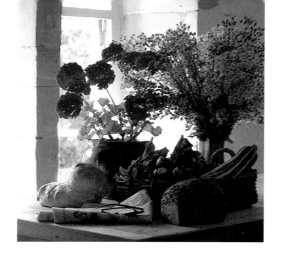

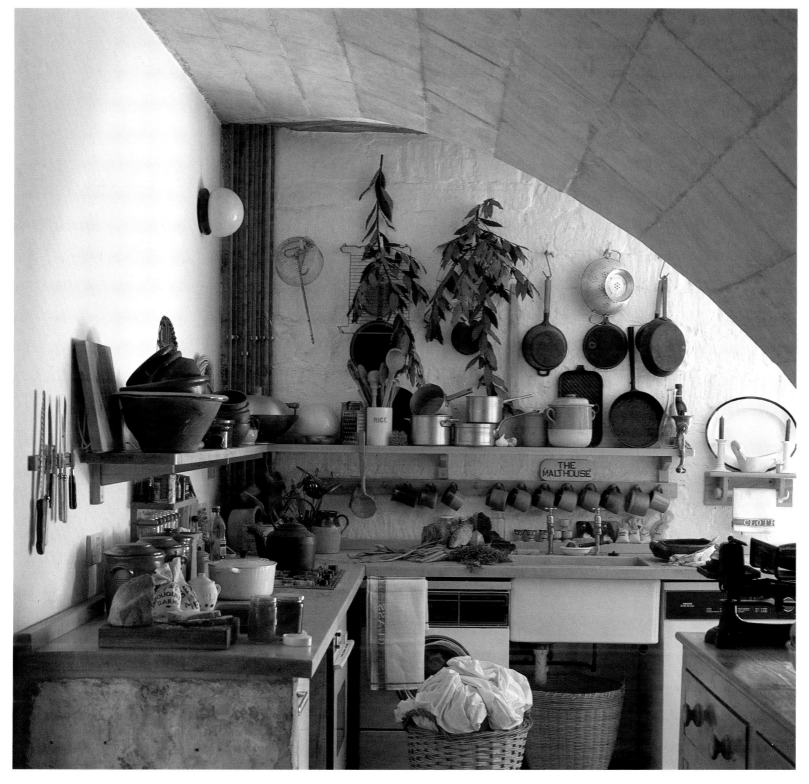

Kitchens

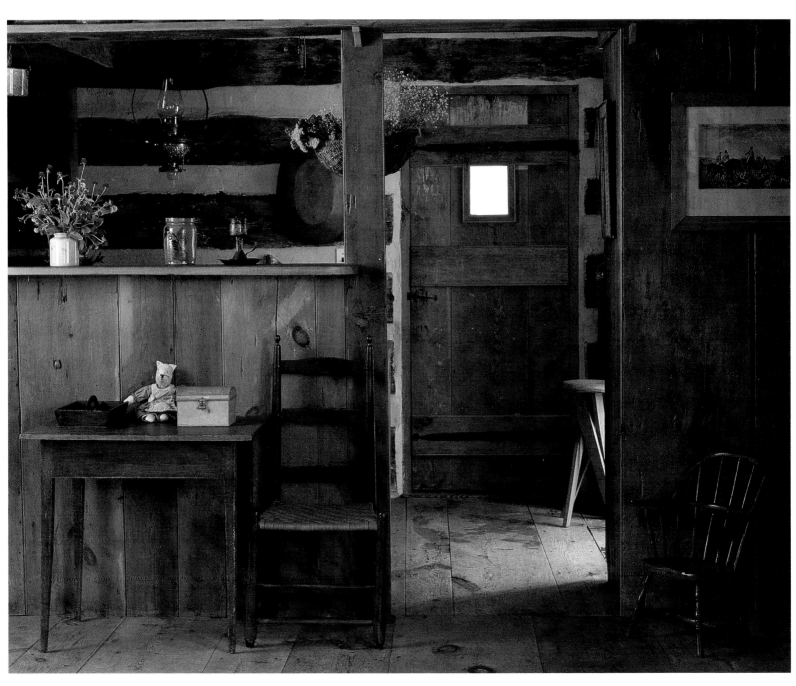

Right:
Details like hinges,
knobs and latches are
the key to creating a
country kitchen that
has all the 20th
century conveniences,
yet captures the
character of an
earlier era.

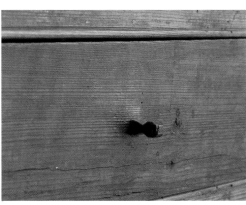

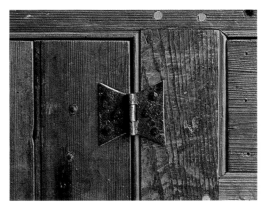

Right and above:
Country homes evolve
over the generations
so well-chosen
improvements can be
a genuine solution.
In this American
kitchen, hand-crafted
pine cabinets
accomodate modern
appliances.

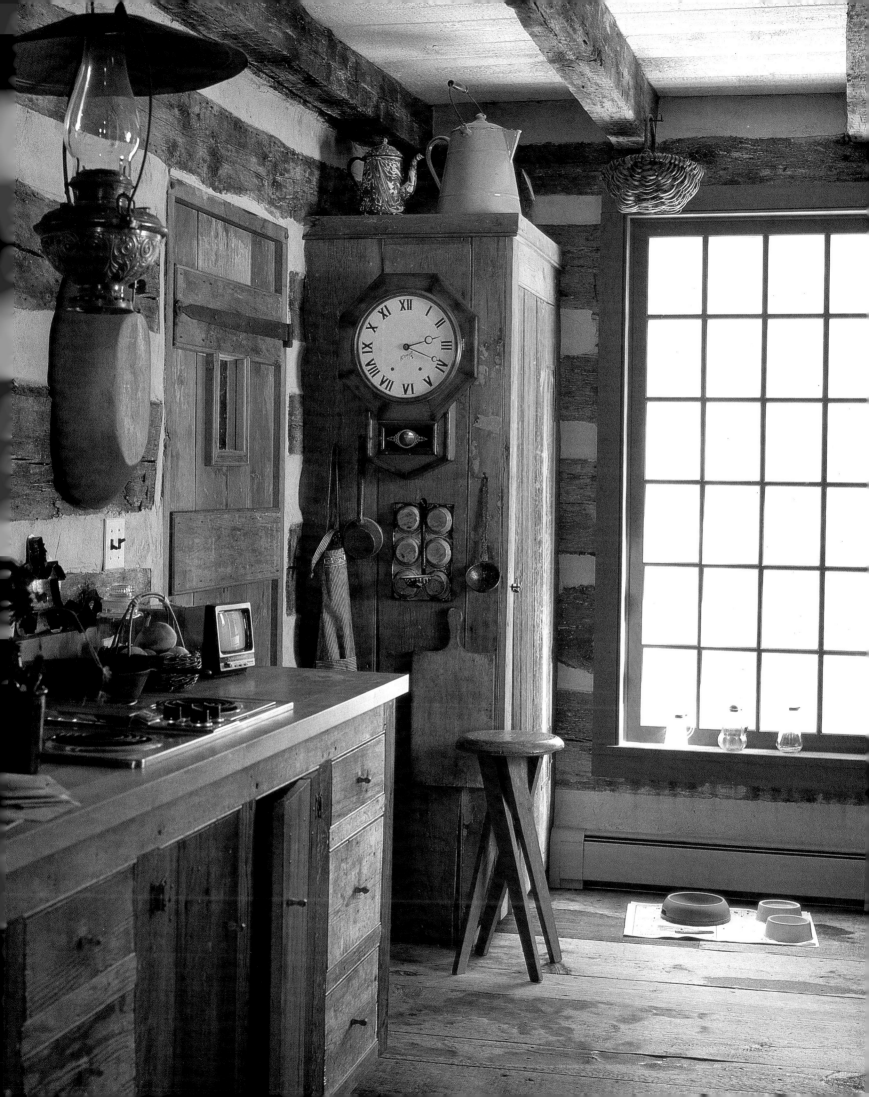

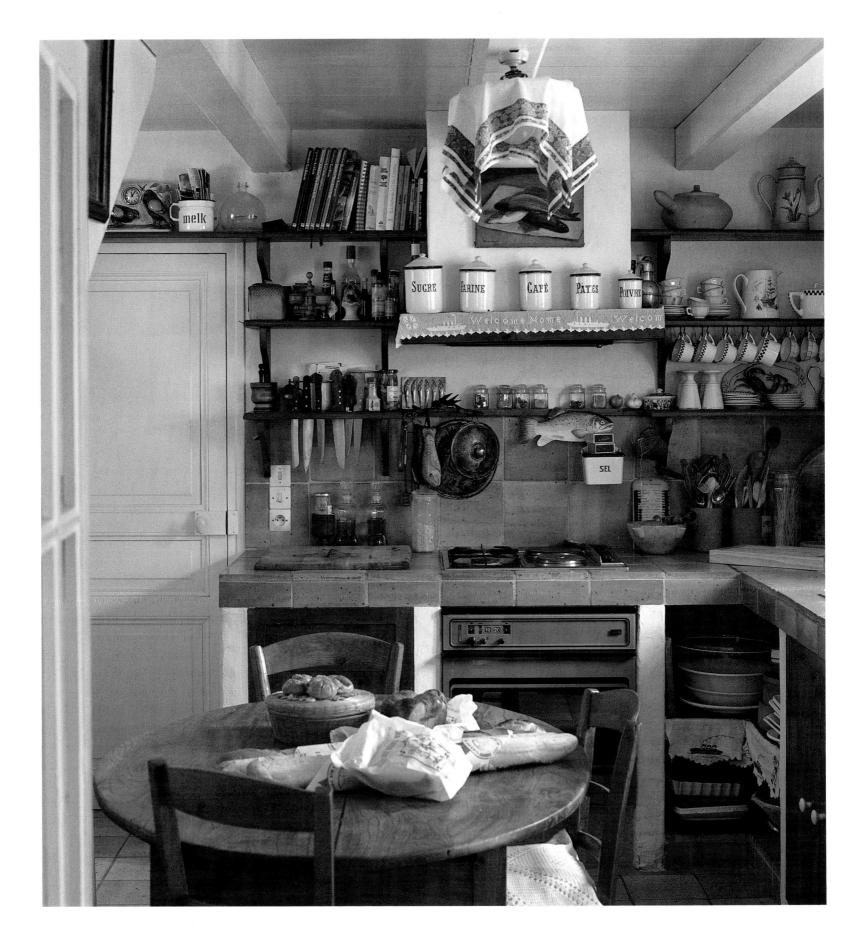

Kitchens

Left:
This French kitchen is workmanlike, with open storage space that leaves nothing hidden, everything to hand. Kitchen knives and tools hang above the counters, while cups are suspended from hooks beneath narrow shelves. Storage jars in graduated sizes march along the cloth that covers the shelf in front of the chimney breast. Recipe books are tucked into a recess near the ceiling. A particularly charming touch is the traditional glass cloth or tea towel shading the light. Local tiles, white-painted woodwork and pine furniture contribute to the natural mood of the room, which seems to have evolved rather than being planned.

Below right:
Creamy sailcloth curtains, simply hung by loops from a pole, screen the kitchen doorway from the heat of the sun. The presence of the sea, visible throughout this house (see pages 34-7), is evident here too. Freshly caught colinets await cleaning and cooking on the drainer and a painting of the local harbour, with its fishing boats and fishermen at work on their nets, hangs above a small shelf like an extra window with a view to the port outside.

Below left:
In this corner of the kitchen a row of copper saucepans, an essential part of the batterie de cuisine *of any self-respecting French cook, hang from small butcher's hooks. To their right, a wooden rack holds jars of herbs and spices. On the sturdy pine table in the foreground a meal is in preparation. True country style makes use of local ingredients – from the wood used to make the table to the food served up on it.*

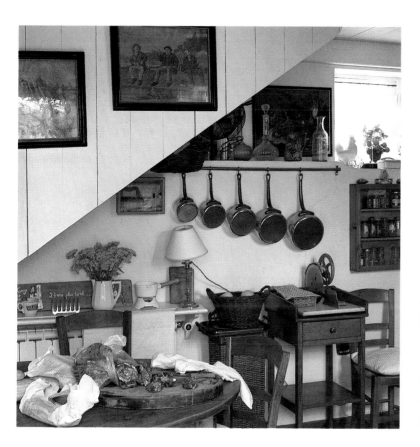
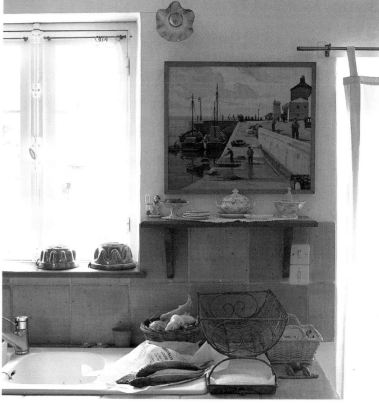

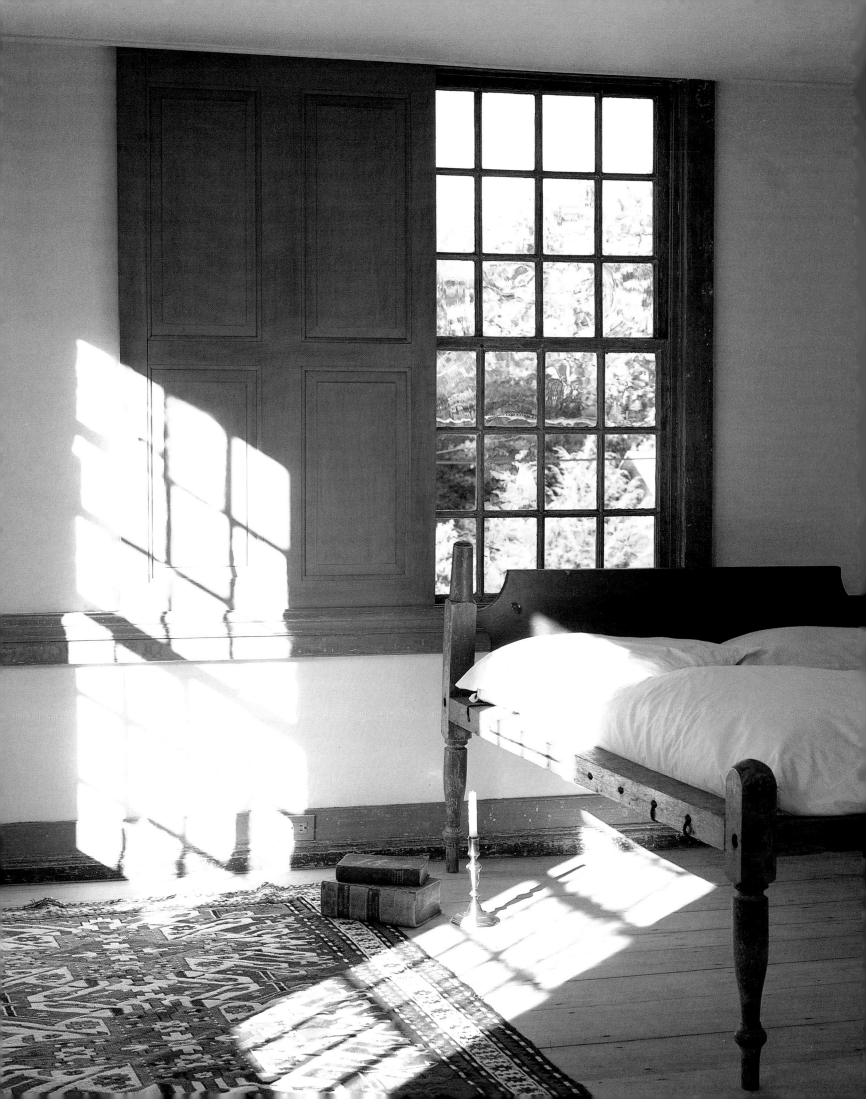

Bedrooms

The bedroom did not come into being until late in the Middle Ages, and even then it served as a sort of reception room as well as a sleeping place. Only the rich had such a chamber – everyone else slept communally on the floor of the same room in which they lived, cooked and ate. By the 18th century in farmhouses all over Europe and America bedrooms had become more private and more hygienic. Washable cottons and linens imported from the Far East replaced furs and tapestries, and cast iron beds that were less of a haven for bugs became popular. During the 19th century a gentle eclecticism evolved – china ornaments, framed water-colours, painted washstands and floral fabrics began to appear. Whether today's room has a four-poster or a simple metal-framed bed, polished floorboards or comfortable rugs, chintz curtains or bare windows, it will conform to one premise: the country bedroom is never grand.

Left:
Windows unfettered with curtains admit maximum sunlight. The 19th century American bed bears its original paint, which tones well with the colour used on the Indian shutter.

Below:
Bright rag rugs and a painted Mexican cupboard bring a catholic mixture of rich colours to the puritan white of the walls and bedcover in this New England barn.

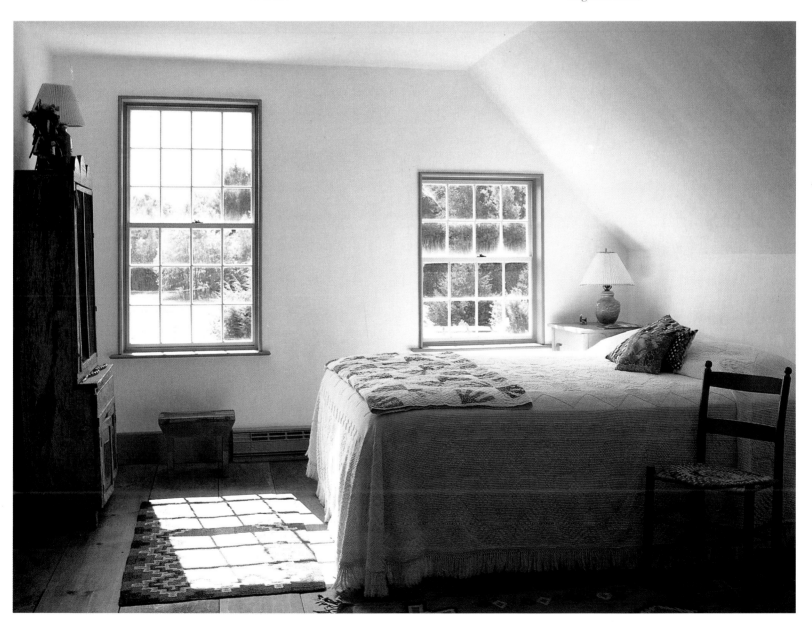

Bedrooms

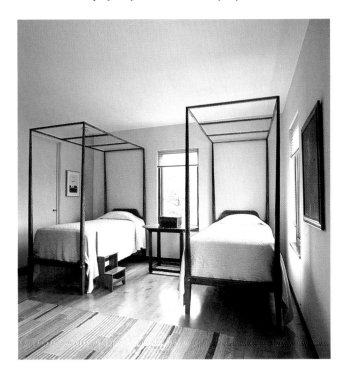

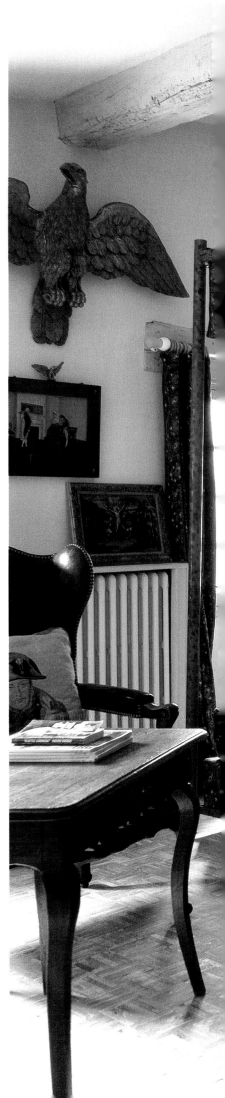

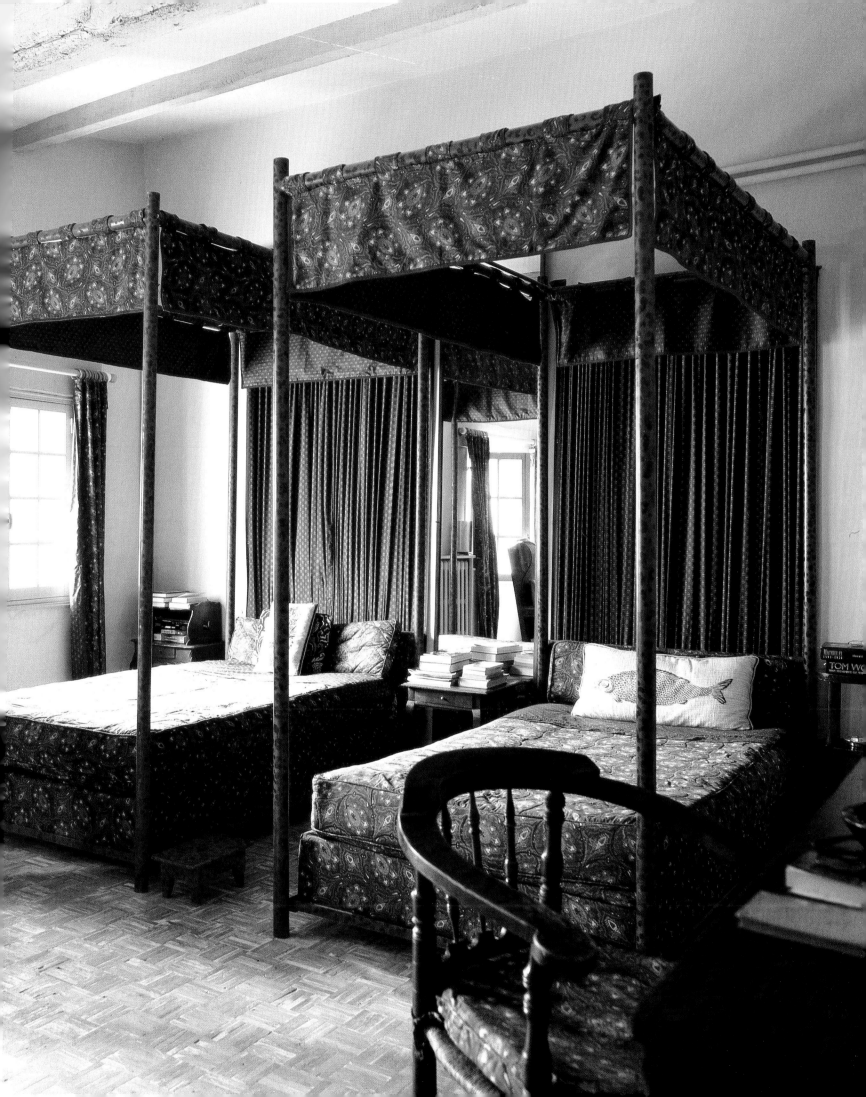

Bedrooms

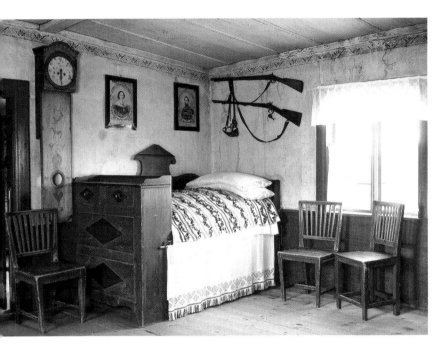

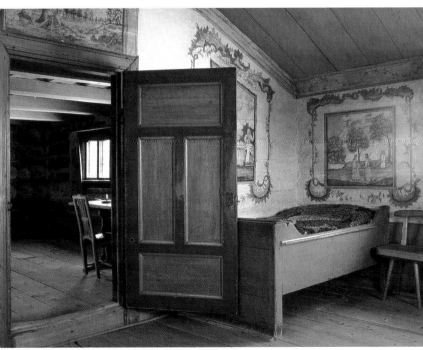

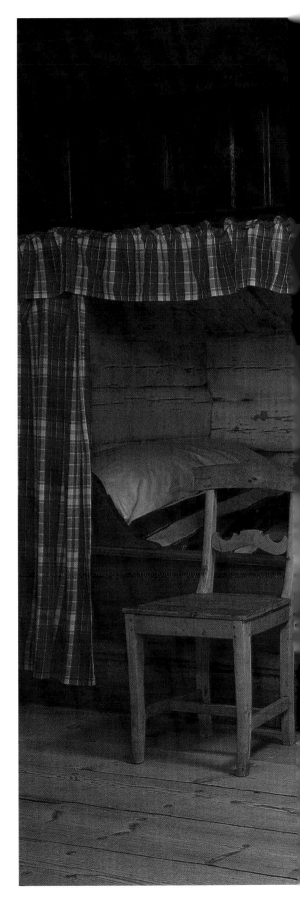

Right:
Country interiors make use of every inch of space. Between these two built-in beds in this 18th century Swedish farmhouse is a fitted cupboard. The wooden railed space at the bottom of the cupboard was used to house the poultry in the coldest winter spells.

Top left:
The Swedish painted pine box bed incorporates a chest at the end. It dates from the early 19th century, as do the clock and chairs.

Bottom left:
In Sweden, farmers used paint to imitate the lavish interior decor of the manor houses. These wall paintings were executed in distemper onto smooth wooden walls to give the impression of pictures in frames hung against wallpaper.

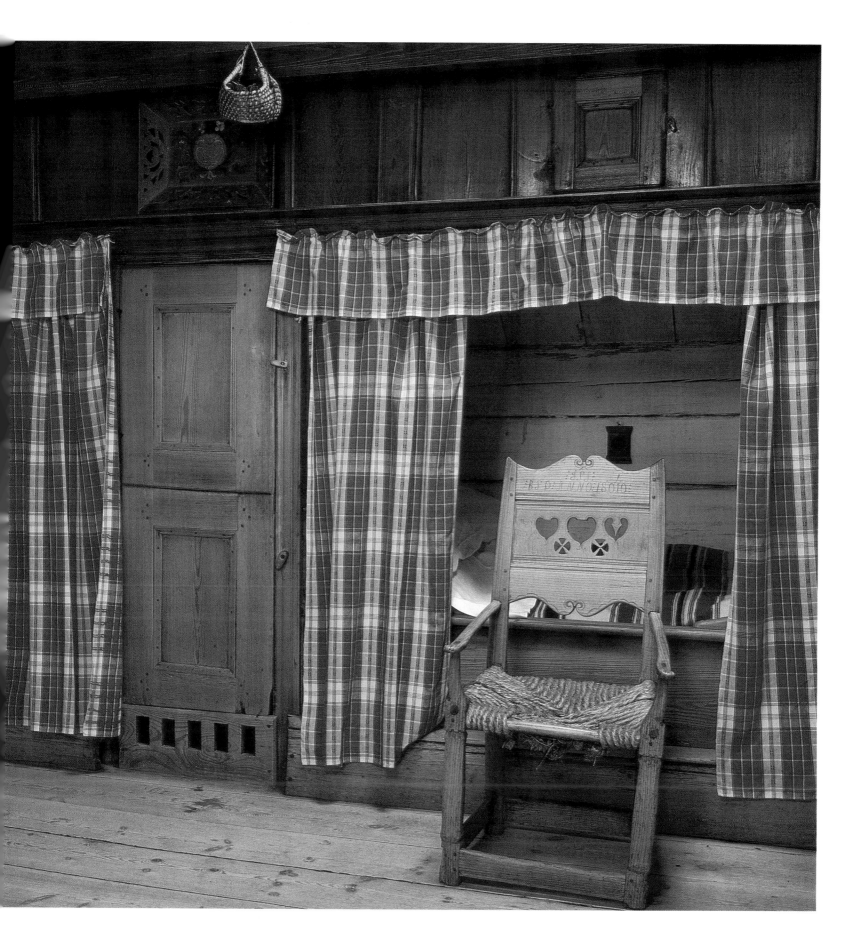

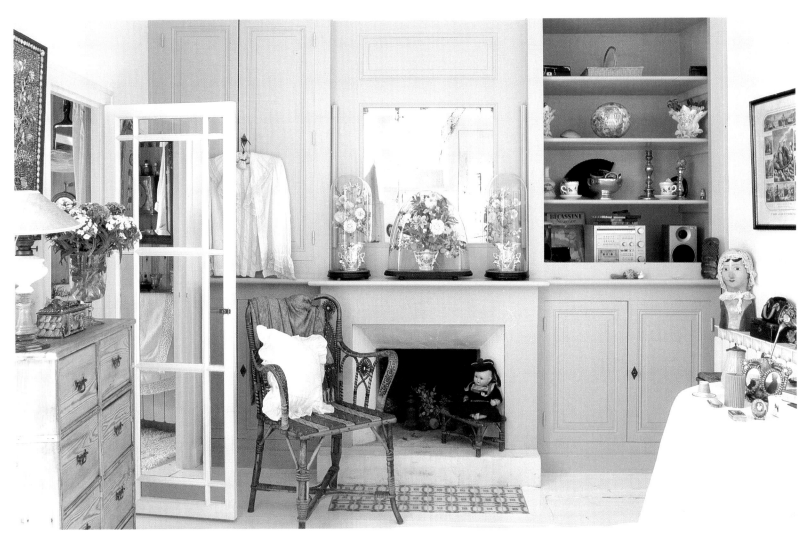

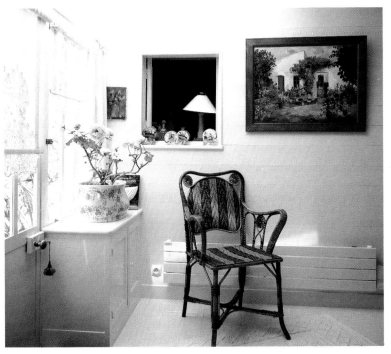

Above:
This restful blue-gray colour
scheme in a French home on the
Atlantic coast was inspired by
paintwork in a nearby church.

Right:
Drifts of crunchy white lace will
enhance any French or English-
style country bedroom.

Right:
Sail-like swathes of white fabric
curtain the glass roof of this
bedroom. The white bedspread,
floorboards and stair treads all
add to the sun-bleached seaside
look. The stairs lead up to an
eyrie-like study in the roof (see
page 34). Above the bed, a
porthole-shaped mirror provides a
nautical finishing touch.

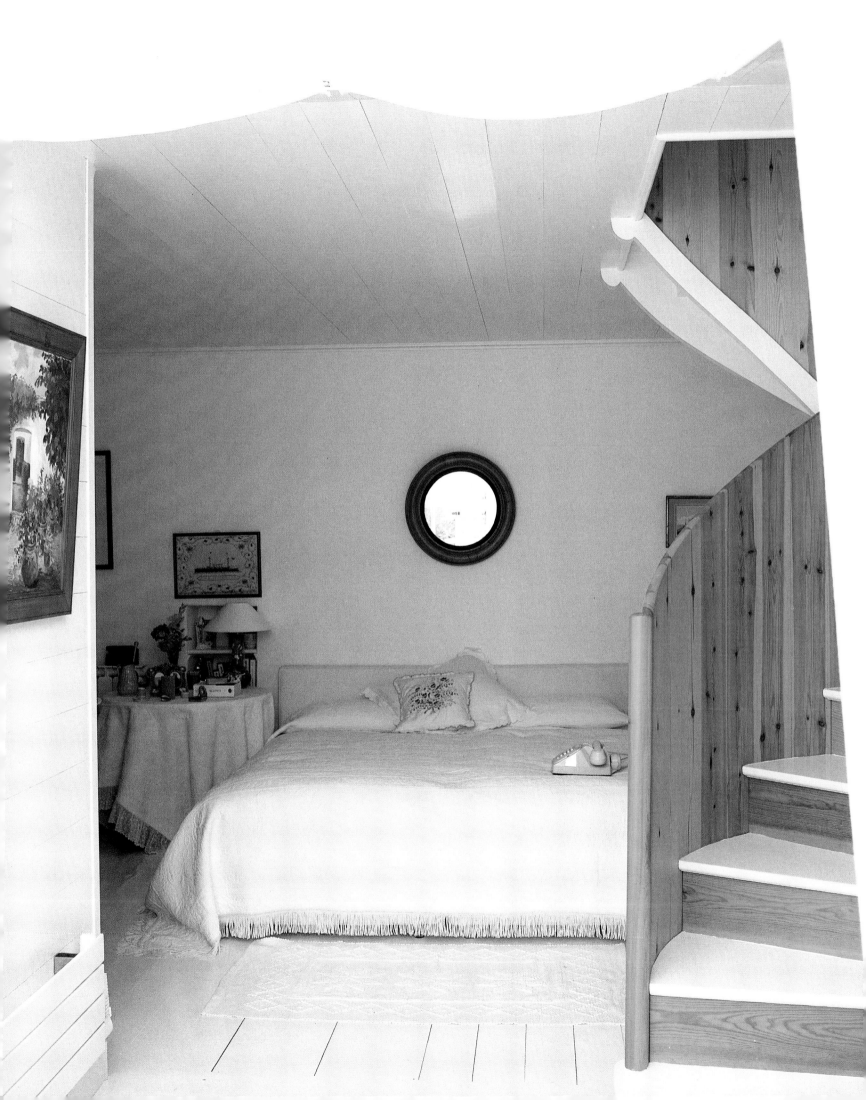

Bathrooms

Although the ancient Egyptians, Greeks and Romans had sophisticated systems of public and private baths, plumbing and aquaducts, most of Europe (and later America) failed to catch onto the idea of personal hygiene until the early 20th century. Only monasteries and great houses had plumbing systems – for example, 16th century Italian nobles had sumptuous bathrooms with hot and cold running water. Meanwhile, most country dwellers made do with a basin and pitcher of water, an outside privy or earth closet and the ubiquitous chamber pot. Ablutions were carried out at the most once a week, on washday, in a tin bath that was placed in front of the range. Often, the whole family bathed one after the other in the same water they had used for the weekly laundry! By the 19th century these arrangements were replaced with plumbed bathrooms in wealthier homes and the 20th century saw their spread to humbler dwellings. Inevitably, these improvements took place in the cities first, only reaching the countryside several years later.

Because the tradition of country bathrooms is so short, there are very few rules to base a room scheme on. As a result, in many homes country style stops at the bathroom door, where a modern look takes over. However, it seems a pity not to continue the mood of the house into the bathroom. The most important factor when designing a country-style bathroom is to consider how it will fit into the rest of the house. If the room has been converted from a bedroom in a large farmhouse, then the luxury of space will allow you to indulge in the most glorious amalgam of 20th century plumbing and 19th century comfort. A rolltop bath in the middle of the room and a glowing fire in a working fireplace will allow you to experience the romance of the cottager's tin bath in front of the range with none of the original discomfort. If space is at a premium, or a Victorian style unsuitable, you could install good quality modern fittings and decorate the walls with natural materials like wood-panelling in cooler climes or hand-fired tiles in warmer regions.

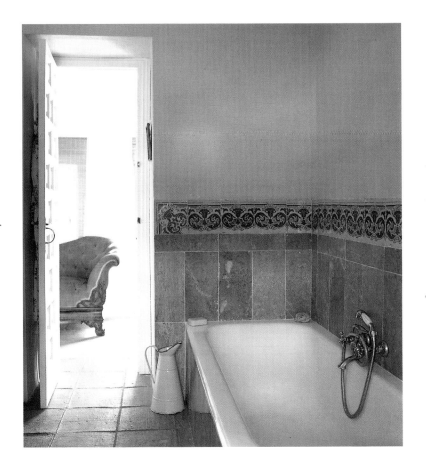

Right:
A country style bathroom should be unpretentious and uncontrived. This pleasing Spanish room, with its ochre-coloured walls, has a basic white bath framed by slips of local marble and a border of Andalucian tiles.

Right:
A restrained use of neutral colours maintains a country mood in this English cloakroom. White-painted tongue-and-grooved boards hide the plumbing, while the wooden floorboards are whitened with a proprietary woodstain. Black towels and basin brackets provide contrast and mahogany accessories warm the scheme.

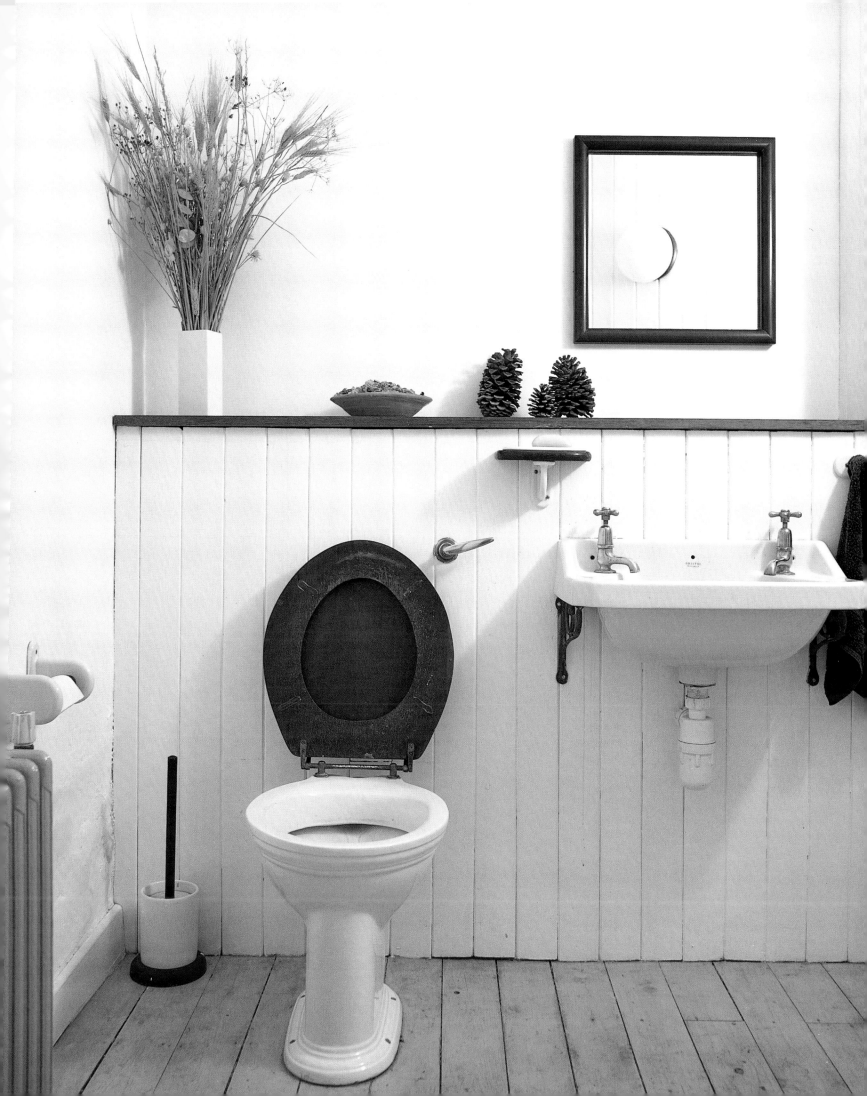

Bathrooms

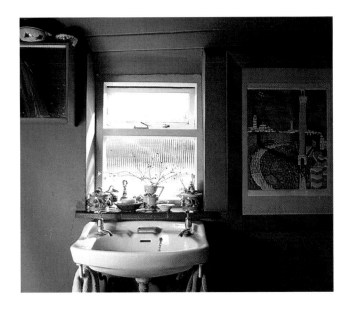

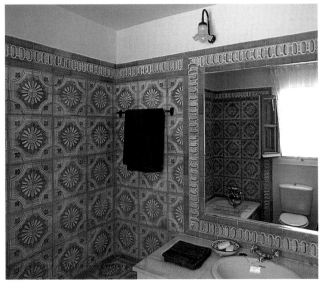

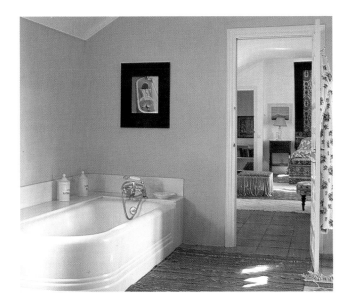

Left:
Glaze-bright colours warm a potter's English country cottage bathroom. The broad windowsill is a perfect resting place for pots that hold bathroom clutter.

Middle left:
A contemporary bathroom acquires a Spanish country atmosphere from modern tiles that are based on the colours and patterns of period faience.

Bottom left:
Walls in a strong Mediterranean blue and a kelim-covered floor enliven this ensuite bathroom, while coordinating it with the bedroom it leads off.

Right:
Wood panelling is more suitable than tiles in chilly English country bathrooms. Vibrant hand-painted decoration adorns the bath panel and chest in this room at Charleston, the country home of the Bloomsbury group.

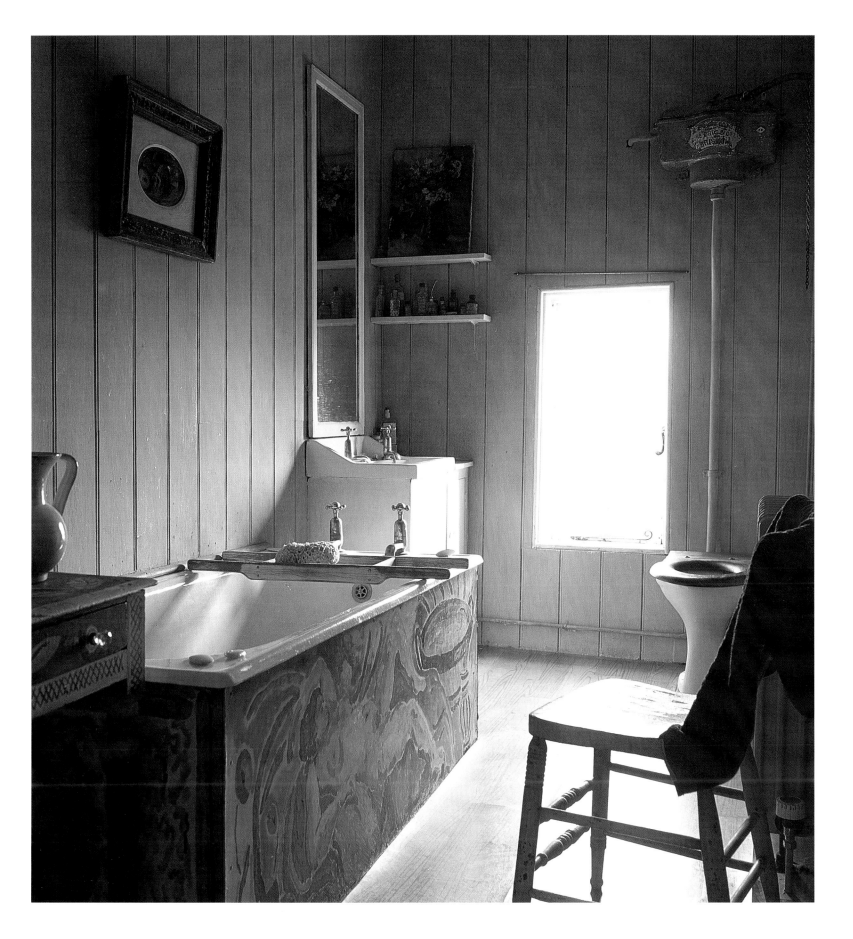

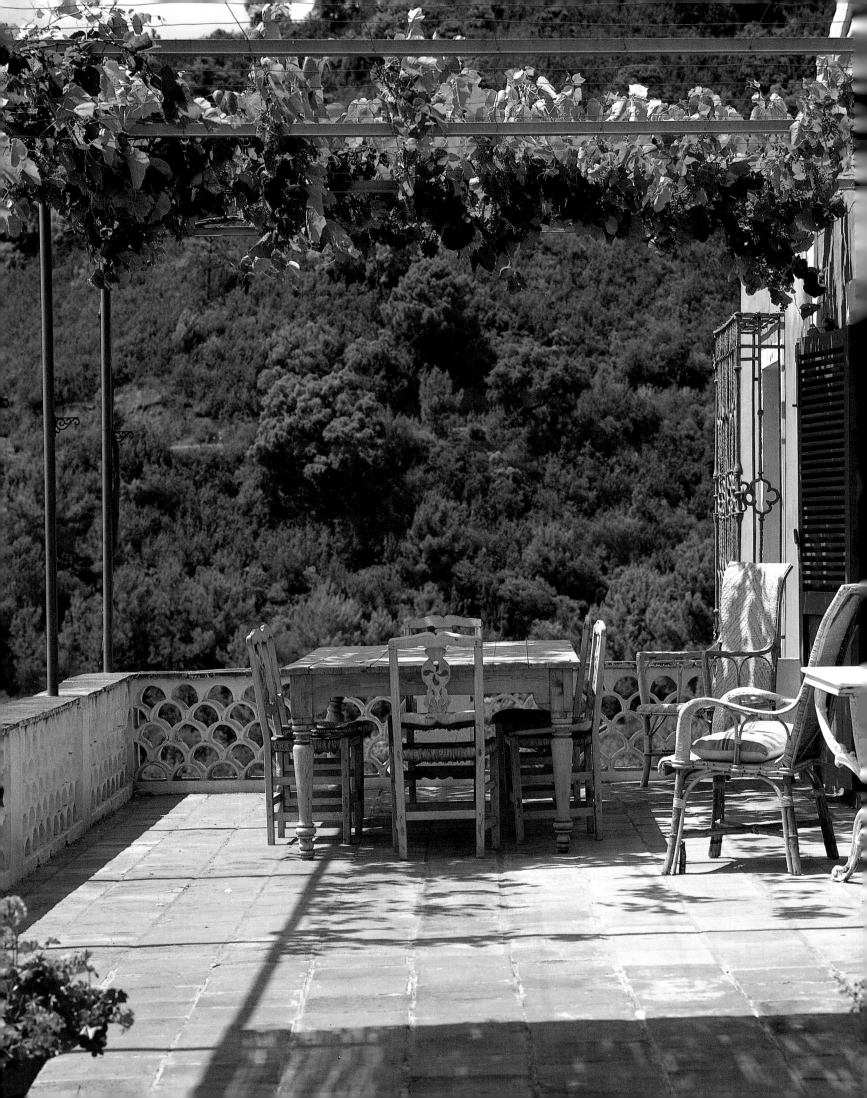

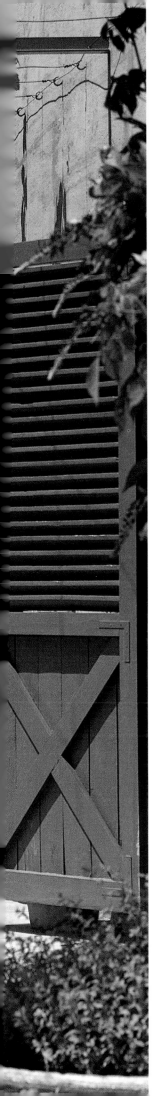

Inside, outside

*I*n hot countries eating in the open is part of everyday life. Simple ingredients served up in the fresh air make the perfect country lunch. Tables are permanently positioned in the full sun of the terrace or under the comfortable shade of an olive tree or grape vine, always ready for the next open-air meal. Verandahs give shelter from the heat of the sun; their screens keep out insects yet permit free passage to cooling breezes. Greenery softens sun-baked terraces – terracotta pots hold bay, or geraniums, daisies and drifts of scented herbs peep out between weathered slabs or tiles.

Cooler climes, with their uncertain weather, have created their own temperate zones by building porches, conservatories, sun rooms and summer houses. These sheltered spots allow occupants to sample the outdoors while protected from winds and rain. Furnishings should be weatherproof: chairs and tables that can be transported outdoors, yet suffer no ill-effects if left out in rain.

Left and below:
Terraces furnished with sun-bleached wooden furniture, and shaded from the blazing midday sun by a well-placed tree or a canopy of brushwood or vines, act as outdoor rooms.

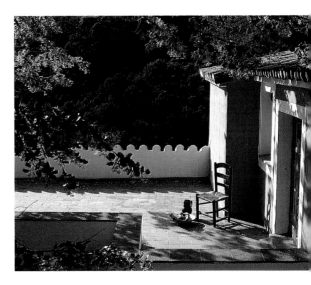

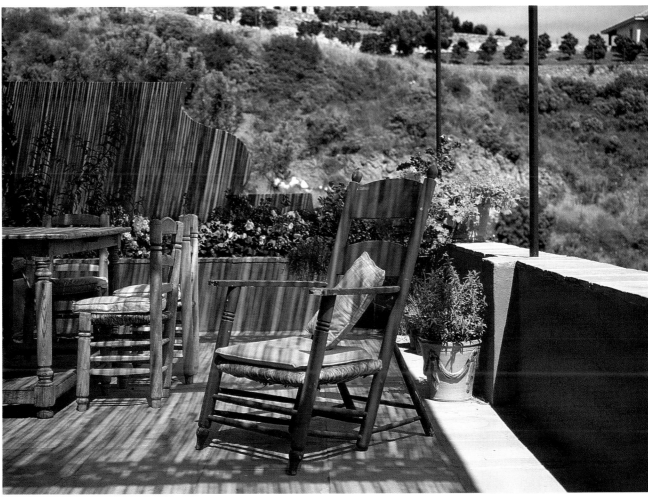

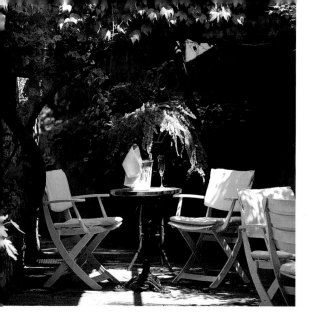
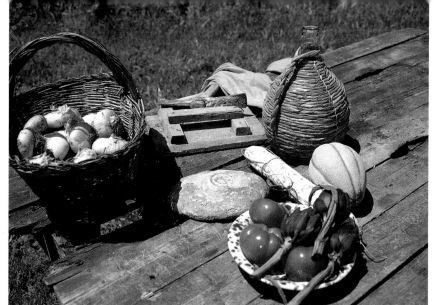
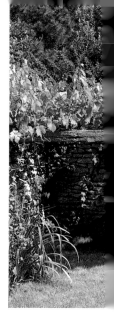
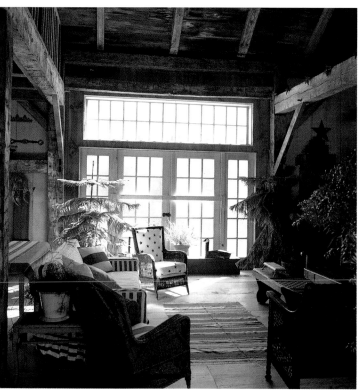
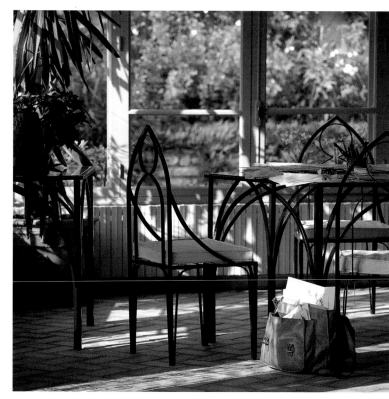
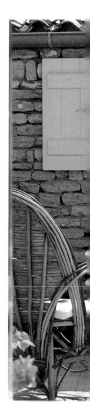

Top row, left to right:
A love of the country usually embraces a love of
the outdoors. In towns, a passion for nature is
expressed in well-tended gardens, verandahs or
roof terraces. These outdoor rooms draw the
living element of flowers, herbs and vegetables
into the home, just as country dwellers are
drawn outdoors whenever the weather permits.
Whether sampled in a country garden, suburban
conservatory or on a city roof terrace, an outdoor
repast is an essential component of this. The
other ingredients are sunshine, informal metal,
wood or wicker furniture, simple crockery and
hearty food and wine.

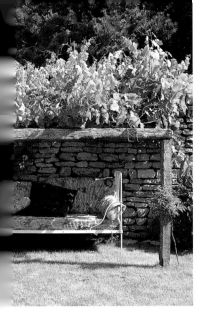

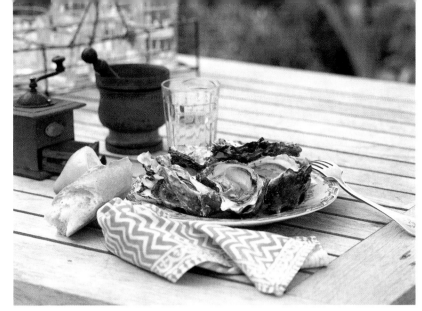

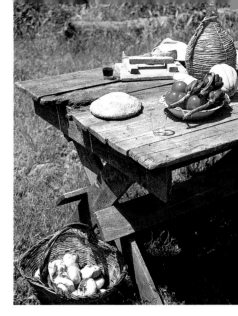

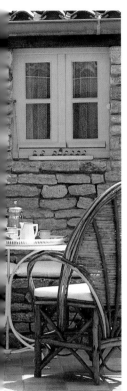

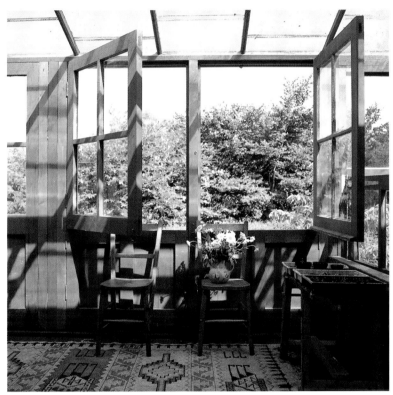

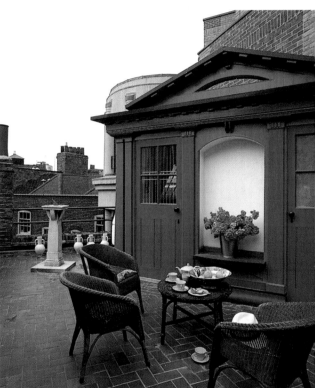

Bottom row, left to right:
Relaxation is the theme of rooms where inside
and outside meet. Capture this mood with well-
worn, comfortably cushioned furniture. For
example, in the French garden arbor, top row
third from left, an iron bedstead piled high
with cushions provides an improvized outdoor
couch. In cooler climes, conservatories
weatherproof outdoor living. Large windows
and an abundance of plants blur the distinction
between outdoors and inside. Adaptability,
another feature of country style, is seen fourth
from left, where cedarwood stable doors fold
back to transform a wintertime conservatory
into a summer sun-deck.

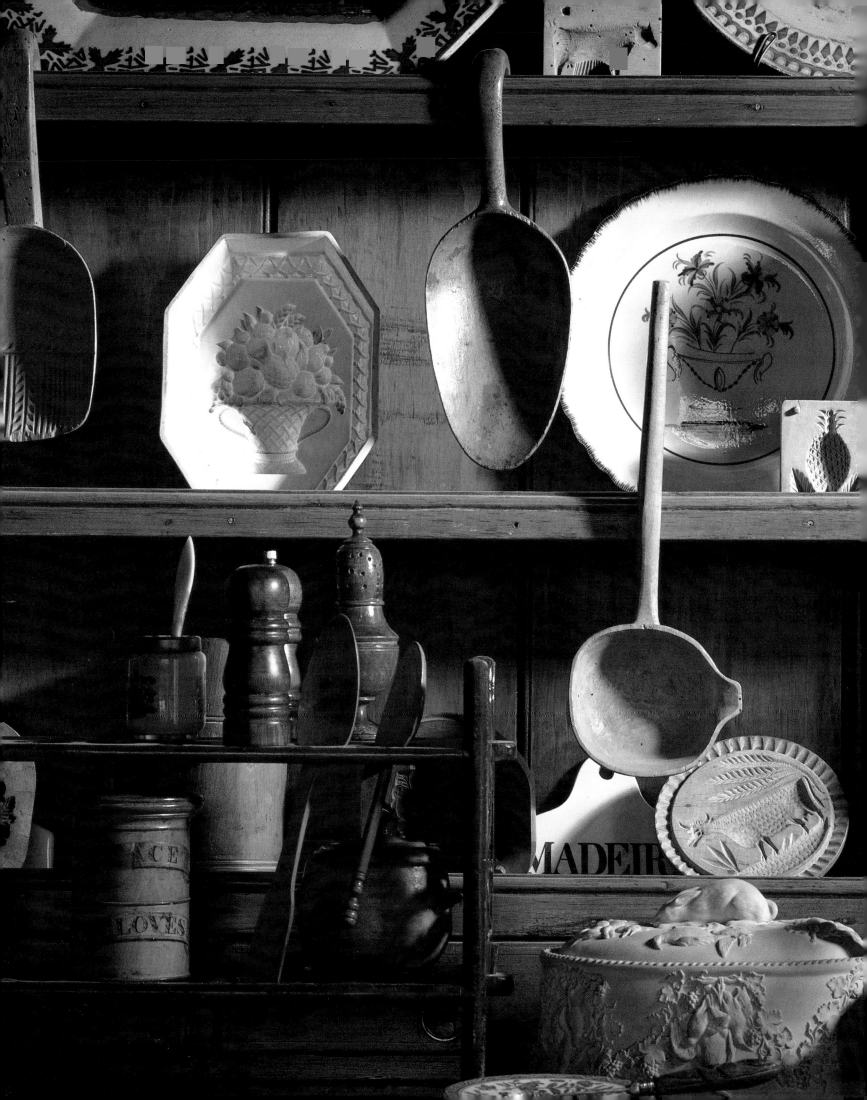

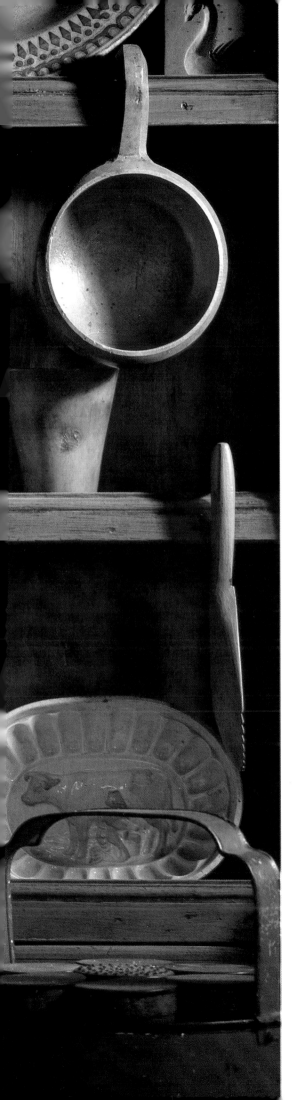

THE ELEMENTS
of Country Style

*C*hoosing the right ingredients is an essential part of creating a successful country style. The roots of the style are found in the rural past, when practicality and necessity dictated shape and form. Walls, woodwork, ceilings and floors should form an appropriate framework for furniture, fabrics and accessories. Take your pick of natural colours, from deep russets to palest sky blue, on simple materials like rough-hewn wood or uneven plaster. Then add vegetable-dyed fabrics, painted or mellow wood furniture and flowers from the local countryside for a harmonious whole.

When buying furnishings, there is no need to keep to a single period. Like the buildings, the elements that make an authentic country style room often span the centuries. You should always be aware of tradition, but you need never feel obliged to follow it slavishly. Country is a living style, not a carefully reconstructed slice of the past. Unlike formal period styles, there is no set of rules that dictates whether a particular piece of furniture or artefact is academically correct. Just as genuine country homes were furnished over the centuries, each generation making their own contribution to the character of the house, so country style today is layered with tradition and memories.

Left:
Country style eschews ornament for ornament's sake. Objects on display in country homes are always useful as well as beautiful. This detail closes in on the contents of the dining room dresser shown on page 55. Its collection of decorative culinary objects includes Portuguese majolica, 18th century English pearlware plates, English saltglaze jelly moulds and 19th century treen butter moulds and scoops.

Furniture

*I*n traditional country interiors much of the furniture would be handed down or made by local craftsmen to designs that did not change for centuries. Simple rustic furniture from different periods, and even from different countries, will happily mix together. Although country furniture was utilitarian, it was not necessarily without ornamentation. The solid, practical pieces were often painted, both to cover the deficiencies of the wood and for the sheer joy of decoration. On some of the most delightful pieces layers of paint are partly worn away to reveal a patchwork of faded colours and raw wood. This look can be copied to improve pieces that look too new. Apply different-coloured coats patchily onto the bare wood, then paint on an even top coat. Rub the paint with damp wet-and-dry paper to reveal colour and grain. Years of continuous use can be simulated by rubbing through to the grain in the areas of most wear. Handle the piece to find where grimy fingers mark doors or drawers, and don't forget to replicate the scuff marks near ground level and the chipped paintwork at corners and edges.

Below:
Contemporary American Shaker furniture has the timeless elegance shared by all well-crafted country pieces. Shaker furniture can be purchased from specialist outlets (see Directory).

Right:
This dark-stained 18th century American ladderback chair originated from the Shenendoah Valley in Virginia. It has a seat that is woven from pliable wood strips.

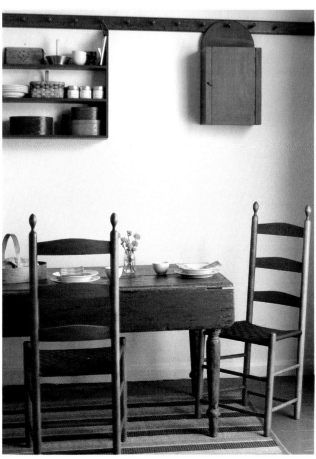

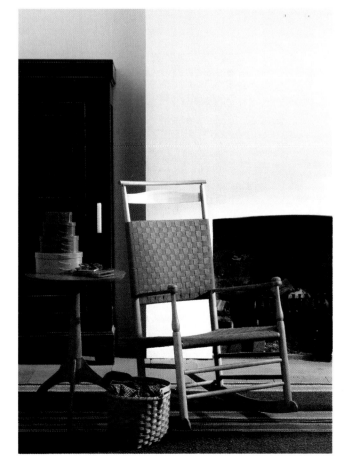

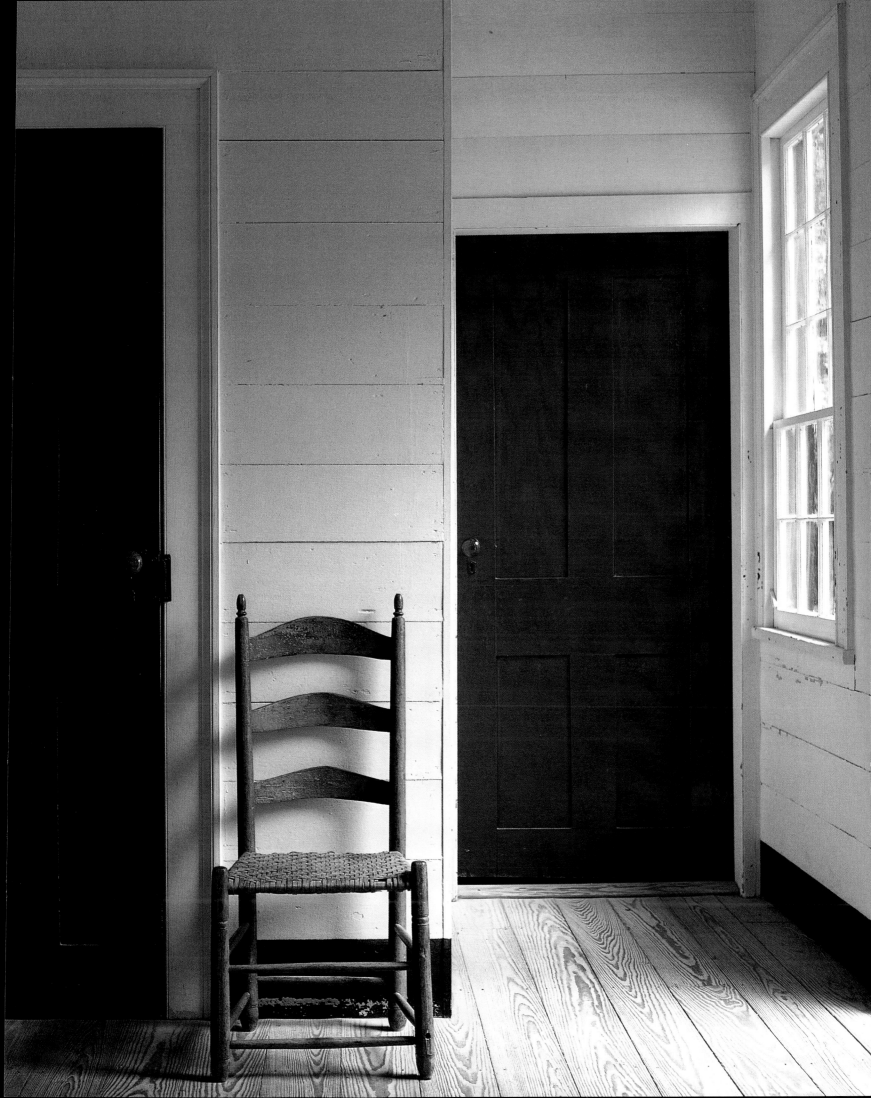

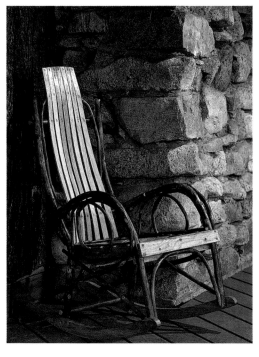

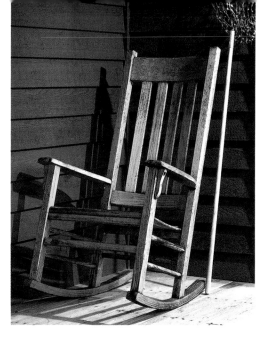

Above and right:
Modern Amish (above) and rustic style (right)
chairs are ideal to furnish an American
country porch or verandah.

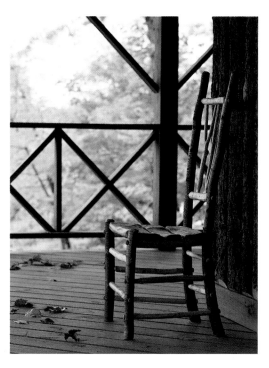

Above:
American Adirondack furniture makers (see
page 146) incorporated organic forms such as
twigs, branches and tree roots into their rustic
designs.

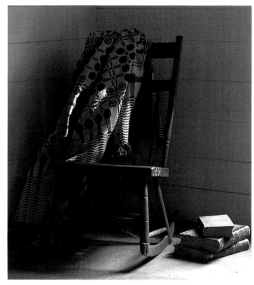

Right:
This rustic style table with a twisted root base,
dating from circa 1900, was made for an
Adirondack cabin at Raquette Lake, New York
State, America.

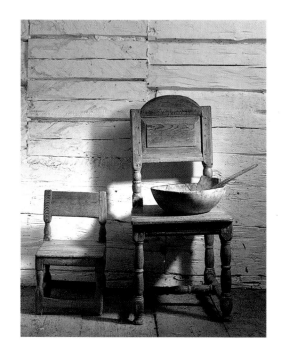

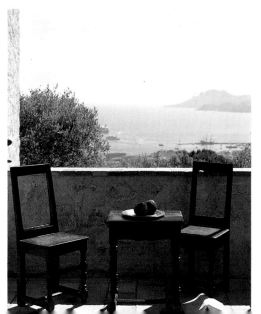

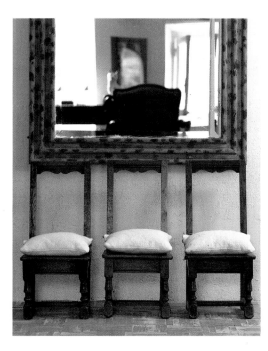

Above:
Rocking chairs like this 19th century one were
an American innovation.

Above:
These rough-hewn mid-19th century pieces from
Sweden are typical of Scandinavian farm
furniture.

Left and above:
Many French chairs seem too elaborate for
country homes, but these 17th century oak ones
are ideal.

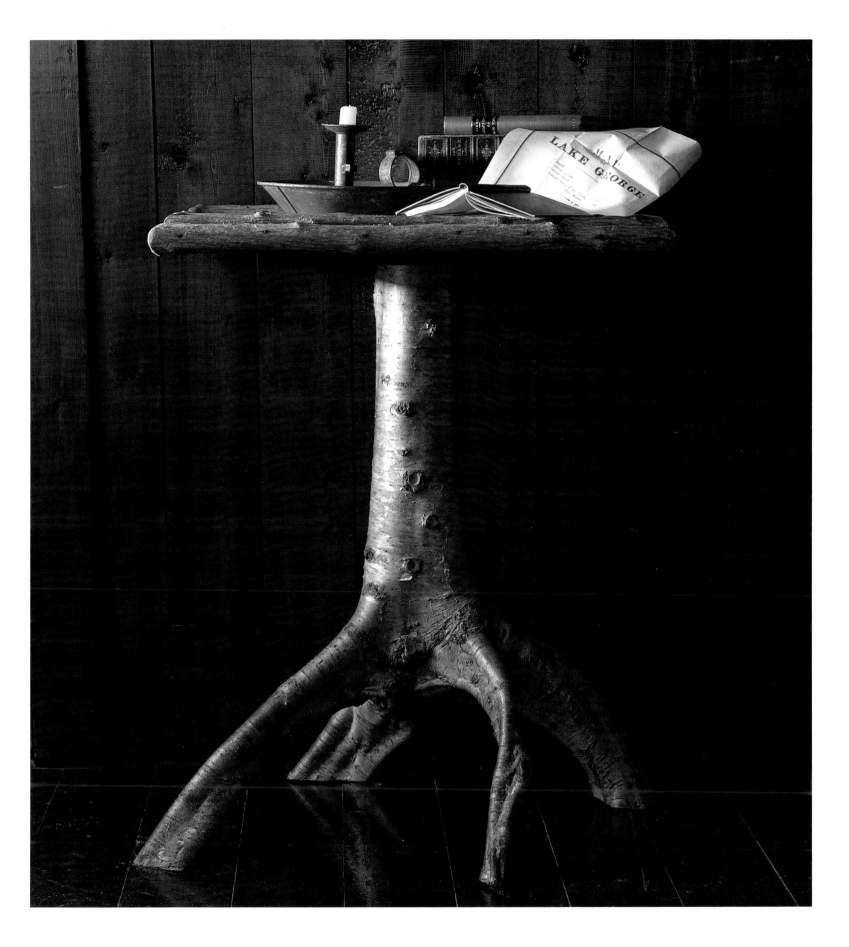

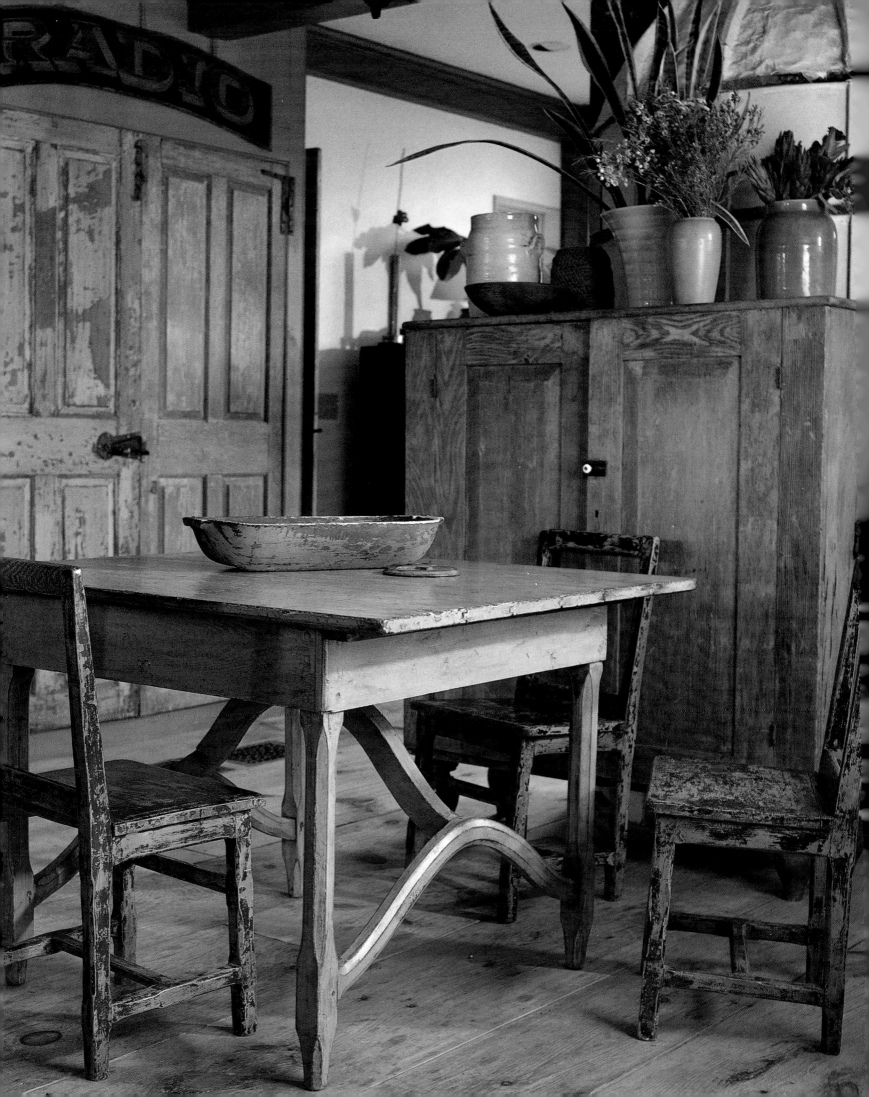

Furniture

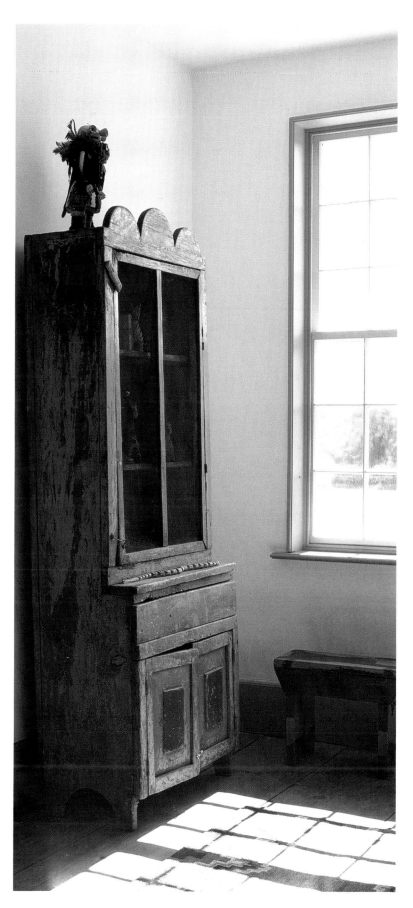

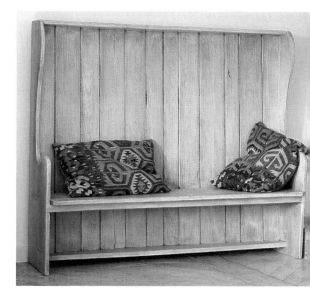

Top right:
This English
mahogany settle was
stripped and then
painted with a white
wood stain. The
stain reacted with
the new wood, giving
the piece a ghostly
blue tone. Although
this was not the
intended result, it is
a mistake that works.

Far left:
This Canadian late
18th century table
and chairs are a
delightful example
of the appeal of a
time-worn painted
finish.

Middle right:
The patina of this
18th century English
fruitwood chair
contrasts with the
scarred paint of the
time-worn dresser.

Bottom right:
An 18th century
French walnut buffet
laden with antique
pewterware.

Left:
Folk furniture, like
this brightly painted
Mexican cupboard
paired with a
Jamaican stool, suits
country style homes.

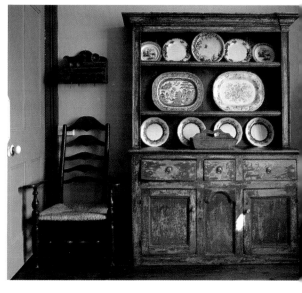

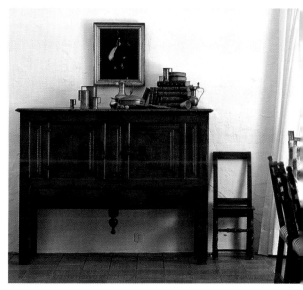

Walls

Below:
Milk paint was used as a flat coat for everything from walls to furniture. Its soft, rich colours have a beauty that ready-mixed paints rarely achieve; they seem to have been mellowed by the years. You can buy milk paint or mix your own. Use equal parts buttermilk or skim milk, lime and pigment and strain to remove lumps.

Right:
Mellow wooden walls are common in American and Scandinavian country homes.

Almost any colour can be used to decorate country walls – it is the way that it is handled, the rough, thick strokes, the easy-going attitude to layers of paint and bulging surfaces, which give them that authentic country look. Earth colours – terracottas, ochres, browns and greens – all blend well with country furniture. In hot countries white spiced with bright colours will freshen a dry, arid environment. While in cooler climates choose between maximizing the hours of daylight by using pale shades or bringing in warmth with rich shades that contrast with the chill of the outside world.

The surface of internal walls will vary, depending on local materials and building traditions. You may find rough stone, untreated or painted brick, wood, plaster, cob or

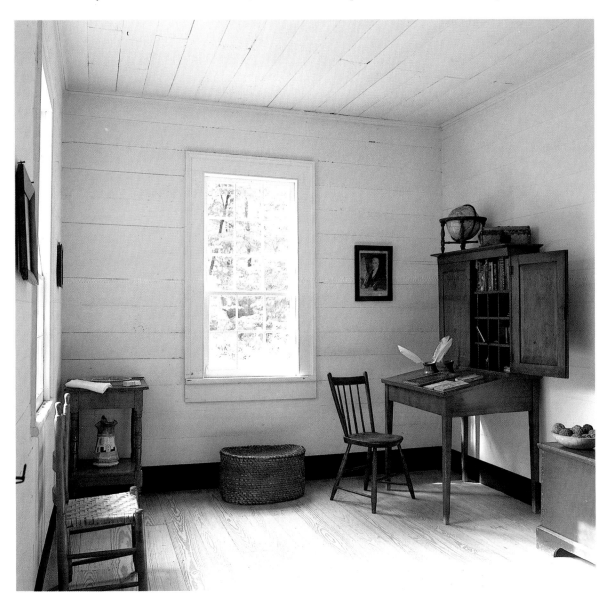

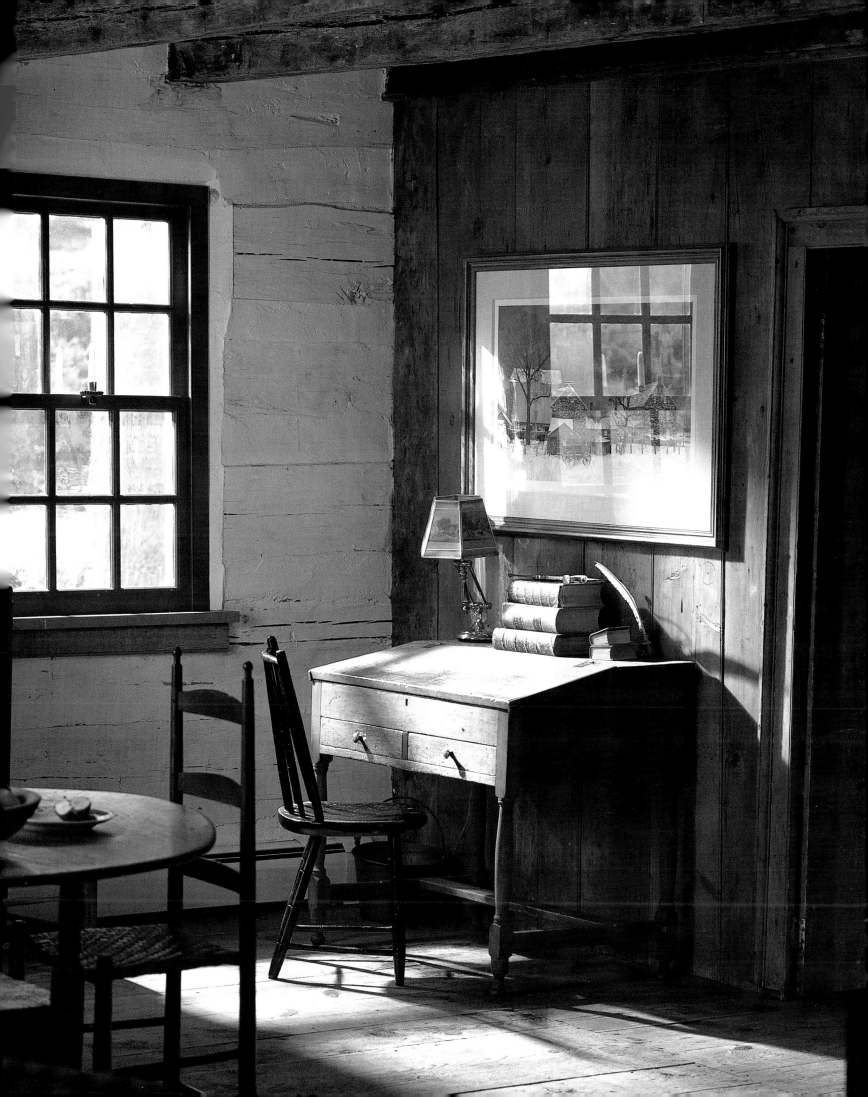

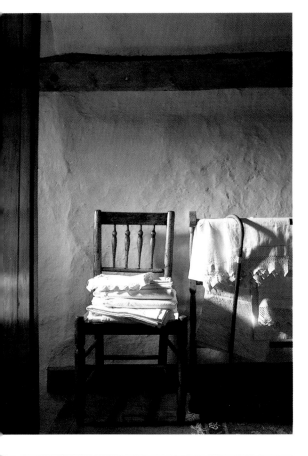

Limewash gives an excellent finish to period walls.

Right:
You can mix your own limewash by adding water to quicklime. Wear protective gloves and goggles as the mixture will bubble and spit. The mix cools to form a thick putty which you then further dilute to the consistency of thin cream by adding more water. Tint this with brick clay for pinky shades and yellow ochre for cream.

Left:
You must mix enough limewash for the whole room as a second batch will never be quite the same colour.

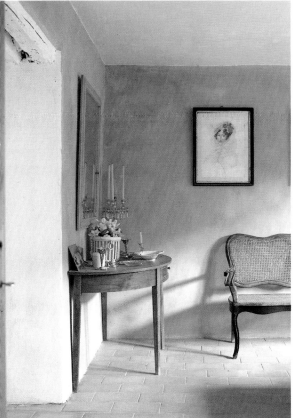

marble. If your country house is a period building, research is necessary before you decorate. Horror stories abound of untold damage caused by owners who did not pay heed to age-old ways. For example, in an English cob house (see p. 49), with its walls filled with a mixture of clay subsoil and chopped straw, a modern paint used inside or out will create a waterproof layer that will encourage condensation and cause great damage to the structure. Instead, such houses should be painted with limewash, a material that dates back to 8,000 BC, doesn't bubble or blister and allows walls to breathe so that damp and minerals can pass through. Specialist suppliers sell limewashes ready for use (see Directory), or you can make your own.

For newer houses there are a number of finishes that will create a country look. You can simulate a rough plaster finish by spreading a thin layer of all-purpose plaster filler or spackle on the wall, with a spatula or filling knife, in random directions. Once dry, colour it using the dry brush technique. Brush on a base coat in a rich shade of water-based paint, working it well into the texture of the plaster, and leave to dry. Dip a fresh brush into white or slightly tinted water-based paint, wipe most of this paint off on waste paper then stroke the brush across the surface of the plaster finish to tone down the base shade. Keep adding dry brush layers until you have created the appropriate dusty bloom of colour.

Another effect worth trying is colourwashing, which imbues even new plasterwork with the appearance of gentle weathering by time and the sun. The method is extremely simple – over a dry, light-coloured base coat apply a very dilute water-based paint colour in generous, random brushstrokes. Let it dry and then apply a second coat to soften and blur any patchiness to a watercolour texture. To colourwash wooden walls brush water-based matte white paint, thinned one to five with water, onto the bare wood to soften the grain. When dry, paint over again in your chosen colour, using a water-based paint, thinned one to five. While this coat is still wet, soften the effect by brushing over it with a dry brush. When completely dry, the wood can be sanded, waxed and polished.

Stencilling can be most effective if you choose traditional designs, whether stylized or naturalistic, that are taken from nature – berries, leaves, flowers or animals.

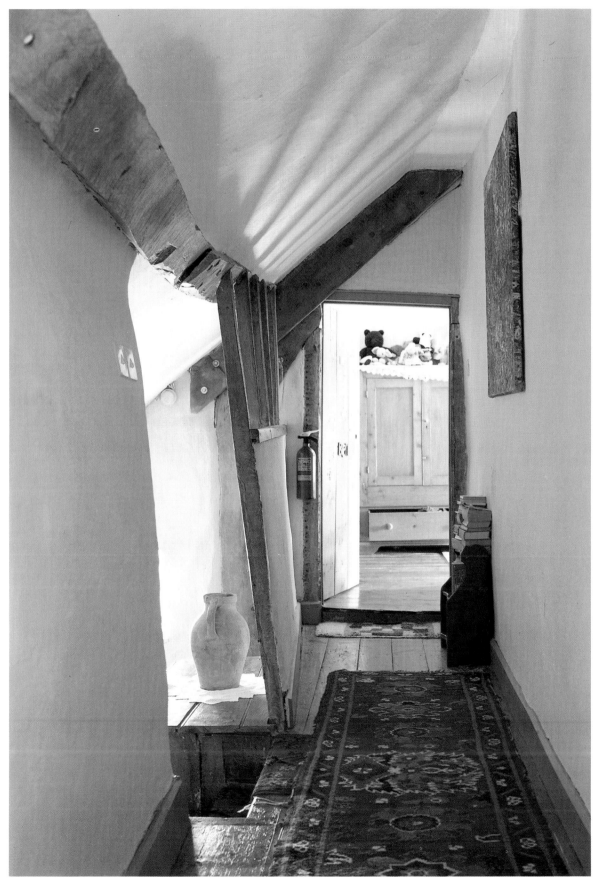

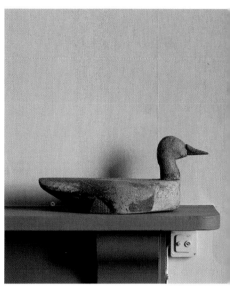

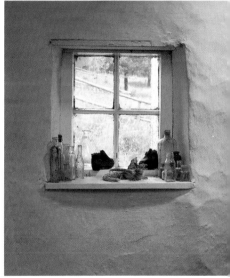

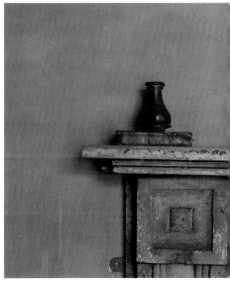

Walls

214

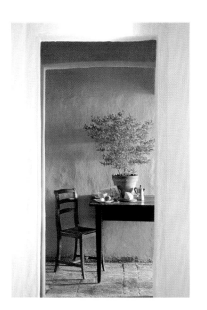

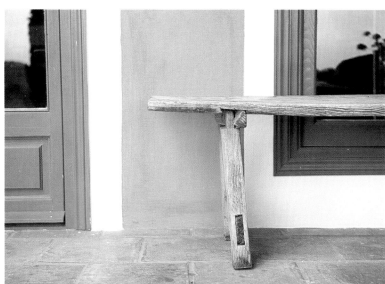

Far right:
Soft, aged shades have been used
to decorate this Canary Islands
salon. The blue-painted woodwork
was scrubbed with soap and water
and then darkened by rubbing in
an oil-based glaze tinted with
burnt sienna oil paint.

Right and below:
Rich colours like these jewel-bright
greens and blues can be found on
Mediterranean walls.

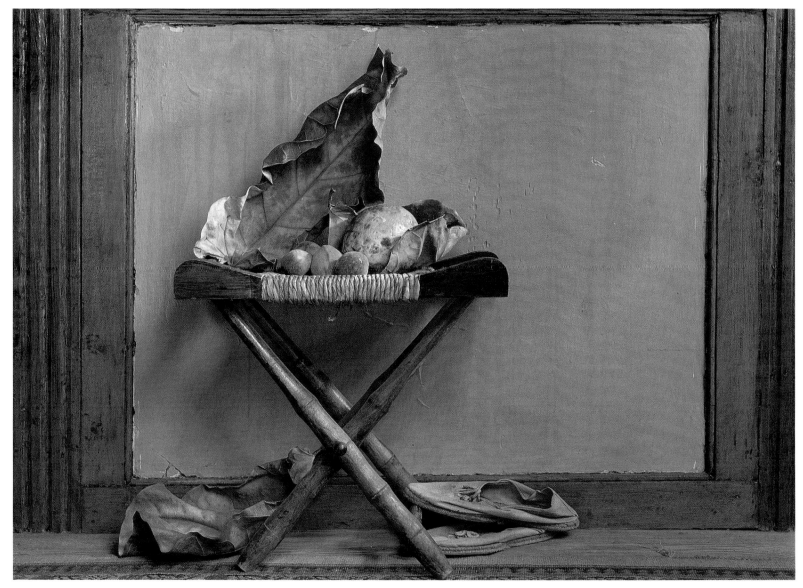

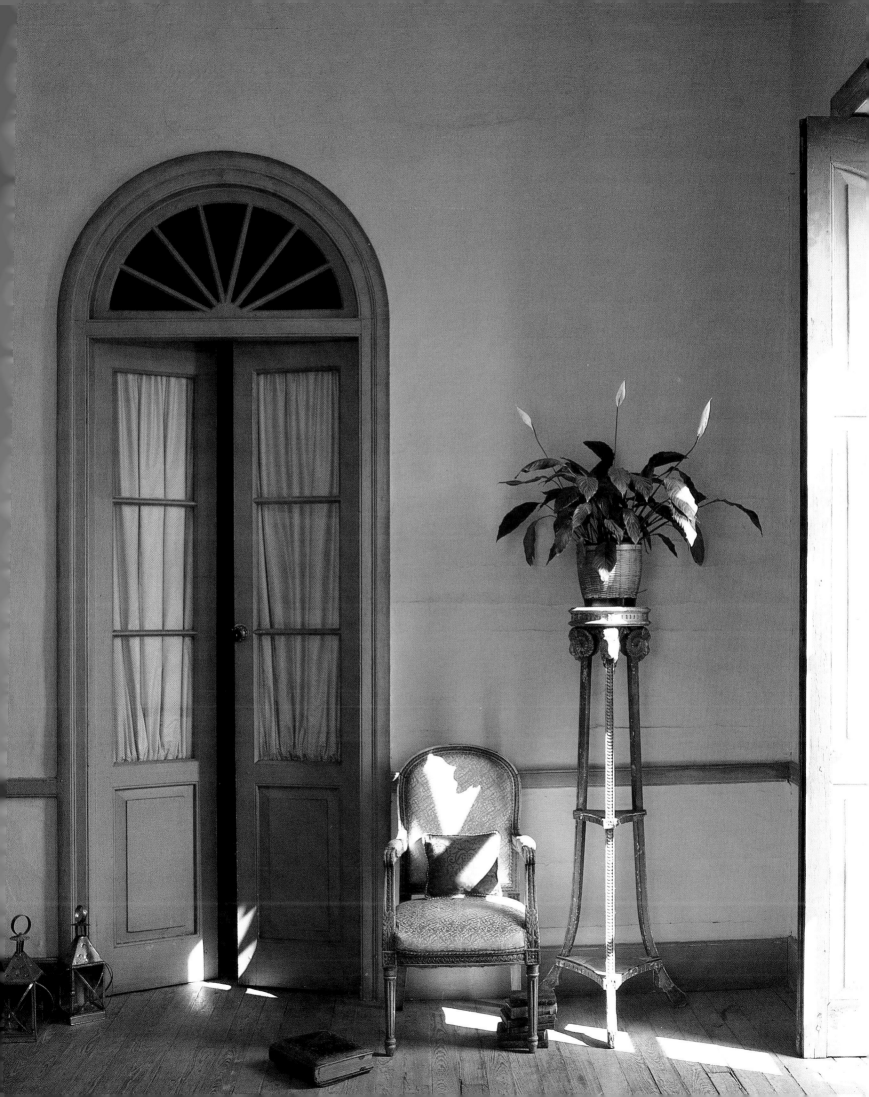

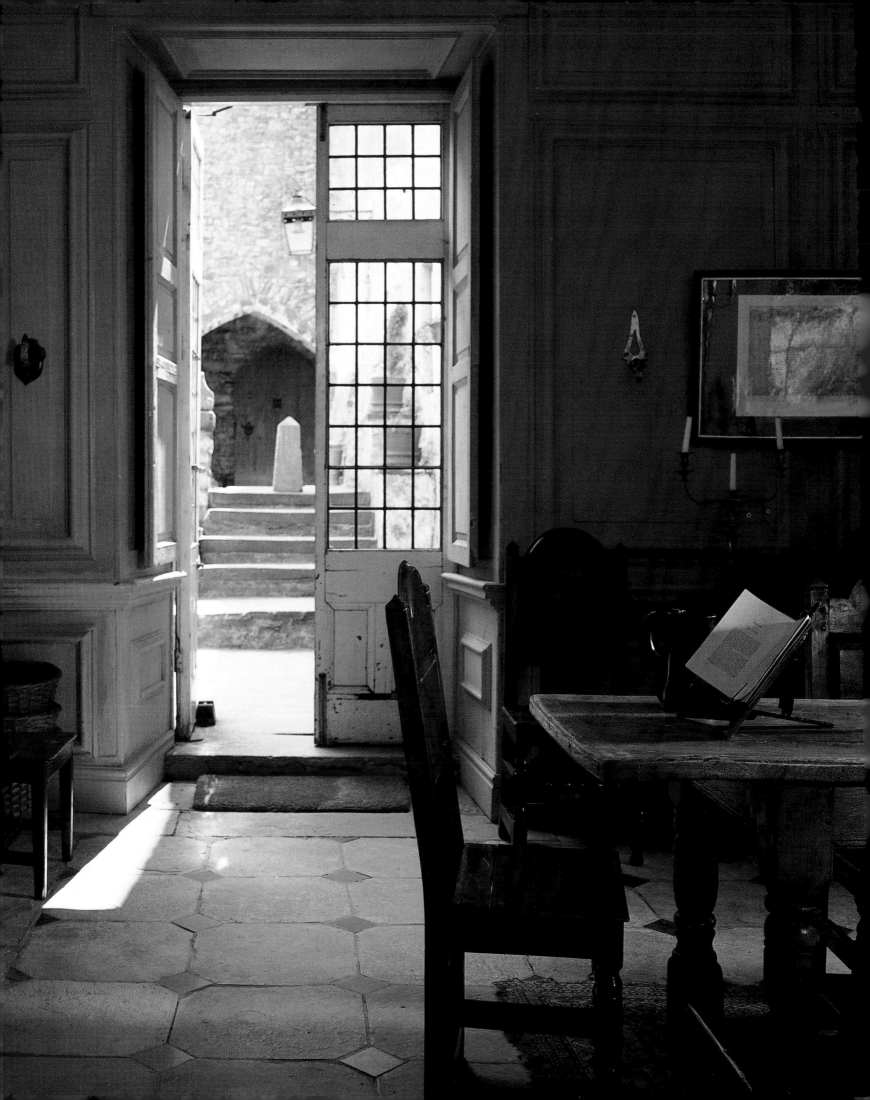

Floors

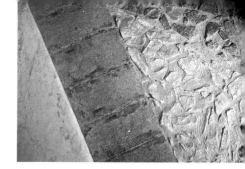

Floors have come a long way since their medieval beginnings as a "marsh" of beaten earth littered with rushes and straw. The hard floors which replaced them are made from a range of materials according to region. In northern, central and western England flagstones are used, whereas in the south and east quarry tiles, bricks or pamments (the East Anglian version of the French Provençal tiles that look like squares of terracotta) are laid. Like Provence, Italy and Spain also use terracotta tiles, but in the rest of France black and white tiles are more usual. The timber-rich Scandinavian countries favour painted or scrubbed wooden floors topped with long, narrow handwoven runners (see page 128). In much of America too, hardwood forests provide the materials for polished floors topped with hooked rugs or painted floorcloths (see pages 156-7).

In old Scandinavian homes the wooden floors were cleaned by rubbing a wet paste of sand into the planks. Over the years, the floors bleached to a pale, matte colour. A similar effect can be achieved by bleaching or pickling. To bleach a wooden floor first strip the old varnish, then scrub bleach into the grain, leaving it for about 15 minutes to take effect and then rinsing off the residue. Repeat this process until the desired lightness is achieved. Then neutralize the surface with a solution of one part vinegar to one part water, rinse with water and leave to dry. For a pickled look, simply paint the floor white or cream and then wipe off most of the paint with a clean, dry rag, working against the grain. This leaves a film of colour over the surface, with more paint filling the crevices and grain.

If you are fortunate enough to inherit a genuinely old floor, resist the temptation to even out any imperfections. And if the floor has to be lifted to lay a damp-proof course it should be relaid with some small irregularities so that it still has original charm. If you don't have a period floor you can lay reclaimed or new tiles or rush matting. Until the middle of the 17th century rush matting was the most common covering for hard or wooden floors. To this day, matting is available in a variety of textures and colours, ranging from pale greenish-cream to mid-brown. That rushes, an integral element of medieval flooring, should later be woven into a substantial material which has remained in use to the present day is symbolic of the timelessness of country style.

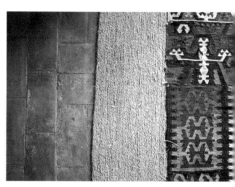

Right, top to bottom:
This detail of a Spanish floor shows a section of its stone chip pattern that is edged in brick.

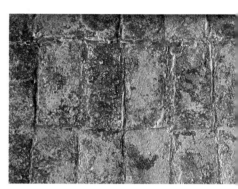

Kelims, or any good woven rug, should not be placed directly on top of boards or tiles because the ridges of the flooring will damage them. Use matting or a purpose-made liner in between rug and floor.

Well-worn brick floors are found in many country homes.

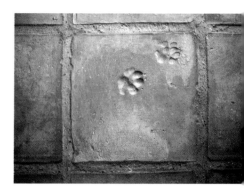

In Spain, laying a tile marked by a cat's paw into a terracotta floor is reputed to bring good luck.

Laying a terracotta-tiled floor will create instant country ambience.

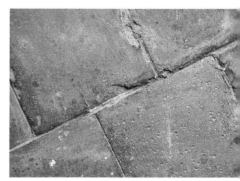

An original country floor made from stamped earth.

Left:
A limestone flagged floor is an attractive feature in many larger English country farmhouses.

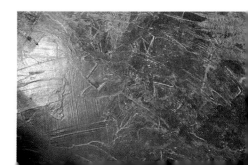

Ceilings

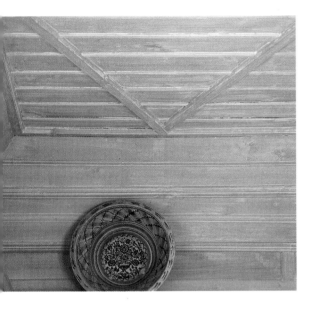

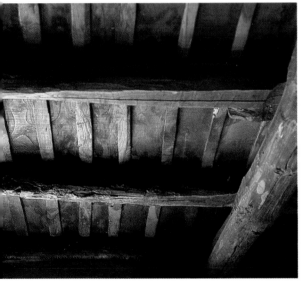

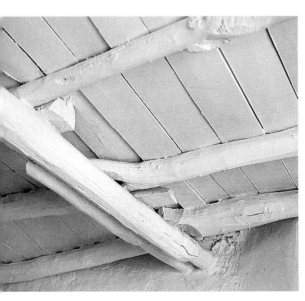

*C*ountry ceiling finishes vary from highly ornamented plasterwork to the unfinished surface that is quite simply the underside of the floor above, complete with exposed joists and floorboards. In converted barns or cottages, ceilings usually match the rest of the building – uneven, irregular and full of character. Resist the temptation to square up old, sloping cottage ceilings as they contribute strongly to the rustic feel of the house.

Try to find out exactly what would be the authentic ceiling for your property. Exposed structural beams or joists should be left in as natural a state as possible. This may mean stripping the wood of inappropriate paints or treacly varnishes. If it is necessary to replace missing or damaged beams use old wood salvaged from other buildings of a similar period. The ceiling is extremely important to the whole appearance of a room and if it is given the wrong finish the whole ambience may well be spoiled.

Even if your house is new, you should strive for imperfection. Country style is the evocation of the humble craftsmanship of working peasants and farmers and is characterized by the slightly uneven handiwork of men who built their own homes with simple tools and local materials.

Top left:
This replacement wooden ceiling in a 19th century house in Spain reconstructs the original design. The wood was painted with limewash, which was rubbed back to give an aged effect.

Middle and bottom left:
A very basic construction in a Spanish cottage. Logs and rough-hewn planks form a ceiling. In the bottom version the planks are also the floor of the room above, while in the middle example additional floorboards are laid on top of them.

Right:
A classic English beamed ceiling in a 16th century farmhouse.

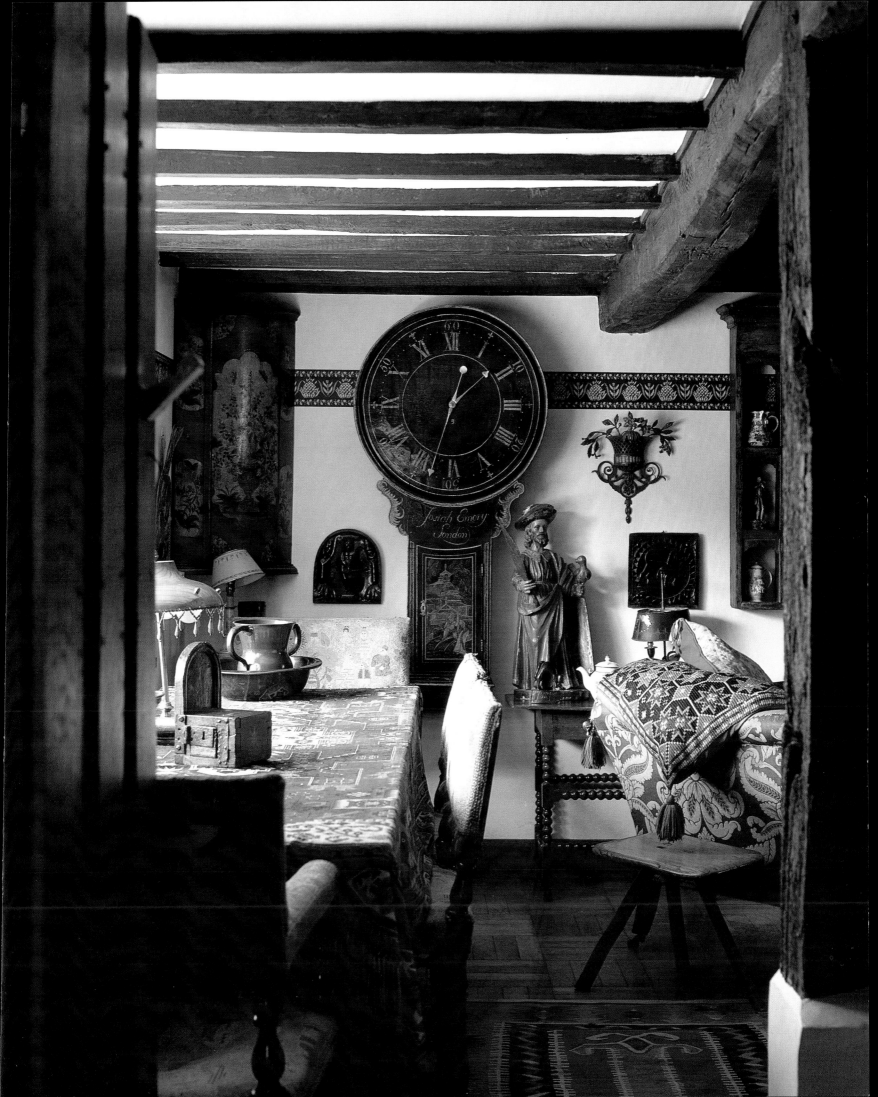

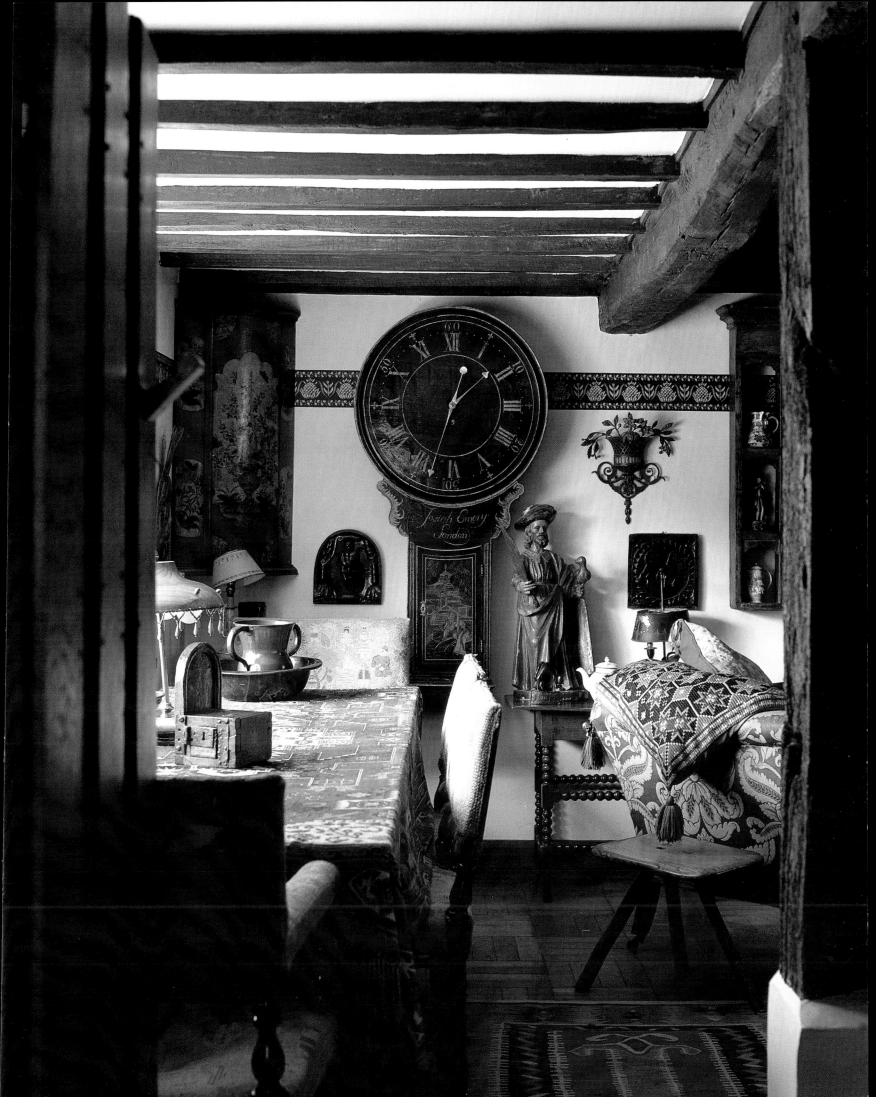

Woodwork

Right:
A natural oak stable door with iron hinges and latches is set against milk-painted (see page 210) wall panelling in this late 18th century American country home.

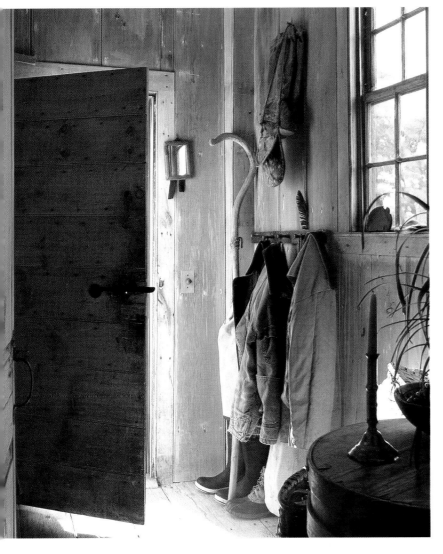

Above:
Whittled wooden coat pegs complement the natural wood-panelled walls and door in this 18th century American mud room.

*M*uch original woodwork has been destroyed in the name of improvement and modernization. And neglect has had its toll too, with damage by weather, rot or insects inflicting irreparable damage. If previous modernization to your country home was carried out inexpensively, original features may remain. For example, old panelled doors and turned staircase balustrades were often made flush with sheets of board and you can prize these off gently to reveal hidden delights beneath.

If woodwork has been ripped out you will need to replace it. You should start by researching the appropriate styles for the period of your house. Make sure that your selection is appropriate for your home's location, too. For example, until well into the 19th century almost all houses were fitted with security shutters. These were installed either inside or outside the house depending on the practice of the region. If you want to replace missing shutters you should find the appropriate design for your area. Do not confuse genuine shutters with the pseudo-country slatted louvres sometimes fixed either side of a window. Without hinges, and rarely of sufficient size to cover the opening, these "improvements" have no discernible purpose and should be removed.

Of all the original joinery in houses, doors probably survived in the largest quantities, yet they have suffered from fashion too. The recent trend for stripped pine does not create an authentic period door. Most softwood doors were intended to be protected by several coats of flat lead paint and then varnished. Because of this the craftsmen who made them did not strive for the same perfection to the finish that they would have with a hardwood. In addition, clumsy gauging of paint from mouldings and the caustic action of the stripping bath itself have detrimental effects on the appearance of the door. If you inherit such doors it is more in keeping to restore the original paintwork. Although lead paint is controversial – it has long been the subject of a campaign to ban its use – it has properties that modern paints do not: greater durability, better period colours, and it ages well. Unlike modern paint, lead paint doesn't seal the wet in but breathes and decomposes very gently and therefore is less liable to encourage rot. If you choose to use lead paint for conservation work, you can obtain it from specialist suppliers (see Directory).

Woodwork

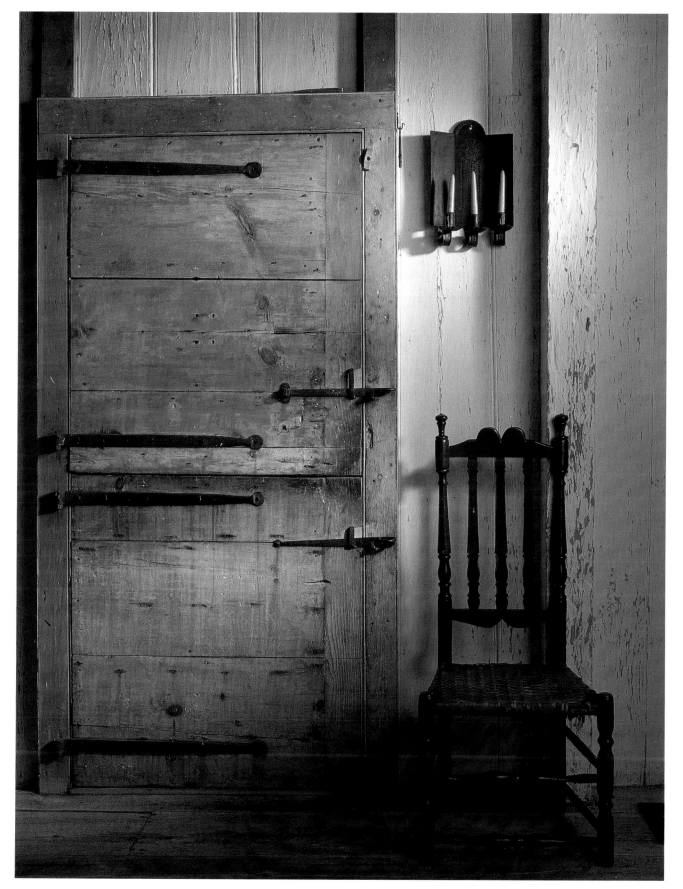

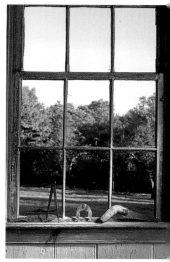

Below:
The paint on the
woodwork is peeling
because the house's
owner, Stephen
Mack, prefers to
leave that which is
worn but original
untouched.

Below:
The paint on the
woodwork is peeling
because the house's
owner, Stephen
Mack, prefers to
leave that which is
worn but original
untouched.

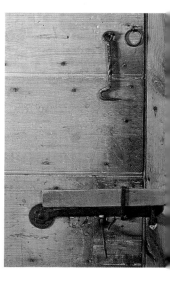

Above:
A detail of the
fastening on an age-
worn late 18th
century American
hardwood door. Old
wrought-iron fittings
are locked by a
wooden wedge.

Woodwork

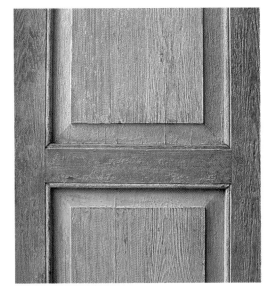

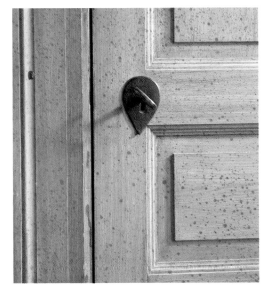

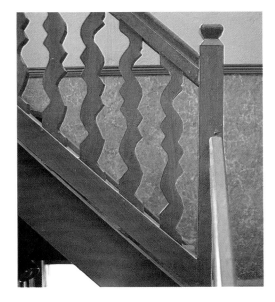

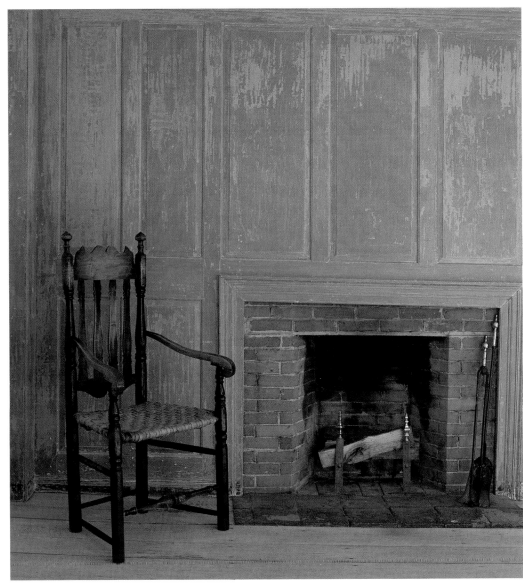

Above:
Five coats of paint were painstakingly scraped off the panelling in this 18th century American room to reveal the original blue-green colour.

Top left:
The paint has worn away to the grain on the middle panels of this shutter.

Middle left:
The speckled appearance of old paintwork can be simulated by flicking droplets of a burnt sienna paint glaze at the surface.

Left:
This stairway from a Canary Islands internal courtyard to a roof terrace has plum-painted banisters carved to an traditional island design.

Woodwork

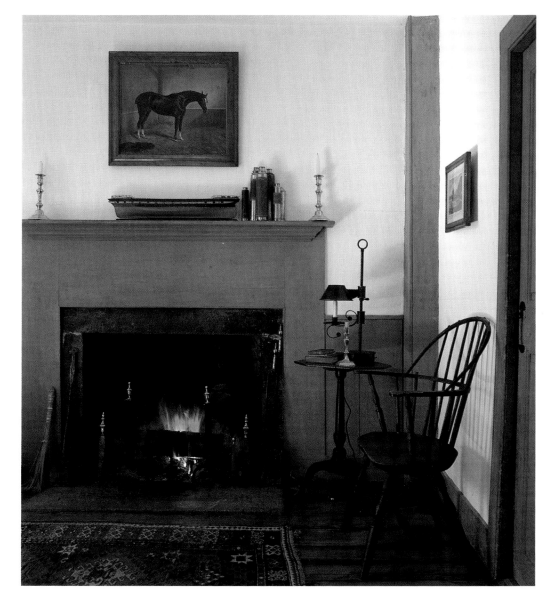

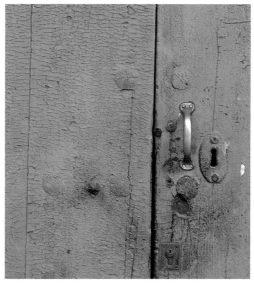

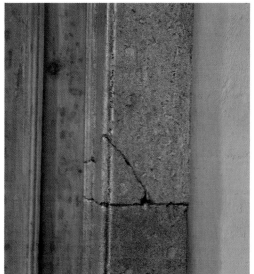

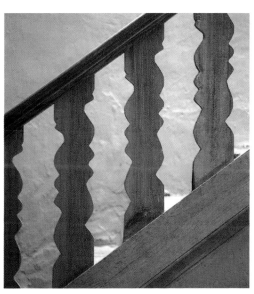

Above:
Soft green-painted woodwork contrasts with milky white walls. An open fire will mellow paintwork to an agreeable aged appearance.

Top and middle right:
Old paint may bubble and blister, but as it ages it develops an attractive patina that modern paints do not.

Right:
Missing banisters can be copied from existing flights. The original of this Spanish stairway is shown opposite.

Plants and containers

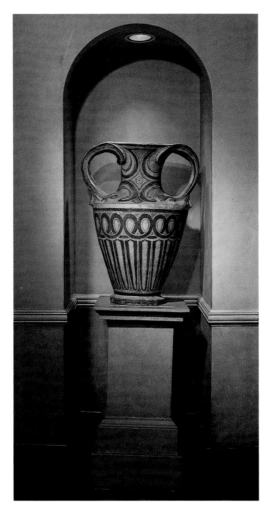

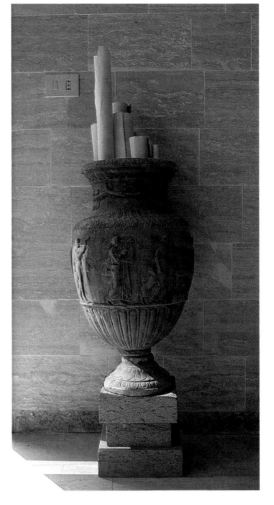

Above:
In this Italian-style hallway a classical alcove,
carved out of a blind wall, frames a boldly
decorated Tuscan urn displayed on a stone-
coloured plinth. The urn could be filled with
dried flowers or bare branches in toning colours.

Above:
The faded tomatoey hue of a generous Etruscan
vase harmonizes with the golden olive tones of
local marble floor and walls in this Tuscan
room. An arrangement of branches or foliage
would complement this container.

*H*uge terracotta urns filled with branches, stone jars crammed with foliage, slipware jugs full of wild flowers, earthernware pots of geraniums, tubs of herbs tumbling over a terrace – the sheer joyous abundance of nature is the hallmark of the country.

In summer, simply pick bunches of fresh flowers from the countryside to bring nature indoors. And in winter cut armfuls of bare branches – japonica, forsythia, hawthorn or birch. Like indoor trees they will bloom and leaf, bringing the changing seasons into the house. You should only use one species per pot and it is important to keep the container well-filled with water as cut foliage is enormously thirsty.

Another winter alternative is dried flowers, gathered and dried in the summer months. They look best in quantity; take the dominant fabric or colour in the room and create an affinity with armfuls of flowers. Choose containers made from natural materials because refined ceramics and glass are often too formal for country rooms. Try terracotta urns, wicker baskets or wooden trugs.

Outside, plant urns, tubs and old stone sinks with a tumble of prolifically growing foliage that will brush your legs with fragrance as you walk past into the garden.

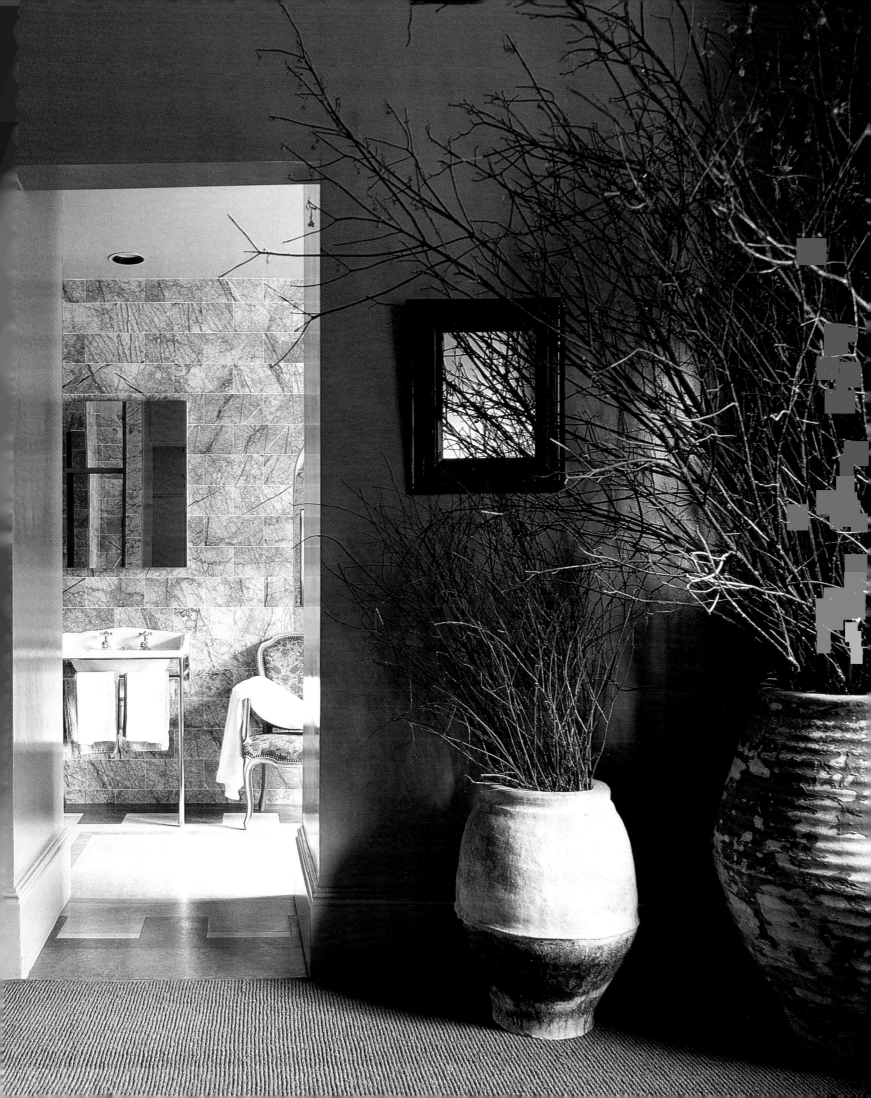

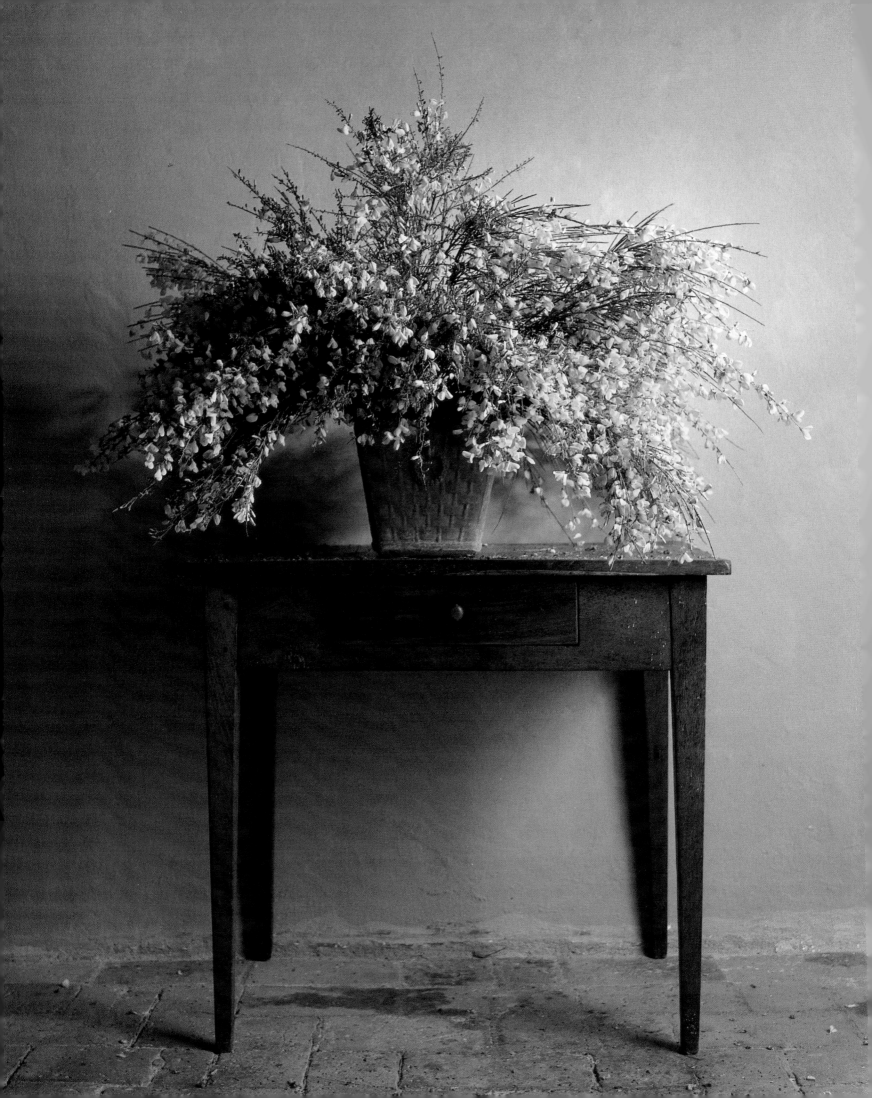

Plants and containers

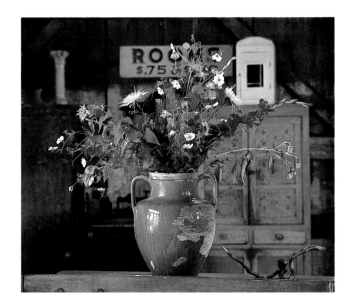

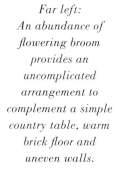

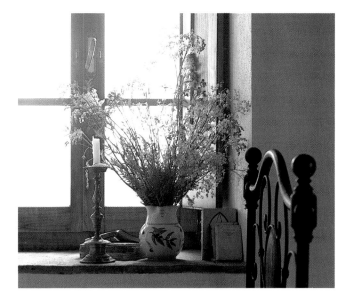

Far left:
An abundance of
flowering broom
provides an
uncomplicated
arrangement to
complement a simple
country table, warm
brick floor and
uneven walls.

Top left:
Containers don't
need to be perfect –
here, the peeling
paint on the
earthenware jug adds
to the charm of the
wild flowers.

Middle left:
Fresh flowers can be
arranged in baskets
if a waterproof liner
is used.

Bottom left:
Small arrangements
will brighten empty
surfaces.

Top right:
"Weeds" from the
hedgerow make
attractive decoration.

Middle right:
Lemon-coloured roses
provide a sharp note
of colour against
mellow wood.

Bottom right:
Lavender in a
Chinese vase
harmonizes with
weathered walls.

Overleaf:
Terracotta pots of
blooms soften a
Spanish terrace.

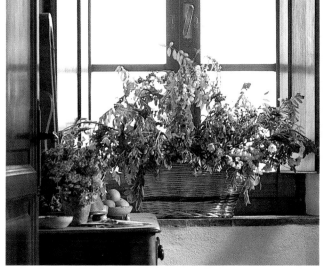

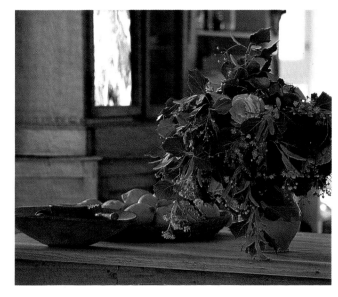

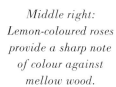

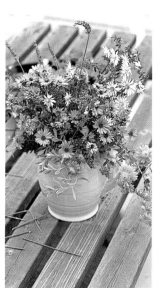

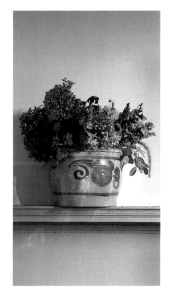

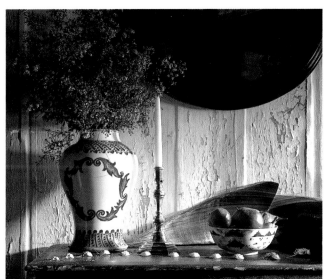

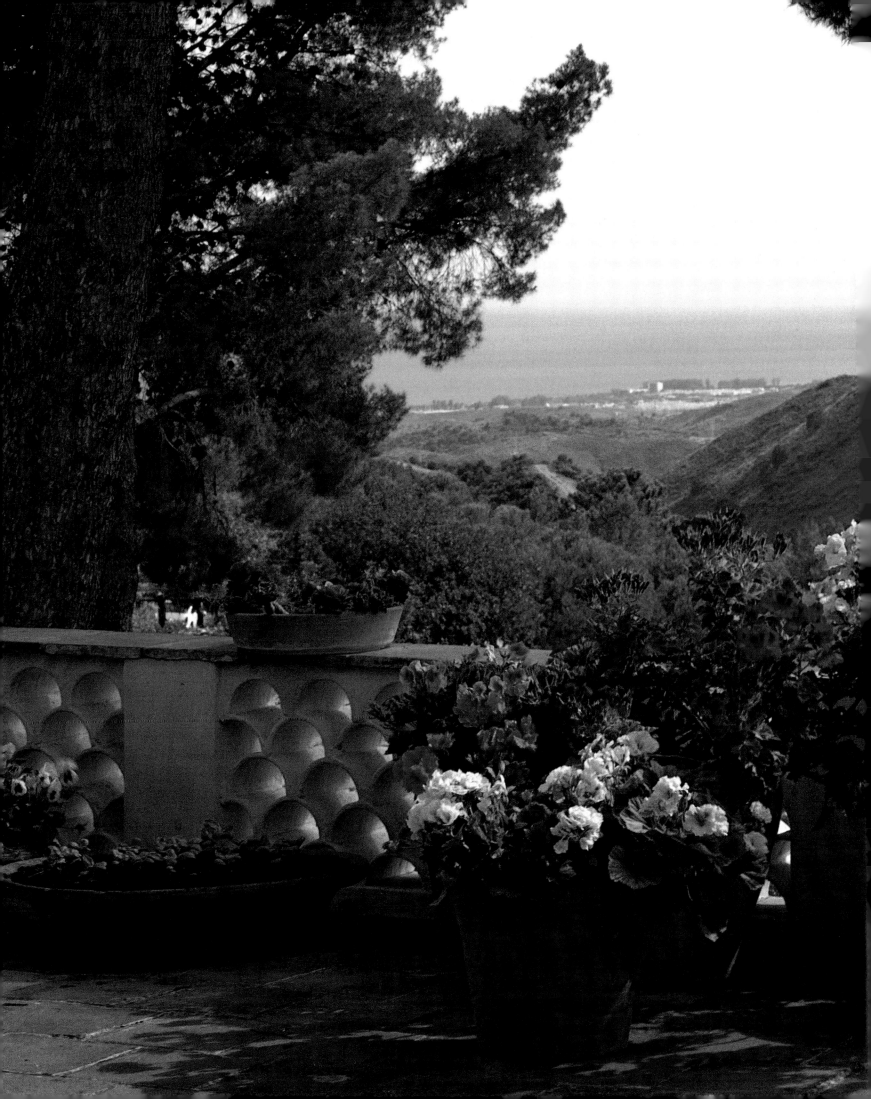

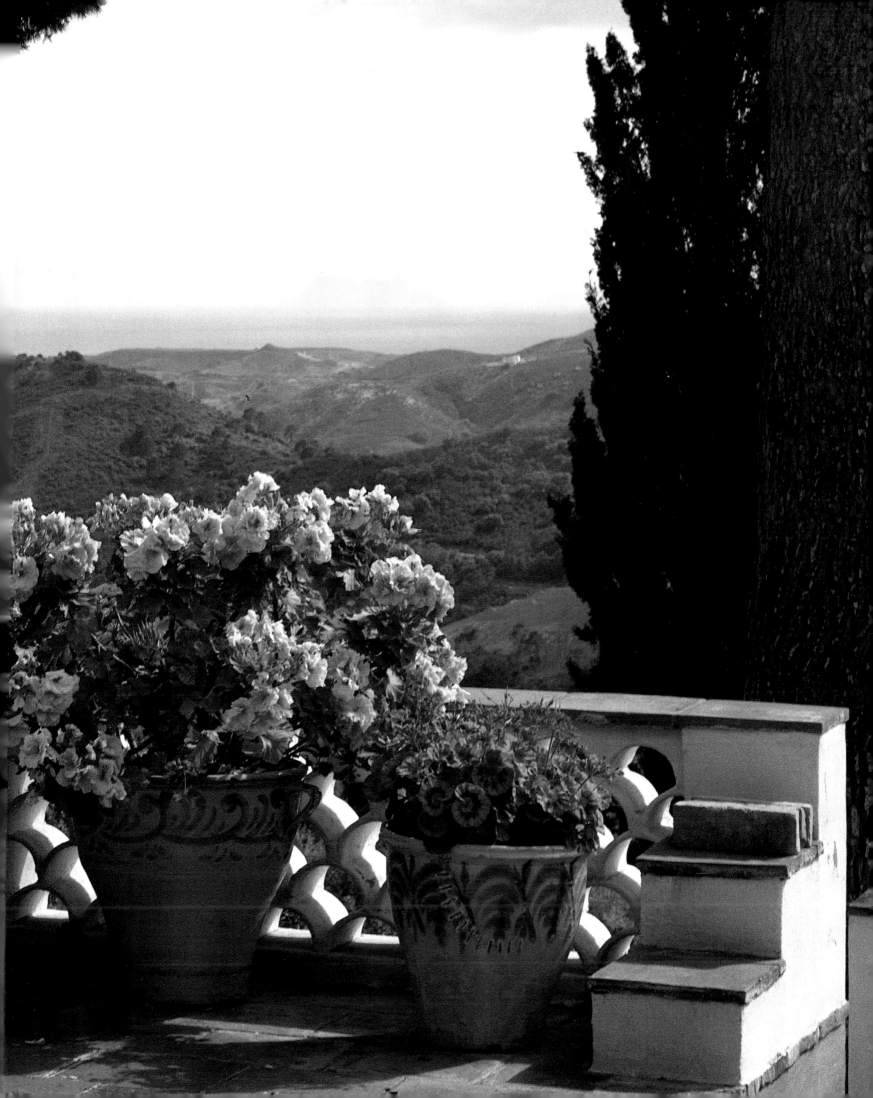

Plants and containers

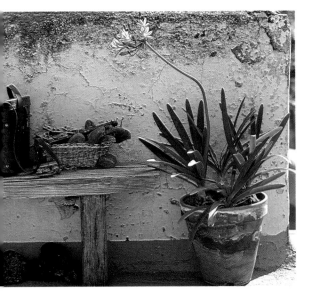

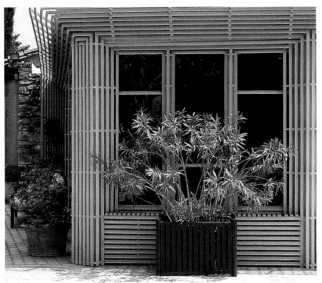

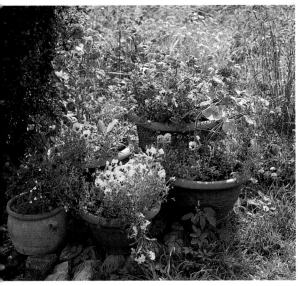

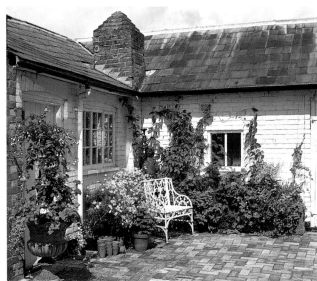

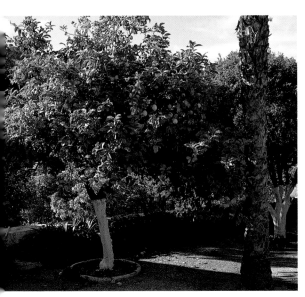

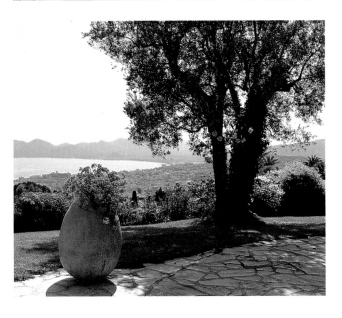

Top row, far left:
An agapanthus flowers on a Canary Islands roof garden.

Top row, left:
The purpose-built container for this palm was built to co-ordinate with the exterior cladding on this French house.

Middle row, far left:
Flowering plants soften the divide between terrace and grass.

Middle row, left:
Pots and plants turn brick walls and paving into a garden corner.

Bottom row, far left:
A lemon tree is contained in a circle of earth on this French terrace.

Bottom row, left:
Crimson geraniums in an old terracotta olive pot brighten the edge of a terrace that overlooks Cannes harbour in the South of France.

Right:
A pair of glossy-leaved bay trees flank a faded green Spanish doorway.

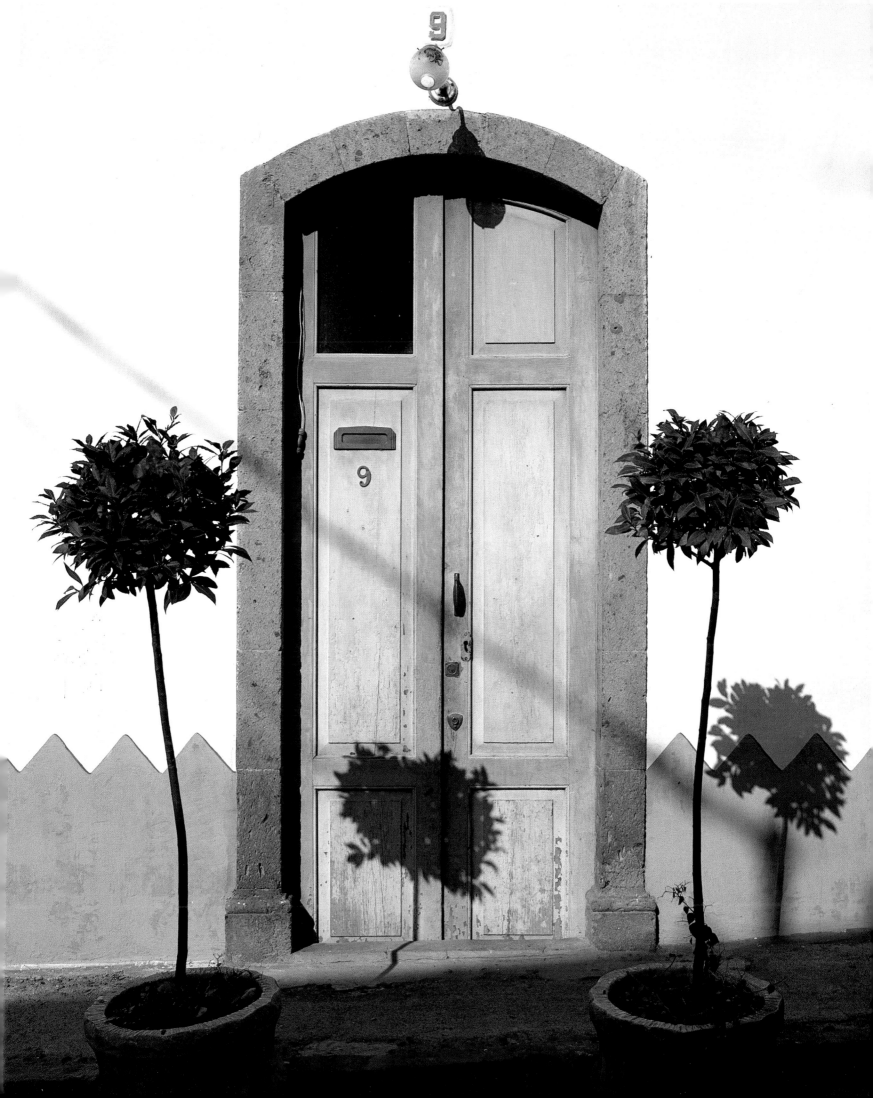

Lighting

Candlelight may lack the wattage of electric lighting – it is said that it takes 120 candles to produce the light of a single electric bulb – but it has a special power of its own in country settings. Although cleverly concealed electric lighting can give a good overall effect, it cannot compare with the warmth of candlelight, especially if it is combined with the movement of flames and the crackling of logs on an open fire.

Candlesticks were made in most materials and a variety of styles. For country homes choose tin, wooden or brass designs; these can be rustic, with a minimum of decoration.

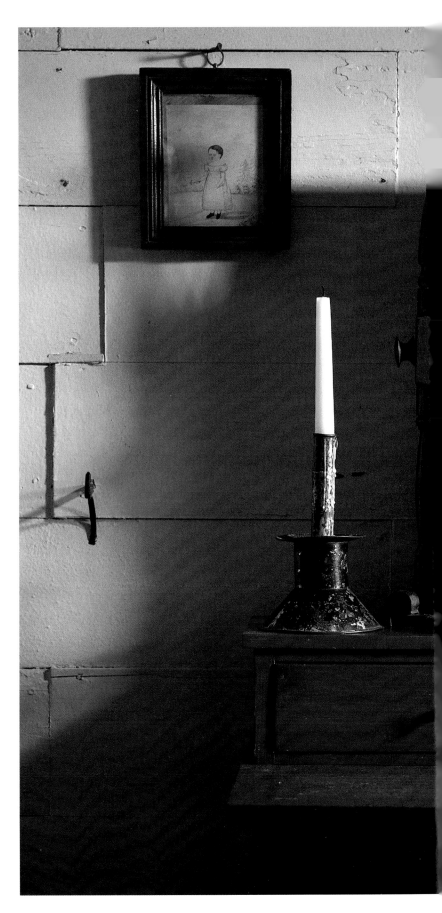

Candles themselves were made from beeswax, whale fat and, in poorer homes, tallow fat. The best candles are still hand-dipped beeswax, or a beeswax mix. However, the ivory-coloured mass-produced ones can be an effective substitute. Beeswax candles are expensive and burn quickly, but they scent the room with a real breath of a country summer.

Candles are not the only lighting conducive to country style – paraffin and storm lamps, pierced tin lanterns and Victorian oil lamps can all be used. And electric lighting can work if carefully handled, with some strategic sources of light casting a sympathetic glow. Choose candlestick lamp bases with low wattage bulbs under a simple shade, traditional brass and green glass desk lamps or generous ceramic, terracotta or wooden table lamps with plain shades for electric lighting that doesn't destroy a country atmosphere.

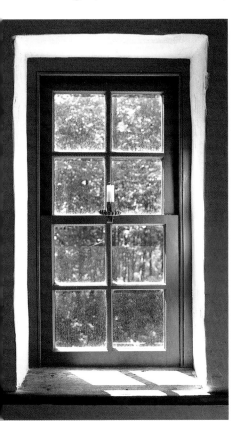

Above:
This wrought iron candleholder that fits onto the window frame was copied by a blacksmith from a traditional American design. At night, the candlelight shines a welcome through the darkness beyond the uncurtained window.

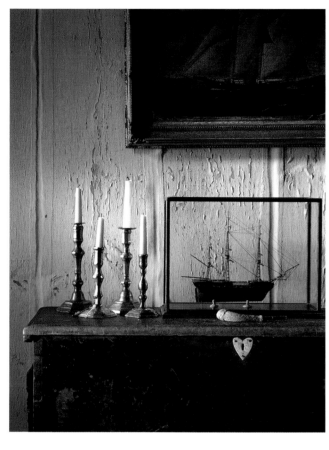

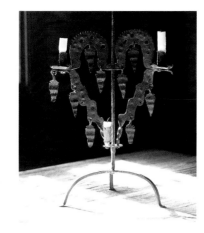

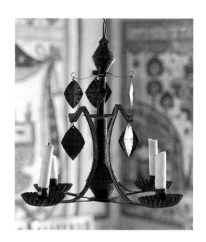

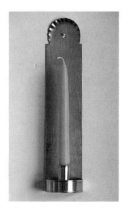

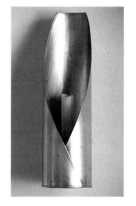

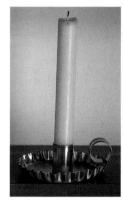

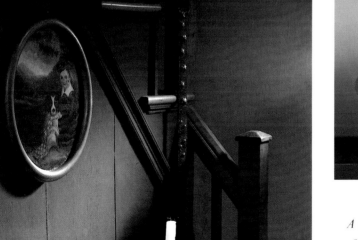

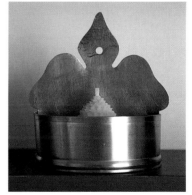

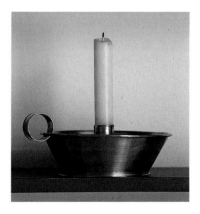

Far left and above:
A selection of tin candleholders. Search for similar antique or modern copies; most countries had their own versions of these attractive but functional designs.

Left:
Brass candlesticks can be used if the design is not too elaborate. These examples illuminate an American barn.

Directory

DECORATIVE ACCESSORIES

BRITAIN

James Burnett-Stewart
70 Southerton Road
London W6 0PH
(081) 748 0335
Traditionally-thrown red earthenware.

The Decoy Gallery
Chewton Magna
Bristol
Avon
(0761) 52075
Suppliers of decoy ducks carving kits.

Folk Art
1 Mill Lane
East Coker
Yeovil
Somerset BA22 9LE
(093) 586 3026
Painted and hand-stencilled pine mirrors inspired by the early naive art of Pennsylvania, USA.

John Galloway
72 Vicars Hill
London SE13
(081) 690 3925
A traditional maker of dyed willow baskets and screens.

Global Village
Roundell Street
South Petherton
Somerset
(0460) 40194
Suppliers of baskets suitable for storage, log baskets or plant holders.

Ben Maurice-Jones
Bob Jones Arcade
293 Westbourne Grove
London W11
(081) 452 6193
Antique and French reed fishing creels.

Neal Street East
5 Neal Street
London WC2
(071) 240 0135
An assortment of baskets from the Far East.

Janice Tchalenko
30 Therapia Road
East Dulwich
London SE22 0SE
(081) 693 1624
Modern ceramics that mix well with country furniture.

Wooden Box Workshop
Ports Farm Barn
Duck Street
Egginton
Derbyshire DE6 6HG
(028373) 2869
Oval wooden boxes made in the Shaker tradition using maple from areas of guaranteed reforestation.

NORTH AMERICA

The Back Door
10 Batchellor Drive
North Brookfield
Massachusetts 05135
Basketweaving kits, reeds.

Baldwin Hardware Co
841 E. Wyomissing Blvd.
Box 15048
Reading
Pennsylvania 19612
Brass hardware.

Basketville
Route 1
Putney
Vermont 05346
Baskets.

Bear Creek Folk Art
P.O. Box 535
Phoenix
Arizona 97535
Folk pots, baskets and textiles.

Cane and Basket Supply Co
1283 South Cochran Avenue
Los Angeles
California 90019
Caning and basketmaking supplies.

Carol's Canery
232 Barnsdale Road W.
Charlottesville
Virginia 22901
Basket kits.

Coker Creek Crafts
P.O. Box 95
Coker Creek
Tennessee 37314
Baskets.

Connecticut Cane Reed Co
P.O. Box 1276
Manchester
Connecticut 06040
Suppliers of cane and reed.

Country Accents
P.O. Box 437
Montoursville
Pennsylvania 17754
Punched tin panels.

Country Folks Ltd
305 Valley Ridge Drive
Timber Valley Estates
Blue Grass
Iowa 52726
Decorative accessories.

Harmon Basket and Woodworks
P.O. Box 1418
Columbia
South Carolina 29202
Baskets, slatted crates.

Historic Hardware Ltd
Box 1327
North Hampton
New Hampshire 03862
Brass hardware.

Historic Housefitters Co
Farm to Malker Road
Brewster
New York 10509
Wrought-iron hardware.

Iron Art
1122 Hamilton Street
P.O. Box 1794
Allentown
Pennsylvania 18105
Cast-iron toys, animals and trivets.

The Past Basket
222 S. Third Street
Geneva
Ilinois 60134
Antique basketware.

Virginia Metalcrafters
1010 E. Main Street
P.O. Box 1068
Waynesboro
Virginia 22980
Brass hardware.

Renovations Supply
Millers Falls
Massachusetts 01349
Hardware.

FLOWERS

BRITAIN

Bugglesden Crafts
St. Michaels
Tenterden
Kent TN30 6TG
(0580) 291129
Dried vines and Kentish hops in 10-ft (3m) lengths.

Robin Day
85 Pimlico Road
London SW1
Natural flower and plant arrangements.

The Flower Arrangers Shop
11 Union Street
Stratford-on-Avon
Warwickshire
(0789) 66318
An extensive range of dried material, silk flowers, foliage and plants.

Sandy James
Moorings
Over Stowey
Nr. Bridgewater
Somerset
(0278) 732446
Dried flower arrangements made to order.

Meadow Herbs Ltd
Upper Clatford
Andover
Hampshire SP11 7LW
(0264) 52998
Hand-made herbal pillows, sachets, coat hangers and accessories. Also stock hand-blended potpourri and aromatic oils.

Martin Robinson Flowers
637 Fulham Road
London SW6
(071) 731 3595
Suppliers of indoor wreaths made of dried herbs.

William E. Selkin Ltd (Floral Magic)
12 Ludlow Hill Road
West Bridgford
Nottingham NG2 6HF
(0602) 232286/7
Suppliers of floral accessories.

Ken Turner
Thomas Goode & Co
Conduit Street
London W1
Natural flower and plant arrangements. Also supply scented candles and pot-pourris.

NORTH AMERICA

Cherchez
862 Lexington Avenue
New York 10021
Potpourris and herbal sachets. Also stock antique linens and other home furnishings.

Delicate Designs
205 Willowgrove South
Tonawanda
New York 14150
Herbal wreaths.

Faith Mountain Herbs
Main Street
Box 199
Sperryville
Virginia 22740
Herbal wreaths and bouquets.

The Newport House
P.O. Box 15415
Richmond
Virginia 23227
Floral supplies, wreath forms, dried botanicals.

Betsy Williams
68 Park Street
Andover
Massachusetts 01810
Wreaths and everlastings.

FLOORING

BRITAIN

Bosanquet-Ives
3 Court Lodge
48 Sloane Square
London SW1
(071) 730 6241
Glastonbury woven cotton stair runners; sisal, coir and seagrass matting.

Bull Ceramics, Descobra Trading Co Ltd
77 Bellgrove Road
Welling, Kent
Importers of Brazilian tiles.

John Caddick and Son Ltd
Spoutfield Tileries
Stoke-on-Trent
ST4 7BX
Quarry tiles.

Candy Tiles Ltd
Heathfield
Newton Abbot
Devon TQ12 6RF
Importers of unglazed Danish floor tiles.

Ceramica
275 London Road
Hazel Grove
Stockport
Cheshire
(061) 483 7356
Hand-painted wall and floor tiles, and pottery.

Conservation Building Products Ltd
Forge Works, Forge Lane
Cradley Heath, Warley
West Midlands
(0384) 69551
Black and red quarry tiles.

Crucial Trading Ltd
P.O. Box 689
London W2 4BX
(05887) 666
Natural fibre floor-coverings including seagrass, sisal and coir.

Cornwise Ltd
168 Old Brompton Road
London SW5 0BA
(071) 373 6890
Extensive selection of ceramic, granite and marble tiles.

J.C. Edwards (Ruabon) Ltd
Streamhill Works
Bromyard
Herefordshire
Quarry tiles.

Fired Earth
102 Portland Road
London W11 4LX
(071) 221 4825
Suppliers of hand-hewn African slate and other wall and floor tiles.
    Also at: Middle Aston, Oxfordshire OX5 3PX. Tel: (0869) 40724. And 37-41 Battersea High Street, London SW11 3JF. Tel: (071) 924 2272.

Hereford Tiles Ltd
Whitestone
Hereford
Herefordshire HR1 3SF
Quarry tiles in several tones.

Junckers Ltd
Clarendon House
London Road
Chelmsford
Essex CM2 0NZ
Manufacturers of bleached beech flooring.

Paris Ceramics
543 Battersea Park Road
London SW11
(071) 228 5785/9
Suppliers of blue English limestone (used for floors since the Middle Ages). Its natural colours vary from greenish-blue to dark bluish-purple.

Reed-Harris Ltd
Riverside House
Carnwath Road
London SW6 2HS
Importers of a range of Italian, Portuguese and German tiles.

Directory

Dennis Ruabon
Haford Tileries
Ruabon
Wrexham
Clwyd, Wales
(0978) 843484
Red and black quarry tiles.

Sinclair Till
793 Wandsworth Road
London SW8
(071) 720 0031
*Design, lay and cut
linoleum of all styles and
designs, from Etruscan
borders to gingham checks.*

Stone Age
67 Dendy Street
London SW12 8DA
(081) 673 7284
Stone floor tiles.

The Tile Gallery
1 Royal Parade
247 Dawes Road
London SW6 7RE
(071) 385 8818/9
*Hand-painted, marble,
slate, granite and terracotta
tiles.*

Trillby Herriott
Byeways
Palesgate Lane
Crowborough
Sussex
(0892) 652967
*Canvas floorcloths with
stencilled designs.*

**World's End Tiles and
Flooring Ltd**
9 Langton Street
London SW10
*Wall and floor tile
suppliers.*

NORTH AMERICA

The Aged Ram
P.O. Box 201
Essex
Vermont 05451
Hooked rugs.

The Barn
P.O. Box 25
Market Street
Lehman
Pennsylvania 18627
Rag rugs.

Capel Inc
Troy
North Carolina 27371
*Area rugs, including
braided, hooked,
needlepoint and rag types.*

Carol Beron Rugs
6 Greene Street
New York 10013
Rag rugs.

Colonial Mills Inc
560 Mineral Springs Avenue
Pawtucket
Rhode Island 02860
Braided rugs.

Country Stenciler
6 Surrey Trail
Sandy Hook
Connecticut 06482
*Canvas floorcloths, wall
stencilling.*

Elizabeth Eakins
1053 Lexington Avenue
New York 10021
Custom-crafted rugs.

Floorcloths by Ingrid
8 Randall Road
Rochester
Massachusetts 02770
Floorcloths.

**Good and Company
Floorclothmakers at
Salzburg Square**
Route 101
Amherst
New Hampshire 03031
Floorcloths.

The Hooking Room
1840 House
237 Pine Point Road
Scarborough
Maine 04074
*Over 200 hooked rug
designs, kits, supplies.*

Import Specialists
82 Wall Street
New York 10005
*Sisal, rag and cotton
dhurrie rugs, mats.*

Lancaster County Folk Art
Pat Horfanius
113 Meadowbrook Lane
Elizabethtown
Pennsylvania 17022
Hooked rugs.

McAdoo Rugs
P.O. Box 847
The Red Mill
N. Bennington
Vermont 05257
Hooked rugs.

Marian B. Miller Kilims
148 E. 28th Street
New York 10016
New and antique kilims.

Mills River
713 Old Orchard Road
Hendersonville
North Carolina 28739
Braided rugs.

John Moshimer
P.O. Box 351
Kennebunkport
Maine 04046
Custom-made hooked rugs.

Mulberry Street Rugs
230 State Street
Williamsport
Pennsylvania 17701
Braided rugs.
Also at: 15135 Sunset Blvd.,
0220 Pacific Palisades,
CA30049.

Dana Nelson
155 Fairview Road
Ellenwood
Georgia 30049
Rag rugs.

Philadelphia Floorcloths
510 Merwyn Road
Narbert
Pennsylvania 19072
Floorcloths.

Ragtime Weavers
4 Jarvis Street
Norwalk
Connecticut 06851
Rag rugs.

Patty Read
3 Alden Street
Camden
Maine 04843
Custom-made rag rugs.

Shyam Ahuja
201 E. 56th Street
New York 10022
*Dhurrie rugs in patchwork
patterns.*

Trans-Oceanic Rugs
919 Third Avenue
New York 10022
*Area rugs, including
hooked rugs.*

Thos. K. Woodard
835 Madison Avenue
New York 10021
*Custom-crafted rugs and
runners.*

Yankee Pride
29 Parkside Cr.
Braintree
Massachusetts 02188
*Rag rugs, hooked rugs,
quilts.*

FURNITURE

BRITAIN

**Andre de Cacqueray
Antiquities**
227 Ebury Street
London SW1
(071) 730 5000
*18th and 19th century
French furniture.*

**Antique Brass Bedstead
Company Ltd**
Baddow Antique Centre
Great Baddow
Chelmsford
Essex CM2 7JW
(0245) 71137
Antique brass bedsteads.

Banyan Trading
412 Didsbury Road
Heaton Mersey
Stockport
Cheshire
(061) 432 6466
Bamboo steamer chairs.

Carter Period Furnishings
Kirkby on Bain
Woodhall Spa
Lincolnshire LN10 6YL
*Period country-style
furniture.*

Chalon
The Plaza
535 Kings Road
London SW10
(071) 351 0008
*Original painted country
furniture plus "Chalon
Originals", a collection of
paint-aged country classics.
For brochures tel: (0458)
252374.*

Codington
Units 23⅜
Block A
Bendon Valley Estate
Haldane Place
London SW18
(081) 874 0013
*Designer and maker of
colonial-style furniture,
including linen chests, spice
chests, peg racks as well as
tables and benches.*

The Conran Shop
Michelin House
Fulham Road
London SW3
(071) 589 7401
*Suppliers of Adirondack
chairs, rattan and cane
furniture.*

Frank Griffiths
Waterside Mill
Waterside
Macclesfield
Cheshire
(0625) 33622
*Importers of steel beds from
Fiesole in Tuscany.*

Guimond Mounter
Bakers Farm
Dulford
Devon
(0884) 6358
*Dealer in antique pine and
country furniture.*

Hampstead Pine Company
238 West End Lane
West Hampstead
London NW6 1LG
(071) 435 4496
*Makers of Irish, Welsh and
Cornish dressers using
reclaimed pine.*

Haycocks at Rosa Danica
Penllwynplan House
Meidrim
Carmarthen
Dyfed SA33 5NX
*Pine cabinets decorated in
traditional Danish style.*

Richard Large
Stone House Antiques
St Marys Street
Painswick
Gloucestershire
(0452) 813540
*Specialist in Windsor chairs
made from yew.*

Laura Ashley Home
7-9 Harriet Street
London SW1
(071) 235 9797
*Country pine, painted and
Gustavian-style furniture.*

Steward Linford
Kitchener Works
Kitchener Road
High Wycombe
Buckinghamshire
HP11 2SJ
(0494) 40408/44
*Maker of classic chairs in
yew and English
hardwoods.*

Lusty Lloyd Loom Ltd
Hoo Lane
Chipping Camden
Gloucestershire GL55 6AU
(0386) 841333
*Makers of authentic-style
new furniture using
traditional methods.*

Marim Cane Collections
Unit 143
Shepherds Bush Centre
London W12
(081) 749 7308
Cane furniture.

Marston and Langinger Ltd
20 Bristol Gardens
Little Venice
London W9 2JQ
(071) 286 7643
*English Willow furniture in
a choice of finishes.*

Pineapple
Clevedon Cottages
Clevedon Works
off London Street
Bath
Avon
(0225) 446181
Twig furniture.

Rope Walk Antiques
18-22 Rope Walk
Rye
East Sussex
(0797) 223486
*Antique pine furniture and
accessories.*

Jill Saunders
46 White Hart Lane
London SW13 0PZ
(081) 878 0400
*Stocks and repairs Lloyd
Loom sofas and chairs.*

The Shaker Shop
25 Harcourt Street
London W1
*Designers and
manufacturers of Shaker-
style furniture and
accessories in maple and
American cherry.*

Somerset Country Furniture
The Old Chapel
Church Street
Ilchester
Somerset
(0935) 841212
*Craftsmen follow 17th, 18th
and 19th century designs to
make copies of British, Irish
and French dressers, plus
simple Shaker-inspired
furniture.*

Stoves Antiques
The Old School
Fen Ditton
Cambridge
Cambridgeshire CB5 8ST
(02205) 5264
*Painted furniture, mainly
pre-1860.*

Directory

Stratford Clock Co Ltd
1301 Stratford Road
Hall Green
Birmingham B29 9AP
(021) 702 2110
Clocks made in oak, black walnut and mahogany, with solid brass movements.

Tobias And The Angel
Whitehart Lane
Barnes
London SW13
Primitive furniture.

Trevor Micklem Antiques
Frog Pool Farm
Moor Wood
Oak Hill, nr. Bath
Avon
(0749) 840754
Early furniture, delft-ware, pottery, pewter, needlework and metalware.

Up Country
The Old Corn Stores
68 St John's Road
Tunbridge Wells
Kent TN4 9PE
(0892) 23341
English and Continental antique country furniture, rural artefacts and decorative items for the home and garden.

Village Collection
42-43 Peascod Street
Windsor
Buckinghamshire
(0753) 855730
Hand-made pine furniture.

Robert Young Antiques
68 Battersea Bridge Road
London
SW11 3AG
(071) 228 7847
Antique country-style furniture.

NORTH AMERICA

Amish Country Collection
R.D. 5
Sunset Valley Road
P.O. Box 5085
New Castle
Pennsylvania 16105
(0101) (412) 652 0789
Willow and slat furniture, folk art, rag rugs.

Barn Raising
P.O. Box 248
Rutledge
Georgia 30663
Reproduction furniture.

Peter Bentson
Bentson-West
325 Pacific Avenue
San Francisco
California 94111
French-style park chairs and outdoor furniture.

Blue Ridge Woodworks
Route 3, Sparta
North Carolina 28675
Pie safes.

Corinne Burke
1 Forest Glen Road
New Paltz
New York 12561
Custom-crafted reproductions.

Cohasset Colonials
Cohasset
Massachusetts 02025
Colonial-style furniture to assemble.

Colonial Williamsburg Foundation
P.O. Box C
Williamsburg
Virginia 23187
(0101) (804) 229 1000
Furniture, fabrics, wallcoverings, lighting and accessories.

Laura C. Copenhaver
c/o Rosemont
Box 149G, Marion
Virginia 24354
Reproduction furniture, coverlets, rugs, quilts, table linen.

Council Craftsman
Box 398
Denton
North Carolina 27239
18th century reproduction upholstered furniture.

Country Primitives
31 South Main Street
Concord
New Hampshire 03301
Reproduction furniture.

Countrystore
P.O. Box 17696
Whitefish Bay
Wisconsin 53217
Willow furniture.

Darrow School
Pittsfield
New Lebanon
New York
Shaker colony school with shop that sells furniture.

Furniture Guild
5095 Riverhill Road
Marietta
Georgia 30067
Reproduction furniture.

Gear Inc
127 Seventh Avenue
New York 10011
Furniture, fabrics, accessories.

Great Meadows Joinery
P.O. Box 392
Wayland
Massachusetts 01778
Custom-made Shaker reproductions.

Historic Charleston Reproductions
105 Broad Street
Charleston
South Carolina 29401
Furniture, fabrics, china and accessories.

Hitchcock Chair
Riverton
Connecticut 06065
Stencilled chairs.

Kramer
P.O. Box 232
Washington
Virginia 22747
Reproduction furniture.

The Lane Co
Altavista
Virginia 24517-0151
The Museum of American Folk Art collection.

Raimondo Lemus
125 Christopher Street
New York 10014
Custom-made Shaker-style reproductions.

Lloyd/Flanders
P.O. Box 500
3010 Tenth Street
Menominee
Michigan 49858
Wicker-like outdoor furniture.

Nichols and Stone
232 Sherman Street
Gardner
Massachusetts 01440
Farm-style furniture.

O'Asian Designs Inc
1100 W. Walnut
Compton
California 90220
Wicker furniture.

Old Hickory
403 S. Noble Street
Shellyville
Indiana 46176
Hickory furniture.

Palacek
P.O. Box 225
Station A
Richmond
California 94808
Wicker furniture.

Reed Bros
6006 Gravenstein Hwy.
Cotati
California 94928
Hand-carved furniture.

Charles P. Rogers
170 Fifth Avenue
New York 10010
Brass beds, iron beds, enamelled beds.

The Seraph-East
P.O. Box 500
Route 20, Sturbridge
Massachusetts 01566
Custom-crafted reproductions.

The Seraph-West
at The 1817 Shoppe
14659 Street
Route 37, Sunbury
Ohio 43074
Custom-crafted reproductions.

Shaker Workshops
P.O. Box 1028
Concord
Massachusetts 01742
Shaker-style furntiture to assemble.

Simms and Thayer
P.O. Box 35
1037 Union Street
North Marshfield
Massachusetts 02059
Custom-crafted reproductions.

Ron Smith
Hissing Goose Gallery
Sun Valley
Idaho 83353
Custom designing, log furniture, different finishes.

Southwood Reproductions
Box 2245
Highway 64-70 East
Hickory
North Carolina 28603
Reproduction 18th century upholstered furniture.

Ruth Stalker
4447 Saint Catherine West
Westmount
Quebec
Canada H32 1RZ
(01046) (514) 931 0822
Primitive and painted Canadian furniture.

Taylor Woodcraft
P.O. Box 245
South River Road
Malta
Ohio 43758
Farm-style tables and chairs.

Charles E. Thibeau
Box 222
Groton
Massachusetts 01450
Custom-crafted reproductions.

Thos. Moser
30 Cobbs Bridge Road
New Gloucester
Maine 04260
Custom-crafted reproductions.

Wentz Farmstead
Montgomery County
Pennsylvania
Country furniture.

Winterthur Museum Reproductions
Winterthur
DE 19735
Furniture, fabrics, wallcoverings, pottery, lighting and accessories.

SCANDINAVIA

Antiklagret Stig Jonsson
Sturegatan 58
Falun
Sweden
(01046) (023) 121 63 or 0
Scandinavian country furniture.

Broberg Antikhandel
Grev Turegatan 56
114 38 Stockholm
Sweden
(01046) (08) 60 40 26 or
Scandinavian country furniture.

Draken Antikhandel
Kopmantorget 2
111 31 Stockholm
Sweden
(01046) (08) 20 26 38
Scandinavian country furniture.

Lars Olsson Antikhandel AB o HB
Kopmangatan 7
111 31 Stockholm
Sweden
(01046) (08) 10 25 00
Scandanavian country furniture and pottery.

Stens Antik
Landsvagsgatan 61
464 00 Mellerud
Sweden
(01046) (0530) 12225
Scandinavian country furniture and pottery.

FRANCE

Dumas and Margit Leger
Sun House
Mas des Sablières
Oppede
France 04580
(01033) (90) 76 90 51
Designers and makers of metal furniture.

KITCHENS

BRITAIN

Aga-Rayburn
P.O. Box 30
Ketley
Telford
Shropshire
(0952) 641100
Stockists of cast-iron stoves and ranges.

Brass Sinks Ltd
The Birches
Deravden Green
Gwent
Wales
(02915) 738
Stockists of a range of solid brass sinks and taps.

Eden Grove
Eden Mews
56 Eden Grove
London N7 8EJ
(071) 607 6376
Kitchens built in old pine and decorated with a variety of specialist paint finishes.

The English Kitchen Company
Elliott House
Greenacres Road
Oldham
Lancashire OL4 1HB
(061) 627 0042
Makers of English-style kitchens.

Directory

Heritage Interiors
4B London Road
Tunbridge Wells
Kent TN1 1DQ
(0892) 511366
Hand-made frosted oak and distressed painted furniture, with multi-colour granite tops. Antique French terracotta floor tiles; hand-painted wall tiles.

Hunter Stoves
Mells, Frome
Somerset
(0373) 812545
Suppliers of wood and solid-fuel stoves.

Kitchen Shop
109 Kenwyn Street
Truro
Cornwall TR1 3DJ
(0872) 72145
Kitchen accessories.

Naturally Wood Ltd
Twyford Road
Bishops Stortford
Hertfordshire CM23 3JL
Natural wood kitchens.

Penny's Mill Designs Ltd
Penny's Mill Nunney
Frome
Somerset BA11 4NP
(0373) 84210
Hand-built bespoke kitchens and other furniture in ash, oak, cherry and maple.

Smallbone Kitchens
Smallbone of Devizes
Hopton Industrial Estate
London Road
Devizes
Wiltshire SN10 2EU
(0734) 591459
Hand-built kitchens.
    Also at: 105-9 Fulham Road, London SW3.

Smith and Wellstood Esse
Bonnybridge
Stirlingshire
(0324) 812171
Cast-iron ranges with double oven and boiler, available in eight colours.

Thermocet UK
Real Fire Heating Centre
Telford Way
Kettering
Northamptonshire
NN16 8UN
(0536) 514964
Traditional stoves and fires.

U.A. Engineering
Canal Street
Sheffield
(0742) 738803
Suppliers of multi-fuel ranges with electrical back-up for main oven.

Winchmore World of Wood
Chiswick Avenue
Mildenhall
Suffolk IP28 7BE
(0638) 712082
Makers of solid wood kitchens in maple and oak.

Woodcraft
16 Fell View
Crossens
Southport
Lancashire PR9 8JX
(0704) 213212
Wooden kitchenware decorated in pokerwork.

Woodgoods
Unit 40
Woolmer Trading Estate
Bordon
Hampshire GU35 9QZ
(04203) 7182/3
Painted country kitchens; also kitchens hand-built in antique pine, oak and ash.

NORTH AMERICA

Consolidated Dutchwest
P.O. Box 1019
Plymouth
Massachusetts 02360
Woodburning stoves.

Elmira Stoveworks
22 Church Street
Elmira
Ontario
Canada N2B 1M3
Woodburning stoves; electrical conversions.

Jotul Usa
353 Forest Avenue
P.O. Box 1157
Portland
Maine 04104
Woodburning stoves.

Tulikivi
P.O. Box 300
Schuyler
Virginia 22969
Soapstone stoves.

Vermont Castings
Prince Street
Randolph
Vermont 05060
Woodburning stoves.

LIGHTING

BRITAIN

Burrell
Woad
The Forge
192 Petersham Road
Nr. Richmond
Surrey TW10 7AD
(081) 332 1602
Metal-work candlestands, candelabras, lamps and mirrors.

Forgeries
The Old Butchery
High Street
Twyford
Winchester
Hampshire
(0962) 712196
A range of hand-made ironmongery.

Light Brigade
18 Regent Street
Cheltenham
Gloucestershire
(0242) 226777
Striped and checked candle shades.

Lion, Witch and Lampshade
89 Ebury Street
London SW1W 9QU
(071) 730 1774
Makers of tole wall brackets.

Paul Micklin
2-3 Market Place
Whittlesey
Peterborough
Cambridgeshire PE7 1AB
(0733) 204355
Stockist of tole imported from France.

Soft Options Interior Design
Studio 12
Lots Road
London SW10
(071) 351 4463
Suppliers of decorative candlestands.

Wilchester County
Stable Cottage
Vicarage Lane
Steeple Ashton
Trowbridge
Wiltshire
(0380) 870764
Hand-made range of "primitive" lighting in reclaimed metal, copied from American designs.

NORTH AMERICA

Authentic Designs
The Mill Road
West Rupert
Vermont 05776
Chandeliers, sconces (reproductions of originals).

Authentic Reproduction Lighting Co
P.O. Box 218
Avon
Connecticut 06001
Chandeliers and sconces (reproductions of original American designs).

Colonial Candle of Cape Cod
Hyannis
Massachusetts 02601
Candles.

Colonial Tin Craft
7805 Railroad Avenue
Cincinnati
Ohio 45243
Pierced tin lighting fixtures.

Essex Forge
5 Old Dennison Road
Essex
Connecticut 06426
Chandeliers, sconces.

Gates Moore
River Road
Silvermine
Norwalk
Connecticut 06850
Chandeliers, sconces.

Harmony Candles and Gifts
G-6429 Flushing Road
Flushing
Michigan 48433
Candles.

Heritage Lanterns
70A Main Street
Yarmouth
Maine 04096
Chandeliers and sconces. Also authentic outdoor lighting fixtures.

Pickwick Papers
4592 Lancaster Road
Granville
Ohio 43023
Lampshades.

Willard and Co
1156 U.S. 50
Cincinnati
Ohio 45150
Chandeliers, sconces, tin lanterns.

PAINTS AND FINISHES

BRITAIN

H.J. Chard and Son
Feeder Lane
Bristol BS2 0JJ
(0272) 777681
Limewashes, plasters, renders etc.

Jackie Lowe
Church Terrace Cottage
Laxfield
Woodbridge
Suffolk IP13 8DL
(098683) 464
A wide range of stencils to order.

George Morris
104 Edith Grove
Chelsea
London SW3
(081) 397 8142
Marble and paint finishes.

John Oliver
33 Pembridge Road
London W11
Paints in traditional colours.

Paper Moon
Unit 2, Brent Trading Estate
390 North Circular Road
London NW10
Decorative wallpaper borders.

Papers and Paints
4 Park Walk
London SW10
(071) 352 8626
Paints in period-style colours.

Potmolen Paints
27 Woodstock Industrial Estate
Warminster
Wiltshire BA12 9DX
(0985) 213960
Conservation-grade limewashes, casein and oil-bound distemper, biodegradable stripper.

Rose of Jericho
14 Station Road
Kettering
Northamptonshire
(0536) 73439
Limewashes, plaster, renders, coatings and paints. Also England's last producer of lead paint (EEC permitting).

Carolyn Warrender
Lower Sloane Street
London SW1
Stencil store. Also runs courses.

NORTH AMERICA

Antique Color Supply Inc
P.O. Box 711
Harvard
Massachusetts 01451
(0101) (617) 456 8398
Milk paints, available in a wide range of colours.

Adele Bishop
P.O. Box 3349
Kinston
North Carolina 28502-3349
Japan paints, brushes, stencil sheets and other related materials.

Favor-Ruhl
23 S. Wabash
Chicago
Illinois 60603
Paints.

Flax's
1699 Market Street
San Francisco
California 94103
Paints.

Grisi Stenciling
P.O. Box 1263-H
Haddonfield
New Jersey 08033
Pre-cut, ready-to-use stencils, stencilling supplies.

Old Fashioned Milk Paint Co
Box 222
Groton
Massachusetts 01450
Milk paints.

Martin Senour Company
1370 Ontario Avenue N.W.
Cleveland
Ohio 44113
Authentic period Williamsburg paint colours.
    Also available at: West Chester Wallpaper and Paint Co, 104 W. Market Street, West Chester, Pennsylvania, 19380.

Stencil House of New Hampshire
P.O. Box 109
Hooksett
New Hampshire 03106
Stencils.

Directory

Texas Art Supply
2001 Montrose
Houston
Texas 77006
Paints.

Wolf's Sons
771 Ninth Avenue
New York
New York 10019
Paints.

CERAMICS AND TABLEWARE

BRITAIN

Divertimenti
45-47 Wigmore Street
London W1
(071) 935 0689
A wide range of tableware, including brightly coloured Mediterranean-style pottery and faience.

Mary Wondrausch
The Pottery
Brickfields
Compton
Nr. Guildford
Surrey GU3 1HZ
(0468) 4097
Slipware pottery – traditional pots, commemorative pieces. Also undertakes individual commissions.

Top Knobs
4 Brunnel Buildings
Newton Abbot
Devon
(0626) 63388
Hand-painted ceramic cupboard and door handles and finger plates.

NORTH AMERICA

J.A. Adams Co
Dorset
Vermont 05251
Wooden bowls, boards.

T. Bagge-Merchant
The Olde Salem Museum Store
626 S. Main Street
Winston-Salem
North Carolina 27101
Moravian-style slipware and sgraffito.

Beaumont Pottery
293 Beech Ridge Road
York
Maine 03909
Stoneware.

Bennington Potters
324 Country Street
Bennington
Vermont 05201
Earthenware, including spatterware.

Boch
Comalco International
P.O. Box 675
Perrysburg
Ohio 43551
Dinnerware, including stickware.

Boston Warehouse
180 Kerry Place
Norwood
Massachusetts 02062
Cookware, kitchenware, kitchen linens.

Lester Breininger
South Church Street
Rebesonia
Pennsylvania 19551
Redware, slipware.

CGS
14180 S.W. 139th Ct.
Miami
Florida 33186
Graniteware.

Colonial Form
11167 Hillis Road
Riverdale
Michigan 48877
Redware.

Gris Pottery
10 W. Main Street
Carpentersville
Illinois 60110
Redware, pottery lamps.

Hall China
34 Wildwood Road
New Rochelle
New York 10804
1930s and 1940s reissues.

Harstone
P.O. Box 2626
Zanesville
Ohio 43701
Earthenware, kitchenware, cookie molds, canisters.

Johnson Bros
41 Madison Avenue
New York 10010
Earthenware.

Louisville Stoneware
731 Brent Street
Louisville
Kentucky 40204
Earthenware, stoneware.

Make Mine Country
1109 E. Willoughby Road
Lansing
Michigan 48910
Spongeware.

Nelson McCoy Pottery
Lancaster
Ohio 43130
Fiesta-type earthenware.

Pfaltzgraff Co
P.O. Box 1069
York
Pennsylvania 17405
Earthenware.

Rowe Pottery
217 Main Street
Box L
Cambridge
Wisconsin 53523
Stoneware.

Van Briggle Pottery
600 S. 21st Street
Colorado Springs
Colorado 80904
Art pottery and earthenware.

Vollmer Products Inc
4522 Macco Drive
San Antonio
Texas 78218
Graniteware.

Trading Co
P.O. Box 669984
Marietta
Georgia 30066
Pottery, decorative accessories.

Westmore Pottery
Route 2
Box 494
Seagrove
North Carolina 27341
Redware.

Wilton Armetale
The Wilton Co.
Columbia
Pennsylvania 17512
Pewter-like metal dinnerware and accessories.

TEXTILES

BRITAIN

Alfies Antique Market
V.S. Habberley
Stall 832
Church Street
London NW8
(071) 723 6066
Antique linens.

Catherine Buckley
302 Westbourne Grove
London W11
(071) 229 8786
Antique fabrics.

Ehrman
21-22 Vicarage Gate
London W8 4AA
(071) 937 5077
Tapestry kits for carpet bags, rugs and wall-hangings.

Hodsoll McKenzie Cloths
52 Pimlico Road
London SW1W 8LP
(071) 730 2877
Fabric supplier – fruit and floral designs on linen.

Gordon Reece Gallery
Finkle Street
Knaresborough
Yorkshire HG5 8AA
(0423) 866219
Stockist of a wide variety of kilims.

Daphne Graham
1 Elystan Street
Chelsea Green
London SW3 3NT
(071) 584 8724
Stockist of a wide variety of kilims.

Hoobags
Unit 3
Kym Road
Bicton Rural Park
Kimbolton
Huntingdon
Cambridgeshire PE18 0HU
(0480) 860679
Nottingham lace tablecloths, napkins and undercloths, doilies and runners.

The Kilim House
951-953 Fulham Road
London SW6 5HY
(071) 731 4912
Old, new, decorative and antique kilims.
Also at: The Kilim Warehouse, 28A Pickett Street, London SW12 Tel: (081) 675 3122.

Christopher Legge
Oriental Carpets
25 Oakthorpe Road
Summertown
Oxford
(0865) 57572
Old and decorative tribal rugs and carpets.

Les Olivades
16 Filmer Road
London SW6
(071) 386 9661
Provençal printed cotton fabrics from France.

Lunn Antiques
86 New Kings Road
London SW6
Wide range of antique lace and cotton furnishings.

The Quilt Workshop
The Old Beet House
Silver Street
Askrigg
Wensleydale
North Yorkshire DL8 3HS
(0969) 50659
Mary Foley Murrell makes patchwork quilts to order in Provençal and American cottons, silks and other materials. Also sells antique quilts.

Souleiado
Fulham Road
London SW6
Provençal printed cotton fabrics from France.

Virginia Antiques
98 Portland Road
London W11 4LQ
(071) 727 9908
Provençal-type fabrics, old linens and lace.

NORTH AMERICA

1817 Shoppe
5606 E. State Road
Route 37
Delaware
Ohio 43015
Homespuns, furnishings, accessories.

Amish Quilts
Lancaster County
Pennsylvania
(0234) 56785
Hand-worked quilts, wall hangings and cushion covers.

Anichini Linea Casa
150 Fifth Avenue
New York 10011
Embellished bed linens.

B and B International
13 Old Orchard Road
Rye Brook
New York 10573
Throws.

Bates Fabrics Inc
Lewiston
Maine 04240
Bedspreads.

Boycan's
P.O. Box 897
Sharon
Pennsylvania 16146
Craft and art supplies, quilt supplies.

Calico Corners
Funwood Inc
Bancroft Mills Drawer 670
Wilmington
Delaware 19899
Printed fabrics.

Carter Canopies
P.O. Box 3372
Eden
North Carolina 27288
Handmade quilts, hand-tied canopies, candlewick bedspreads.

Chicago Weaving Corp.
5900 Northwest Hwy.
Chicago
Illinois 60631
Homespun table linens.

Churchill Weavers
P.O. Box 30
Berea
Kentucky 40403
Blankets and throws.

Claesson Co
Route 1
Neddick
Maine 03902
Lace valances and panels.

Colonial Maid
One Depot Plaza
Mamaroneck
New York 10543
Curtains.

Colonial of Cape Cod
Box 670
Hyannis
Maine 02601
Table linens, candles.

Company Store
500 Company Store Road
P.O. Box 2167
Lacrosse
Wisconsin 54602
Down comforters, bedding.

Country Curtains
at the Red Lion Inn
Stockbridge
Massachusetts 01262
Curtains.

238

Faribo Blankets
1500 N.W. Second
Avenue
Faribault
MN 55021
Blankets.

Garnett Hill
Franconia
New Hampshire 03580
Flannel sheets, down comforters.

Ginny's Stitchins
106 Braddock Road
Williamsburg
Virginia 23185
Candlewicking, cross-stitch pieces.

Goodwin Guild Weavers
Blowing Rock Crafts
P.O. Box 314
Corning Road
Blowing Rock
North Carolina 28605
Blankets, throws.

Great Coverups
P.O. Box 1368
West Hartford
Connecticut 06107
Curtains.

Greer Fabrics
Cushing Corners Road
P.O. Box 165
Freedom
New Hampshire 03836
Homespun fabrics.

Hands All Around
971 Lexington
Avenue
New York 10021
New quilts.

Harrisville Designs
Harrisville
New Hampshire 03450
Blankets.

Hinson and Co
27-35 Jackson Avenue
Long Island City
New York 11101
Fabrics, wallcoverings.

Howard Kaplan's French Country Store
35 E. 10th Street
New York 10003
French country fabrics, accessories, pottery.

Kennebunk Weavers
Suncook
New Hampshire 03275
Blankets, throws.

Lanz
Charles Bay Linens
8680 Hayden Place
P.O. Box 5266
Culver City
California 90231
Flannel sheets.

Laura Ashley
P.O. Box 891
Mahwah
New Jersey 07430-9990
English country fabrics, wallcoverings and furniture.

Le Jacquard Francais
200 Lovers Lane
Culpepper
Virginia 22701
French linens, towels.

Lion Knitting Mills
3256 W. 25th Street
Cleveland
Ohio 44109
Knitted throws.

Milos Marketing
111 W. 40th Street
New York 10018
Flannel sheets.

Motif Designs
20 Jones Street
New Rochelle
New York 10801
Fabrics, wallcoverings.

Mystic Valley Traders
400 Massachusetts Avenue
Arlington
Massachusetts 02174
Bedcoverings, throws.

New Hampshire Blanket
Main Street
Harrisville
New Hampshire 03450
Blankets.

Now Designs
540 Hampshire Street
San Francisco
California 94110
Domestic linens.

Jane Olson
4645 W. Rosecrans Ave.
Hawthorne
California 90250
Supplies for hooked rugs.

Paper White Ltd
Box 956
Fairfax
California 94930
White cutwork and lace trimmed bed linens.

Pierre Deux
870 Madison Avenue
New York 10021
French Provençal fabrics, faience dinnerware.

Poly-Commodity Corp.
175 Great Neck Road
Great Neck
New York 11021
Flannel sheets.

Quilts Unlimited
203 East Washington Street
P.O. Box 1210
Lewisburg
West Virginia 24901
Quilts, quilting supplies.

Raintree Designs
979 Third Avenue
New York 10022
English and French country fabrics, wallcoverings.

Ritz
40 Portland Road
W. Conshonocken
Pennsylvania 19428
Homespun-style kitchen linens.

Rue de France
78 Thames Street
Newport
Rhode Island 02840
Lace panels, curtains.

Scandia Down
1040 Independence Drive
Seattle
Washington 98188
Down comforters, pillows, duvet covers.

The Scarlet Letter
P.O. Box 397
Sullivan
Wisconsin 53178
Sampler kits.

Smith
295 Fifth Avenue
New York 10010
Homespun linens and pillows.

Stevens Linen Associates
P.O. Box 220
Webster
Massachusetts 01570
Throws.

The Stitchery
204 Worcester Street
Wellesley
Massachusetts 02181
Candlewicking, cross-stitch kits and supplies.

Three Weavers
1206 Brooks Street
Houston
Texas 77009
Throws.

FRANCE

Ebene
38 Boulevard Victor Hugo
Saint Rémy-de-Provence
(01033) (90) 92 36 10
Authentic Provençal fabric and furniture.

Espace Bechard
1 Avenue Jean Charmasson
L'Ilse Sur Sarque
Les Baux
Dealer in old Provençal fabrics.

PLACES WITH COUNTRY STYLE

NORTH AMERICA

Adirondack Museum
Blue Mountain Lake
New York 12812
(0101) (518) 352 7311
Museum depicting the history and art of the Adirondack region.

Atlanta Historic Society
3101 Andrews Drive N.W.
Atlanta, Georgia 30305
(0101) (404) 261 1837
Two historic houses: Tullie Smith House, an 1840s plantation farm house, and the Swan House, an Anglo-Palladian mansion built in 1928. Plus gardens, woodlands and museum exhibits.

Dekalb Historic Society
Old Courthouse
Decatur, Atlanta
Georgia 30030
(0101) (404) 373 1088
The Mary Gay house, Swanton House, log cabins and rustic barns all historically furnished.

Seaside
P.O. Box 4730
Santa Rosa Beach
Florida 32459
(0101) (904) 231 4224 Fax:
(0101) (904) 231 2219
A new town on Florida's Northwest coast. Cottages and luxury suites available for rent. Call, fax or write SEASIDE for information.

FRANCE

L'Aubergade
52 Rue Royale
47270 Puymirol
(01033) (53) 95 31 46
Michel and Maryse Trama's Michelin-starred restaurant, situated in a 13th century house in Puymirol (a small limestone village ten miles/ 16 kilometres from Agen).

Chateau de Courances
Par Milly La Foret
Dpt 91490
(01033) (1) 64 98 41 18
One hour south of Paris; open to the public by arrangement.

Chateau d'O
Mortree 61570
Orne
(01033) (33) 35 33 56
Open to the public daily – not Tuesday – winter 2-5.30, summer 2-6.30. Three miles (five kilometres) from Surdon station.

Le Moulin de Mougins
424 Chemin de Moulin
06250 Mougins
(01033) (93) 75 78 24
16th century olive-mill restaurant presided over by master chef Roger Vergé.

SPAIN

El Molino del Carmen
Barrio Alto 67
Gaucin
Malaga
(01034) (52) 15 12 77
A beautifully converted olive mill in an unspoilt mountain village with all rooms looking over the Mediterranean and North Africa. Contact Jancis Page as above or Sarah Potter of Gaucin Travel in London – (071) 627 0570 – for details of accommodation.

SCANDINAVIA

Skansen Open Air Museum
Skansen
Djurgarden
Stockholm
Sweden
(01046) (8) 663 0500
Museum of authentic Scandinavian Country buildings.

FRANCE

L'Aubergade

ITALY

Castello di Argiano
S. Angelo in Colle
Siena
(01039) (577) 86 41 13
Tiny medieval village perched on top of a hill – available for film locations. Contact Sarah and Giuseppe Sesti as above.

INTERIOR DESIGNERS

Christophe Gollut
116 Fulham Road
London SW3 6HU
(071) 370 4101
Furniture of the 18th and 19th centuries used in eclectic Continental-influenced interiors.

Tony Heaton
The Malt House
Sydney Buildings
Bath BA2 6BZ
(0225) 466936
Offers an international interior design service for a wide range of clients and projects, domestic and commercial.

Dick Dumas for Sunhouse
Rue d'Apt
Isle sur la Sorgue
Vancluse, France
(010 33) (90) 38 24 77
Decorator and designer of furniture. Dumas's shop, Sunhouse, is filled with original Dick dumas designs.

Stephen Mack
Stephen Mack Associates
Chase Hill Farm
Ashaway
Rhode Island 02804, USA
(0101) (401) 377 8041
Specializes in the reconstruction and restoration of 17th and 18th century buildings.

Jaime Parlade
San Juan Bosco 6
Marbella
Spain
(01034) (52) 77 05 01
and 27 Ruiz de Alarcon,
Madrid
(01034) (12) 48 51 63
International architect and designer providing complete interior and exterior service.

Index/Acknowledgments

The Authors and Publishers would like to thank the following house owners, interior designers, antique dealers, museums, restaurants and hotels for allowing special photography for this book.

Adirondack Museum, Bull Cottage, Blue Mountain Lake, NY 12812, USA. (0101) (518) 352 7311.

Atlanta Historic Society, 3101 Andrews Drive NW, Atlanta, Georgia 30305, USA. (0101) (404) 261 1837.

André de Cacqueray Antiquities, 227 Ebury Street, London SW1. (071) 730 5000.

Dekalb Historic Society, Old Courthouse, Decatur, Atlanta, Georgia 30030, USA. (0101) (404) 373 1088.

Christophe Gollut, 116 Fulham Road, London SW3 6HU. (071) 370 4101.

Tony Heaton, The Malt House, Sydney Buildings, Bath BA2 6BZ. (0225) 466936.

Jane and Terry Macey, Jatz Clothes, Somerset. (0749) 86565.

Stephen Mack, Stephen Mack Associates, Chase Hill Farm, Ashaway, Rhode Island 02804, USA. (0101) (401) 377 8041.

Trevor Micklem, Trevor Micklem Antiques Ltd, Frog Pool Farm, Moor Wood, Oakhill, Nr Bath, Avon BA3 5BN. (0749) 840754.

Guimund Mounter and Ana Simons, Bakers Farm, Dulford, Devon. (08846) 358.

Lars Olsson, Antikhandel, Kapmangatan 7, 111 31 Stockholm, Sweden. (01046) (8) 10 25 00.

Jancis Page, El Molino del Carmen, Barrio Alto 67, Gaucin, Malaga, Spain. (01034) (52) 15 12 77.

Jaime and Janetta Parlade, San Juan Bosco 6, Marbella, Spain. (01034) (52) 77 05 01. And 27 Ruiz de Alarcon, Madrid.

Seaside, PO Box 4730, Santa Rosa Beach, Florida 32459, USA. (0101) (904) 231 4224.

Sarah and Giuseppe Sesti, Castello di Argiano, S. Angelo in Colle, Siena, Italy. (01039) (577) 86 41 13.

Skansen Open Air Museum, Skansen, Djurgarden, Stockholm. (01046) (8) 663 0500.

Maryse et Michel Trama, L'Aubergade, 52 rue Royale, 47270 Puymirol, France. (01033) (53) 95 31 46.

Roger Vergé, Le Moulin de Mougins, 424 Chemin de Moulin, 06250 Mougins, France. (01033) (93) 75 78 24.

Michael Wakelin and Helen Linfield, Wakelin and Linfield, 10 New Street, Petworth, W. Sussex. (0798) 42417.

Stephen Weeks, Penhow Castle, Penhow, Nr Newport, Gwent, NP6 3AD. (0633) 400800 or 400469 (information).

Mary Wondrausch, The Pottery, Brickfields, Compton, Nr Guildford, Surrey GU3 1HZ. (0468) 4097.

The following people also kindly allowed us to photograph their homes:

Stephen Andrews RCA, Maria Pilar Aritio, Jean and Vony Becker, Liz and Jim Cherry, Dick Dumas, Mrs Jessie Famous, Maria Luisa Larranaga Condesa Vda de Foixa, Marquise de Ganay, Jenny Hall, Mme Jacques de Lacratelle, Robert and Illene Ligday, M et Mme Daniel Pons, Jacqueline Ryder, Peter and Silvie Schofield, Scott Shepard, Lars and Ursula Sjoberg, Sally Spillane and Robinson Leech.